Taste*of*Home.
SKINNY
INSTANT POT® & SLOW COOKER COOKBOOK

TASTE OF HOME BOOKS • RDA ENTHUSIAST BRANDS, LLC • MILWAUKEE, WI

Visit us at *tasteofhome.com* for other *Taste of Home*
books and products.

INTERNATIONAL STANDARD BOOK NUMBER:
978-1-61765-922-5

LIBRARY OF CONGRESS CONTROL NUMBER:
2019947875

EXECUTIVE EDITOR: Mark Hagen
SENIOR ART DIRECTOR: Raeann Thompson

COVER PHOTOGRAPHER: Dan Roberts
COVER SET STYLIST: Stacey Genaw
COVER FOOD STYLIST: Josh Rink

PICTURED ON FRONT COVER: Steak Fajitas, p. 200
PICTURED ON BACK COVER: Sesame Pulled Pork
Sandwiches, 145; Slow Cooker Ham & Eggs, p. 8; Strawberry
Sorbet Sensation, p. 235; Southwestern Breakfast Casserole,
p. 37; Creamy Cauliflower Soup, p. 239; and Slow Cooker
BBQ Chicken, p. 121

Printed in China
1 3 5 7 9 10 8 6 4 2

BOOK ONE

SKINNY INSTANT POT®
Lighten up with 100 dishes made in a one-pot cooker.

Today's home cooks turn to their Instant Pots for comforting meals and beat-the-clock convenience. Now you can use these popular appliances to eat healthy as well!

With this book, you'll discover 100 delectable recipes that will satisfy everyone at the table—while cutting back on calories, carbs, fat, sugar and sodium.

From busy weeknight suppers to impressive weekend dinner parties, you'll find dishes that satisfy without straying from healthy-eating goals. In fact, these family-friendly staples are so flavor packed, no one will realize they're eating light! So, what are you waiting for? Get cooking with *Skinny Instant Pot* today and see how delicious eating right can be.

BOOK TWO

SKINNY SLOW COOKER
Cook smart, eat smart, lose weight, feel great!

Everyone could use a little help when it comes to eating right, so why not rely on your slow cooker? Keep your commitment to setting a healthy table by serving up these comforting classics.

This mouthwatering collection makes it a snap to enjoy hearty slow-cooked dishes that are so tasty, no one will realize they're eating light. Best of all, these satisfying recipes simmer on their own during the day, so a sensational, healthy meal is ready when you walk through the door.

You'll even find two bonus chapters that round out slow-cooked entrees, making it a snap to create comforting menus that keep calories and fat at bay.

Taste of Home
SKINNY
INSTANT POT®

BOOK ONE

TASTE OF HOME BOOKS • RDA ENTHUSIAST BRANDS, LLC • MILWAUKEE, WI

CONTENTS

GET SOCIAL WITH US!

LIKE US: facebook.com/tasteofhome | **PIN US:** pinterest.com/taste_of_home

FOLLOW US: @tasteofhome | **TWEET US:** twitter.com/tasteofhome

TO FIND A RECIPE: tasteofhome.com

TO SUBMIT A RECIPE: tasteofhome.com/submit

TO FIND OUT ABOUT OTHER *TASTE OF HOME* PRODUCTS: shoptasteofhome.com

INSTANT POT® 101

Let's get cooking! It's a snap to simmer a winner any night of the week when you have an Instant Pot and your copy of *Skinny Instant Pot Cookbook* at the ready. These popular devices are a great way for today's cooks to prepare healthy meals. Best of all, each recipe found here was tested in an Instant Pot by the Taste of Home Test Kitchen and reviewed by a registered dietitian, so you're guaranteed success.

WHAT IS AN INSTANT POT?

People may use "instant pot" to refer to any electric pressure cooker, but Instant Pot is actually the brand name for a popular line of electric pressure cookers. The cooker is an airtight pot that cooks food quickly using steam pressure. When it comes to selecting an electric pressure cooker, there are actually several brands and sizes to choose from.

PICK YOUR POT

When determining the best device for you, consider how many people you cook for. This will help narrow the selection to the cooker that's the right size for your needs. Next think about the features various models offer. For example: Is a yogurt-making option something you'd use regularly?

GET TO KNOW THE DESIGN

Electric pressure cookers have a lid that forms an airtight seal to create pressure; an inner pot that holds the food; and an outer pot with a control panel. For the most part, the buttons on the control panel are to help you set a cooking time. For example, if there is a "fish" button, pressing it will likely mean your food will cook for a short time. Some electric pressure cookers have a saute feature and others even offer a sterilize function. Most also include a slow-cook option, which allows you to cook your food slowly instead of pressure-cooking it.

THE PRESSURE'S ON

No matter what cooker you're using, you'll need to learn how to release the pressure safely. Because the escaping steam is hot enough to burn you, it's imperative you read and understand the directions that come with your pot for releasing pressure. Generally speaking, you'll either use a quick-release method (which involves pressing a handle or button) or the natural-release method (where the cooker cools down and releases pressure naturally). Always make sure the hole on top of the pressure-release is facing away from you before pressing the release button. And remember that the quick-release method is not suitable for soups (or anything with a large liquid volume) and cereals (or any dish with a high starch content), because quick-release may cause food to splatter out with the steam.

KEEP IT CLEAN

Follow the manufacturer's directions for cleaning your electric pressure cooker and review the tips and ideas on page 8, and you'll be cooking with it for years to come.

GET THE MOST OUT OF YOUR INSTANT POT®

Today's home cooks are turning to Instant Pots for everything from appetizers to desserts. But are they getting the ultimate out of these incredible kitchen helpers? Review these handy tips and see how you can save even more time and effort when using your Instant Pot.

LEARN HOW TO BOIL WATER (SERIOUSLY)

As soon as you get your cooker, start out by learning how to boil water in it. Pour about 1 cup of water into the inner pot so you will gain a sense of where the maximum fill line is. Seal the lid and select a short cook time. Within 5 minutes, the water should heat up and build pressure, at which point the pressure will release naturally. This is also a good time to learn how to use the quick-release method.

TRY THE RICE COOKER FUNCTION

You can use your pot as a rice cooker. It takes about the same amount of time as cooking on the stovetop, with walk-away convenience, easy cleanup and perfect results every time.

USE IT AS A STEAMER

Looking for a side of steamed veggies? Don't forget that these devices make great steamers. You can even use your Instant Pot to steam hard-boiled eggs—and you won't believe how easy they are to peel.

UP YOUR GAME WITH THE SAUTE FUNCTION

This is one of the reasons people love Instant Pots. The saute function browns meats in the inner pot without dirtying a pan on the stovetop. You can also use this function on the low setting to simmer foods. This means you can simmer stock or beans after pressure-cooking them. And that means you can make super fast soups and stews—all in one pot.

SAVE TIME WITH QUICK-RELEASE

To save time, let the pot cool down slightly, then manually release the pressure. The steam will be very hot, so be careful when moving the release to vent. A cool, wet towel placed on the lid can help speed up the release. Read the release directions that came with your cooker.

The best way to make the most of all-in-one cookers is to first understand what they can do and how they can save you time. A little bit of know-how goes a long way! Turn the page for more tips and hints on using your device.

HOW PRESSURE-COOKING WORKS FOR YOU

Pressure cookers build up hot steam and raise the pressure and temperature to simulate long braising, boiling or simmering. The resulting flavor is just as terrific as if you stood and stirred a bubbling pot all day.

LEARN THE BEST PRACTICES

Using a multipurpose cooker requires some reading and practice, so be patient. It will definitely be worth it in the end. Keep these hints in mind when using your cooker:

- Read the instruction manual for your electric pressure cooker before you make anything. Not all brands and models are the same, so get to know your pot!

- For food safety and efficiency, the total amount of food and liquid should never exceed the maximum level (also known as the max line or the fill line) indicated in the pot.

- Make sure the pressure-release valve is closed before you start cooking. Even the pros at the *Taste of Home* Test Kitchen have forgotten to close the valve and returned to find the pot venting instead of building pressure.

- The pressure-release valve is supposed to feel loose to the touch. The pressure-release handle works simply by applying pressure on the release pipe. Since the contact between the handle and the pipe is not fully sealed, the valve may release a little bit of steam while the food cooks.

- The power cord on some models is removable, which makes the appliance easier to store. If you plug it in and the light does not go on, check the cord. Is it attached securely? When the cooker isn't in use, consider storing the cord in the inner pot.

- After each use, remove and clean the rubber sealing ring, pressure-release valve and anti-block shield. See pages 10 and 11 for more on cleaning your electric pressure cooker.

- If your pot starts to smell like food even after cleaning it, put the sealing ring through the dishwasher. If that doesn't work, try steam cleaning: Pour 2 cups water and 1 Tbsp. lemon zest into the inner pot. Place the lid and run the steam program for 2 minutes. Carefully remove the sealing ring and let it air dry.

- Consider purchasing a separate sealing ring, using one for savory foods and one for sweet treats or foods with delicate flavors.

ARE YOU PLUGGED IN?

STORE CORD IN POT

TO CLEAN, REMOVE RUBBER SEALING RING

SNAP SEAL BACK

FAMILY COOKS SHARE THEIR BEST INSTANT POT® SECRETS

We asked Instant Pot fans to share their favorite hints and tips. Here's how they get the most out of an all-in-one cooker:

THINK BEFORE YOU COOK.

Before you begin cooking, determine if using the Instant Pot is the best method for the job. Not every dish is faster with the Instant Pot; however, the appliance will almost always save you active time. Instead of supervising the entree, you can be playing outside with the kids, relaxing or whipping up a yummy dessert while the main dish simmers.

HIT THE SAUTE FUNCTION EARLY.

Preheating your electric pressure cooker saves valuable time, so turn on the saute function while you prepare the ingredients. Slice and dice your veggies, and your Instant Pot will be ready to saute when you are.

CALCULATE PASTA COOKING TIME.

Check the recommended time for cooking noodles to al dente in boiling water. Halve that time for Instant Pot cooking.

SUBSTITUTE HEALTHY BROWN RICE.

To substitute brown rice for regular white long grain, try increasing the cooking liquid by ¼ cup and the cook time by 5 minutes.

ADD THICKENER TO SAUCES.

Because there's no evaporation when you cook with an Instant Pot, braised recipes may have excess liquid. Try bumping up the cornstarch or flour a bit when adapting such recipes to all-in-one cookers.

TRY THESE "HARD-BOILED" EGGS.

Crack a few eggs into a baking dish, then pour a cup of water into your Instant Pot. Set the dish on the trivet insert inside the Instant Pot and pressure-cook on high for 5 minutes. When done, chop up the "egg loaf" for a head start on egg salad.

TURN THE HANDLES INTO LID HOLDERS.

The newer models' lid handles do double duty, holding the Instant Pot open with the lid out of the way. This feature is great for the buffet line. You also can store your Instant Pot this way to ensure the inside fully dries.

LET YOUR INSTANT POT® SHINE

Millions of home cooks have fallen in love with the Instant Pot; maybe you're one of them! If you love something, you need to take care of it. In the case of your all-in-one cooker, that means cleaning and drying it properly each and every time you use it.

Always unplug the device before washing. With the exception of the exterior cooker, or outer pot, all of the Instant Pot's parts are dishwasher safe, making life even easier.

You can allow the parts to dry in the dishwasher, or dry them by hand. Be sure everything, particularly the sealing ring, is completely dry before reassembling and storing.

See the pointers at right for even more washing and cleaning strategies.

WHAT TO WASH AFTER EVERY USE

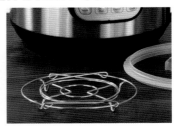

INNER POT: The inner pot is made of stainless steel, so you can wash it in warm, soapy water or set it in the dishwasher. Since the food touches the pot directly, you'll definitely need to wash this pot after every use.

TRIVET INSERT: Since the trivet sits in the inner pot and makes direct contact with the food, you'll need to wash this each time you cook with it. The rack will easily fit in the dishwasher, but feel free to wash by hand and dry completely.

PRESSURE-RELEASE VALVE AND FLOAT VALVE: It's important to wipe food particles off these valves. You don't want anything blocking them, because that would hinder the steam from releasing when you are cooking future meals.

ANTI-BLOCK SHIELD: This is something that many cooks forget to clean. Remove shield from lid. After hand-washing it, wipe with a soft cloth and dry completely. Make sure to secure it in place on the lid before using the appliance again.

SEALING RING: The sealing ring can absorb food odors, so you'll want to clean this after every use. Wash it by hand or toss it in the dishwasher. Make sure it's completely dry before setting it back on the lid. The ring is key to sealing the lid onto the pot and building pressure.

WHAT TO WASH OCCASIONALLY

EXTERIOR: Wipe the exterior of your Instant Pot with a damp cloth as needed. It's important not to submerge the cooker in water since it contains the heating element. When you need to clean the inside of the cooker (not to be confused with the inner pot), use a damp cloth.

LID: After carefully removing the sealing ring and the anti-block shield, wash the lid on the top rack of your dishwasher. It is not necessary to clean the lid after every use, but it's not a bad idea to give it a good wipe with a clean kitchen towel or cotton cloth between washes.

CONDENSATION CUP: This little cup collects the moisture that's created during the cooling process. It doesn't get particularly dirty, so a periodic wash is all it needs. You should check the cup regularly, however, and keep it clean with a quick wipe every now and again.

DEEP-CLEANING BASICS

Show your Instant Pot some extra attention by giving it a deep clean every so often.

INNER POT: To refresh the inner pot, pour 1 cup of white vinegar into it and let sit for 5 minutes. Pour the vinegar out and rinse. If you start to see water stains, use a nonabrasive scouring cleanser to remove them.

SEALING RING: Give the ring a deep clean by adding 2 cups white vinegar and 1 tablespoon lemon zest to the inner pot and running the steam program for 2 minutes. Remove the sealing ring and let it air-dry completely.

SNACKS & APPETIZERS

Got a case of the munchies? Just because you're cutting calories doesn't mean you can't enjoy a savory bite now and then. Perfect for parties and casual nibbles alike, these fast and easy ideas always put hunger in its place.

PARTY PLANNING MADE EASY

Planning is important so you can enjoy your own party. Whether hosting a formal soiree or casual get-together, remember to have fun.

The most important factor to keep in mind when throwing a party is to be sure everyone has a great time—and that includes you! Keep the following ideas in mind for a stress-free bash.

Start by planning healthy appetizers that vary in color, texture and flavor. Serve sweet and spicy, crisp and chewy, hot and cold. Include several make-ahead starters to avoid last-minute prep.

The number of appetizers per person will vary according to the length of the event, the number of guests and the other items on your menu.

For cocktails before dinner, plan on serving 3-4 types of appetizers with enough for 4-5 pieces per person.

For an open house buffet, plan on 4-5 types of appetizers and 4-6 pieces per person.

For a light dinner of finger foods, plan on 6-8 appetizer types and roughly 14-16 pieces per person.

EASY WAY TO IMPRESS

Cheese balls, dips and spreads that contain low-fat cream cheese should stand at room temperature for 15 minutes before serving. They will be easier to spread and far more flavorful.

Dust sweet appetizers with a tiny bit of confectioners' sugar or cocoa powder for a light yet pretty presentation.

Tightly wrap all refrigerated make-ahead appetizers to help them retain optimal texture and flavor.

Keep cold appetizers chilled by setting the serving dish in a bowl of ice. Replenish the ice as it melts.

Prep fresh finger foods to bake and serve in batches.

DO'S AND DONT'S FOR THE PERFECT PARTY

A few simple things can make or break a good time. Run through this list before your guests arrive.

- **Do play music** in the background to set the mood but still allow for easy conversation.

- **Do create an open floor plan** so guests can easily walk from one room to the next. Consider stowing away pieces of furniture that are in the way.

- **Do arrange chairs** in groups that encourage conversation.

- **Don't stash the trash containers** but set them out strategically to prevent clutter from building up.

- **Don't hide the coasters** if you want your guests to use them. Have plenty available and place them in noticeable locations.

- **Don't keep clutter** on tables and other surfaces. Give guests room to easily set down their glasses and plates.

HOW MUCH FOOD? HOW MANY DRINKS?

Planning how much food to serve doesn't have to be daunting!
Here's a quick guide to how many drinks and how much food to stock.

APPETIZERS

Each guest at a dinner party will have about six appetizers (12 if it's a cocktail party). Stock up on bulk items like nuts, pretzels and olives that can fill in any shortfall without drawing attention.

ENTREES AND SIDES

The list below estimates a serving size per person. Remember, the more options you offer, the smaller each portion will be. Given a spread of healthy yet tempting dishes, guests will take a little of each instead of a lot of just one.

- **Poultry, fish or meat:**
  6 ounces
- **Grains:** 1.5 ounces as a side dish,
  2 ounces as a main dish

- **Potatoes:** 5 ounces
- **Vegetables:** 4 ounces
- **Beans:** 2 ounces
- **Green salad:** 1 ounce
- **Bread:** 1-2 pieces

DRINKS

Several factors govern how many beverages you'll need, including the type of party, its duration and your guests. For a 2-hour party:

- **Ice:** 1 pound per person
- **Nonalcoholic beverages:**
  One drink per person if alcohol is provided, three per person if alcohol isn't
- **Champagne:** 1.5 glasses per person for cocktails, three glasses per person at dinner

- **Wine:** One bottle of wine for every two adult guests
- **Spirits:** Three drinks per person (you'll get roughly 17 drinks per bottle)

DESSERTS

No matter how big the dinner, there's always room for dessert—especially at the holidays, when everyone looks forward to their favorite cakes or pies. Figure per guest:

- **Cake, tart or pastry:** 1 slice
- **Creamy desserts:** 4 ounces
- **Ice cream:** 5 ounces
- **Cookies:** 5-6 cookies—but because these are the ultimate "just one more" treat, err on the side of plenty. Also take the size of your cookies into account.

CURRIED CHICKEN MEATBALL WRAPS

My strategy to get picky kids to eat healthy: Let everyone assemble their dinner at the table. We love these easy meatball wraps topped with crunchy veggies and peanuts, sweet raisins and a creamy dollop of yogurt.
—Jennifer Beckman, Falls Church, VA

Prep: 35 min.
Cook: 10 min.
Makes: 2 dozen

- 1 **large egg,**
  lightly beaten
- 1 **small onion,**
  finely chopped
- ½ **cup Rice Krispies**
- ¼ **cup golden raisins**
- ¼ **cup minced**
  fresh cilantro
- 2 **tsp. curry powder**
- ½ **tsp. salt**
- 1 **lb. lean ground chicken**
- 2 **Tbsp. olive oil**

SAUCE

- 1 **cup plain yogurt**
- ¼ **cup minced**
  fresh cilantro

WRAPS

- 24 **small Bibb or Boston**
  lettuce leaves
- 1 **medium carrot,**
  shredded
- ½ **cup golden raisins**
- ½ **cup chopped**
  salted peanuts

1. In a large bowl, combine the first 7 ingredients. Add chicken; mix lightly but thoroughly (mixture will be soft). With wet hands, shape mixture into 24 balls (about 1¼-in.). Select saute or browning setting on a 6-qt. electric pressure cooker. Adjust for medium heat; add oil. When oil is hot, brown meatballs in batches; remove and keep warm. Add 1 cup water to pressure cooker. Cook 1 minute, stirring to loosen browned bits from pan. Press cancel.

2. Place trivet insert in pressure cooker. Place meatballs on trivet, overlapping if needed. Lock lid; close pressure-release valve. Adjust to pressure-cook on high for 7 minutes. Quick-release pressure.

3. In a small bowl, mix sauce ingredients. To serve, place 2 tsp. sauce and 1 meatball in each lettuce leaf; top with remaining ingredients. If desired, serve with additional minced fresh cilantro.

1 WRAP: 82 cal., 4g fat (1g sat. fat), 22mg chol., 88mg sod., 6g carb. (4g sugars, 1g fiber), 6g pro. **DIABETIC EXCHANGES:** 1 lean meat, ½ starch.

CILANTRO-LIME CHICKEN WITH SCOOPS

I came up with this recipe when I was preparing for a large party and wanted a healthy Tex-Mex chicken appetizer. The dish can be made ahead of time, and leftovers make for a tasty next-day burrito filling.
—Lori Terry, Chicago, IL

Prep: 15 min.
Cook: 10 min.
Makes: 16 servings

1 lb. boneless skinless chicken breasts
½ cup reduced-sodium chicken broth
2 Tbsp. lime juice
2 tsp. chili powder
1½ cups frozen petite corn (about 5 oz.), thawed
1½ cups chunky salsa
1½ cups finely shredded cheddar cheese
1 medium sweet red pepper, finely chopped
4 green onions, thinly sliced
Baked tortilla chip scoops
Minced fresh cilantro

1. Place chicken in a 6-qt. electric pressure cooker; add broth, lime juice and chili powder. Lock lid; close pressure-release valve. Adjust to pressure-cook on high for 7 minutes. Quick-release pressure. A thermometer inserted in chicken should read at least 165°.

2. Remove chicken; discard cooking juices. Shred chicken with 2 forks; return to pressure cooker. Select saute setting and adjust for low heat. Add corn and salsa; cook and stir until heated through, about 5 minutes. Press cancel.

3. Transfer to a large bowl; stir in cheese, red pepper and green onions. Serve with tortilla scoops; sprinkle with cilantro.

¼ **CUP CHICKEN MIXTURE:** 97 cal., 4g fat (2g sat. fat), 26mg chol., 202mg sod., 6g carb. (2g sugars, 1g fiber), 9g pro. **DIABETIC EXCHANGES:** 1 medium-fat meat.

ASIAN WRAPS

This recipe is similar to other Asian wraps but packed with even more deliciously healthy flavor. Instead of ordering Chinese, why not try making these yourself?
—Melissa Hansen, Ellison Bay, WI

Prep: 30 min.
Cook: 10 min.
Makes: 1 dozen

- 2 lbs. boneless skinless chicken breast halves
- ¼ cup reduced-sodium soy sauce
- 6 Tbsp. water, divided
- ¼ cup ketchup
- ¼ cup honey
- 2 Tbsp. minced fresh gingerroot
- 2 Tbsp. sesame oil
- 1 small onion, finely chopped
- 2 Tbsp. cornstarch
- 12 round rice papers (8 in.)
- 3 cups broccoli coleslaw mix
- ¾ cup crispy chow mein noodles

TEST KITCHEN TIP
Rice papers are chewy translucent sheets most often used to hold a combination of savory ingredients. Look for them in the Asian or international aisle.

1. Place chicken in a 6-qt. electric pressure cooker. In a small bowl, whisk soy sauce, ¼ cup water, ketchup, honey, ginger and oil; stir in onion. Pour over the chicken. Lock lid; close pressure-release valve. Adjust to pressure-cook on high for 7 minutes. Quick-release pressure. Press cancel. A thermometer inserted in chicken should read at least 165°. Remove chicken; shred with 2 forks. Set aside.

2. In a small bowl, mix cornstarch and remaining 2 Tbsp. water until smooth; gradually stir into pressure cooker. Select saute setting and adjust for low heat. Simmer, stirring constantly, until thickened, 1-2 minutes. Remove sauce from pressure cooker. Toss shredded chicken with ¾ cup sauce; reserve remaining sauce for serving.

3. Fill a large shallow dish partway with water. Dip a rice paper wrapper into water just until pliable, about 45 seconds (do not soften completely); allow excess water to drip off.

4. Place wrapper on a flat surface. Layer ¼ cup coleslaw, ⅓ cup chicken mixture and 1 Tbsp. noodles across bottom third of wrapper. Fold in both sides of wrapper; fold bottom over filling, then roll up tightly. Place on a serving plate, seam side down. Repeat with remaining ingredients. Serve with reserved sauce.

1 WRAP: 195 cal., 5g fat (1g sat. fat), 42mg chol., 337mg sod., 21g carb. (8g sugars, 1g fiber), 17g pro. **DIABETIC EXCHANGES:** 2 lean meat, 1½ starch, ½ fat.

TROPICAL PULLED PORK SLIDERS

I used what I had in my cupboard to make this Hawaiian-style pork filling, and the results were fantastic. It's a delicious way to fuel a party.
—Shelly Mitchell, Gresham, OR

Prep: 15 min.
Cook: 50 min. + releasing
Makes: 24 servings

- 1 boneless pork shoulder butt roast (3 lbs.), halved
- 2 garlic cloves, minced
- ½ tsp. lemon-pepper seasoning
- 1 can (20 oz.) unsweetened crushed pineapple, undrained
- ½ cup orange juice
- 1 jar (16 oz.) mango salsa
- 24 whole wheat dinner rolls, split

1. Rub roast with garlic and lemon pepper. Transfer to a 6-qt. electric pressure cooker; top with pineapple and orange juice. Lock lid; close pressure-release valve. Adjust to pressure-cook on high for 50 minutes. Let pressure release naturally. A thermometer inserted in pork should read at least 145°.

2. Remove roast; cool slightly. Skim fat from cooking juices. Shred pork with 2 forks. Return pork and cooking juices to pressure cooker. Stir in salsa; heat through. Serve with rolls.

FREEZE OPTION: Freeze cooled meat mixture and juices in freezer containers. To use, partially thaw in refrigerator overnight. Heat through in a saucepan, stirring occasionally and adding a little water if necessary.

1 SLIDER: 211 cal., 7g fat (2g sat. fat), 34mg chol., 349mg sod., 23g carb. (7g sugars, 3g fiber), 13g pro. **DIABETIC EXCHANGES:** 2 medium-fat meat, 1½ starch.

WHY YOU'LL LOVE IT...

"This was very good! I will be adding this to my summer rotation and camping cookbook. Easy to make and delicious, a nice change from traditional pulled pork. Thanks for sharing!"
—PATTY2222, TASTEOFHOME.COM

LIGHT DEVILED EGGS

Our updated version of a classic appetizer uses only half the egg yolks of traditional deviled eggs and calls for soft bread crumbs to help firm up the filling. Light ingredients lower the fat grams even more.
—*Taste of Home* Test Kitchen

Prep: 20 min.
Cook: 5 min. + releasing
Makes: 16 servings

  8 **large eggs**
  ¼ **cup fat-free mayonnaise**
  ¼ **cup reduced-fat sour cream**
  2 **Tbsp. soft bread crumbs**
  1 **Tbsp. prepared mustard**
  ¼ **tsp. salt**
      Dash white pepper
  4 **pimiento-stuffed olives, sliced**
      Paprika, optional

1. Place trivet insert and 1 cup water in a 6-qt. electric pressure cooker. Set the eggs on trivet. Lock lid; close pressure-release valve. Adjust to pressure-cook on high for 5 minutes. Let pressure release naturally for 5 minutes; quick-release any remaining pressure. Immediately place eggs in a bowl of ice water to cool. Remove shells.

2. Cut eggs lengthwise in half. Remove yolks; refrigerate 8 yolk halves for another use. Set whites aside. In a small bowl, mash remaining yolks. Stir in mayonnaise, sour cream, bread crumbs, mustard, salt and pepper. Stuff or pipe into egg whites. Garnish with sliced olives. If desired, sprinkle with paprika.

1 STUFFED EGG HALF: 32 cal., 2g fat (1g sat. fat), 46mg chol., 132mg sod., 1g carb. (1g sugars, 0 fiber), 3g pro.

TEST KITCHEN TIP
Amp up flavor without adding fat or calories when you stir your favorite chopped fresh herb into the ingredients for the filling. Try garden-fresh parsley, basil, chives or thyme.

HEALTHY STEAMED DUMPLINGS

My family loves Chinese food, but it's hard to find healthy choices in restaurants or at the grocery store, so I make my own. The recipe makes a lot; I freeze big batches so we can enjoy these dumplings later.
—Melody Crain, Houston, TX

Prep: 45 min.
Cook: 10 min./batch
Makes: 30 dumplings

- ½ **cup finely shredded Chinese or napa cabbage**
- 2 **Tbsp. minced fresh cilantro**
- 2 **Tbsp. minced chives**
- 1 **large egg, lightly beaten**
- 4 **tsp. rice vinegar**
- 2 **garlic cloves, minced**
- 1½ **tsp. sesame oil**
- ½ **tsp. salt**
- ½ **tsp. ground ginger**
- ½ **tsp. Chinese five-spice powder**
- ¼ **tsp. grated lemon zest**
- ¼ **tsp. pepper**
- ¾ **lb. lean ground turkey**
- 30 **pot sticker or gyoza wrappers**
- 9 **Chinese or napa cabbage leaves**
  Sweet chili sauce, optional

1. In a large bowl, combine the first 12 ingredients. Add turkey; mix lightly but thoroughly.

2. Place 1 Tbsp. filling in center of each pot sticker wrapper. (Cover remaining wrappers with a damp paper towel until ready to use.) Moisten wrapper edge with water. Fold the wrapper over filling; seal edges, pleating the front side several times to form a pleated pouch. Stand dumplings on a work surface to flatten bottoms; curve slightly to form crescent shapes, if desired.

3. Place trivet the insert and 1 cup water in a 6-qt. electric pressure cooker. Line trivet with 3 cabbage leaves. Arrange 10 dumplings over cabbage (do not stack). Lock lid; close pressure-release valve. Adjust to pressure-cook on high for 7 minutes; quick-release pressure. A thermometer inserted in dumpling should read at least 165°.

4. Transfer dumplings to a serving plate; keep warm. Discard cabbage and cooking juices. Repeat with additional water, remaining cabbage and dumplings. If desired, serve with the chili sauce.

FREEZE OPTION: Cover and freeze cooled dumplings on parchment-lined baking sheets until firm. Transfer to a large freezer container. To use, microwave dumplings, covered, for 30-45 seconds or until heated through.

1 DUMPLING: 37 cal., 1g fat (0 sat. fat), 14mg chol., 74mg sod., 3g carb. (0 sugars, 0 fiber), 3g pro.

CAPONATA

This Italian eggplant dip preps quickly and actually gets better as it stands. Serve it warm or at room temperature. Try adding a little leftover caponata to scrambled eggs for a savory breakfast the next day.
—Nancy Beckman, Helena, MT

Prep: 20 min.
Cook: 5 min.
Makes: 6 cups

- 2 medium eggplants, cut into ½-in. pieces
- 1 can (14½ oz.) diced tomatoes, undrained
- 1 medium onion, chopped
- ½ cup dry red wine
- 12 garlic cloves, sliced
- 3 Tbsp. extra virgin olive oil
- 2 Tbsp. red wine vinegar
- 4 tsp. capers, undrained
- 5 bay leaves
- 1½ tsp. salt
- ¼ tsp. coarsely ground pepper
  French bread baguette slices, toasted
  Optional toppings: Fresh basil leaves, toasted pine nuts and additional olive oil

1. Place the first 11 ingredients in a 6-qt. electric pressure cooker (do not stir). Lock lid; close pressure-release valve. Adjust to pressure-cook on high for 3 minutes. Quick-release the pressure.

2. Cool slightly; discard bay leaves. Serve with toasted baguette slices. If desired, serve with toppings.

¼ CUP: 34 cal., 2g fat (0 sat. fat), 0 chol., 189mg sod., 5g carb. (2g sugars, 2g fiber), 1g pro.

DID YOU KNOW?
You can make this light bite in your slow cooker. Simply cook the first 11 ingredients on high for 3 hours. Stir together and cook another 2 hours or until the veggies are tender. Discard the bay leaves and serve with the baguettes. Garnish with the toppings, if desired.

BREAKFAST & BRUNCH

Load up on a filling breakfast that keeps your mind off fatty meals the rest of the day. Your Instant Pot® makes it easy. Simply turn the page and learn how delicious it is to brighten up your morning routine.

TAKE MORNINGS TO NEW HEIGHTS

Nothing impresses more than an incredible breakfast or brunch. Whether you're feeding just a few on a busy weekday morning or hosting a crowd for a memorable feast, these eye-opening dishes make every morning a bit more special. Turn here for breakfast favorites made easy as well as tasty new ways to celebrate the day.

EGGS TO THE RESCUE

Few ingredients are as versatile and economical as eggs. That's probably why they're one of the most popular ingredients for your favorite morning fare. Combine eggs with a couple of kitchen staples, and the breakfast possibilities are endless. We have included dozens of egg basics and tips on the following pages to help you make your very best breakfast dishes!

BUYING EGGS
Select eggs with unbroken shells from the refrigerator case. Check the grade: AA, A or B. The higher grades have thicker whites and more nicely shaped yolks.

Read the date on the carton. The USDA requires the carton to display the packing date using the Julian calendar (Jan. 1 is "1" and Dec. 31 is "365"). Other dates on the carton (not required by the USDA) are the sell-by date and the best-by or use-by date. Egg cartons that do not display the USDA shield are governed by individual state standards.

Refrigerate eggs as soon as possible after purchase, discarding any with cracked shells. Always store eggs on an inside shelf in the egg carton. The cartons cushion the eggs and help prevent moisture loss and odor absorption. Do not reuse cartons.

SPECIALTY EGGS
Several types of specialty eggs are commonly available, such as organic, vegetarian, pasteurized, free-range and cage-free. The added cost to produce these eggs is often reflected in their higher price.

Organic Eggs are from hens given feed grown without conventional pesticides, fungicides, herbicides or commercial fertilizers. Organic eggs must meet the standards set by the National Organic Standards Board.

Vegetarian Eggs are from hens fed without animal byproducts.

Pasteurized Eggs are heat-treated to kill salmonella that may be on the shell or in the eggs. Because of the heat treatment, these eggs may have slightly lower levels of heat-sensitive vitamins, such as thiamine and riboflavin.

Free-Range Eggs are from uncaged hens with access to the outdoors.

Cage-Free Eggs are from hens raised indoors without cages.

SHELL COLOR
The color of the eggshell is based on the breed of the chicken and doesn't reflect the contents of the egg itself. Brown and white eggs have identical nutritional values and cook the same.

EGG SIZE EQUIVALENTS

The recipes in this cookbook were tested with large eggs. Use the following guidelines for substituting other egg sizes for large eggs.

EGG SIZE	SUBSTITUTION
1 LARGE EGG	1 JUMBO, 1 EXTRA-LARGE OR 1 MEDIUM
2 LARGE EGGS	2 JUMBO, 2 EXTRA-LARGE, 2 MEDIUM OR 3 SMALL
3 LARGE EGGS	2 JUMBO, 3 EXTRA-LARGE, 3 MEDIUM OR 4 SMALL
4 LARGE EGGS	3 JUMBO, 4 EXTRA-LARGE, 5 MEDIUM OR 5 SMALL

3 WAYS TO CRACK AN EGG

ON THE COUNTER: Gently but firmly rap the egg's equator squarely against the countertop. Use your thumbs to press inward and separate the shell, then pour the yolk and white into a bowl.

WITH TWO EGGS: Hold an egg in each hand. Tap the eggs together at their equators. One egg will crack. Use your thumbs to press inward and separate the shell.

ONE-HANDED: Hold the egg in one hand. Position your thumb and index finger above the egg's equator and your middle and ring fingers below it. Sharply crack the egg against the side of a bowl. Immediately pull the eggshell apart using your thumb and middle finger.

TIPS FOR STORING EGGS

- Refrigerate egg whites in an airtight container up to 4 days.

- Refrigerate unbroken egg yolks covered with water in an airtight container up to 2 days.

- Freeze whole eggs by lightly beating them until blended, then pouring them into an airtight, freezer-safe container. Freeze up to 1 year.

- Freeze egg whites in an airtight container up to 1 year.

- Freeze egg yolks by lightly beating ¼ cup yolks with ⅛ tsp. salt or 1½ tsp. corn syrup. Pour into a freezer container and store up to 1 year. Use yolks with added salt in savory dishes and yolks with corn syrup for desserts.

FOOD SAFETY WITH EGGS

- Cook eggs until whites and yolks are firm. For dishes that use eggs as an ingredient, such as casseroles, cook until the internal temperature reaches 160°. Discard any egg dishes that have been left at room temperature for more than 2 hours.

CHERRY-ALMOND OATMEAL

Breakfast doesn't get much easier than when you take advantage of your all-in-one cooker and some fruit and nuts for a yummy way to start your day.
—Geraldine Saucier, Albuquerque, NM

Prep: 10 min. + standing
Cook: 5 min. + releasing
Makes: 6 servings

- 4 **cups vanilla almond milk**
- 1 **cup steel-cut oats**
- 1 **cup dried cherries**
- ⅓ **cup packed brown sugar**
- ½ **tsp. salt**
- ½ **tsp. ground cinnamon**

1. In a 6-qt. electric pressure cooker, combine all ingredients. Lock lid; close pressure-release valve. Adjust to pressure-cook on high for 5 minutes. Let pressure release naturally.

2. Let stand 10 minutes before serving (oatmeal will thicken upon standing). If desired, serve with additional almond milk.

¾ **CUP:** 296 cal., 4g fat (0 sat. fat), 0 chol., 304mg sod., 62g carb. (40g sugars, 4g fiber), 4g pro.

TEST KITCHEN TIP
Nutritionally, steel-cut oats are about the same as rolled oats, so take your pick. Skip instant oatmeal mixes, which have a lot of added sugar.

SOUTHWESTERN BREAKFAST CASSEROLE

I created this recipe for a breakfast-for-dinner meal one day, and it's also become a favorite on chilly mornings. Such a wonderful aroma! Extra-sharp cheddar cheese allows you to use less while boosting the flavor.
—Lisa Renshaw, Kansas City, MO

Prep: 20 min. + standing
Cook: 20 min. + releasing
Makes: 4 servings

2 large eggs, room temperature
4 large egg whites, room temperature
⅔ cup fat-free milk
1½ tsp. chili powder
¼ tsp. ground cumin
¼ tsp. cayenne pepper
¼ tsp. pepper
¾ cup canned black beans, rinsed and drained
½ cup frozen corn, thawed
½ cup cubed fully cooked ham
½ cup shredded extra-sharp cheddar cheese
¼ cup canned chopped green chiles
3 slices whole wheat bread, lightly toasted and cubed
Pico de gallo, optional

1. In a large bowl, whisk together the first 7 ingredients. Stir in beans, corn, ham, cheese and chiles. Stir in toasted bread cubes to moisten.

2. Transfer to a greased 1½-qt. baking dish. Place trivet insert and 1 cup water in pressure cooker. Cover baking dish with foil. Fold an 18x12-in. piece of foil lengthwise into thirds to make a sling. Use the sling to lower the dish onto the trivet.

3. Lock lid; close pressure-release valve. Adjust to pressure-cook on high for 20 minutes. Let pressure release naturally for 10 minutes; quick-release any remaining pressure. Using foil sling, carefully remove baking dish. Uncover and let stand 10 minutes before serving. If desired, serve with pico de gallo.

1¼ CUPS: 257 cal., 9g fat (4g sat. fat), 118mg chol., 661mg sod., 23g carb. (4g sugars, 4g fiber), 21g pro. **DIABETIC EXCHANGES:** 3 lean meat, 1½ starch.

RAISIN NUT OATMEAL

There's no better feeling than starting off the day with a nourishing breakfast. I love that the oats, fruit and spices in this homey meal cook together on their own.
—Valerie Sauber, Adelanto, CA

Prep: 10 min. + standing
Cook: 5 min. + releasing
Makes: 6 servings

  3 cups vanilla almond
     milk
  ¾ cup steel-cut oats
  ¾ cup raisins
  3 Tbsp. brown sugar
4½ tsp. butter
  ¾ tsp. ground cinnamon
  ½ tsp. salt
  1 large apple, peeled
     and chopped
  ¼ cup chopped pecans

1. In a 6-qt. electric pressure cooker, combine first 7 ingredients. Lock lid; close pressure-release valve. Adjust to pressure-cook on high for 5 minutes. Let pressure release naturally.

2. Stir in apple. Let stand 10 minutes before serving (oatmeal will thicken upon standing). Spoon oatmeal into bowls; sprinkle with pecans.

¾ **CUP:** 272 cal., 9g fat (2g sat. fat), 8mg chol., 298mg sod., 47g carb. (29g sugars, 4g fiber), 4g pro.

WHY YOU'LL LOVE IT...

"I tried this recipe with almond milk and it was fabulous! My entire family loved it! So delicious!"
—HON1HON1, TASTEOFHOME.COM

EGGS IN PURGATORY

Tomatoes and red pepper flakes add spicy zing to these saucy eggs. Serve them with toasted bread or sauteed polenta rounds for an unforgettable morning meal.
—Nick Iverson, Denver, CO

Prep: 30 min.
Cook: 5 min.
Makes: 4 servings

- 2 cans (14½ oz. each) fire-roasted diced tomatoes, undrained
- 1 medium onion, chopped
- ½ cup water
- 2 Tbsp. canola oil
- 2 garlic cloves, minced
- 2 tsp. smoked paprika
- ½ tsp. sugar
- ½ tsp. crushed red pepper flakes
- ¼ cup tomato paste
- 4 large eggs
- ¼ cup shredded Manchego or Monterey Jack cheese
- 2 Tbsp. minced fresh parsley
- 1 tube (18 oz.) polenta, sliced and warmed, optional

1. Place the first 8 ingredients in a 6-qt. electric pressure cooker. Lock lid; close pressure-release valve. Adjust to pressure-cook on high for 4 minutes. Quick-release pressure. Press cancel.

2. Select saute setting and adjust for low heat. Add tomato paste; simmer, uncovered, until mixture is slightly thickened, about 10 minutes, stirring occasionally.

3. With the back of a spoon, make 4 wells in sauce. Break an egg into each well; sprinkle with cheese. Cover (do not lock lid). Simmer until egg whites are completely set and yolks begin to thicken but are not hard, 8-10 minutes. Sprinkle with parsley. If desired, serve with polenta.

1 SERVING: 255 cal., 14g fat (4g sat. fat), 193mg chol., 676mg sod., 20g carb. (9g sugars, 3g fiber), 11g pro. **DIABETIC EXCHANGES:** 1½ fat, 1 starch, 1 medium-fat meat.

APPLE PIE STEEL-CUT OATMEAL

I absolutely love this one-dish oatmeal. The steel-cut oats have so much flavor and texture. My family loves to sprinkle toasted pecans on top.
—Angela Lively, Conroe, TX

Prep: 10 min. + standing
Cook: 5 min. + releasing
Makes: 8 servings

  6 cups water
1½ cups steel-cut oats
1½ cups unsweetened
      applesauce
  ¼ cup maple syrup
1½ tsp. ground cinnamon
  ½ tsp. ground nutmeg
  ⅛ tsp. salt
  1 large apple, chopped
      Optional toppings:
      Sliced apples and
      toasted pecans

1. In a 6-qt. electric pressure cooker, combine the first 7 ingredients. Lock lid; close pressure-release valve. Adjust to pressure-cook on high for 5 minutes. Let the pressure release naturally.

2. Stir in chopped apple. Let stand 10 minutes before serving (oatmeal will thicken upon standing). If desired, top servings with sliced apples, pecans and additional syrup.

1¼ CUPS: 171 cal., 2g fat (0 sat. fat), 0 chol., 39mg sod., 36g carb. (13g sugars, 4g fiber), 4g pro.

TEST KITCHEN TIP
Boost the protein power in this oatmeal with a dollop of vanilla Greek yogurt. Not only will it add layers of flavor and texture, but it will help you stay full longer.

HAWAIIAN BREAKFAST HASH

Breakfast is our favorite meal, and we love a wide variety of dishes. This hash brown recipe is full of flavor and possibilities. Top it with some eggs or spinach for another twist!
—Courtney Stultz, Weir, KS

Prep: 30 min.
Cook: 5 min.
Makes: 6 servings

- 4 **bacon strips, chopped**
- 1 **Tbsp. canola or coconut oil**
- 2 **large sweet potatoes (about 1½ lbs.), peeled and cut into ½-in. pieces**
- 1 **cup water**
- 2 **cups cubed fresh pineapple (½-in. cubes)**
- ½ **tsp. salt**
- ¼ **tsp. chili powder**
- ¼ **tsp. paprika**
- ¼ **tsp. pepper**
- ⅛ **tsp. ground cinnamon**

1. Select the saute or browning setting on a 6-qt. electric pressure cooker; adjust for medium heat. Add bacon; cook and stir until crisp. Remove with a slotted spoon; drain on paper towels. Discard drippings.

2. Add oil to pressure cooker. When oil is hot, brown sweet potato pieces in batches. Remove from pressure cooker. Add water to pressure cooker. Cook 1 minute, stirring to loosen browned bits from pan. Press cancel. Place steamer basket in pressure cooker.

3. Stir pineapple and seasonings into potatoes; transfer to steamer basket. Lock lid; close pressure-release valve. Adjust to pressure cook on high for 2 minutes. Quick-release pressure. Sprinkle with the bacon.

⅔ **CUP:** 194 cal., 5g fat (1g sat. fat), 6mg chol., 309mg sod., 35g carb. (17g sugars, 4g fiber), 4g pro. **DIABETIC EXCHANGES:** 2 starch, 1 fat.

GRUYERE & PROSCIUTTO STRATA

Prosciutto, sweet onions and Gruyere combine for a perfect brunch dish that's extra flavorful for a lighter dish, and the recipe's just the right size for us.
—Patti Lavell, Islamorada, FL

Prep: 15 min. + standing
Cook: 20 min. + releasing
Makes: 5 servings

- 1 tsp. canola oil
- 2 oz. thin slices prosciutto, chopped
- 1 large sweet onion, chopped (2 cups)
- ½ cup egg substitute
- 1¼ cups 2% milk
- ⅛ tsp. ground mustard
  Dash pepper
- 4 cups cubed French bread
- ¾ cup shredded Gruyere or Swiss cheese, divided

1. Select saute setting on a 6-qt. electric pressure cooker and adjust for medium heat; add oil. When oil is hot, cook and stir prosciutto until crisp, about 3 minutes. Remove from pan with a slotted spoon. Add onion to pressure cooker; cook and stir until tender, 4-5 minutes. Press cancel.

2. In a large bowl, whisk egg substitute, milk, mustard and pepper. Stir in bread, half the cheese, and onions. Reserve 2 Tbsp. cooked prosciutto for topping; stir the remaining prosciutto into bread mixture.

3. Transfer to a greased 1½-qt. baking dish. Wipe pressure cooker clean. Place trivet insert and 1 cup water in pressure cooker. Cover baking dish with foil. Fold an 18x12-in. piece of foil lengthwise into thirds, making a sling. Use the sling to lower the dish onto the trivet.

4. Lock lid; close pressure-release valve. Adjust to pressure-cook on high for 20 minutes. Let pressure release naturally for 10 minutes; quick-release any remaining pressure. Using foil sling, carefully remove baking dish. Sprinkle with remaining cheese and prosciutto; cover and let stand 10 minutes.

1 CUP: 241 cal., 10g fat (5g sat. fat), 34mg chol., 557mg sod., 22g carb. (8g sugars, 1g fiber), 16g pro. **DIABETIC EXCHANGES:** 2 medium-fat meat, 1½ starch, 1 fat.

HOMEMADE CHUNKY APPLESAUCE

This applesauce is so easy. My family loves the things I make from scratch, and it's good knowing exactly what I'm putting in it!
—Marilee Cardinal, Burlington, NJ

Prep: 10 min.
Cook: 5 min. + releasing
Makes: 5 cups

- **7** medium McIntosh, Empire or other apples (about 3 lbs.)
- ½ cup sugar
- ½ cup water
- **1** Tbsp. lemon juice
- ¼ tsp. almond or vanilla extract

1. Peel, core and cut each apple into 8 wedges. Cut each wedge crosswise in half; place in a 6-qt. electric pressure cooker. Add remaining ingredients.

2. Lock lid; close pressure-release valve. Adjust to pressure-cook on high for 3 minutes. Let pressure release naturally. Mash apples with a potato masher or use an immersion blender until desired consistency is reached.

¾ **CUP:** 139 cal., 0 fat (0 sat. fat), 0 chol., 0 sod., 36g carb. (33g sugars, 2g fiber), 0 pro.

WHY YOU'LL LOVE IT...

"Super easy, loved the flavor. I added just a touch of cinnamon also."
—HOTFUDGESUNDAE, TASTEOFHOME.COM

CINNAMON BLUEBERRY FRENCH TOAST

Healthy and hearty! That's the best way to describe this satisfying breakfast. It's one dish worth jumping out of bed for.
—Angela Lively, Conroe, TX

Prep: 15 min. + standing
Cook: 20 min. + releasing
Makes: 4 servings

  2 **large eggs**
1⅓ **cups 2% milk**
  3 **Tbsp. sugar**
  1 **tsp. ground cinnamon**
  1 **tsp. vanilla extract**
¼ **tsp. salt**
  6 **cups cubed French**
    bread (about 6 oz.)
¾ **cup fresh or frozen**
    blueberries
    Maple syrup

HEALTH TIP
Swap whole wheat for white French bread to increase the fiber in this recipe. If you can't find it, cube 100% whole wheat buns.

1. Whisk together the first 6 ingredients. Arrange half the bread cubes in a greased 1½-qt. baking dish. Top with half the blueberries and half the milk mixture. Repeat layers.

2. Place trivet insert and 1 cup water in a 6-qt. electric pressure cooker. Cover baking dish with foil. Fold an 18x12-in. piece of foil lengthwise into thirds, making a sling. Use the sling to lower the dish onto the trivet.

3. Lock lid; close pressure-release valve. Adjust to pressure-cook on high for 20 minutes. Let pressure release naturally for 10 minutes; quick-release any remaining pressure. Using foil sling, carefully remove baking dish. Let stand 10 minutes. Serve with syrup.

1 SERVING: 273 cal., 6g fat (2g sat. fat), 100mg chol., 479mg sod., 44g carb. (19g sugars, 2g fiber), 11g pro.

RHUBARB COMPOTE WITH YOGURT

My grandma made rhubarb compote and always had some in the freezer when I came to visit. This breakfast is a tribute to her. No two batches of rhubarb are exactly alike, so make sure to taste your compote before you chill it. It should be tart, but sometimes it needs a little extra sugar.
—Michael Hoffman, Brooklyn, NY

Prep: 10 min. + chilling
Cook: 5 min. + releasing
Makes: 6 servings

- 2 **cups finely chopped fresh rhubarb**
- ⅓ **cup water**
- ¼ **cup sugar**
- 3 **cups reduced-fat plain Greek yogurt**
- 2 **Tbsp. honey**
- ¾ **cup sliced almonds, toasted**

1. Place rhubarb, water and sugar in a 6-qt. electric pressure cooker. Lock lid; close pressure-release valve. Adjust to pressure-cook on high 3 minutes. Let pressure release naturally for 10 minutes, then quick-release any remaining pressure. Transfer to a bowl; cool slightly. Refrigerate until cold.

2. In a small bowl, whisk yogurt and honey until blended. Spoon into serving dishes. Top with compote; sprinkle with the almonds.

½ CUP YOGURT WITH ABOUT 2 TBSP. COMPOTE AND 2 TBSP. ALMONDS: 216 cal., 8g fat (2g sat. fat), 7mg chol., 49mg sod., 23g carb. (20g sugars, 2g fiber), 14g pro. **DIABETIC EXCHANGES:** 1 starch, 1 reduced-fat milk, 1 fat.

SIDE DISHES

When it's time to round out a healthy meal, let
your one-pot cooker do the work. From classic
sides to ethnic favorites, these trimmed-down
dishes make any menu a bit more special.

FARM-FRESH PICKIN'S
Here's what's best to buy according to the season.

SPRING
Artichokes, Arugula, Asparagus, Avocados, Butter Lettuce, Chard, Green Beans, Mango, Morel Mushrooms, Parsnips, Radishes, Rhubarb, Snap Peas, Spinach, Strawberries

SUMMER
Apricots, Baby Carrots, Cherries, Cucumbers, Bell Peppers, Blueberries, Boysenberries, Cantaloupe, Corn, Eggplant, Figs, Green Beans, Key Limes, Lima Beans, Long Beans, Melon, Okra, Onions, Peaches, Pineapple, Raspberries, Snap Peas, Snow Pea , Tomatoes, Watermelon, Zucchini

FALL

Acorn Squash, Apples, Beets, Broccoli, Cauliflower, Celery, Cranberries, Endive, Garlic, Ginger, Grapes, Jalapeno Peppers, Kohlrabi, Mushrooms, Pears, Potatoes, Pumpkin, Quince, Sweet Potatoes

WINTER
Brussels Sprouts, Cabbage, Dates, Grapefruit, Horseradish, Kale, Mandarin Oranges, Passion Fruit, Radicchio, Tangerines, Turnips, Winter Squash

WHAT'S DOES YOUR PRODUCE LABEL MEAN?

GMO AND NON-GMO
GMO stands for genetically modified organism. Produce labeled GMO has been engineered via DNA modification to be larger or more abundant, or to withstand drought or insect damage. Produce labeled non-GMO has not been modified in this way.

NATURAL
In theory, foods with this label are produced simply, without food additives, antibiotics, added colors or artificial sweeteners. That said, the Food and Drug Administration has no official regulations about manufacturers' use of the "natural" label.

USDA ORGANIC
This label signifies crops grown without the use of pesticides or chemicals and without genetic modification. If you see this logo on packaging, it's got the official stamp of approval from the U.S. Department of Agriculture.

WHY ORGANICS COST MORE
- Organic foods take longer to grow, with no chemicals or hormones to speed things up.
- Organic farms are typically smaller than traditional ones.
- Organic farming is usually more labor-intensive.

GUIDE TO RICE & GRAINS

Rice is used in many cuisines around the globe. In fact, there are more than 40,000 known types of rice in the world. As North American interest in world cuisines has increased, the selection and availability of rice varieties has expanded on our supermarket shelves.

WHITE & BROWN RICE

The most common types of rice used in American cooking are white and brown. White rice can be stored indefinitely in an airtight container. Brown rice should be stored at room temperature for no more than 6 months. For longer storage, refrigerate or freeze.

ARBORIO RICE

This is a medium-grain rice used for making risotto. When cooked into creamy textured risotto, it has a chewy center.

AROMATIC RICE

Also know as fragrant rice, aromatic rice has an incredible perfume while cooking and a very distinctive flavor. Each type—basmati, Black Japonica, jasmine and Texmati—has its own cooking characteristics, which can change from one growing season to the next.

WILD RICE

This is not actually rice; it's a marsh grass grain. Wild rice can be stored indefinitely in an airtight container. Rinse wild rice before cooking to remove any dirt or debris. Note that wild rice may not absorb all of the cooking liquid before it becomes tender. Drain off any liquid that remains in the pot.

COOKING RICE & GRAINS

The chart at right tells you more about a variety of grains and their uses. You might want to cook them or rice on the stovetop while using your one-pot cooker for an entree. Bring water, ¼ tsp. salt (if desired) and 1 Tbsp. butter (if desired) to a boil in a 2-qt. saucepan. Stir in the rice or grain; return to a boil. Cover and reduce heat to a simmer. Cook for the time given on the package or until tender. Fluff with a fork and serve.

BROWN RICE: EASY AS 1, 2, 3

The standard ratio for long grain rice (white or brown) is 1-2-3:
1 cup uncooked rice
+ 2 cups liquid
= 3 cups cooked rice.

Brown rice takes 40-50 minutes to cook but has about four times the fiber of white rice. Quick and instant brown rice cook in about 10 minutes and are just as healthy, so take a shortcut!

GRAIN	DESCRIPTION	STORAGE
BARLEY	A flavorful, chewy alternative to white rice, pearl, quick-cooking and Scotch barley can be found in supermarkets. Pearl barley has the double outer hull and bran layer removed. Quick-cooking barley is precooked pearl barley. Scotch barley has been processed less than pearl barley and retains some of its bran layer.	Store barley in an airtight container in a cool, dry place. Barley can also be stored in the refrigerator or freezer.
BUCKWHEAT	Buckwheat is not related to wheat, which means it is gluten-free. The black triangular seeds are sold as groats, buckwheat grits, kasha or buckwheat flour. Groats are kernels with the inedible black shells removed. Grits are finely ground unroasted groats. Kasha is roasted groats that have been cracked into coarse, medium or fine grains. Buckwheat flour, used for noodles, pancakes and breads, is made of ground groats.	Store opened buckwheat products in a cool, dry place (in warm climates, use the refrigerator or freezer). Always store buckwheat flour in the refrigerator.
BULGUR	This whole wheat grain is processed like converted rice. Kernels are cleaned, steam-cooked, dried and cracked or ground into pieces. Bulgur is ready to eat after soaking in water or broth for about 30 minutes. Bulgur comes in coarse, medium and fine grains. Coarse bulgur is used for stuffings and pilafs; medium for cereals, breads and stews; and fine for tabbouleh, cereals and breads.	Store opened packages of bulgur in a cool, dry place for up to 1 month. In warm climates, store it in the refrigerator or freezer.
CORNMEAL	Dried corn is hulled and finely ground between steel rollers or two stones to make meal. Stone-ground cornmeal is coarser than steel-ground and has a shorter shelf life. Look for white and yellow cornmeal in supermarkets and for blue cornmeal in specialty markets. Self-rising cornmeal has added baking powder and salt and cannot be used interchangeably with plain cornmeal. Use cornmeal for breads, muffins and polenta.	Store stone-ground cornmeal in the refrigerator for up to 4 months. Use steel-ground cornmeal before the use-by date on the package.
GRITS	Grits is a term used to describe coarsely ground dried corn, oats or rice. Today, it typically refers to coarsely ground dried hominy (field corn). Hominy grits are sold as regular grits, quick-cooking grits and, with the shortest cooking time, instant grits.	Use before the use-by date on the package.
MILLET	This grain makes a healthy side dish. Look for it in health-food stores and some grocery stores. Pearl millet comes in white, yellow, red or gray. To cook as a substitute for rice, simmer ½ cup millet in 1½ cups water in a covered saucepan for about 25 minutes until fluffy.	Store millet in an airtight container in a cool, dry place for several months.
HOMINY	Dried corn with the hull and germ removed through a process of soaking in an alkaline solution, typically lye or slacked lime, is called hominy. It's available canned or dried. When ground, it is often referred to as grits.	Use before the use-by date on the package.
OATS	Popular and readily available, oats are a grain and breakfast cereal. The most common oat products are Scottish or steel-cut, old-fashioned, quick-cooking and instant. Scottish oats have been processed less than the old-fashioned oats. Old-fashioned oats have been flattened by rollers; quick-cooking oats are flattened and cut into small pieces; instant oats have been precooked, dried, and cut even smaller. Oat bran is the outer bran layer of the grain and is high in fiber. Old-fashioned and quick-cooking oats can be used interchangeably in baked goods. Instant oats cannot be used interchangeably with other oat products.	Once opened, oats should be stored in a cool, dry place. In warm climates, store them in the freezer or refrigerator. Use by the package use-by date.
QUINOA	Quinoa has a more complete protein than most grains. The flattened oval grains come in a variety of colors, most commonly white, pale gold, black and red. Look for quinoa in the grains, rice or organic food aisles of grocery stores. Rinse under cold running water before cooking. For a more pronounced flavor, toast in a skillet before cooking. Quinoa is done when the grains are translucent and the germ spirals out to form a crunchy tail. Quinoa has a mild taste and a fluffy texture.	Store uncooked quinoa in a cool, dry place. In warm climates, store it in the refrigerator or freezer.

SUMMER SQUASH

We love squash, but I got tired of fixing plain old squash and cheese. I decided to jazz it up a bit. This was a huge hit with the family.
—Joan Hallford, North Richland Hills, TX

Prep: 20 min.
Cook: 5 min.
Makes: 8 servings

- 1 lb. medium yellow summer squash
- 1 lb. medium zucchini
- 2 medium tomatoes, chopped
- 1 cup vegetable broth
- ¼ cup thinly sliced green onions
- ½ tsp. salt
- ¼ tsp. pepper
- 1½ cups Caesar salad croutons, coarsely crushed
- ½ cup shredded cheddar cheese
- 4 bacon strips, cooked and crumbled

1. Cut squash into ¼-in.-thick slices; place in a 6-qt. electric pressure cooker. Add tomatoes, broth, green onions, salt and pepper. Lock lid; close pressure-release valve. Adjust to pressure-cook on high for 1 minute. Quick-release pressure. Remove squash with a slotted spoon.

2. To serve, top with croutons, cheese and bacon.

¾ **CUP:** 111 cal., 6g fat (2g sat. fat), 12mg chol., 442mg sod., 10g carb. (4g sugars, 2g fiber), 6g pro. **DIABETIC EXCHANGES:** 1 vegetable, 1 fat.

SICILIAN STEAMED LEEKS

I love the challenge of developing recipes for my garden leeks, a delicious but underused vegetable. This Italian-flavored dish is an all-time favorite.
—Roxanne Chan, Albany, CA

Prep: 10 min.
Cook: 5 min.
Makes: 6 servings

- 1 large tomato, chopped
- 1 small navel orange, peeled, sectioned and chopped
- 2 Tbsp. minced fresh parsley
- 2 Tbsp. sliced Greek olives
- 1 tsp. capers, drained
- 1 tsp. red wine vinegar
- 1 tsp. olive oil
- ½ tsp. grated orange zest
- ½ tsp. pepper
- 6 medium leeks (white portion only), halved lengthwise, cleaned
  Crumbled feta cheese

1. Combine the first 9 ingredients; set aside. Place trivet insert and 1 cup water in a 6-qt. electric pressure cooker. Set leeks on trivet. Lock lid; close pressure-release valve. Adjust to pressure-cook on high for 2 minutes. Quick-release pressure.

2. Transfer leeks to a serving platter. Spoon tomato mixture over top; sprinkle with cheese.

1 SERVING: 83 cal., 2g fat (0 sat. fat), 0 chol., 77mg sod., 16g carb. (6g sugars, 3g fiber), 2g pro. **DIABETIC EXCHANGES:** 1 starch, ½ fat.

TEST KITCHEN TIP
To prepare leeks, remove any withered outer leaves. Trim root end. Cut off and discard the green upper leaves at the point where the pale green becomes dark green. Leeks often contain sand between their many layers. If leeks are to be sliced or chopped, cut the leek open lengthwise down one side and rinse under cold running water, separating the leaves.

SPAGHETTI SQUASH WITH TOMATOES

This squash is tempting as a side dish, but you can also top it with canned tuna to serve as an entree. I use my own home-canned tomatoes for the best flavor. It's easy, tasty and light!
—Carol Chase, Sioux City, IA

Prep: 15 min.
Cook: 10 min.
Makes: 10 servings

- 1 **medium spaghetti squash, halved lengthwise, seeds removed**
- 1 **can (14 oz.) diced tomatoes, drained**
- ¼ **cup sliced green olives with pimientos**
- 1 **tsp. dried oregano**
- ½ **tsp. salt**
- ½ **tsp. pepper**
- ½ **cup shredded cheddar cheese**
- ¼ **cup minced fresh basil**

1. Place trivet insert and 1 cup water in a 6-qt. electric pressure cooker. Set the squash on trivet, overlapping as needed to fit. Lock lid; close pressure-release valve. Adjust to pressure-cook on high for 7 minutes. Quick-release pressure. Press cancel.

2. Remove squash and trivet from pressure cooker; drain cooking liquid from pressure cooker. Using a fork, separate squash into strands resembling spaghetti, discarding skin. Return squash to pressure cooker. Stir in tomatoes, olives, oregano, salt and pepper. Select saute setting and adjust for low heat. Cook and stir until heated through, about 3 minutes. Top with cheese and basil.

¾ **CUP:** 92 cal., 3g fat (1g sat. fat), 6mg chol., 296mg sod., 15g carb. (1g sugars, 4g fiber), 3g pro. **DIABETIC EXCHANGES:** 1 starch, ½ fat.

PRESSURE-COOKER DRESSING

Here's an easy dressing that's perfect for special get-togethers. It's a modern take on an old-fashioned side dish that everyone loves.
—Rita Nodland, Bismarck, ND

Prep: 15 min. + standing
Cook: 10 min. + releasing
Makes: 8 servings

- 2 **Tbsp. olive oil**
- 1 **medium celery rib, chopped**
- 1 **small onion, chopped**
- 2 **cups reduced-sodium chicken broth**
- 1 **tsp. poultry seasoning**
- ¼ **tsp. salt**
- ¼ **tsp. pepper**
- 8 **cups unseasoned stuffing cubes**

1. Select saute setting on a 6-qt. electric pressure cooker. Adjust for medium heat; add oil. When oil is hot, cook and stir celery and onion until crisp-tender, 3-4 minutes. Press cancel. Stir in broth and seasonings. Gently stir in stuffing cubes; toss to combine. Transfer to a greased 1½-qt. baking dish.

2. Place trivet insert and 1 cup water in pressure cooker. Cover baking dish with foil. Fold an 18x12-in. piece of foil lengthwise into thirds, making a sling. Use the sling to lower the dish onto the trivet.

3. Lock lid; close pressure-release valve. Adjust to pressure-cook on high for 15 minutes. Let pressure release naturally for 10 minutes; quick-release any remaining pressure. Using foil sling, carefully remove baking dish. Let stand 10 minutes.

½ **CUP:** 225 cal., 5g fat (0 sat. fat), 0 chol., 634mg sod., 40g carb. (3g sugars, 3g fiber), 8g pro.

BUFFALO WING POTATOES

I was getting tired of mashed potatoes and baked spuds, so I decided to create something new. This potluck-ready recipe is an easy and delicious twist on the usual potato dish.
—Summer Feaker, Ankeny, IA

Prep: 15 min.
Cook: 5 min.
Makes: 6 servings

  2 lbs. Yukon Gold
       potatoes, cut into
       1-in. cubes
  1 small sweet yellow
       pepper, chopped
  ½ small red onion,
       chopped
  ¼ cup Buffalo wing sauce
  ½ cup shredded
       cheddar cheese
     Optional toppings:
       Crumbled cooked
       bacon, sliced green
       onions and sour cream

1. Place steamer basket and 1 cup water in a 6-qt. electric pressure cooker. Set potatoes, yellow pepper and onion in basket. Lock lid; close pressure-release valve. Adjust to pressure-cook on high for 3 minutes. Quick-release pressure. Press cancel.

2. Remove vegetables to a serving bowl; discard cooking liquid. Add Buffalo wing sauce to vegetables; gently stir to coat. Sprinkle with cheese. Cover and let stand until cheese is melted, 1-2 minutes. If desired, top with bacon, green onions and sour cream.

¾ **CUP:** 182 cal., 4g fat (2g sat. fat), 9mg chol., 382mg sod., 32g carb. (3g sugars, 3g fiber), 6g pro. **DIABETIC EXCHANGES:** 2 starch, ½ fat.

WHY YOU'LL LOVE IT...

"Such a delicious recipe! Don't skip the green onions or bacon! Would be great for a picnic or potluck."
—LPH, TASTEOFHOME.COM

MUSHROOM RICE PILAF

A few modifications to our Great-Aunt Bernice's easy pilaf recipe made it a much-requested item for potlucks, barbecues and family get-togethers. It'll become a favorite in your home and with your gang, too!
—Amy Williams, Rialto, CA

Prep: 20 min.
Cook: 5 min. + releasing
Makes: 6 servings

 ¼ cup butter
 1 cup medium grain rice
 ½ lb. sliced baby
   portobello mushrooms
 6 green onions, chopped
 2 garlic cloves, minced
 1 cup water
 4 tsp. beef base

1. Select saute setting on a 6-qt. electric pressure cooker. Adjust for medium heat; add butter. When butter is hot, cook and stir rice until lightly browned, 3-5 minutes. Press cancel. Add mushrooms, green onions and garlic. In a small bowl, whisk water and beef base; pour over rice mixture.

2. Lock lid; close pressure-release valve. Adjust to pressure-cook on high for 4 minutes. Let pressure release naturally. If desired, serve with additional green onions.

⅔ **CUP:** 209 cal., 8g fat (5g sat. fat), 20mg chol., 519mg sod., 30g carb. (2g sugars, 1g fiber), 4g pro. **DIABETIC EXCHANGES:** 2 starch, 2 fat.

ROSEMARY BEETS

We're a family of beet eaters. For a simple side, I use a one-dish cooker and let the beets mellow with rosemary and thyme.
—Nancy Heishman, Las Vegas, NV

Prep: 20 min. + cooling
Cook: 20 min. + releasing
Makes: 8 servings

- 5 **large fresh beets (about 3½ lbs.)**
- 1 **Tbsp. olive oil**
- 1 **medium red onion, chopped**
- 2 **garlic cloves, minced**
- 1 **medium orange, peeled and chopped**
- ⅓ **cup honey**
- ¼ **cup white balsamic vinegar**
- 1 **Tbsp. minced fresh rosemary or 1 tsp. dried rosemary, crushed**
- 2 **tsp. minced fresh thyme or ¾ tsp. dried thyme**
- ¾ **tsp. salt**
- ½ **tsp. Chinese five-spice powder**
- ½ **tsp. coarsely ground pepper**
- 1 **cup crumbled feta cheese**

1. Place trivet insert and 1 cup water in a 6-qt. electric pressure cooker. Scrub beets, trimming tops to 1 in.; set on trivet. Lock lid; close pressure-release valve. Adjust to pressure-cook on high for 20 minutes. Let pressure release naturally. Press cancel.

2. Remove beets and cool enough to handle. Remove trivet; discard cooking juices. Wipe pot clean. Peel and cut beets into wedges.

3. Select saute setting; adjust for medium heat. Add oil. When oil is hot, cook and stir red onion until crisp-tender, 4-5 minutes. Add garlic; cook 1 minute longer. Stir in orange, honey, vinegar, rosemary, thyme, salt, Chinese five-spice, pepper and beets; heat through. Press cancel. Serve warm, or refrigerate and serve cold. Serve with a slotted spoon; sprinkle with cheese.

¾ **CUP:** 200 cal., 4g fat (2g sat. fat), 8mg chol., 511mg sod., 37g carb. (31g sugars, 5g fiber), 6g pro. **DIABETIC EXCHANGES:** 2 vegetable, 1 starch, 1 fat.

BLACK-EYED PEAS WITH HAM

Here's a regional favorite I grew to love after moving to the South. You'll never want to eat canned black-eyed peas again! Serve the dish as a side with grilled chicken, or make it your main course and round out the meal with greens and cornbread.
—Tammie Merrill, Wake Forest, NC

Prep: 10 min.
Cook: 20 min. + releasing
Makes: 10 servings

- 1 pkg. (16 oz.) dried black-eyed peas
- 4 cups water
- 1 cup cubed fully cooked ham
- 1 medium onion, finely chopped
- 3 garlic cloves, minced
- 2 tsp. seasoned salt
- 1 tsp. pepper
  Thinly sliced green onions, optional

1. Rinse and sort the black-eyed peas. Transfer to a 6-qt. electric pressure cooker. Stir in water, ham, onion, garlic, seasoned salt and pepper. Lock lid; close pressure-release valve. Adjust to pressure-cook on high for 18 minutes. Let pressure release naturally for 10 minutes; quick-release any remaining pressure.

2. Serve with a slotted spoon. If desired, sprinkle with sliced green onions.

FREEZE OPTION: Freeze cooled pea mixture in freezer containers. To use, partially thaw in refrigerator overnight. Heat through in a saucepan, stirring occasionally and adding a little water if necessary.

¾ **CUP:** 76 cal., 1g fat (0 sat. fat), 8mg chol., 476mg sod., 11g carb. (2g sugars, 3g fiber), 7g pro. **DIABETIC EXCHANGES:** 1 starch.

CHICKPEA TAGINE

While traveling through Morocco, my wife and I fell in love with the complex flavors of the many tagines we tried, so we came up with this no-fuss dish. It's great alongside grilled fish, or add shredded cooked chicken in the last 10 minutes for a change-of-pace entree.
—Raymond Wyatt, West St. Paul, MN

Prep: 30 min.
Cook: 5 min.
Makes: 12 servings

- 2 Tbsp. olive oil
- 2 garlic cloves, minced
- 2 tsp. paprika
- 1 tsp. ground ginger
- 1 tsp. ground cumin
- ½ tsp. salt
- ¼ tsp. pepper
- ¼ tsp. ground cinnamon
- 1 small butternut squash (about 2 lbs.), peeled and cut into ½-in. cubes
- 2 medium zucchini, cut into ½-in. pieces
- 1 can (15 oz.) chickpeas or garbanzo beans, rinsed and drained
- 1 medium sweet red pepper, coarsely chopped
- 1 medium onion, coarsely chopped
- 12 dried apricots, halved
- ½ cup water
- 2 to 3 tsp. harissa chili paste
- 2 tsp. honey
- 1 can (14.5 oz.) crushed tomatoes, undrained
- ¼ cup chopped fresh mint leaves
  Plain Greek yogurt, optional

1. Select saute setting on a 6-qt. electric pressure cooker. Adjust for medium heat; add oil. When oil is hot, add garlic, paprika, ginger, cumin, salt, pepper and cinnamon; cook and stir until fragrant, about 1 minute. Press cancel.

2. Add squash, zucchini, chickpeas, red pepper, onion, apricot halves, water, harissa and honey. Lock lid; close pressure-release valve. Adjust to pressure-cook on high for 3 minutes. Quick-release pressure. Press cancel. Gently stir in tomatoes and mint; heat through.

3. If desired, top with yogurt and additional mint, olive oil and honey.

¾ CUP: 127 cal., 3g fat (0 sat. fat), 0 chol., 224mg sod., 23g carb. (9g sugars, 6g fiber), 4g pro. DIABETIC EXCHANGES: 1½ starch, ½ fat.

WHY YOU'LL LOVE IT...

"I never had tagine before, but this recipe intrigued me. It was delicious and so easy to make! We ate it over quinoa, and it was delicious! I will definitely make it again!"
—KATIE, TASTEOFHOME.COM

SMOKY WHITE BEANS & HAM

I had never made or even eaten this dish before meeting my husband. Now I make it at least once a week. I serve it with some homemade sweet cornbread. Delicious!
—Christine Duffy, Sturgis, KY

Prep: 15 min.
Cook: 30 min. + releasing
Makes: 10 servings

- 1 **lb. dried great northern beans**
- 3 **smoked ham hocks (about 1½ lbs.)**
- 3 **cans (14½ oz. each) reduced-sodium chicken or beef broth**
- 2 **cups water**
- 1 **large onion, chopped**
- 1 **Tbsp. onion powder**
- 1 **Tbsp. garlic powder**
- 2 **tsp. pepper**
  Thinly sliced green onions, optional

1. Rinse and sort beans. Transfer to a 6-qt. electric pressure cooker. Add the ham hocks. Stir in broth, water, onion and seasonings. Lock lid; close pressure-release valve. Adjust to pressure-cook on high for 30 minutes. Let the pressure release naturally for 10 minutes; quick-release any remaining pressure. Press cancel.

2. When cool enough to handle, remove meat from bones; cut ham into small pieces and return to pressure cooker. Serve with a slotted spoon. Sprinkle with green onions if desired.

⅔ **CUP:** 196 cal., 2g fat (0 sat. fat), 8mg chol., 594mg sod., 32g carb. (2g sugars, 10g fiber), 15g pro. **DIABETIC EXCHANGES:** 2 starch, 2 lean meat.

FISH, SEAFOOD & MEATLESS

Whether you enjoy pasta with clam sauce, stuffed peppers or fish fillets baked to perfection, you'll savor the fresh favorites that follow. Best of all, each pares down calories, fat and sodium while keeping the focus on flavor.

DEEP DIVE INTO FISH

Brush up on your vocabulary, then get cooking!

DRESSED FISH
Ready to cook; has been gutted and scaled. It still has its head and tail.

FILLETS
Come from the side of the fish and are boneless. They may or may not be skinless.

FLATFISH
Has both eyes on top of a flat body. Flounder, sole, turbot and halibut are flatfish. Generally, flatfish is sold as fillets; halibut is typically sold as steaks.

FRESHWATER FISH
Are from streams, rivers and freshwater lakes.

LEAN FISH
Has a low fat content — it can be as low as 2.5% fat. Lean fish has a delicate texture and mild flavor. Due to the low fat content, it can dry out easily during cooking and is best cooked with some liquid or fat. Cooking by steaming methods including pressure cooking is recommended. If it is basted during cooking, it can also be baked, broiled or grilled.

MEDIUM-FAT FISH
Has a fat content around 6%. Its texture is firmer than lean fish and it has a neutral flavor. This type of fish withstands high temperatures and can be pressure cooked, baked, broiled, grilled or pan-fried.

HIGH-FAT FISH
Has a fat content of more than 6% and can be as high as 50%. Due to the high fat content, these fish have a meaty texture and a rich flavor. These fish stay moist during cooking and are suitable for pressure cooking, baking, broiling or grilling.

PAN-DRESSED FISH
A dressed fish with the head and tail removed.

ROUNDFISH
Has a round body and eyes on both sides of its head. They are sold pan-dressed or dressed, and as steaks or fillets.

SALTWATER FISH
Fish from seas or oceans.

STEAKS
Cross sections of large roundfish containing part of the backbone; usually steaks are ½ to 1 in. thick.

WHOLE FISH
Need to be gutted and scaled before cooking.

HOW TO TEST DONENESS TEMPERATURE
Fish doneness varies by the type of fish being cooked.

- The USDA recommends an internal temperature of 145°. A general rule is to cook fish for 10 minutes per every inch of thickness, measured at the thickest area. Start checking for doneness about 2 minutes before the recommended cooking time, because overcooked fish becomes tough and dry.

- For fish fillets, insert a fork at an angle into the thickest portion of fish and gently part the meat. When it is opaque and flakes into sections, it's cooked completely. But if the fish is still translucent, it's undercooked.

- For whole fish, insert a fork along the backbone and the top fillet. The fish is done when the fillet lifts easily from the bones.

- For mahi mahi and swordfish, cook until the flesh just turns opaque.

- For fresh tuna, cook to medium-rare or until slightly pink in the center. Longer cooking reduces the flavor.

KEEP IT FRESH

WHEN BUYING FISH, LOOK FOR:
- Fresh fish fillets or steaks that are firm with moist-looking flesh that bounces back when pressed.
- Shiny, bright skin.
- Whole fish with clear eyes (not sunken or cloudy) and a firm body that is springy to the touch.
- Fish with a mild aroma.
- Frozen fish in packages that are frozen solid, tightly sealed and free of freezer burn and odor.
- An appropriate substitute if your market does not carry the type of fish you want. It's best to swap fish with one that has about the same fat content as the fish in the recipe: lean, medium-fat or high-fat.

GENERAL GUIDELINES FOR PURCHASE WEIGHT AND SERVINGS
- 1 lb. whole fish = 1 serving
- 1 lb. pan-dressed fish = 2 servings
- 1 lb. steaks or fillets = 3-4 servings

REFRIGERATOR DEFROSTING
- Place the package on a tray to catch any liquid or juices.
- Defrosting time will vary depending on the weight and the thickness of the package.
- For a 1-lb. package, allow at least 12 hours.

COLD WATER DEFROSTING
- Place the fish or seafood in a leakproof plastic bag and seal.
- Submerge the sealed bag in a pan or dish of cold tap water.
- Change the water every 30 minutes.
- Allow 1-2 hours of thawing time per pound.

KEEP FISH FRESH
Fish stays freshest when stored on ice. To keep it ice-cold without mess or damaging the fish's texture, place frozen gel packs or blue ice blocks in a container, then put the wrapped fish on top. Use within a few days. Always wash the ice packs with hot soapy water before reuse.

WHY CHOOSE A MEATLESS DIET?

PROTEIN HEALTH
A plant-based diet is typically antioxidant-rich, high in fiber and low in cholesterol. Many choose vegetarian food to reduce cholesterol and lower blood pressure; to help prevent many cancers such as colon, breast, stomach, esophageal, lung and prostate; and to help control diabetes.

WEIGHT LOSS
In a well-balanced vegetarian diet, weight loss is a possibility. However, like any other diet, a vegetarian diet high in calories from nuts, full-fat dairy and junk food may result in weight gain.

BUDGET
Forgoing meat and adding more economical staples, such as grains and dried legumes, can lower grocery bills.

RESPECT FOR LIFE
Many vegans feel that all living beings, including animals, have value, and they oppose using animals to serve any human need, whether for food, clothing, household goods or product testing.

ENVIRONMENTAL CONCERNS
Some people refrain from consuming meat to help the environment. They believe humans should eat grains or crops rather than using farmland to grow a vast quantity of grain or grass to feed animals, producing a smaller volume of animal protein. "Food animals" also create animal waste. A vegetarian diet helps reduce the planet's carbon footprint.

RELIGIOUS BELIEFS
Various religions have dietary guidelines that restrict the consumption of some kinds of meat or even all meat.

CHICKPEA & POTATO CURRY

I make chana masala, the classic Indian dish, in my one-pot cooker. Browning the onion, ginger and garlic first really makes the sauce amazing.
—Anjana Devasahayam, San Antonio, TX

Prep: 25 min.
Cook: 5 min. + releasing
Makes: 6 servings

- 1 Tbsp. canola oil
- 1 medium onion, chopped
- 2 garlic cloves, minced
- 2 tsp. minced fresh gingerroot
- 2 tsp. ground coriander
- 1 tsp. garam masala
- 1 tsp. chili powder
- ½ tsp. salt
- ½ tsp. ground cumin
- ¼ tsp. ground turmeric
- 2½ cups vegetable stock
- 2 cans (15 oz. each) chickpeas or garbanzo beans, rinsed and drained
- 1 can (15 oz.) crushed tomatoes
- 1 large baking potato, peeled and cut into ¾-in. cubes
- 1 Tbsp. lime juice
    Chopped fresh cilantro
    Hot cooked rice
    Optional: Sliced red onion and lime wedges

1. Select saute setting on a 6-qt. electric pressure cooker. Adjust for medium heat; add oil. When oil is hot, cook and stir onion until crisp-tender, 2-4 minutes. Add garlic, ginger and dry seasonings; cook and stir 1 minute. Add stock to pressure cooker. Cook 30 seconds, stirring to loosen browned bits from pan. Press cancel. Stir in chickpeas, tomatoes and potato.

2. Lock lid; close pressure-release valve. Adjust to pressure-cook on high for 3 minutes. Let pressure release naturally for 10 minutes; quick-release any remaining pressure.

3. Stir in lime juice; sprinkle with cilantro. Serve with rice and, if desired, red onion and lime wedges.

1¼ **CUPS:** 240 cal., 6g fat (0 sat. fat), 0 chol., 767mg sod., 42g carb. (8g sugars, 9g fiber), g pro.

DID YOU KNOW?
Garam masala is a rich blend of ground spices that often include peppercorns, cumin, coriander, fennel, cloves and cardamom. You can find garam masala in the spice aisle of most grocery stores.

STEAMED MUSSELS WITH PEPPERS

Here's a worthy way to use your Instant Pot. Serve French bread along with the mussels to soak up the deliciously seasoned broth. If you like your food spicy, add the jalapeno seeds.
—*Taste of Home* Test Kitchen

Prep: 30 min.
Cook: 5 min.
Makes: 4 servings

- 2 lbs. fresh mussels, scrubbed and beards removed
- 2 Tbsp. olive oil
- 1 jalapeno pepper, seeded and chopped
- 3 garlic cloves, minced
- 1 bottle (8 oz.) clam juice
- ½ cup white wine or additional clam juice
- ⅓ cup chopped sweet red pepper
- 3 green onions, sliced
- ½ tsp. dried oregano
- 1 bay leaf
- 2 Tbsp. minced fresh parsley
- ¼ tsp. salt
- ¼ tsp. pepper
  French bread baguette, sliced, optional

1. Tap mussels; discard any that do not close. Set aside. Select saute setting on a 6-qt. electric pressure cooker. Adjust for medium heat; add oil. When oil is hot, cook and stir chopped jalapeno until crisp-tender, 2-3 minutes. Add garlic; cook for 1 minute longer. Press cancel. Stir in mussels, clam juice, wine, red pepper, green onions, oregano and bay leaf. Lock lid; close pressure-release valve. Adjust to pressure-cook on high 2 minutes. Quick-release pressure.

2. Discard bay leaf and any unopened mussels. Sprinkle with parsley, salt and pepper. If desired, serve with baguette slices.

12 MUSSELS: 293 cal., 12g fat (2g sat. fat), 65mg chol., 931mg sod., 12g carb. (1g sugars, 1g fiber), 28g pro.

TEST KITCHEN TIP
Purchase mussels that are alive and fresh. Mussel shells should be damp and shiny, and they should smell like the ocean. For a more substantial serving, consider buying ¾ to 1 lb. mussels per person.

SPICE TRADE BEANS & BULGUR

A rich blend of treasured spices turn nutritious bulgur and chickpeas into a tangy stew with just the right amount of heat. I think the hint of sweetness from golden raisins makes a perfect accent.
—Faith Cromwell, San Francisco, CA

Prep: 30 min.
Cook: 15 min.
Makes: 10 servings

- 3 Tbsp. canola oil, divided
- 1½ cups bulgur
- 2 medium onions, chopped
- 1 medium sweet red pepper, chopped
- 5 garlic cloves, minced
- 1 Tbsp. ground cumin
- 1 Tbsp. paprika
- 2 tsp. ground ginger
- 1 tsp. pepper
- ½ tsp. ground cinnamon
- ½ tsp. cayenne pepper
- 1 carton (32 oz.) vegetable broth
- 2 Tbsp. soy sauce
- 1 can (28 oz.) crushed tomatoes
- 1 can (14½ oz.) diced tomatoes, undrained
- 1 can (15 oz.) garbanzo beans or chickpeas, rinsed and drained
- ½ cup golden raisins
- 2 Tbsp. brown sugar
  Minced fresh cilantro, optional

1. Select saute setting on a 6-qt. electric pressure cooker. Adjust for medium heat; add 1 Tbsp. oil. When oil is hot, cook and stir bulgur until lightly browned, 2-3 minutes. Remove from pressure cooker.

2. Heat remaining 2 Tbsp. oil in pressure cooker. Cook and stir onions and red pepper until crisp-tender, 2-3 minutes. Add garlic and seasonings; cook 1 minute longer. Press cancel. Add broth, soy sauce and bulgur to pressure cooker.

3. Lock lid; close pressure-release valve. Adjust to pressure-cook on low for 12 minutes. Quick-release pressure. Press cancel. Select saute setting and adjust for low heat. Add the tomatoes, beans, raisins and brown sugar; simmer, uncovered, until mixture is slightly thickened and heated through, about 10 minutes, stirring occasionally. If desired, sprinkle with the minced cilantro.

1¼ CUPS: 245 cal., 6g fat (0 sat. fat), 0 chol., 752mg sod., 45g carb. (15g sugars, 8g fiber), 8g pro.

SIMPLE POACHED SALMON

I love this recipe because it's healthy and almost effortless. The salmon always cooks to perfection and is ready in hardly any time!
—Erin Chilcoat, Central Islip, NY

Prep: 10 min.
Cook: 5 min.
Makes: 4 servings

- 2 cups water
- 1 cup white wine
- 1 medium onion, sliced
- 1 celery rib, sliced
- 1 medium carrot, sliced
- 2 Tbsp. lemon juice
- 3 fresh thyme sprigs
- 1 fresh rosemary sprig
- 1 bay leaf
- ½ tsp. salt
- ¼ tsp. pepper
- 4 salmon fillets (1¼ in. thick and 6 oz. each)
  Lemon wedges

1. Combine the first 11 ingredients in a 6-qt. electric pressure cooker; top with salmon. Lock lid; close the pressure-release valve. Adjust to pressure cook on high for 3 minutes. Quick-release pressure. A thermometer inserted in fish should read at least 145°.

2. Remove fish from pressure cooker. Serve warm or cold with lemon wedges.

1 SALMON FILLET: 270 cal., 16g fat (3g sat. fat), 85mg chol., 115mg sod., 0 carb. (0 sugars, 0 fiber), 29g pro. **DIABETIC EXCHANGES:** 4 lean meat.

MANCHESTER STEW

While in college, I studied abroad. A vegetarian at the time, I was pleasantly surprised by how delicious and diverse vegetarian food in Britain could be. After returning to the States I re-created my favorite meal from my favorite restaurant and named it after the University of Manchester. When the enticing aroma fills the kitchen, I'm back in England!
—Kimberly Hammond, Kingwood, TX

Prep: 25 min.
Cook: 5 min. + releasing
Makes: 6 servings

- 2 Tbsp. olive oil
- 2 medium onions, chopped
- 2 garlic cloves, minced
- 1 tsp. dried oregano
- 1 cup dry red wine
- 1 lb. small red potatoes, quartered
- 1 can (16 oz.) kidney beans, rinsed and drained
- ½ lb. sliced fresh mushrooms
- 2 medium leeks (white portion only), sliced
- 1 cup fresh baby carrots
- 2½ cups water
- 1 can (14½ oz.) no-salt-added diced tomatoes
- 1 tsp. dried thyme
- ½ tsp. salt
- ¼ tsp. pepper
  Fresh basil leaves

1. Select saute setting on a 6-qt. electric pressure cooker. Adjust for medium heat; add oil. When oil is hot, cook and stir onions until crisp-tender, 2-3 minutes. Add garlic and oregano; cook and stir 1 minute longer. Stir in wine. Bring to a boil; cook until liquid is reduced by half, 3-4 minutes. Press cancel.

2. Add potatoes, beans, mushrooms, leeks and carrots. Stir in water, tomatoes, thyme, salt and pepper. Lock lid; close pressure-release valve. Adjust to pressure-cook on high for 3 minutes. Let pressure release naturally for 10 minutes; quick-release any remaining pressure. Top with basil leaves.

1⅔ **CUPS:** 221 cal., 5g fat (1g sat. fat), 0 chol., 354mg sod., 38g carb. (8g sugars, 8g fiber), 8g pro. **DIABETIC EXCHANGES:** 2 starch, 1 vegetable, 1 fat.

LENTIL STEW

This vegetarian stew is perfect when you want to take a little break from meat. Adding the cream at the end gives the dish a wonderfully smooth texture.
—Michelle Collins, Suffolk, VA

Prep: 45 min.
Cook: 15 min. + releasing
Makes: 8 servings (2¾ qt.)

- 2 Tbsp. canola oil
- 2 large onions, thinly sliced, divided
- 8 plum tomatoes, chopped
- 2 Tbsp. minced fresh gingerroot
- 3 garlic cloves, minced
- 2 tsp. ground coriander
- 1½ tsp. ground cumin
- ¼ tsp. cayenne pepper
- 3 cups vegetable broth
- 2 cups dried lentils, rinsed
- 2 cups water
- 1 can (4 oz.) chopped green chiles
- ¾ cup heavy whipping cream
- 2 Tbsp. butter
- 1 tsp. cumin seeds
- 6 cups hot cooked basmati or jasmine rice
  Optional: Sliced green onions or minced fresh cilantro

1. Select saute setting on a 6-qt. electric pressure cooker. Adjust for medium heat; add oil. When oil is hot, cook and stir half the onions until crisp-tender, 2-3 minutes. Add tomatoes, ginger and garlic, coriander, cumin and cayenne; cook and stir 1 minute longer. Press cancel. Stir in broth, lentils, water, green chiles and remaining onion.

2. Lock lid; close pressure-release valve. Adjust to pressure cook on high for 15 minutes. Let pressure release naturally. Just before serving, stir in the cream. In a small skillet, heat butter over medium heat. Add cumin seeds; cook and stir until golden brown, for 1-2 minutes. Add to lentil mixture.

3. Serve with rice. If desired, sprinkle with sliced green onions or minced cilantro.

1⅓ CUPS STEW WITH ¾ CUP RICE: 497 cal., 16g fat (8g sat. fat), 33mg chol., 345mg sod., 73g carb. (5g sugars, 8g fiber), 17g pro.

CLAM SAUCE

I serve this bright and fresh clam sauce often, usually with pasta; however, it's also delectable as a warm dip for special get-togethers.
—Frances Pietsch, Flower Mound, TX

Prep: 10 min.
Cook: 5 min.
Makes: 4 cups

- 4 Tbsp. butter
- 2 Tbsp. olive oil
- ½ cup finely chopped onion
- 8 oz. fresh mushrooms, chopped
- 2 garlic cloves, minced
- 2 cans (10 oz. each) whole baby clams
- ½ cup water
- ¼ cup sherry
- 2 tsp. lemon juice
- 1 bay leaf
- ¾ tsp. dried oregano
- ½ tsp. garlic salt
- ¼ tsp. white pepper
- ¼ tsp. Italian seasoning
- ¼ tsp. black pepper
- 2 Tbsp. chopped fresh parsley
  Hot cooked pasta
  Grated Parmesan cheese, additional lemon juice, minced parsley optional

1. Select saute setting on a 6-qt. electric pressure cooker. Adjust for medium heat; add butter and oil. When hot, cook and stir onion 2 minutes. Add mushrooms and garlic; cook 1 minute longer. Press cancel.

2. Drain clams, reserving liquid; coarsely chop. Add clams, reserved clam juice and the next 9 ingredients to pressure cooker. Lock lid; close pressure-release valve. Adjust to pressure-cook on high 2 minutes. Quick-release pressure.

3. Discard bay leaf; stir in parsley. Serve with pasta. If desired, serve with grated Parmesan cheese and additional lemon juice and parsley.

½ **CUP:** 138 cal., 10g fat (4g sat. fat), 40mg chol., 580mg sod., 5g carb. (1g sugars, 0 fiber), 7g pro.

TOMATO-POACHED HALIBUT

Simple halibut with a burst of lemon comes together easily. Serve it with bread or, even better, try it with polenta or angel hair pasta.
—Danna Rogers, Westport, CT

Prep: 15 min.
Cook: 5 min.
Makes: 4 servings

- 1 **Tbsp. olive oil**
- 2 **poblano peppers, finely chopped**
- 1 **small onion, finely chopped**
- 1 **can (14½ oz.) fire-roasted diced tomatoes, undrained**
- 1 **can (14½ oz.) no-salt-added diced tomatoes, undrained**
- ½ **cup water**
- ¼ **cup chopped pitted green olives**
- 3 **garlic cloves, minced**
- ¼ **tsp. pepper**
- ⅛ **tsp. salt**
- 4 **halibut fillets (4 oz. each)**
- ⅓ **cup chopped fresh cilantro**
- 4 **lemon wedges Crusty whole grain bread, optional**

1. Select saute setting on a 6-qt. electric pressure cooker. Adjust for medium heat; add oil. When oil is hot, cook and stir poblano peppers and onion until crisp-tender, 2-3 minutes. Press cancel. Stir in tomatoes, water, olives, garlic, pepper and salt. Top with fillets.

2. Lock the lid; close pressure-release valve. Adjust to pressure cook on high for 3 minutes. Quick-release pressure. A thermometer inserted in fish should read at least 145°.

3. Sprinkle with cilantro. Serve with lemon wedges and, if desired, bread.

1 FILLET WITH 1 CUP SAUCE: 215 cal., 7g fat (1g sat. fat), 56mg chol., 614mg sod., 16g carb. (7g sugars, 3g fiber), 23g pro. **DIABETIC EXCHANGES:** 3 lean meat, 1 starch, ½ fat.

FISH STEW

I love fish and chowder, so this stew is a favorite of mine. It's made without cream or whole milk so I don't have to worry about extra fat or calories.
—Jane Whittaker, Pensacola, FL

Prep: 25 min.
Cook: 5 min. + releasing
Makes: 8 servings (3 qt.)

- 1 lb. potatoes (about 2 medium), peeled and finely chopped
- 1 can (14½ oz.) diced tomatoes, undrained
- 1 can (10½ oz.) condensed cream of celery soup, undiluted
- 1 pkg. (10 oz.) frozen corn, thawed
- 1½ cups frozen lima beans, thawed
- 1½ cups vegetable or chicken broth
- 1 large onion, finely chopped
- 1 celery rib, finely chopped
- 1 medium carrot, finely chopped
- ½ cup white wine or additional vegetable broth
- 4 garlic cloves, minced
- 1 bay leaf
- 1 tsp. lemon-pepper seasoning
- 1 tsp. dried parsley flakes
- 1 tsp. dried rosemary, crushed
- ½ tsp. salt
- 1 lb. cod fillets, cut into 1-in. pieces
- 1 can (12 oz.) fat-free evaporated milk

1. Combine the first 16 ingredients in a 6-qt. electric pressure cooker; top with cod. Lock lid; close pressure-release valve. Adjust to pressure-cook on high for 2 minutes.

2. Let pressure release naturally. Discard bay leaf. Stir in milk until heated through.

1½ **CUPS:** 233 cal., 3g fat (1g sat. fat), 25mg chol., 701mg sod., 36g carb. (11g sugars, 5g fiber), 18g pro. **DIABETIC EXCHANGES:** 2 starch, 2 lean meat.

TEST KITCHEN TIP
Feel free to try this recipe with a pound of any variety fish fillets. Just be sure the fish is cut into 1-in. pieces for even cooking.

STUFFED PEPPERS

Here's a good-for-you dinner that's also a meatless meal-in-one classic. Add a salad and in just moments, the family will be running to the table.
—Michelle Gurnsey, Lincoln, NE

Prep: 15 min.
Cook: 5 min. + releasing
Makes: 4 servings

  4 **medium sweet
      red peppers**
  1 **can (15 oz.) black beans,
      rinsed and drained**
  1 **cup shredded pepper
      jack cheese**
  ¾ **cup salsa**
  1 **small onion, chopped**
  ½ **cup frozen corn**
  ⅓ **cup uncooked
      converted long
      grain rice**
1¼ **tsp. chili powder**
  ½ **tsp. ground cumin
      Reduced-fat sour
      cream, optional**

1. Place trivet insert and 1 cup water in a 6-qt. electric pressure cooker.

2. Cut and discard tops from peppers; remove seeds. In a large bowl, mix beans, cheese, salsa, onion, corn, rice, chili powder and cumin; spoon into peppers. Set peppers on trivet.

3. Lock lid; close pressure-release valve. Adjust to pressure-cook on high for 5 minutes. Let pressure release naturally. If desired, serve with sour cream.

1 STUFFED PEPPER: 333 cal., 10g fat (5g sat. fat), 30mg chol., 582mg sod., 45g carb. (8g sugars, 8g fiber), 15g pro. **DIABETIC EXCHANGES:** 2 starch, 2 lean meat, 2 vegetable, 1 fat.

WHY YOU'LL LOVE IT...

"This is one of my favorite vegetarian dishes! My family loves it! So glad I discovered this dish! Thank you!"
—LOURENA, TASTEOFHOME.COM

PORK DINNERS

When it comes to lighter meals, pork is a natural choice. Whether you're looking for a quick weeknight supper or an impressive entree for weekend guests, pork offers the versatility, ease and flavor today's cooks crave.

GUIDE TO PORK

When it comes to serving up meals that are lean, tender and satisfying, pork is a natural choice. Find new ways to serve ribs, roasts, chops, ham and more.

PORK PURCHASING GUIDELINES

- Pork with firm meat, a pink color and a small amount of fat on the surface.

- A package with no holes, tears or excess liquid, which may indicate improper handling and storage.

- A sell-by date on the package that is later than the day of your purchase. If it is the same date, use the meat that day or freeze it for later.

- For the leanest pork options, opt for any cut of loin.

GENERAL GUIDELINES FOR PORK PURCHASE WEIGHT AND SERVINGS

- 4 oz. of uncooked, boneless pork = 3 oz. cooked serving

- 1 lb. of any boneless cuts = 4 servings

- 1 lb. bone-in roasts, chops or ham = 2½-3 servings

- 1 lb. spareribs = about 1¼ servings

HOW LEAN IS PORK?

Some of the leanest cuts of pork are boneless loin roasts or chops, boneless sirloin roasts or chops, and bone-in pork loin chops. Ounce for ounce, pork tenderloin is as lean as boneless skinless chicken breast.

QUICK & VERSATILE

Considering which cut of pork to use will help set a meal on the table quicker. For instance, lean pork tenderloin can be grilled in less than half an hour. Cut it into medallions or cutlets, pork makes super-fast stovetop entrees. Don't forget about chops, such as ½-in.-thick rib or loin chops. Cooked on the stovetop, they can be ready in a flash. And for stir-fries or pork strips make a delicious choice.

To make sure pork is done and safe to eat, consider these basic guidelines:

- Whole cuts of fresh pork are safe when cooked to 145° with a 3-5 minute rest time.

- If you like a firmer texture, cook pork to temperatures above 145°.

- Cook ground pork to a minimum of 160°.

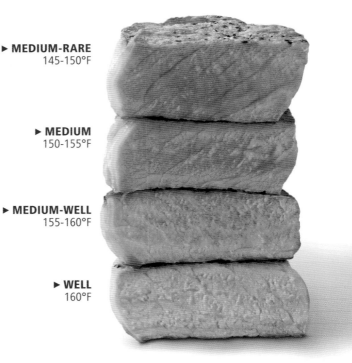

► **MEDIUM-RARE**
145-150°F

► **MEDIUM**
150-155°F

► **MEDIUM-WELL**
155-160°F

► **WELL**
160°F

PORK DONENESS PHOTO COURTESY OF
NATIONAL PORK BOARD DES MOINES, IOWA USA

PORK DINNERS MADE EASY

Planning a healthy meal is a snap when pork plays a starring role on the menu. Use this chart for compatible menu ideas when you are looking to round out the main courses in this chapter.

PORK RECIPE
Pork Chops,
Page 110

MENU ADD-ONS
- Sweet potatoes
- Sugar-free iced tea

PORK RECIPE
Pork Chops & Acorn Squash,
Page 114

MENU ADD-ONS
- Vegetable soup
- Bran muffins

PORK RECIPE
Mushroom Pork Ragout,
Page 113

MENU ADD-ONS
- Spinach salad
- Lemon sherbet

PORK RECIPE
Spicy Pork & Squash Ragu,
Page 117

MENU ADD-ONS
- Fruit salad
- Broiled eggplant

PORK RECIPE
Pork & Apple Curry,
Page 118

MENU ADD-ONS
- Whole grain naan
- Green tea

PORK RECIPE
Sweet Onion & Cherry
Pork Chops, Page 121

MENU ADD-ONS
- Steamed green beans
- Sugar-free vanilla pudding

PORK RECIPE
Pork Satay with
Rice Noodles, Page 122

MENU ADD-ONS
- Cucumber salad
- Fortune cookies

PORK RECIPE
Teriyaki Pork Roast,
Page 125

MENU ADD-ONS
- Roasted Brussels sprouts
- Brown rice

PORK RECIPE
Red Beans & Rice,
Page 126

MENU ADD-ONS
- Baked tortilla chips
- Salsa

PORK RECIPE
Pork Tacos with
Mango Salsa, Page 129

MENU ADD-ONS
- Grilled corn
- Fat-free refried beans

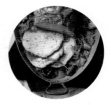

PORK RECIPE
Pork with Prunes and
Apples, Page 130

MENU ADD-ONS
- Wild rice
- Roasted asparagus

PORK CUTS

Know your pork! Consider this at-a-glance guide when deciding which cut makes the most sense for your family favorites.

▶ TENDER ◀ LESS TENDER

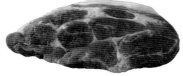

▲ SHOULDER
BLADE STEAK

▶ SHOULDER
SHOULDER ARM PORK
ROAST, BONE-IN

▲ LOIN
BACK RIBS,
BABY

▲ PICNIC
PICNIC
SHOULDER

▲ LOIN
PORK
TENDERLOIN

▲ LOIN
COUNTRY-STYLE
SPARERIBS

▲ SHOULDER
BLADE ROAST,
BONELESS

▲ LOIN
PORK TOP LOIN
CHOP, NEW YORK

◀ LOIN
BONELESS
SIRLOIN
ROAST

◀ SHOULDER
GROUND
PORK

◀ LOIN
SIRLOIN CHOP

▲LOIN
CENTER CUT
ROAST

▲ SIDE
ST. LOUIS-
STYLE RIBS

▼ LOIN
CENTER
RIB ROAST

▲SIDE
SPARERIBS

▼ SIDE
BACON

▲ LOIN
PORK RIB CHOP,
RIBEYE

► SIDE
PORK
BELLY

◄ LOIN
LOIN CHOP
(PORTERHOUSE)

◄SIDE
CANADIAN-STYLE
BACON

▼ LEG
SANDWICH
STEAKS

▲LEG
SMOKED
HAM

PORK CHOPS

Everyone will enjoy these fork-tender pork chops with a creamy gravy...and no one will suspect they're eating light! Serve the chops with a green vegetable or a salad.
—Sue Bingham, Madisonville, TN

Prep: 15 min.
Cook: 5 min.
Makes: 4 servings

- ½ **cup all-purpose flour, divided**
- ½ **tsp. ground mustard**
- ½ **tsp. garlic-pepper blend**
- ¼ **tsp. seasoned salt**
- 4 **boneless pork loin chops (4 oz. each)**
- 2 **Tbsp. canola oil**
- 1 **can (14½ oz.) chicken broth, divided**

1. In a shallow bowl, mix ¼ cup flour, mustard, garlic pepper and seasoned salt. Add 1 pork chop at a time, and toss to coat; shake off excess.

2. Select saute or browning setting on a 6-qt. electric pressure cooker. Adjust for medium heat; add canola oil. When oil is hot, brown pork in batches. Add 1½ cups broth to pressure cooker. Cook for 30 seconds, stirring to loosen browned bits from pan. Press cancel. Return all to pressure cooker.

3. Lock lid; close pressure-release valve. Adjust to pressure-cook on high for 3 minutes. Quick-release pressure. A thermometer inserted in pork should read at least 145°. Press cancel. Remove pork to serving plate and keep warm.

4. In a small bowl, mix remaining ¼ cup flour and ¼ cup broth until smooth; stir into pressure cooker. Select saute setting and adjust for low heat. Simmer, stirring constantly, until thickened, 1-2 minutes. Serve with pork.

1 PORK CHOP WITH ⅓ CUP GRAVY: 257 cal., 14g fat (3g sat. fat), 57mg chol., 606mg sod., 8g carb. (0 sugars, 0 fiber), 23g pro. **DIABETIC EXCHANGES:** 3 lean meat, 1½ fat, ½ starch.

MUSHROOM PORK RAGOUT

This savory pork for two comes together quickly with a tomato gravy and noodles. It's a nice change from regular pork roast. I serve it with broccoli or green beans on the side.
—Connie McDowell, Greenwood, DE

Prep: 20 min.
Cook: 10 min.
Makes: 2 servings

1 pork tenderloin (¾ lb.)
⅛ tsp. salt
⅛ tsp. pepper
1½ cups sliced fresh
    mushrooms
¾ cup canned crushed
    tomatoes
¾ cup reduced-sodium
    chicken broth, divided
⅓ cup sliced onion
1 Tbsp. chopped
    sun-dried tomatoes
    (not packed in oil)
1¼ tsp. dried savory
1 Tbsp. cornstarch
1½ cups hot cooked
    egg noodles

1. Rub pork with salt and pepper; cut in half. Place in a 6-qt. electric pressure cooker. Top with mushrooms, tomatoes, ½ cup broth, onion, sun-dried tomatoes and savory.

2. Lock lid; close pressure-release valve. Adjust to pressure-cook on high for 6 minutes. Quick-release pressure. A thermometer inserted in pork should read at least 145°. Press cancel.

3. Remove pork; keep warm. In a small bowl, mix cornstarch and remaining broth until smooth; stir into pressure cooker. Select saute setting and adjust for low heat. Simmer, stirring constantly, until thickened, 1-2 minutes. Slice pork; serve with sauce and noodles.

FREEZE OPTION: Place sliced pork and vegetables in freezer containers; top with sauce. Cool and freeze. To use, partially thaw in refrigerator overnight. Heat through in a covered saucepan, stirring gently and adding a little broth if necessary.

1 SERVING: 387 cal., 8g fat (2g sat. fat), 119mg chol., 613mg sod., 37g carb. (8g sugars, 4g fiber), 43g pro. **DIABETIC EXCHANGES:** 5 lean meat, 2 vegetable, 1 starch.

PORK CHOPS & ACORN SQUASH

My husband and I are crazy for the squash we grow in our garden. For a sweet and tangy dish, we pressure-cook it with pork chops and orange juice.
—Mary Johnson, Coloma, WI

Prep: 15 min.
Cook: 5 min.
Makes: 6 servings

- 6 **boneless pork loin chops (4 oz. each)**
- 2 **medium acorn squash, halved lengthwise, seeded and sliced**
- ½ **cup packed brown sugar**
- ½ **cup reduced-sodium chicken broth**
- 2 **Tbsp. butter, melted**
- 1 **Tbsp. orange juice**
- ¾ **tsp. salt**
- ¾ **tsp. browning sauce, optional**
- ½ **tsp. grated orange zest**

Place the pork chops in a 6-qt. electric pressure cooker; add squash. In a small bowl, mix the remaining ingredients; pour over squash. Lock lid; close pressure-release valve. Adjust to pressure-cook on high for 4 minutes. Quick-release pressure. A thermometer inserted in pork should read at least 145°.

1 SERVING: 349 cal., 11g fat (5g sat. fat), 65mg chol., 416mg sod., 42g carb. (23g sugars, 3g fiber), 24g pro.

TEST KITCHEN TIP
Select acorn squash that feel heavy for their size and are free of blemishes and cuts. The skin should be dark and glossy.

SPICY PORK & SQUASH RAGU

This recipe is a marvelously spicy combo perfect for cooler weather. It's so satisfying after a day spent outdoors.
—Monica Osterhaus, Paducah, KY

Prep: 20 min.
Cook: 15 min. + releasing
Makes: 10 servings

- 2 **cans (14½ oz. each) stewed tomatoes, undrained**
- 1 **pkg. (12 oz.) frozen cooked winter squash, thawed**
- 1 **large sweet onion, cut into ½-in. pieces**
- 1 **medium sweet red pepper, cut into ½-in. pieces**
- ¾ **cup reduced-sodium chicken broth**
- 1½ **tsp. crushed red pepper flakes**
- 2 **lbs. boneless country-style pork ribs**
- 1 **tsp. salt**
- ¼ **tsp. garlic powder**
- ¼ **tsp. pepper**
  Hot cooked pasta
  Shaved Parmesan cheese, optional

1. Combine first 6 ingredients in a 6-qt. electric pressure cooker. Sprinkle ribs with salt, garlic powder and pepper; place in pressure cooker. Lock lid; close pressure-release valve. Adjust to pressure-cook on high for 15 minutes. Let pressure release naturally for 10 minutes; quick-release any remaining pressure.

2. Remove cover; stir to break pork into smaller pieces. Serve with pasta. If desired, top with Parmesan cheese.

FREEZE OPTION: Freeze cooled sauce in freezer containers. To use, partially thaw in refrigerator overnight. Heat through in a saucepan, stirring occasionally.

1 CUP RAGU: 196 cal., 8g fat (3g sat. fat), 52mg chol., 469mg sod., 13g carb. (6g sugars, 2g fiber), 18g pro. **DIABETIC EXCHANGES:** 2 lean meat, 1 starch.

PORK & APPLE CURRY

Here's a gentle curry dish that's won't overwhelm more delicate palates. For fun, try varying the garnish—add a few chopped peanuts or a little chutney, for instance.
—Nancy Reck, Mill Valley, CA

Prep: 15 min.
Cook: 10 min.
Makes: 8 servings

- 2 lbs. boneless pork loin roast, cut into 1-in. cubes
- 1 small onion, chopped
- ½ cup orange juice
- 1 Tbsp. curry powder
- 1 tsp. chicken bouillon granules
- 1 garlic clove, minced
- ½ tsp. salt
- ½ tsp. ground ginger
- ¼ tsp. ground cinnamon
- 1 medium apple, peeled and chopped
- 2 Tbsp. cornstarch
- 2 Tbsp. cold water
  Hot cooked rice, optional
- ¼ cup raisins
- ¼ cup sweetened shredded coconut, toasted

1. In a 6-qt. electric pressure cooker, combine the first 9 ingredients. Lock lid; close pressure-release valve. Adjust to pressure-cook on high for 3 minutes. Quick-release the pressure. A thermometer inserted in pork should read at least 145°. Press cancel.

2. Add apple to pressure cooker. In a small bowl, combine cornstarch and water until smooth; stir into pressure cooker. Select saute setting and adjust for low heat. Simmer, stirring constantly, until thickened and apple is tender, 3-5 minutes.

3. If desired, serve with rice. Sprinkle with raisins and coconut.

⅔ **CUP:** 174 cal., 6g fat (2g sat. fat), 57mg chol., 287mg sod., 8g carb. (4g sugars, 1g fiber), 22g pro. **DIABETIC EXCHANGES:** 3 lean meat, ½ starch.

WHY YOU'LL LOVE IT...

"Pork and apple curry is one my family simply loves and makes any time we can. It's usually served over rice, which is just fine with all of us, as we love rice dishes."
—TKARINAS, TASTEOFHOME.COM

SWEET ONION & CHERRY PORK CHOPS

When I want to jump-start supper, I opt for these tender pork chops. The sweet and savory cherry sauce makes this recipe a keeper. Try serving it with wild rice pilaf.
—Stephanie Ray, Naples, FL

Prep: 15 min.
Cook: 5 min.
Makes: 4 servings

- 1 **cup fresh or frozen pitted tart cherries, thawed**
- 1 **cup reduced-sodium chicken broth**
- ¼ **cup chopped sweet onion**
- 2 **Tbsp. honey**
- 1 **tsp. seasoned salt**
- ½ **tsp. pepper**
- 4 **boneless pork loin chops (5 oz. each)**
- 1 **Tbsp. cornstarch**
- 1 **Tbsp. cold water**

1. In a 6-qt. electric pressure cooker, combine the first 6 ingredients; top with pork chops. Lock lid; close pressure-release valve. Adjust to pressure-cook on high for 3 minutes. Quick-release pressure. A thermometer inserted in pork should read at least 145°. Press cancel.

2. Remove pork to a serving platter; keep warm. In a small bowl, mix cornstarch and water until smooth; stir into the pressure cooker. Select saute setting and adjust for low heat. Simmer, stirring constantly, until thickened, 1-2 minutes. Serve with pork.

1 PORK CHOP WITH ¼ CUP CHERRY MIXTURE: 259 cal., 8g fat (3g sat. fat), 68mg chol., 567mg sod., 17g carb. (14g sugars, 1g fiber), 29g pro. **DIABETIC EXCHANGES:** 4 lean meat, 1 starch, ½ fat.

PORK SATAY WITH RICE NOODLES

I love the addition of peanuts to savory recipes. Intensify the flavor by sprinkling with minced fresh cilantro and chopped peanuts for that restaurant-quality look and taste.
—Stephanie Anderson, Horseheads, NY

Prep: 20 min.
Cook: 5 min.
Makes: 6 servings

1½ lbs. boneless pork loin chops, cut into 2-in. pieces
¼ tsp. pepper
1 medium onion, halved and sliced
⅓ cup creamy peanut butter
¼ cup reduced-sodium soy sauce
½ tsp. onion powder
½ tsp. garlic powder
½ tsp. hot pepper sauce
1 can (14½ oz.) reduced-sodium chicken broth, divided
3 Tbsp. cornstarch
9 oz. uncooked thick rice noodles
Optional: Minced fresh cilantro and chopped peanuts

1. Sprinkle pork with pepper. Place in a 6-qt. electric pressure cooker; top with onion. In a small bowl, mix peanut butter, soy sauce, onion powder, garlic powder and pepper sauce; gradually add 1½ cups broth. Pour over onion.

2. Lock the lid; close pressure-release valve. Adjust to pressure-cook on high for 3 minutes. Quick-release pressure. A thermometer inserted in pork should read at least 145°. Press cancel. Remove pork chops from pressure cooker and keep warm.

3. In a small bowl, mix cornstarch and remaining ¼ cup broth until smooth; stir into pressure cooker. Select saute setting and adjust for low heat. Simmer, stirring constantly, until thickened, 1-2 minutes. Add pork; heat through.

4. Meanwhile, cook rice noodles according to package directions; drain. Serve with pork mixture. If desired, sprinkle with cilantro and peanuts.

1 SERVING: 427 cal., 14g fat (4g sat. fat), 55mg chol., 754mg sod., 44g carb. (3g sugars, 2g fiber), 29g pro.

TERIYAKI PORK ROAST

I'm always looking for no-fuss recipes, so I was thrilled to find this one. The tender teriyaki pork has become a family favorite.
—Roxanne Hulsey, Gainesville, GA

Prep: 10 min.
Cook: 30 min. + releasing
Makes: 10 servings

- ¾ cup unsweetened apple juice
- 2 Tbsp. sugar
- 2 Tbsp. reduced-sodium soy sauce
- 1 Tbsp. white vinegar
- 1 tsp. ground ginger
- ¼ tsp. garlic powder
- ⅛ tsp. pepper
- 1 boneless pork loin roast (about 3 lbs.), halved
- 8 tsp. cornstarch
- 3 Tbsp. cold water

1. Combine the first 7 ingredients in a 6-qt. electric pressure cooker. Add roast and turn to coat. Lock lid; close pressure-release valve. Adjust to pressure-cook on high for 25 minutes. Let pressure release naturally for 10 minutes; quick-release any remaining pressure. A thermometer inserted in pork should read at least 145°. Press cancel.

2. Remove pork to a serving platter; keep warm. In a small bowl, mix the cornstarch and water until smooth; stir into pressure cooker. Select saute setting and adjust for low heat. Simmer, stirring constantly, until thickened, 1-2 minutes. Serve with the pork.

FREEZE OPTION: Place sliced pork roast in freezer containers; top with sauce. Cool and freeze. To use, partially thaw in refrigerator overnight. Heat through in a covered saucepan, stirring gently and adding a little water if necessary.

4 OZ. COOKED PORK: 198 cal., 6g fat (2g sat. fat), 68mg chol., 155mg sod., 7g carb. (4g sugars, 0 fiber), 27g pro. **DIABETIC EXCHANGES:** 4 lean meat, ½ starch.

RED BEANS & RICE

My family loves New Orleans-style cooking, so I make this dish often. I appreciate how simple it is, and the smoky ham flavor is scrumptious.
—Celinda Dahlgren, Napa, CA

Prep: 20 min.
Cook: 45 min. + releasing
Makes: 6 servings

- 3 cups water
- 2 smoked ham hocks (about 1 lb.)
- 1 cup dried red beans
- 1 medium onion, chopped
- 1½ tsp. minced garlic
- 1 tsp. ground cumin
- 1 medium tomato, chopped
- 1 medium green pepper, chopped
- 1 tsp. salt
- 4 cups hot cooked rice

1. Place the first 6 ingredients in a 6-qt. electric pressure cooker. Lock lid; close pressure-release valve. Adjust to pressure-cook on high for 35 minutes.

2. Let pressure release naturally. Press cancel. Remove ham hocks; cool slightly. Remove meat from bones. Finely chop meat and return to pressure cooker; discard bones. Stir in the tomato, green pepper and salt. Select saute setting and adjust for low heat. Simmer, stirring constantly, until pepper is tender, 8-10 minutes. Serve with rice.

FREEZE OPTION: Freeze cooled bean mixture in freezer containers. To use, partially thaw in refrigerator overnight. Microwave, covered, on high in a microwave-safe dish until heated through, gently stirring and adding a little water if necessary.

⅔ CUP BEAN MIXTURE WITH ⅔ CUP RICE: 216 cal., 2g fat (0 sat. fat), 9mg chol., 671mg sod., 49g carb. (3g sugars, 12g fiber), 12g pro.

PORK TACOS WITH MANGO SALSA

I've made quite a few tacos in my day, but you can't beat the tender filling made in a pressure cooker. These are by far the best pork tacos we've had—and we've tried plenty. Make the mango salsa from scratch if you have time!
—Amber Massey, Argyle, TX

Prep: 25 min.
Cook: 5 min.
Makes: 12 servings

- 2 Tbsp. white vinegar
- 2 Tbsp. lime juice
- 3 cups cubed fresh pineapple
- 1 small red onion, coarsely chopped
- 3 Tbsp. chili powder
- 2 chipotle peppers in adobo sauce
- 2 tsp. ground cumin
- 1½ tsp. salt
- ½ tsp. pepper
- 1 bottle (12 oz.) dark Mexican beer
- 3 lbs. pork tenderloin, cut into 1-in. cubes
- ¼ cup chopped fresh cilantro
- 1 jar (16 oz.) mango salsa
- 24 corn tortillas (6 in.), warmed
  Optional toppings: Cubed fresh pineapple, cubed avocado and queso fresco

1. Puree the first 9 ingredients in a blender; stir in beer. In a 6-qt. electric pressure cooker, combine pork and pineapple mixture. Lock the lid; close pressure-release valve. Adjust to pressure-cook on high for 3 minutes. Quick-release pressure. A thermometer inserted into pork should read at least 145°. Stir to break up pork.

2. Stir cilantro into salsa. Using a slotted spoon, serve pork mixture in tortillas; add salsa and toppings as desired.

FREEZE OPTION: Freeze cooled meat mixture and cooking juices in freezer containers. To use, partially thaw in refrigerator overnight. Heat through in a saucepan, stirring occasionally.

2 TACOS: 284 cal., 6g fat (2g sat. fat), 64mg chol., 678mg sod., 30g carb. (5g sugars, 5g fiber), 26g pro. **DIABETIC EXCHANGES:** 3 lean meat, 2 starch.

WHY YOU'LL LOVE IT...

"This was so easy to prepare, and it was super good. The leftovers in the freezer will be so good. Meat was very tender and the blend of the spices was just perfect."
—BONITO15, TASTEOFHOME.COM

PORK WITH PRUNES & APPLES

The classic flavors of herbes de Provence, apples and dried plums make this easy entree taste like a hearty meal at a French country cafe. For a truly traditional meal, serve the pork with braised lentils.
—Suzanne Banfield, Basking Ridge, NJ

Prep: 20 min. + standing
Cook: 35 min. + releasing
Makes: 10 servings

- 1 **boneless pork loin roast (3 to 4 lbs.)**
- 2 **Tbsp. all-purpose flour**
- 1 **Tbsp. herbes de Provence**
- 1½ **tsp. salt**
- ¾ **tsp. pepper**
- 2 **Tbsp. olive oil**
- 1 **cup apple cider or unsweetened apple juice**
- 2 **medium onions, halved and thinly sliced**
- 1 **cup beef stock**
- 2 **bay leaves**
- 2 **large tart apples, peeled and chopped**
- 1 **cup pitted dried plums**

1. Halve roast. Mix flour, herbes de Provence, salt and pepper; rub over pork. Select saute or browning setting on a 6-qt. electric pressure cooker. Adjust for medium heat; add 1 Tbsp. oil. When oil is hot, brown a roast half on all sides. Remove; repeat with remaining pork and oil.

2. Add cider to pressure cooker. Cook 1 minute, stirring to loosen browned bits from pan. Press cancel. Add onions, stock, bay leaves and roast.

3. Lock lid; close pressure-release valve. Adjust to pressure-cook on high for 25 minutes. Let pressure release naturally for 10 minutes; quick-release any remaining pressure. A thermometer inserted in pork should read at least 145°. Press cancel. Remove roast and onions to a serving platter, discarding bay leaves; tent with foil.

4. Select saute setting and adjust for low heat. Add apples and plums; simmer, uncovered, until the apples are tender, 6-8 minutes, stirring occasionally. Serve with roast.

4 OZ. COOKED PORK WITH ¾ CUP FRUIT MIXTURE: 286 cal., 9g fat (3g sat. fat), 68mg chol., 449mg sod., 22g carb. (13g sugars, 2g fiber), 28g pro.

POULTRY FAVORITES

Chicken and turkey save the day whenever time is tight, particularly when your one-pot cooker is in the mix. Consider these full-flavored entrees when you're watching the clock and the scale.

PICKING THE RIGHT POULTRY

When purchasing chicken and turkey, be sure you understand your options.

BASTED OR SELF-BASTED
Chicken or turkey that has been injected or marinated with a solution of water, broth or stock that contains some form of fat, such as butter, plus spices and flavor enhancers.

BROILER/FRYER
A chicken about 7 weeks old that weighs 2½-4½ pounds.

CAPON
A castrated male chicken between 4 and 8 months old that weighs 4-7 pounds.

CHICKEN LEG
The attached drumstick and thigh.

CHICKEN QUARTER
A quarter of the chicken, which may be the leg or breast quarter. The leg quarter contains the drumstick, thigh and portion of the back. The breast quarter contains the breast, wing and portion of the back.

CORNISH GAME HEN
A small broiler/fryer that is less than 30 days old and weighs 1¼-1½ pounds.

CUT-UP CHICKEN
A broiler/fryer that has been cut into two breast halves, two thighs, two drumsticks and two wings. It may or may not have the back.

DRUMMETTE
First section of a chicken wing.

DRUMSTICK
The lower portion of the leg.

FREE-RANGE OR FREE-ROAMING
The poultry was not confined to a chicken house but was allowed outside to forage for food.

FRESH POULTRY
Uncooked poultry that has never been commercially stored below 26°.

GIBLETS
The heart, liver, neck and gizzard.

HEN OR TOM TURKEY
Indicates whether the turkey was female (hen) or male (tom). Tom turkeys are usually larger than hen turkeys. They are equally tender.

HERITAGE TURKEY
These turkey breeds were developed over hundreds of years across the U.S. and Europe, and they're identified in the American Poultry Association's Turkey Standard of Perfection of 1874. Heritage turkeys take longer to raise and are more expensive. Cooks seek them out for their richer flavor and moister meat.

NATURAL
This label means the product does not contain artificial flavors, colors, chemical preservatives or other artificial or synthetic ingredients.

ORGANIC
The poultry was raised by a producer certified by the National Organic Program in compliance with USDA organic regulations.

ROASTER
A chicken between 3 and 5 months old that weighs 5-7 pounds.

SPLIT CHICKEN
A broiler/fryer that has been cut in half lengthwise.

HANDY AT-A-GLANCE HINTS

WHEN BUYING, LOOK FOR:

- Fresh, moist meat. The skin color of chicken ranges from white to deep yellow. Color is an indication of the chicken's diet, not freshness.

- Duck and goose in the freezer case. The holiday season is usually the best time to find them fresh.

- A package with no holes, tears or excessive liquid, which may indicate improper handling and storage.

- A sell-by date on the package that is later than the day of your purchase. If it is the same date, use the meat that day or freeze it for later.

REFRIGERATOR DEFROSTING:

- Place a tray under the meat to catch any liquid.

- Defrosting time will vary depending on the weight and thickness of the poultry.

- For bone-in parts or a small whole chicken, allow at least 1-2 days.

- For duck or goose parts, allow at least 1 day.

- For a whole duck or goose, allow at least 2 days.

- For a whole turkey or large whole chicken, allow 24 hours for every 4 pounds.

DONENESS TEMPERATURES AS MEASURED WITH A FOOD THERMOMETER:

165° Ground chicken and ground turkey

165° Chicken and turkey boneless breast minimum temperature

165° Stuffing

170° Chicken and turkey bone-in breast

170° Chicken and turkey boneless thighs

170°-175° Whole chicken and turkey as measured in thickest part of thigh

170°-175° Chicken and turkey legs, drumsticks and bone-in thighs

180° Duck, goose, pheasant

TYPE OF POULTRY	SERVINGS PER POUND
CHICKEN, WHOLE	1-2
CHICKEN PARTS (BONE-IN, SKIN-ON)	2-3
CHICKEN BREASTS (BONELESS SKINLESS)	3-4
TURKEY, WHOLE (12 LBS. OR LESS)	1
TURKEY, WHOLE (12 LBS. OR MORE)	2
TURKEY PARTS (THIGHS, BONE-IN BREASTS)	2-3
TURKEY BREAST (BONELESS)	3-4
DUCK, WHOLE	1
GOOSE, WHOLE	1
CORNISH GAME HENS	1-2 (PER HEN)

FOUR FAST, EASY WAYS TO SHRED CHICKEN

- After cooking boneless skinless chicken breasts in the electric pressure cooker, use a hand mixer right in the pot to quickly shred the meat for recipes.

- Cut cooked chicken into chunks and add it to a stand mixer with the paddle attachment. A few seconds on medium-low speed is just enough to shred it.

- Use 2 large forks to pull cooked chicken in opposite directions.

- After the chicken has cooled a little, pull it into shreds with your hands.

CAJUN-STYLE BEANS & SAUSAGE

Beans and rice make the perfect meal because they're well-balanced, an excellent source of protein and easy to prepare. Sausage adds full flavor to the recipe, and traditional pork sausage lovers won't even notice the switch to chicken sausage.
—Robin Haas, Cranston, RI

Prep: 25 min.
Cook: 5 min. + releasing
Makes: 8 servings

- 1 pkg. (12 oz.) fully cooked spicy chicken sausage links, halved lengthwise and cut into ½-in. slices
- ¾ cup reduced-sodium chicken broth
- 2 cans (16 oz. each) red beans, rinsed and drained
- 2 cans (14½ oz. each) diced tomatoes, undrained
- 3 medium carrots, chopped
- 1 large onion, chopped
- 1 large green pepper, chopped
- ½ cup chopped roasted sweet red peppers
- 3 garlic cloves, minced
- 1 tsp. Cajun seasoning
- 1 tsp. dried oregano
- ½ tsp. dried thyme
- ½ tsp. pepper
- 5⅓ cups cooked brown rice

1. Select saute or browning setting on a 6-qt. electric pressure cooker. Adjust for medium heat; brown sausage. Add broth; cook 1 minute, stirring to loosen browned bits. Press cancel. Stir in beans, tomatoes, vegetables, garlic and seasonings.

2. Lock lid; close pressure-release valve. Adjust to pressure-cook on high for 5 minutes. Let pressure release naturally for 10 minutes; quick-release any remaining pressure. Serve with hot brown rice.

FREEZE OPTION: Freeze cooled meat mixture in freezer containers. To use, partially thaw in refrigerator overnight. Microwave, covered, on high in a microwave-safe dish until heated through, stirring gently and adding a little water if necessary.

1 CUP SAUSAGE AND BEAN MIXTURE WITH ⅔ CUP RICE: 377 cal., 5g fat (1g sat. fat), 33mg chol., 826mg sod., 63g carb. (7g sugars, 10g fiber), 18g pro.

MUSHROOM CHICKEN & PEAS

This meal-in-one recipe was inspired by some amazingly fresh mushrooms I found at our local farmers market. When you start with the best ingredients, you just can't go wrong.
—Jenn Tidwell, Fair Oaks, CA

Prep: 10 min.
Cook: 10 min.
Makes: 4 servings

- 4 **boneless skinless chicken breast halves (6 oz. each)**
- 1 **envelope onion mushroom soup mix**
- ½ **lb. baby portobello mushrooms, sliced**
- 1 **medium onion, chopped**
- ¾ **cup water**
- 4 **garlic cloves, minced**
- 2 **cups frozen peas, thawed**

1. Place chicken in a 6-qt. electric pressure cooker. Sprinkle with soup mix, pressing to help seasonings adhere. Add mushrooms, onion, water and garlic. Lock lid; close pressure-release valve. Adjust to pressure-cook on high for 6 minutes.

2. Quick-release pressure. Press cancel. A thermometer inserted in chicken should read at least 165°. Select saute setting and adjust for low heat. Add peas; simmer, uncovered, until peas are tender, 3-5 minutes, stirring occasionally.

1 CHICKEN BREAST HALF WITH ¾ CUP VEGETABLE MIXTURE: 282 cal., 5g fat (1g sat. fat), 94mg chol., 558mg sod., 18g carb. (6g sugars, 4g fiber), 41g pro. **DIABETIC EXCHANGES:** 5 lean meat, 1 starch, 1 vegetable.

TEST KITCHEN TIP
Make frozen peas a staple in your home. They're perfect to toss into pasta dishes, salads, soups, stews and casseroles. Best of all, they thaw quickly under warm water, making it a snap to add a bit of color (and nutrition) to your dishes.

HERBED TURKEY BREASTS

Here tender turkey breast is enhanced with an array of flavorful herbs in this juicy, flavorful and comforting dish. What a fabulous way to save time on holiday meals.
—Laurie Mace, Los Osos, CA

Prep: 25 min. + marinating
Cook: 20 min. + releasing
Makes: 12 servings

   1 can (14½ oz.)
       chicken broth
 ½ cup lemon juice
 ¼ cup packed
       brown sugar
 ¼ cup fresh sage
 ¼ cup fresh thyme leaves
 ¼ cup lime juice
 ¼ cup cider vinegar
 ¼ cup olive oil
   1 envelope onion
       soup mix
   2 Tbsp. Dijon mustard
   1 Tbsp. minced fresh
       marjoram
1½ tsp. paprika
   1 tsp. garlic powder
   1 tsp. pepper
 ½ tsp. salt
   2 boneless skinless
       turkey breast halves
       (2 lbs. each)
       Lemon wedges,
         optional

1. In a blender, process the first 15 ingredients until blended. Place turkey in a bowl or shallow dish; pour marinade over turkey and turn to coat. Refrigerate, covered, 8 hours or overnight, turning occasionally.

2. Transfer turkey and marinade to a 6-qt. electric pressure cooker. Lock lid; close pressure-release valve. Adjust to pressure-cook on high for 20 minutes.

3. Let pressure release naturally for 10 minutes; quick-release any remaining pressure. A thermometer inserted in turkey breasts should read at least 165°. Remove the turkey from pressure cooker; tent with foil. Let stand 10 minutes before slicing. If desired, top with additional fresh thyme and marjoram and serve with lemon wedges.

5 OZ. COOKED TURKEY: 219 cal., 5g fat (1g sat. fat), 87mg chol., 484mg sod., 5g carb. (3g sugars, 0 fiber), 36g pro. **DIABETIC EXCHANGES:** 5 lean meat.

GARLIC CHICKEN & BROCCOLI

This simple riff on a classic Chinese chicken dish proves you can savor the takeout taste you crave while still eating right.
—Connie Krupp, Racine, WI

Prep: 15 min.
Cook: 5 min.
Makes: 8 servings

- 2 lbs. boneless skinless chicken breasts, cut into 1-in. pieces
- 4 cups fresh broccoli florets
- 4 medium carrots, julienned
- 1 can (8 oz.) sliced water chestnuts, drained
- 6 garlic cloves, minced
- 3 cups reduced-sodium chicken broth
- ¼ cup reduced-sodium soy sauce
- 2 Tbsp. brown sugar
- 2 Tbsp. sesame oil
- 2 Tbsp. rice vinegar
- ½ tsp. salt
- ½ tsp. pepper
- ⅓ cup cornstarch
- ⅓ cup water
  Hot cooked rice

1. Place the first 5 ingredients in a 6-qt. electric pressure cooker. In a large bowl, mix broth, soy sauce, brown sugar, sesame oil, vinegar, salt and pepper; pour over chicken mixture. Lock lid; close pressure-release valve. Adjust to pressure-cook on high for 3 minutes. Quick-release pressure. Press cancel. A thermometer inserted in chicken should read at least 165°.

2. Remove chicken and vegetables; keep warm. In a small bowl, mix cornstarch and water until smooth; stir into cooking juices. Select saute setting and adjust for low heat. Simmer, stirring constantly, until thickened, 1-2 minutes. Serve with chicken, vegetables and hot cooked rice.

FREEZE OPTION: Place chicken and vegetables in freezer containers; top with sauce. Cool and freeze. To use, partially thaw in refrigerator overnight. Microwave, covered, on high in a microwave-safe dish until heated through, stirring gently and adding a little broth or water if necessary.

1 CUP: 241 cal., 6g fat (1g sat. fat), 63mg chol., 798mg sod., 19g carb. (8g sugars, 3g fiber), 26g pro. **DIABETIC EXCHANGES:** 3 lean meat, 1 vegetable, ½ starch, ½ fat.

AUTUMN APPLE CHICKEN

Chicken with apples and barbecue sauce fills the whole house with the most delicious aroma! This is a meal you won't want to wait to dig into.

—Caitlyn Hauser, Brookline, NH

Prep: 25 min.
Cook: 20 min. + releasing
Makes: 4 servings

- 4 **bone-in chicken thighs (about 1½ lbs.), skin removed**
- ¼ **tsp. salt**
- ¼ **tsp. pepper**
- 1 **Tbsp. canola oil**
- ½ **cup apple cider or juice**
- 1 **medium onion, chopped**
- ⅓ **cup barbecue sauce**
- 1 **Tbsp. honey**
- 1 **garlic clove, minced**
- 2 **medium Fuji or Gala apples, coarsely chopped**

1. Sprinkle chicken with salt and pepper. Select saute or browning setting on a 6-qt. electric pressure cooker. Adjust for medium heat; add oil. When oil is hot, brown chicken; remove and keep warm.

2. Add apple cider, stirring to loosen browned bits from pan. Stir in the onion, barbecue sauce, honey, garlic and chicken. Press cancel. Lock lid; close pressure-release valve. Adjust to pressure-cook on high for 10 minutes. Let pressure release naturally for 5 minutes; quick-release any remaining pressure. Press cancel. A thermometer inserted in chicken should read at least 170°.

3. Remove chicken; keep warm. Select saute setting and adjust for low heat. Add apples; simmer, stirring constantly, until apples are tender, about 10 minutes. Serve with chicken.

1 CHICKEN THIGH WITH ½ CUP APPLE MIXTURE: 340 cal., 13g fat (3g sat. fat), 87mg chol., 458mg sod., 31g carb. (24g sugars, 3g fiber), 25g pro. **DIABETIC EXCHANGES:** 4 lean meat, 1½ starch, ½ fruit.

CHICKEN WITH RAISINS & CAPERS

Capers, golden raisins and fresh basil give this dish a sweetly savory flavor.
And what's even better than that? The kids love it!
—Nadine Mesch, Mount Healthy, OH

Prep: 25 min.
Cook: 10 min.
Makes: 8 servings

- 2 **Tbsp. olive oil, divided**
- 8 **boneless skinless chicken thighs (4 oz. each)**
- 1 **tsp. salt**
- 1 **tsp. pepper**
- ½ **cup Marsala wine**
- ½ **lb. sliced fresh mushrooms**
- 1 **medium sweet red pepper, thinly sliced**
- 1 **medium onion, thinly sliced**
- 1 **can (14½ oz.) diced tomatoes, undrained**
- ½ **cup golden raisins**
- 2 **Tbsp. capers, drained**
- ¼ **cup chopped fresh basil Hot cooked couscous**

1. Select saute or browning setting on a 6-qt. electric pressure cooker. Adjust for medium heat; add 1 Tbsp. oil. Sprinkle the chicken with salt and pepper. When oil is hot, brown chicken in batches. Add wine to pressure cooker. Cook 1 minute and stir to loosen browned bits from pan. Press cancel. Return chicken to pressure cooker.

2. Stir mushrooms, red pepper, onion, and tomatoes, raisins and capers into pressure cooker. Lock lid; close pressure-release valve. Adjust to pressure-cook on high for 6 minutes. Quick-release pressure. A thermometer inserted in chicken should read at least 170°. Sprinkle with basil before serving. Serve with hot cooked couscous.

FREEZE OPTION: Place chicken and vegetables in freezer containers; top with cooking juices. Cool and freeze. To use, partially thaw in refrigerator overnight. Heat through in a covered saucepan, stirring gently and adding a little water if necessary.

1 SERVING: 250 cal., 12g fat (3g sat. fat), 76mg chol., 494mg sod., 13g carb. (9g sugars, 2g fiber), 23g pro. **DIABETIC EXCHANGES:** 3 lean meat, 1 starch, 1 fat.

INDIAN-STYLE CHICKEN & VEGETABLES

This easy Indian-influenced dish is one just about everyone will love. Feel free to add more or less tikka masala sauce according to your taste.
—Erica Polly, Sun Prairie, WI

Prep: 15 min.
Cook: 5 min.
Makes: 8 servings

- 2 lbs. boneless skinless chicken thighs, cubed
- 2 medium sweet potatoes, peeled and cut into 1½-in. pieces
- 2 medium sweet red peppers, cut into 1-in. pieces
- 3 cups fresh cauliflowerets
- 2 jars (15 oz. each) tikka masala curry sauce
- ½ cup water
- ¾ tsp. salt
  Minced fresh cilantro, optional
  Naan flatbreads, warmed

In a 6-qt. electric pressure cooker, combine the chicken and vegetables; add sauce, water and salt. Lock lid; close pressure-release valve. Adjust to pressure-cook on high for 3 minutes. Quick-release pressure. A thermometer inserted in chicken should read at least 170°. If desired, top with cilantro; serve with warmed naan.

FREEZE OPTION: Omitting cilantro and naan, freeze cooled chicken and vegetable mixture in freezer containers. To use, partially thaw in refrigerator overnight. Microwave, covered, on high in a microwave-safe dish until heated through, stirring gently and adding a little water if necessary. If desired, sprinkle with cilantro. Serve with warmed naan.

1¼ CUPS: 334 cal., 15g fat (4g sat. fat), 80mg chol., 686mg sod., 25g carb. (12g sugars, 5g fiber), 25g pro. DIABETIC EXCHANGES: 3 lean meat, 2 fat, 1½ starch.

TEST KITCHEN TIP
Tikka masala is a reddish orange sauce sometimes used in Indian dishes. The spicy ingredient can be found in the ethnic foods aisle of larger grocery stores.

ITALIAN TURKEY BREAST

This recipe makes some of the most succulent turkey I've ever eaten. High in lean protein, it's a smart entree for special occasions.
—Jessica Kunz, Springfield, IL

Prep: 25 min. + standing
Cook: 25 min. + releasing
Makes: 14 servings

- 1 lb. carrots, cut into 2-in. pieces
- 2 medium onions, cut into wedges
- 3 celery ribs, cut into 2-in. pieces
- 1 can (14½ oz.) chicken broth
- 1 bone-in turkey breast (6 to 7 lbs.), thawed and skin removed
- 2 Tbsp. olive oil
- 1½ tsp. seasoned salt
- 1 tsp. Italian seasoning
- ½ tsp. pepper

1. Place vegetables and broth in a 6-qt. electric pressure cooker. Brush turkey with oil; sprinkle with seasonings. Place over vegetables.

2. Lock lid; close pressure-release valve. Adjust to pressure-cook on high for 25 minutes. Let pressure release naturally for 10 minutes; quick-release any remaining pressure. A thermometer inserted in turkey breast should read at least 170°. Remove turkey from pressure cooker; tent with foil. Let stand 10 minutes before slicing.

1 SERVING: 308 cal., 13g fat (3g sat. fat), 106mg chol., 409mg sod., 5g carb. (2g sugars, 1g fiber), 41g pro. **DIABETIC EXCHANGES:** 5 lean meat, ½ fat.

SPICY LIME CHICKEN

This tender chicken with a light lime flavor is ideal as a taco filling, but my son also loves it spooned over cooked rice and finished off with his favorite taco toppings.
—Christine Hair, Odessa, FL

Prep: 10 min.
Cook: 10 min.
Makes: 6 servings

- 4 **boneless skinless chicken breast halves (6 oz. each)**
- 2 **cups chicken broth**
- 3 **Tbsp. lime juice**
- 1 **Tbsp. chili powder**
- 1 **tsp. grated lime zest**
  Fresh cilantro leaves, optional

DID YOU KNOW?
You can make your own chili powder. Just combine ¼ cup paprika with 1 Tbsp. each garlic powder, onion powder and dried oregano. Stir in 2 tsp. cumin.

1. Place chicken in a 6-qt. electric pressure cooker. Combine broth, lime juice and chili powder; pour over chicken. Lock lid; close pressure-release valve. Adjust to pressure-cook on high for 6 minutes.

2. Quick-release pressure. A thermometer inserted in chicken should read at least 165°.

3. Remove the chicken. When cool enough to handle, shred meat with 2 forks; return to pressure cooker. Stir in lime zest. If desired, serve with cilantro.

FREEZE OPTION: Freeze cooled meat mixture in freezer containers. To use, partially thaw in refrigerator overnight. Microwave, covered, on high in a microwave-safe dish until heated through, stirring gently and adding a little broth if necessary.

1 SERVING: 132 cal., 3g fat (1g sat. fat), 64mg chol., 420mg sod., 2g carb. (1g sugars, 1g fiber), 23g pro. **DIABETIC EXCHANGES:** 3 lean meat.

SPRING-THYME CHICKEN STEW

During a particularly long winter, we were in need of something warm and bright. This stew always reminds me of the days Mom made her chicken soup for me.
—Amy Chase, Vanderhoof, BC

Prep: 25 min.
Cook: 10 min.
Makes: 4 servings

1 lb. small red
   potatoes, halved
1 large onion,
   finely chopped
¾ cup shredded carrots
6 garlic cloves, minced
2 tsp. grated lemon zest
2 tsp. dried thyme
½ tsp. salt
¼ tsp. pepper
1½ lbs. boneless skinless
   chicken thighs, cut
   into 1-in. pieces
2 cups reduced-sodium
   chicken broth, divided
2 bay leaves
3 Tbsp. all-purpose flour
2 Tbsp. minced
   fresh parsley

1. Place potatoes, onion and carrots in a 6-qt. electric pressure cooker. Top with garlic, lemon zest, thyme, salt and pepper. Place chicken over top. Add 1¾ cups broth and bay leaves.

2. Lock lid; close pressure-release valve. Adjust to pressure-cook on high for 5 minutes. Quick-release pressure. Press cancel. A thermometer inserted in chicken should read at least 170°.

3. Remove chicken; keep warm. Discard bay leaves. In a small bowl, mix flour and remaining ¼ cup broth until smooth; stir into pressure cooker. Select saute setting and adjust for low heat. Simmer, stirring constantly, until slightly thickened, for 1-2 minutes. Return chicken to pressure cooker; heat through. Sprinkle servings with parsley.

1 SERVING: 389 cal., 13g fat (3g sat. fat), 113mg chol., 699mg sod., 31g carb. (4g sugars, 4g fiber), 37g pro. **DIABETIC EXCHANGES:** 5 lean meat, 2 vegetable, 1½ starch.

SAUCY BARBECUE CHICKEN THIGHS

Barbecued chicken gets a makeover in this recipe. The combination of ingredients makes for a mellow, not-too-sweet flavor that's more grown-up than the original and super over rice, pasta or potatoes.
—Sharon Fritz, Morristown, TN

Prep: 15 min.
Cook: 10 min.
Makes: 6 servings

- 6 **boneless skinless chicken thighs (about 1½ lbs.)**
- ½ tsp. **poultry seasoning**
- 1 **medium onion, chopped**
- 1 **can (14½ oz.) diced tomatoes, undrained**
- 1 **can (8 oz.) tomato sauce**
- ½ cup **barbecue sauce**
- ¼ cup **water**
- ¼ cup **orange juice**
- 1 tsp. **garlic powder**
- ¾ tsp. **dried oregano**
- ½ tsp. **hot pepper sauce**
- ¼ tsp. **pepper**
  Hot cooked brown rice, optional

1. Place chicken in a 6-qt. electric pressure cooker; sprinkle with poultry seasoning. Top with onion and tomatoes. In a small bowl, mix the tomato sauce, barbecue sauce, water, orange juice and seasonings; pour over top.

2. Lock lid; close pressure-release valve. Adjust to pressure-cook on high for 10 minutes. Quick-release pressure. A thermometer inserted in chicken should read at least 170° If desired, serve with rice.

FREEZE OPTION: Place cooked chicken mixture in freezer containers. Cool and freeze. To use, partially thaw in refrigerator overnight. Microwave, covered, on high in a microwave-safe dish until heated through, gently stirring and adding a little water if necessary.

1 SERVING: 240 cal., 9g fat (2g sat. fat), 76mg chol., 582mg sod., 18g carb. (12g sugars, 2g fiber), 23g pro. **DIABETIC EXCHANGES:** 3 lean meat, 1 starch.

WHY YOU'LL LOVE IT...

"This was surprisingly good, especially considering how easy the prep is. Definitely recommend serving over rice. Lots of sauce. Very yummy."
—CHRIS, TASTEOFHOME.COM

LEMON CHICKEN WITH BASIL

No matter when I eat it, this tangy chicken dish always reminds me of summer meals with friends and family. The recipe produces a lot of lovely sauce; serve it as is or spoon it over some lightly herbed couscous.
—Deborah Posey, VA Beach, VA

Prep: 10 min.
Cook: 10 min.
Makes: 4 servings

- 4 **boneless skinless chicken breast halves (6 oz. each)**
- 2 **medium lemons**
- 1 **bunch fresh basil leaves (¾ oz.)**
- 2 **cups chicken stock**

TEST KITCHEN TIP
Lemon zest is the outer peel or rind. To remove the zest, peel thin strips with a small sharp knife, being careful not to include the white bitter membrane, and mince finely. You can also take the whole fruit and rub it over a hand grater.

1. Place the chicken in a 6-qt. electric pressure cooker. Finely grate enough zest from lemons to measure 4 tsp. Cut lemons in half; squeeze juice. Add zest and juice to pressure cooker.

2. Tear fresh basil leaves directly into pressure cooker; add chicken stock. Lock lid; close pressure-release valve. Adjust to pressure-cook on high for 6 minutes. Quick-release pressure. A thermometer inserted in chicken should read at least 165°. When cool enough to handle, shred meat with 2 forks; return to pressure cooker. If desired, stir in additional lemon zest and chopped basil. Serve with a slotted spoon.

FREEZE OPTION: Place chicken and cooking liquid in freezer containers. Cool and freeze. To use, partially thaw in the refrigerator overnight. Microwave, covered, on high in a microwave-safe dish until heated through, stirring gently.

5 OZ. COOKED CHICKEN: 200 cal., 4g fat (1g sat. fat), 94mg chol., 337mg sod., 3g carb. (1g sugars, 0 fiber), 37g pro. **DIABETIC EXCHANGES:** 5 lean meat.

ORANGE CHIPOTLE CHICKEN

The citrus in this delicious chicken entree keeps things fresh and lively. We're big on spice in our house, so sometimes I use two chipotle peppers.
—Deborah Biggs, Omaha, NE

Prep: 15 min.
Cook: 10 min.
Makes: 6 servings

- ½ cup plus 2 Tbsp. cold water, divided
- ½ cup thawed orange juice concentrate
- ¼ cup barbecue sauce
- 1 chipotle pepper in adobo sauce
- ¼ tsp. salt
- ¼ tsp. garlic powder
- 6 boneless skinless chicken breast halves (6 oz. each)
- ¼ cup chopped red onion
- 4 tsp. cornstarch Grated orange zest

1. Place ½ cup water, orange juice concentrate, barbecue sauce, chipotle pepper, salt and garlic powder in a blender; cover and process until blended.

2. Place chicken and onion in a 6-qt. electric pressure cooker; top with juice mixture. Lock lid; close pressure-release valve. Adjust to pressure-cook on high for 6 minutes.

3. Quick release pressure. Press cancel. A thermometer inserted in chicken should read at least 165°. Remove the chicken from pressure cooker; keep warm.

4. In a small bowl, mix cornstarch and remaining 2 Tbsp. water until smooth; gradually stir into pressure cooker. Select the saute setting and adjust for low heat. Simmer, stirring constantly, until thickened, 1-2 minutes. Spoon over chicken; top with orange zest.

FREEZE OPTION: Place chicken in freezer containers; top with sauce. Cool and freeze. To use, partially thaw in refrigerator overnight. Heat through in a covered saucepan, stirring gently and adding a little water if necessary.

1 CHICKEN BREAST WITH ¼ CUP SAUCE: 246 cal., 4g fat (1g sat. fat), 94mg chol., 315mg sod., 15g carb. (11g sugars, 1g fiber), 35g pro. **DIABETIC EXCHANGES:** 5 lean meat, 1 starch.

RED PEPPER CHICKEN

Chicken breasts are treated to black beans, red peppers and juicy tomatoes in this southwestern supper. We love it served with rice cooked in chicken broth—and it would also make a fun filling for tacos or burritos.
—Piper Spiwak, Vienna, VA

Prep: 15 min.
Cook: 15 min.
Makes: 4 servings

- **4 boneless skinless chicken breast halves (4 oz. each)**
- **1 can (15 oz.) no-salt-added black beans, rinsed and drained**
- **1 can (14½ oz.) Mexican stewed tomatoes, undrained**
- **1 jar (12 oz.) roasted sweet red peppers, drained and cut into strips**
- **1 large onion, chopped**
- **½ cup water**
  Pepper to taste
  Hot cooked rice

1. Place chicken in a 6-qt. electric pressure cooker. In a bowl, combine beans, tomatoes, red peppers, onion, water and pepper; pour over chicken. Lock lid; close pressure-release valve. Adjust to pressure-cook on high for 5 minutes.

2. Quick-release pressure. Press cancel. A thermometer inserted in chicken should read at least 165°. Remove the chicken and keep warm. Select saute setting; adjust for low heat. Simmer cooking juices until thickened, 8-10 minutes. Serve with rice and chicken.

FREEZE OPTION: Place chicken and bean mixture in freezer containers; top with cooking juices. Cool and freeze. To use, partially thaw in refrigerator overnight. Microwave, covered, on high in a microwave-safe dish until heated through, stirring gently and adding a little broth or water if necessary.

1 CHICKEN BREAST HALF WITH 1 CUP BEAN MIXTURE: 288 cal., 3g fat (1g sat. fat), 63mg chol., 657mg sod., 28g carb. (8g sugars, 7g fiber), 30g pro. **DIABETIC EXCHANGES:** 3 lean meat, 1½ starch, 1 vegetable.

COUNTRY CAPTAIN CHICKEN

Whether it was brought by a British sailor or not, the recipe for Country Captain Chicken has been around Georgia since the 1800s. Traditionally served over rice, it's also delicious with noodles or mashed potatoes.
—Suzanne Banfield, Basking Ridge, NJ

Prep: 25 min.
Cook: 10 min.
Makes: 8 servings

- 1 large onion, chopped
- 1 medium sweet red pepper, chopped
- 2 garlic cloves, minced
- 3 lbs. boneless skinless chicken thighs
- ½ cup chicken broth
- 1 Tbsp. brown sugar
- 1 Tbsp. curry powder
- 1 tsp. ground ginger
- 1 tsp. ground cinnamon
- 1 tsp. dried thyme
- 1 can (14½ oz.) diced tomatoes, undrained
- ½ cup golden raisins or raisins
  Hot cooked rice
  Chopped fresh parsley, optional

1. Place onion, red pepper and garlic in a 6-qt. electric pressure cooker; top with chicken. In a small bowl, whisk broth, brown sugar and seasonings; pour over chicken. Top with tomatoes and raisins. Lock lid; close pressure-release valve. Adjust to pressure-cook on high for 6 minutes.

2. Quick-release pressure. A thermometer inserted in chicken should read at least 170°. Thicken cooking juices if desired. Serve with rice and if desired, parsley.

FREEZE OPTION: Place chicken and vegetables in freezer containers; top with cooking juices. Cool and freeze. To use, partially thaw in refrigerator overnight. Heat through in a covered saucepan, stirring gently and adding a little broth if necessary.

1 SERVING: 298 cal., 13g fat (3g sat. fat), 114mg chol., 159mg sod., 13g carb. (9g sugars, 2g fiber), 32g pro. **DIABETIC EXCHANGES:** 4 lean meat, 1 vegetable, ½ starch.

CHICKEN CHOP SUEY

If you're in for a busy evening, here's a wonderful way to ensure you can still have a healthful supper. It's tasty, traditional—and quick, too.
—Melody Littlewood, Royal City, WA

Prep: 20 min.
Cook: 5 min.
Makes: 9 servings

1½ lbs. boneless skinless chicken thighs, cut into 2-in. pieces
½ lb. sliced fresh mushrooms
2 celery ribs, sliced
1 medium onion, chopped
1 can (14 oz.) bean sprouts, rinsed and drained
1 can (8 oz.) bamboo shoots, drained
1 can (8 oz.) sliced water chestnuts, drained
½ cup frozen shelled edamame
1 can (14½ oz.) reduced-sodium chicken broth
½ cup reduced-sodium soy sauce
1 Tbsp. minced fresh gingerroot
¼ tsp. crushed red pepper flakes
¼ cup cornstarch
¼ cup cold water
Hot cooked rice

1. Place chicken in a 6-qt. electric pressure cooker. Top with mushrooms, celery, onion, bean sprouts, bamboo shoots, water chestnuts and edamame. In a small bowl, combine the broth, soy sauce, ginger and pepper flakes. Pour over chicken and vegetables.

2. Lock lid; close pressure-release valve. Adjust to pressure-cook on high for 3 minutes. Quick-release pressure. Press cancel. A thermometer inserted in chicken should read at least 170°.

3. Select saute setting and adjust for low heat. In a small bowl, mix cornstarch and water until smooth; stir into the chicken mixture. Simmer, stirring constantly, until thickened, 1-2 minutes. Serve with rice.

1 CUP: 182 cal., 6g fat (2g sat. fat), 50mg chol., 709mg sod., 13g carb. (3g sugars, 2g fiber), 19g pro. **DIABETIC EXCHANGES:** 2 lean meat, 1 vegetable, ½ starch.

DID YOU KNOW?
Edamame come from the soybean that is harvested early, before the beans become hard. The young beans are parboiled and frozen to retain their freshness and can be found in the freezer section of grocery stores.

GENERAL TSO'S STEW

I love Asian food and wanted a chili-style soup with flavors of General Tso. You can use any meat you like—I used leftover pork, but it's great with turkey, chicken or ground meats.
—Lori McLain, Denton, TX

Prep: 10 min.
Cook: 10 min.
Makes: 6 servings

- 1 cup tomato juice
- ½ cup water
- ½ cup pickled cherry peppers, chopped
- 2 Tbsp. soy sauce
- 2 Tbsp. hoisin sauce
- 1 Tbsp. peanut oil
- 1 to 2 tsp. crushed red pepper flakes
- 1 lb. boneless skinless chicken breast halves
- 1½ cups chopped onion
- 1 cup chopped fresh broccoli
- ¼ cup chopped green onions
- 1 tsp. sesame seeds, toasted

1. In a 6-qt. electric pressure cooker, combine the first 7 ingredients. Top with chicken, onion and broccoli. Lock lid; close pressure-release valve. Adjust to pressure-cook on high for 6 minutes. Quick-release pressure. Press cancel. A thermometer inserted in chicken should read at least 165°.

2. Remove chicken; shred with 2 forks. Return to pressure cooker; heat through. Top with green onions and sesame seeds to serve.

FREEZE OPTION: Freeze cooled stew in freezer containers. To use, partially thaw in refrigerator overnight. Heat through in a saucepan, stirring occasionally and adding a little water if necessary.

1 CUP: 159 cal., 5g fat (1g sat. fat), 42mg chol., 762mg sod., 10g carb. (5g sugars, 2g fiber), 18g pro. **DIABETIC EXCHANGES:** 2 lean meat, 2 vegetable, ½ fat.

BEEF ENTREES

Hearty…satisfying…comforting…those are
just a few of the ways to describe the following
stick-to-your-ribs meals. After all, eating healthy
doesn't have to mean cutting out red meat,
so dig in and enjoy tonight!

BEEF 101

It's true! You can trim down meals and continue to enjoy meaty entrees. Follow these tips to learn how.

WHEN BUYING BEEF, LOOK FOR:

- Bright cherry red color in cuts and ground beef. Avoid meat with gray or brown patches.

- Packages free of holes, tears or excessive liquid, which may indicate improper handling and storage.

- Creamy pink color and fine-grain texture in veal. Avoid discolored or dried-out meat.

- A sell-by date on the package that is later than the day of your purchase. If it's the same date, use the meat that day or freeze it for later.

GENERAL GUIDELINES FOR PURCHASE WEIGHT AND SERVINGS

- 1 lb. bone-in roast = roughly 2½ servings

- 1 lb. boneless cut with some fat to be trimmed = about 2½-3½ servings

- 1 lb. lean boneless cut (such as eye of round, flank steak or tenderloin) = 3-4 servings

- 1 lb. bone-in steak = 2 servings

BUYING AND COOKING GROUND BEEF

Ground beef comes from a combination of beef cuts. It is often labeled with the cut of meat that it is ground from, such as ground chuck or ground round. Ground beef also can be labeled according to the fat content of the ground mixture or the percentage of lean meat to fat, such as 85% or 90% lean. The higher the percentage, the leaner the meat. When buying and cooking ground beef:

- Purchase only the amount you need; 1 lb. of ground beef serves 3-4.

- Select ground beef that is bright red in color and is in a tightly sealed package. Purchase ground beef before the sell-by date.

- Handle the mixture as little as possible when shaping hamburgers, meat loaves or meatballs to keep the final product light in texture.

- Cook ground beef until it is well-done and no longer pink. For patties and loaves, where it is difficult to judge color, make sure a thermometer reads 160° before serving.

DEFROSTING GUIDELINES

The thicker the package, the longer it will take to defrost. Here are some guidelines for defrosting beef or veal in the refrigerator:

- For ½ to ¾-in.-thick ground beef or veal patties, allow at least 12 hours.

- For a large roast or a thick pot roast, allow about 6 hours per pound.

- For steaks, allow 12-24 hours.

- For 1 to 1½-in.-thick meat cuts or packages of ground beef or veal, allow at least 24 hours.

RUBS

A rub is a blend of dry seasonings, such as fresh or dried herbs and spices, that coats the surface of uncooked meat to add flavor. Rubs add a lot of flavor without fat, but they do not tenderize meats.

MARINADES

A marinade is mixture of liquid and seasonings used to coat meat before cooking. Marinades both flavor and tenderize meats, but may add more calories, fat and sodium than rubs.

- To truly tenderize meat, a marinade needs an acidic ingredient like lemon juice, vinegar, yogurt or even wine. For the best results, coat the meat completely in the marinade.

- Allow from 6-24 hours to tenderize cuts such as large steaks or roasts. Smaller cuts like cubes or thin steaks can be marinated for a few hours. Used for more than 24 hours, a tenderizing marinade can make the meat mushy.

- Marinate meat at room temperature for no longer than 30 minutes. For longer times marinate meat in the refrigerator.

BEEF UP YOUR MENUS

You'll save time in the kitchen—in addition to calories, fat, sodium and carbohydrates—when you follow these no-fuss menus. Pick an entree below, then simply plan on the side dishes that go with them.

BEEF RECIPE
Beef Burritos with
Green Chiles, Page 176

MENU ADD-ONS
• Avocado slices
• Roasted corn

BEEF RECIPE
Burgundy Beef,
Page 179

MENU ADD-ONS
• Steamed green beans
• Wedge salad

BEEF RECIPE
Spicy Vegetable Stew,
Page 180

MENU ADD-ONS
• Whole wheat bread
• Sugar-free iced tea

BEEF RECIPE
Coffee Beef Roast,
Page 183

MENU ADD-ONS
• Roasted carrots
• Cooked noodles

BEEF RECIPE
Shredded Beef Lettuce
Cups, Page 184

MENU ADD-ONS
• Cucumber slices
• Tomato wedges

BEEF RECIPE
Spice-Braised Pot Roast,
Page 187

MENU ADD-ONS
• Roasted broccoli
• Bran muffins

BEEF RECIPE
Beef Daube Provencal,
Page 188

MENU ADD-ONS
• Sauteed asparagus
• Fat-free vanilla pudding

BEEF RECIPE
Mushroom Pot Roast,
Page 191

MENU ADD-ONS
• Corn
• Angel food cake

BEEF RECIPE
Beef Roast with Asian Black
Bean Sauce, Page 192

MENU ADD-ONS
• Steamed edamame
• Fortune cookies

BEEF RECIPE
Beef & Rice Cabbage Rolls,
Page 195

MENU ADD-ONS
• Cooked rice
• Roasted cauliflower

BEEF RECIPE
Caribbean Pot Roast,
Page 196

MENU ADD-ONS
• Pita bread
• Steamed okra

BEEF RECIPE
Beefy Cabbage & Bean
Stew, Page 199

MENU ADD-ONS
• 7-grain bread
• Spinach salad

BEEF CUTS

Don't be overwhelmed by the many cuts of beef available today. Simply check here before visiting the butcher.

▶ TENDER ▶ LESS TENDER

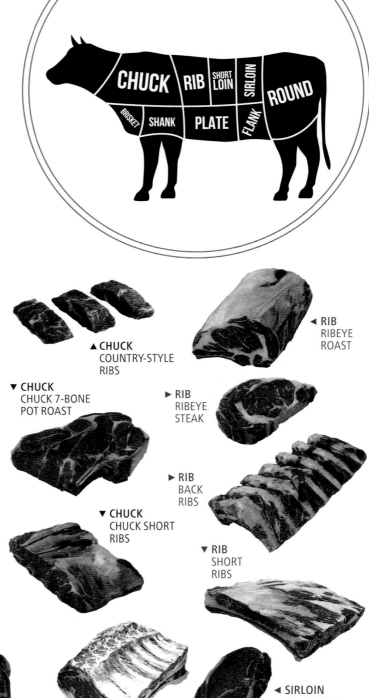

▶ **CHUCK**
CHUCK ARM
POT ROAST

▶ **CHUCK**
CHUCK SHOULDER
POT ROAST,
BONELESS

▲ **CHUCK**
COUNTRY-STYLE
RIBS

◀ **RIB**
RIBEYE
ROAST

▼ **CHUCK**
CHUCK SHOULDER
STEAK, BONELESS

▼ **CHUCK**
CHUCK 7-BONE
POT ROAST

▶ **RIB**
RIBEYE
STEAK

▶ **RIB**
BACK
RIBS

▶ **CHUCK**
CHUCK MOCK
TENDER
STEAK

▼ **CHUCK**
CHUCK SHORT
RIBS

▼ **RIB**
SHORT
RIBS

▶ **CHUCK**
CHUCK POT
ROAST,
BONELESS

▶ **RIB**
RIB ROAST,
LARGE END

◀ **SIRLOIN**
TOP SIRLOIN
STEAK,
BONELESS

▶ **SHORT LOIN**
TOP LOIN
(STRIP) STEAKS

◀ **ROUND**
ROUND
STEAK,
BONELESS

◀ **FLANK**
FLANK
STEAK

▶ **SHORT LOIN**
T-BONE
STEAK

▶ **ROUND**
EYE ROUND
ROAST

▼ **FLANK**
FLANK STEAK,
TRIMMED

◀ **ROUND**
ROUND TIP
ROAST,
CAP OFF

▼ **OTHER CUTS**
GROUND BEEF

▲ **SHORT LOIN**
PORTERHOUSE
STEAK

▶ **BRISKET**
BRISKET,
WHOLE,
BONELESS

▼ **OTHER CUTS**
CUBE STEAKS

▲ **SHORT LOIN**
TENDERLOIN

◀ **BRISKET**
BRISKET,
POINT HALF

▼ **OTHER CUTS**
BEEF STRIPS

▼ **SHORT LOIN**
TENDERLOIN ROAST

▼ **PLATE**
HANGER
STEAK

▶ **SIRLOIN**
BOTTOM
SIRLOIN,
TRI-TIP
ROAST

◀ **OTHER CUTS**
BEEF STEW
MEAT

▼ **PLATE**
INSIDE SKIRT
STEAK

▶ **OTHER CUTS**
KABOB
MEAT

▼ **OTHER CUTS**
SPECIAL TRIM

▲ **ROUND**
TOP ROUND STEAK

▲ **PLATE**
OUTSIDE
SKIRT STEAK

BEEF BURRITOS WITH GREEN CHILES

Here's a family favorite that gets mouths watering simply with its heavenly aroma! Hearty and flavorful, it's quick comfort food.
—Sally J. Pahler, Palisade, CO

Prep: 20 min.
Cook: 1 hour 20 min. + releasing
Makes: 14 servings

- 4 cans (7 oz. each) whole green chiles, undrained
- 1 can (28 oz.) diced tomatoes, undrained
- 1 large onion, diced
- 1 boneless beef chuck roast (4 lbs.)
- 2 garlic cloves, minced
- 1 tsp. salt
- 2 tsp. ground cumin
- 1 tsp. cayenne pepper
- 14 whole wheat tortillas (8 in.), warmed
  Optional toppings:
    Shredded cheddar cheese, salsa, sour cream, sliced ripe olives

1. Drain chiles, reserving liquid. Coarsely chop chiles; place in a 6-qt. electric pressure cooker. Add the tomatoes, onion and reserved drained liquid. Cut roast in half. Combine the garlic, salt, cumin and cayenne; rub over the roast. Place in pressure cooker. Lock the lid; close pressure-release valve. Adjust to pressure-cook on high for 80 minutes. Let pressure release naturally for 10 minutes; quick-release any remaining pressure. A thermometer inserted in the beef should read at least 165°.

2. Remove the roast; shred with 2 forks. Return to pressure cooker; heat through. Using a slotted spoon, serve in tortillas, with toppings if desired.

FREEZE OPTION: Freeze the cooled meat mixture and juices in freezer containers. To use, partially thaw in refrigerator overnight. Heat through in a saucepan, stirring occasionally and adding a little water if necessary.

1 BURRITO: 355 cal., 13g fat (5g sat. fat), 84mg chol., 499mg sod., 28g carb. (4g sugars, 4g fiber), 30g pro. **DIABETIC EXCHANGES:** 4 lean meat, 2 starch, ½ fat.

BURGUNDY BEEF

When my adult children come for dinner, this is the recipe I turn to first. They all just love it!
—Urilla Cheverie, Andover, MA

Prep: 10 min.
Cook: 25 min. + releasing
Makes: 10 servings

- 4 lbs. beef top sirloin steak, cut into 1-in. cubes
- 3 large onions, sliced
- 1 cup water
- 1 cup burgundy wine or beef broth
- 1 cup ketchup
- ¼ cup quick-cooking tapioca
- ¼ cup packed brown sugar
- ¼ cup Worcestershire sauce
- 4 tsp. paprika
- 1½ tsp. salt
- 1 tsp. minced garlic
- 1 tsp. ground mustard
- 2 Tbsp. cornstarch
- 3 Tbsp. cold water
  Hot cooked noodles

1. Combine the first 12 ingredients in a 6-qt. electric pressure cooker. Lock lid; close pressure-release valve. Adjust to pressure-cook on high for 20 minutes. Let pressure release naturally for 10 minutes; quick-release any remaining pressure. Press cancel.

2. Combine cornstarch and cold water until smooth; stir into pressure cooker. Select saute setting and adjust for low heat. Simmer, stirring constantly, until thickened, 1-2 minutes. Serve with noodles.

FREEZE OPTION: Place beef in freezer containers; top with sauce. Cool and freeze. To use, partially thaw in refrigerator overnight. Heat through in a covered saucepan, stirring gently and adding a little water if necessary.

1 CUP: 347 cal., 8g fat (3g sat. fat), 74mg chol., 811mg sod., 24g carb. (15g sugars, 1g fiber), 40g pro.

SPICY BEEF VEGETABLE STEW

This zesty ground beef and vegetable soup is flavorful and comes together so quickly. It makes a complete meal when served with warm cornbread, sourdough or French bread, if you can squeak in a few more calories.
—Lynnette Davis, Tullahoma, TN

Prep: 10 min.
Cook: 5 min. + releasing
Makes: 8 servings (3 qt.)

- 1 lb. lean ground beef (90% lean)
- 3½ cups water
- 1 jar (24 oz.) meatless pasta sauce
- 1 pkg. (16 oz.) frozen mixed vegetables
- 1 can (10 oz.) diced tomatoes and green chiles, undrained
- 1 cup chopped onion
- 1 cup sliced celery
- 1 tsp. beef bouillon granules
- 1 tsp. pepper

Select saute or browning setting on a 6-qt. electric pressure cooker; adjust for medium heat. Cook beef until no longer pink, 6-8 minutes, breaking into crumbles; drain. Stir in the remaining ingredients. Lock lid; close pressure-release valve. Adjust to pressure-cook on high for 5 minutes. Let pressure release naturally.

FREEZE OPTION: Freeze cooled stew in freezer containers. To use, partially thaw in refrigerator overnight. Heat through in a saucepan, stirring occasionally and adding a little water if necessary.

1½ **CUPS:** 177 cal., 5g fat (2g sat. fat), 35mg chol., 675mg sod., 19g carb. (8g sugars, 5g fiber), 15g pro. **DIABETIC EXCHANGES:** 2 lean meat, 1 starch.

WHY YOU'LL LOVE IT...

"What I loved most about this recipe is everything in it is something I have in my stock of food—there was nothing else I had to go and buy. It is amazing, really good."
—BONITO15, TASTEOFHOME.COM

COFFEE BEEF ROAST

Your morning brew is the key to this flavorful roast that simmers until it's fall-apart tender. Try it once, and I'm sure you'll cook it again.
—Charles Trahan, San Dimas, CA

Prep: 15 min.
Cook: 55 min. + releasing
Makes: 6 servings

2 tsp. canola oil
1 beef sirloin tip roast
   (2½ lbs.), halved
1½ cups brewed coffee
1½ cups sliced fresh
   mushrooms
⅓ cup sliced green onions
2 garlic cloves, minced
1 tsp. liquid smoke,
   optional
½ tsp. salt
½ tsp. chili powder
¼ tsp. pepper
¼ cup cornstarch
⅓ cup cold water

1. Select the saute or browning setting on a 6-qt. electric pressure cooker. Adjust for medium heat; add 1 tsp. oil. When oil is hot, brown a roast half on all sides. Remove; repeat with remaining beef and oil. Add coffee to pressure cooker. Cook 1 minute, stirring to loosen browned bits from the pan. Press cancel. Add mushrooms, green onions, garlic, liquid smoke if desired, salt, chili powder, pepper and beef.

2. Lock lid; close pressure-release valve. Adjust to pressure-cook on high for 50 minutes. Let pressure release naturally. A thermometer inserted in beef should read at least 145°. Press cancel.

3. Remove the roast and vegetables to a serving platter; tent with foil. Let stand 10 minutes before slicing. Reserve 2 cups cooking juices; discard the remaining juices. Transfer back to pressure cooker. In a small bowl, mix cornstarch and water until smooth; stir into pressure cooker. Select saute setting and adjust for low heat. Simmer, stirring constantly, until thickened, 1-2 minutes. Serve with roast and vegetables.

FREEZE OPTION: Place the sliced pot roast and vegetables in freezer containers; top with the sauce. Cool and freeze. To use, partially thaw in the refrigerator overnight. Heat through in a covered saucepan, stirring gently and adding a little water if necessary.

5 OZ. COOKED BEEF: 281 cal., 10g fat (3g sat. fat), 120mg chol., 261mg sod., 6g carb. (1g sugars, 0 fiber), 39g pro. **DIABETIC EXCHANGES:** 5 lean meat, ½ starch.

SHREDDED BEEF LETTUCE CUPS

I love this light yet lively dinner for busy days filled with swim lessons and outdoor activities. If you can't find Bibb or Boston, try green leaf lettuce—it's less sturdy but works in a pinch.
—Elisabeth Larsen, Pleasant Grove, UT

Prep: 20 min.
Cook: 40 min. + releasing
Makes: 8 servings

- 3 **medium carrots, chopped**
- 2 **medium sweet red peppers, chopped**
- 1 **medium onion, chopped**
- 1 **boneless beef chuck roast (2 lbs.)**
- 1 **can (8 oz.) unsweetened crushed pineapple, undrained**
- ½ **cup reduced-sodium soy sauce**
- 2 **Tbsp. brown sugar**
- 2 **Tbsp. white vinegar**
- 1 **garlic clove, minced**
- ½ **tsp. pepper**
- 3 **Tbsp. cornstarch**
- 3 **Tbsp. water**
- 24 **Bibb or Boston lettuce leaves**
  Sliced green onions, optional

1. Combine carrots, red peppers and onion in a 6-qt. pressure cooker. Top with roast. In a small bowl, combine pineapple, soy sauce, brown sugar, vinegar, garlic and pepper; pour over roast. Lock lid; close pressure-release valve. Adjust to pressure-cook on high for 40 minutes. Let pressure release naturally. Press cancel. Remove roast from pressure cooker. Cool slightly; shred roast with 2 forks.

2. Skim fat from cooking juices; return juices and vegetables to pressure cooker. In a small bowl, mix cornstarch and water until smooth; stir into pressure cooker. Select saute setting and adjust for low heat. Simmer, stirring constantly, until thickened, 1-2 minutes. Return shredded meat to pressure cooker; heat through.

3. Serve in lettuce leaves. If desired, sprinkle with onions.

FREEZE OPTION: Freeze the cooled meat mixture and sauce in freezer containers. To use, partially thaw in refrigerator overnight. Heat through in a saucepan, stirring occasionally and adding a little water if necessary.

3 LETTUCE CUPS: 270 cal., 11g fat (4g sat. fat), 74mg chol., 641mg sod., 17g carb. (10g sugars, 2g fiber), 24g pro. **DIABETIC EXCHANGES:** 3 lean meat, 1 starch.

SPICE-BRAISED POT ROAST

Herbs and spices give this beef an excellent flavor. I often serve the roast over egg noodles or with mashed potatoes, using the juices as a gravy.
—Loren Martin, Big Cabin, OK

Prep: 15 min.
Cook: 50 min. + releasing
Makes: 8 servings

- 1 **boneless beef chuck roast (2½ lbs.), halved**
- 1 **can (14½ oz.) diced tomatoes, undrained**
- 1 **medium onion, chopped**
- ½ **cup water**
- ¼ **cup white vinegar**
- 3 **Tbsp. tomato puree**
- 1 **Tbsp. poppy seeds**
- 1 **bay leaf**
- 2¼ **tsp. sugar**
- 2 **tsp. Dijon mustard**
- 2 **garlic cloves, minced**
- ½ **tsp. salt**
- ½ **tsp. ground ginger**
- ½ **tsp. dried rosemary, crushed**
- ½ **tsp. lemon juice**
- ¼ **tsp. ground cumin**
- ¼ **tsp. ground turmeric**
- ¼ **tsp. crushed red pepper flakes**
- ⅛ **tsp. ground cloves**
  Hot cooked egg noodles

1. Place beef roast in a 6-qt. electric pressure cooker. Mix all remaining ingredients except egg noodles; pour over roast. Lock lid; close pressure-release valve. Adjust to pressure-cook on high for 50 minutes. Let pressure release naturally. A thermometer inserted in beef should read at least 145°.

2. Discard bay leaf. If desired, skim fat and thicken cooking juices. Serve pot roast with noodles and juices.

FREEZE OPTION: Place the pot roast in freezer containers; top with cooking juices. Cool and freeze. To use, partially thaw in refrigerator overnight. Heat through in a covered saucepan, stirring gently and adding a little water if necessary.

1 SERVING: 272 cal., 14g fat (5g sat. fat), 92mg chol., 320mg sod., 6g carb. (4g sugars, 1g fiber), 29g pro. **DIABETIC EXCHANGES:** 4 lean meat, ½ starch.›

TEST KITCHEN TIP
If you can insert a carving fork into the thickest part of the roast easily, it is near done. If it's cooked until it falls apart, the meat is actually overcooked and will be stringy, tough and dry.

BEEF DAUBE PROVENCAL

My dinner is perfect for us on chilly nights, especially after we've been out chopping wood. The melt-in-your-mouth goodness makes it a staple in my menu rotation.
—Brenda Ryan, Marshall, MO

Prep: 30 min.
Cook: 30 min. + releasing
Makes: 8 servings

- 1 **boneless beef chuck roast or venison roast (about 2 lbs.), cut into 1-in. cubes**
- 1½ tsp. salt, divided
- ½ tsp. coarsely ground pepper, divided
- 2 tsp. olive oil
- 2 cups chopped carrots
- 1½ cups chopped onion
- 12 garlic cloves, crushed
- 1 Tbsp. tomato paste
- 1 cup dry red wine
- 1 can (14½ oz.) diced tomatoes, undrained
- ½ cup beef broth
- 1 tsp. chopped fresh rosemary
- 1 tsp. chopped fresh thyme
- 1 bay leaf
  Dash ground cloves
  Hot cooked pasta or mashed potatoes

1. Sprinkle the beef with ½ tsp. salt and ¼ tsp. pepper. Select saute or browning setting on a 6-qt. electric pressure cooker. Adjust for medium heat; add oil. When oil is hot, brown beef in batches.

2. Add carrots, onions and garlic to pressure cooker; cook and stir until golden brown, 4-6 minutes. Add tomato paste; cook and stir until fragrant, about 1 minute. Add red wine, stirring to loosen browned bits. Return the beef to pressure cooker. Add tomatoes, broth, rosemary, thyme, bay leaf, cloves and remaining 1 tsp. salt and ¼ tsp. pepper. Press cancel.

3. Lock lid; close pressure-release valve. Adjust to pressure-cook on high for 30 minutes. Let pressure release naturally for 10 minutes; quick-release any remaining pressure. A thermometer inserted in the beef should read at least 160°. Discard the bay leaf. Serve with hot cooked pasta. If desired, sprinkle with additional thyme.

FREEZE OPTION: Place the beef and vegetables in freezer containers; top with cooking juices. Cool and freeze. To use, partially thaw in the refrigerator overnight. Heat through in a covered saucepan, stirring gently and adding a little broth if necessary.

1 CUP BEEF MIXTURE: 248 cal., 12g fat (4g sat. fat), 74mg chol., 652mg sod., 10g carb. (5g sugars, 2g fiber), 24g pro. **DIABETIC EXCHANGES:** 3 lean meat, 1 vegetable.

MUSHROOM POT ROAST

Packed with wholesome veggies and tender beef, this is an entree that will delight all ages. Serve mashed potatoes alongside to soak up every last drop of gravy.
—Angie Stewart, Topeka, KS

Prep: 25 min.
Cook: 65 min. + releasing
Makes: 10 servings

- 1 boneless beef chuck roast (3 to 4 lbs.)
- ½ tsp. salt
- ¼ tsp. pepper
- 1 Tbsp. canola oil
- 1½ cups dry red wine or reduced-sodium beef broth
- 1½ lbs. sliced fresh shiitake mushrooms
- 2½ cups thinly sliced onions
- 1½ cups reduced-sodium beef broth
- 1 can (8 oz.) tomato sauce
- ¾ cup chopped peeled parsnips
- ¾ cup chopped celery
- ¾ cup chopped carrots
- 8 garlic cloves, minced
- 2 bay leaves
- 1½ tsp. dried thyme
- 1 tsp. chili powder
- ¼ cup cornstarch
- ¼ cup water
- Mashed potatoes

1. Halve roast; sprinkle with salt and pepper. Select saute or browning setting on a 6-qt. electric pressure cooker. Adjust for medium heat; add 1½ tsp. oil. When oil is hot, brown a roast half on all sides. Remove; repeat with remaining beef and 1½ tsp. oil. Add wine to pressure cooker. Cook 2 minutes, stirring to loosen browned bits from pan. Press cancel. Return beef to pressure cooker.

2. Add mushrooms, onions, broth, tomato sauce, parsnips, celery, carrots, garlic, bay leaves, thyme and chili powder. Lock lid; close pressure-release valve. Adjust to pressure-cook on high for 60 minutes. Let the pressure release naturally for 10 minutes; quick-release any remaining pressure. Press cancel. A thermometer inserted in the beef roast should read at least 160°.

3. Remove meat and vegetables to a serving platter; keep warm. Discard the bay leaves. Skim fat from cooking juices; transfer back to pressure cooker. In a small bowl, mix the cornstarch and water until smooth; stir into cooking juices. Select saute setting and adjust for low heat. Simmer, stirring constantly, until thickened, 1-2 minutes. Serve with mashed potatoes, meat and vegetables.

FREEZE OPTION: Place the roast and vegetables in freezer containers; top with cooking juices. Cool and freeze. To use, partially thaw in the refrigerator overnight. Heat through in a covered saucepan, stirring gently and adding a little broth if necessary.

4 OZ. COOKED BEEF WITH ⅔ CUP VEGETABLES AND ½ CUP GRAVY: 316 cal., 15g fat (5g sat. fat), 89mg chol., 373mg sod., 16g carb. (4g sugars, 4g fiber), 30g pro. **DIABETIC EXCHANGES:** 4 lean meat, 2 vegetable, 1½ fat.

BEEF ROAST WITH ASIAN BLACK BEAN SAUCE

I love stir-fry with black bean sauce. This recipe takes the same delicious flavor and combines it with fork-tender pot roast.
—Judy Lawson, Chelsea, MI

Prep: 25 min.
Cook: 70 min. + releasing
Makes: 10 servings

- 1 boneless beef chuck roast (3 to 4 lbs.)
- ½ tsp. salt
- ½ tsp. pepper
- 1 Tbsp. olive oil
- 1 cup reduced-sodium beef broth
- 1 medium onion, cut into 1-in. pieces
- ½ lb. sliced fresh mushrooms
- 8 oz. fresh snow peas, trimmed
- ¾ cup Asian black bean sauce
- 2 Tbsp. cornstarch
- 2 Tbsp. cold water
  Hot cooked rice
- 4 green onions, sliced

1. Halve roast; sprinkle with salt and pepper. Select saute or browning setting on a 6-qt. electric pressure cooker. Adjust for medium heat; add 1½ tsp. oil. When oil is hot, brown a roast half on all sides. Remove; repeat with remaining beef and 1½ tsp. oil.

2. Add beef broth to pressure cooker. Cook 2 minutes, stirring to loosen browned bits from the pan. Press cancel. Return all to pressure cooker; add onion.

3. Lock the lid and close pressure-release valve. Adjust to pressure-cook on high for 60 minutes. Let the pressure release naturally for 10 minutes; quick-release any remaining pressure. Press cancel. A thermometer inserted in beef should read at least 160°.

4. Remove roast; keep warm. Add mushrooms, snow peas and black bean sauce to pressure cooker. Select saute setting and adjust for low heat. Cook and stir until the vegetables are tender; 6-8 minutes.

5. In a small bowl, mix the cornstarch and cold water until smooth; stir into pressure cooker. Simmer, stirring constantly, until thickened, 1-2 minutes. Serve with roast, hot cooked rice and green onions.

1 SERVING: 286 cal., 14g fat (5g sat. fat), 89mg chol., 635mg sod., 9g carb. (4g sugars, 1g fiber), 29g pro. **DIABETIC EXCHANGES:** 4 lean meat, ½ starch, ½ fat.

BEEF & RICE CABBAGE ROLLS

My family can't wait for dinner when I'm serving my tasty cabbage rolls. The dish comes together easily and always satisfies.
—Lynn Bowen, Geraldine, AL

Prep: 45 min.
Cook: 20 min.
Makes: 6 servings

12 cabbage leaves
 1 cup cooked brown rice
 ¼ cup finely chopped onion
 1 large egg, lightly beaten
 ¼ cup fat-free milk
 ½ tsp. salt
 ¼ tsp. pepper
 1 lb. lean ground beef (90% lean)
 ½ cup plus 2 Tbsp. water, divided
 1 can (8 oz.) tomato sauce
 1 Tbsp. brown sugar
 1 Tbsp. lemon juice
 1 tsp. Worcestershire sauce
 2 Tbsp. cornstarch

1. In batches, cook cabbage in boiling water 3-5 minutes or until crisp-tender. Drain; cool slightly. Trim the thick vein from the bottom of each cabbage leaf, making a V-shaped cut.

2. In a large bowl, combine rice, onion, egg, milk, salt and pepper. Add beef; mix lightly but thoroughly. Place about ¼ cup beef mixture on each cabbage leaf. Pull together the cut edges of leaf to overlap; fold over filling. Fold in the sides and roll up.

3. Place trivet insert and ½ cup water in a 6-qt. electric pressure cooker. Set 6 rolls on the trivet, seam side down. In a bowl, mix tomato sauce, brown sugar, lemon juice and Worcestershire sauce; pour half the sauce over cabbage rolls. Top with remaining rolls and sauce.

4. Lock lid; close pressure-release valve. Adjust to pressure-cook on high for 15 minutes. Quick-release pressure. Press cancel. A thermometer inserted in the beef should read at least 160°.

5. Remove the rolls to a serving platter; keep warm. Remove trivet. In a small bowl, mix cornstarch and remaining 2 Tbsp. water until smooth; stir into pressure cooker. Select the saute setting and adjust for low heat. Simmer, stirring constantly, until thickened, 1-2 minutes. Serve with rolls.

2 CABBAGE ROLLS: 219 cal., 8g fat (3g sat. fat), 78mg chol., 446mg sod., 19g carb. (5g sugars, 2g fiber), 18g pro. **DIABETIC EXCHANGES:** 2 lean meat, 1 starch.

CARIBBEAN POT ROAST

This tropical dish is definitely an all-year recipe. Sweet potatoes, orange zest and baking cocoa are my surprise ingredients.
—Jenn Tidwell, Fair Oaks, CA

Prep: 30 min.
Cook: 55 min. + releasing
Makes: 10 servings

- 1 Tbsp. canola oil
- 1 boneless beef chuck roast (2½ lbs.), halved
- ½ cup water
- 2 medium sweet potatoes, cubed
- 2 large carrots, sliced
- 1 large onion, chopped
- ¼ cup chopped celery
- 1 can (15 oz.) tomato sauce
- 2 garlic cloves, minced
- 1 Tbsp. all-purpose flour
- 1 Tbsp. sugar
- 1 Tbsp. brown sugar
- 1 tsp. ground cumin
- ¾ tsp. salt
- ¾ tsp. ground coriander
- ¾ tsp. chili powder
- ¾ tsp. grated orange zest
- ¾ tsp. baking cocoa
- ½ tsp. dried oregano
- ⅛ tsp. ground cinnamon

1. Select the saute or browning setting on a 6-qt. electric pressure cooker. Adjust for medium heat; add 1½ tsp. oil. When the oil is hot, brown a roast half on all sides. Remove; repeat with remaining beef and oil.

2. Add water to pressure cooker. Cook 30 seconds, stirring to loosen browned bits from the pan. Press cancel. Place the sweet potatoes, carrots, onion and celery in pressure cooker; top with beef. Combine remaining ingredients; pour over top.

3. Lock lid; close pressure-release valve. Adjust to pressure-cook on high for 55 minutes. Let pressure release naturally. A thermometer inserted in beef should read at least 145°.

FREEZE OPTION: Place the pot roast and vegetables in freezer containers; top with cooking juices. Cool and freeze. To use, partially thaw in the refrigerator overnight. Heat through in a covered saucepan, stirring gently and adding a little water if necessary.

3 OZ. COOKED BEEF WITH ½ CUP VEGETABLE MIXTURE : 282 cal., 13g fat (4g sat. fat), 74mg chol., 442mg sod., 18g carb. (8g sugars, 3g fiber), 24g pro. **DIABETIC EXCHANGES:** 3 lean meat, 1 starch, 1 vegetable, ½ fat.

BEEFY CABBAGE & BEAN STEW

While we were on a small-group quilting retreat, a friend of mine surprised everyone with this wonderful stew for dinner. We all loved it and have since passed the recipe around for others to enjoy—now I'm passing it on to you.
—Melissa Glancy, La Grange, KY

Prep: 30 min.
Cook: 5 min.
Makes: 6 servings

½ lb. lean ground beef (90% lean)
3 cups shredded cabbage or angel hair coleslaw mix
1 can (16 oz.) red beans, rinsed and drained
1 can (14½ oz.) diced tomatoes, undrained
1 can (8 oz.) tomato sauce
¾ cup water
¾ cup salsa or picante sauce
1 medium green pepper, chopped
1 small onion, chopped
3 garlic cloves, minced
1 tsp. ground cumin
½ tsp. pepper

1. Select saute or browning setting on a 6-qt. electric pressure cooker; adjust for medium heat. Cook beef until no longer pink, 6-8 minutes, breaking into crumbles; drain. Press cancel. Return beef to pressure cooker.

2. Stir in the remaining ingredients. Lock lid; close pressure-release valve. Adjust to pressure-cook on high for 3 minutes. Quick-release pressure.

FREEZE OPTION: Freeze the cooled stew in freezer containers. To use, partially thaw in refrigerator overnight. Heat through in a saucepan, stirring occasionally and adding a little water if necessary.

1 CUP: 177 cal., 4g fat (1g sat. fat), 24mg chol., 591mg sod., 23g carb. (5g sugars, 7g fiber), 13g pro. **DIABETIC EXCHANGES:** 2 lean meat, 1 starch, 1 vegetable.

STEAK FAJITAS

I've enjoyed cooking since I was a girl growing up in the Southwest, and I think fajitas are an easy way to add some wallop to ho-hum dinner lineups. This simply delicious main dish is an excellent option if you're looking for something new to serve.
—Janie Reitz, Rochester, MN

Prep: 20 min.
Cook: 5 min.
Makes: 6 servings

- 2 Tbsp. canola oil
- 1½ lbs. beef top sirloin steak, cut into thin strips
- 1 large onion, julienned
- 1 large sweet red pepper, julienned
- 1 garlic clove, minced
- ½ cup reduced-sodium beef broth
- 2 Tbsp. lemon juice
- 1½ tsp. ground cumin
- 1 tsp. seasoned salt
- ½ tsp. chili powder
- ¼ to ½ tsp. crushed red pepper flakes
- 12 mini flour tortillas (5 in.), warmed
  Optional toppings: Shredded cheddar cheese, fresh cilantro leaves, sliced jalapeno pepper and avocado

1. Select saute or browning setting on a 6-qt. electric pressure cooker. Adjust for medium heat; add oil. When the oil is hot, brown beef. Press cancel. Place onions, peppers and garlic on meat. Top with broth, lemon juice and seasonings.

2. Lock lid; close pressure-release valve. Adjust to pressure-cook on high for 3 minutes. Quick-release the pressure. A thermometer inserted in beef should read at least 160°. Using tongs, serve with tortillas and toppings as desired.

2 FAJITAS: 337 cal., 14g fat (4g sat. fat), 46mg chol., 554mg sod., 21g carb. (2g sugars, 3g fiber), 28g pro. **DIABETIC EXCHANGES:** 4 lean meat, 1½ starch, 1 fat.

WHY YOU'LL LOVE IT...

"This recipe is truly fabulous! It's my go-to for fajitas and I use it for chicken, too. I'll even double the recipe, so there's extra to make quick-and-easy quesadillas for dinner the next night."
—MAMATRICIA, TASTEOFHOME.COM

SWISS STEAK

Swiss steak has a been a standby for family cooks for decades, and this fuss-free version promises to keep the dish popular for years to come. Best of all, it's low in calories and fat.
—Sarah Burks, Wathena, KS

Prep: 10 min.
Cook: 20 min.
Makes: 6 servings

1½ lbs. beef round steak, cut into 6 pieces
½ tsp. salt
¼ tsp. pepper
1 medium onion, cut into ¼-in. slices
1 celery rib, cut into ½-in. slices
2 cans (8 oz. each) tomato sauce

Sprinkle the steak with salt and pepper. Place the onion in a 6-qt. electric pressure cooker. Top with the celery, tomato sauce and steak. Lock lid; close pressure-release valve. Adjust to pressure-cook on high for 20 minutes. Let pressure release naturally for 5 minutes; quick-release any remaining pressure. A thermometer inserted in steak should read at least 145°.

1 SERVING: 167 cal., 4g fat (1g sat. fat), 63mg chol., 581mg sod., 6g carb. (2g sugars, 2g fiber), 27g pro. **DIABETIC EXCHANGES:** 3 lean meat, 1 vegetable.

ROUND STEAK ITALIANO

My mom used to make a similar version of this wonderful dish, and I've always enjoyed it. The gravy is especially dense and flavorful.
—Deanne Stephens, McMinnville, OR

Prep: 15 min.
Cook: 20 min.
Makes: 8 servings

- 2 **lbs. beef top round steak**
- 1 **can (8 oz.) tomato sauce**
- ½ **cup reduced-sodium beef broth**
- 2 **Tbsp. onion soup mix**
- 2 **Tbsp. canola oil**
- 2 **Tbsp. red wine vinegar**
- 1 **tsp. ground oregano**
- ½ **tsp. garlic powder**
- ¼ **tsp. pepper**
- 8 **medium potatoes (7 to 8 oz. each)**
- 1 **Tbsp. cornstarch**
- 1 **Tbsp. cold water**

1. Cut steak into serving-size pieces; place in a 6-qt. electric pressure cooker. In a large bowl, combine tomato sauce, broth, soup mix, oil, vinegar, oregano, garlic powder and pepper; pour over meat. Scrub and pierce potatoes; place over meat.

2. Lock lid; close pressure-release valve. Adjust to pressure-cook on high for 15 minutes. Quick-release pressure. Press cancel. A thermometer inserted into beef should read at least 160°. Remove meat and potatoes; keep warm.

3. For gravy, skim fat from cooking juices; return to pressure cooker. In a small bowl, mix cornstarch and cold water until smooth; stir into pressure cooker. Select the saute setting and adjust for low heat. Simmer, stirring constantly, until thickened, 1-2 minutes. Serve with meat and potatoes.

1 SERVING: 353 cal., 7g fat (2g sat. fat), 64mg chol., 357mg sod., 41g carb. (2g sugars, 5g fiber), 31g pro. **DIABETIC EXCHANGES:** 4 lean meat, 3 starch, ½ fat.

BEEF & BEANS

This deliciously spicy steak with beans and rice will have your family and friends asking for more. It's a perennial favorite in my recipe collection.
—Marie Leamon, Bethesda, MD

Prep: 10 min.
Cook: 15 min.
Makes: 8 servings

1½ lbs. boneless
   round steak
1 Tbsp. prepared mustard
1 Tbsp. chili powder
½ tsp. salt
¼ tsp. pepper
1 garlic clove, minced
2 cans (14½ oz. each)
   diced tomatoes,
   undrained
1 medium onion,
   chopped
½ cup water
1 tsp. beef bouillon
   granules
1 can (16 oz.) kidney
   beans, rinsed
   and drained
   Hot cooked rice

1. Cut steak into thin strips. Combine mustard, chili powder, salt, pepper and garlic in a bowl; add steak and toss to coat. Transfer to a 6-qt. electric pressure cooker; add tomatoes, onion, water and bouillon.

2. Lock lid; close pressure-release valve. Adjust to pressure-cook on high for 15 minutes. Quick-release pressure. Stir in the beans; heat through. Serve with rice.

1 CUP: 185 cal., 3g fat (1g sat. fat), 48mg chol., 574mg sod., 16g carb. (5g sugars, 5g fiber), 24g pro. **DIABETIC EXCHANGES:** 3 lean meat, 1 starch.

DID YOU KNOW?
Canned beans are packed with a lot of sodium in order to extend their shelf life. Be sure to rinse and drain the beans before using them in recipes.

SOUPS & SANDWICHES

Who can resist the incomparable pairing
of soup and sandwich? Now you don't have to,
regardless of your healthy-eating goals. Let your
one-pot cooker do the work and settle in for
a delectable duo of flavor.

CLASSIC COMBO NEVER FAILS

Cutting calories and fat doesn't have to mean missing out on soups and sandwiches. Read up on these definitions and pointers for meal planning made easy.

STOCK
Usually made with meaty bones (possibly roasted), meat and vegetables. Stock is clear and free of fat, offering a very subtle flavor.

CONSOMME
A completely defatted and clarified stock. It has a very rich flavor and, because of its high gelatin content, will set up when chilled.

BROTH
A light, thin soup made from simmering meats, poultry, fish or vegetables. Broths and stocks may be used interchangeably, but broths have less body.

CHILI
A hearty dish usually made with tomatoes and chili powder, but some chili dishes are white. The variations on chili seem endless. A chili can be mild, hot or anywhere in between. It may include ground beef, stew meat, sausage or poultry, or be meatless.

CREAMED SOUP
Pureed soup with a smooth, silky texture. Most focus on a single vegetable. It may be thickened with flour or potatoes and can be made with or without cream.

GUMBO
A hearty stewlike soup usually served with white rice that starts with a dark roux of flour and oil or butter. It may contain shellfish, chicken, sausage, ham, tomatoes, onions, garlic, sweet peppers and/or celery. Okra is used as a thickening agent in addition to the roux.

DO YOU HAVE TO SOAK BEANS WHEN USING A PRESSURE COOKER FOR SOUP?

Soaking beans overnight—or using the quick-soak technique—is so well ingrained in our minds that it's become a given. But do you really need to take this step when cooking with a pressure cooker?

Almost any from-scratch bean recipe starts with the same instructions: Soak beans in cold water overnight, or use the quicker method and soak them in warm water for an hour. You may have noticed that not all pressure-cooker recipes call for the standard soaking. Feeling confused? Don't be!

The high temperatures reached inside electric pressure cookers dramatically decrease the cooking time of beans. They may cook as much as 75 percent faster! That's why many recipes might skip the soaking step. The beans can cook from a dried state in the time it takes a tough cut of meat to tenderize.

Keep in mind that thin-skinned beans such as black-eyed peas, pintos and black beans yield the best results when you skip the soak method. If you want to speed things up, though, using canned or presoaked beans always results in a fully cooked pressure-cooker soup without much fuss.

SANDWICH PIZAZZ

Add a little extra punch to ordinary sandwiches, wraps and pitas by replacing the butter or full-fat mayo with one of these quick-to-fix spreads.

GARLIC MAYO — Microwave 8 peeled garlic cloves and 1 tsp. olive oil, uncovered, on high for 20-30 seconds or until garlic is softened. Transfer to a blender. Add 1 Tbsp. each lemon juice and Dijon mustard, ¾ cup light mayonnaise and 2 Tbsp. plain fat-free yogurt; cover and process until blended.

MAYO WITH A KICK — Mix ⅓ cup light mayonnaise with ⅓-½ tsp. prepared horseradish, ½ tsp. minced chives and ¼-½ tsp. garlic powder.

BLAZING MUSTARD — Combine ½ cup ground mustard, 1½ tsp. sugar and ½ tsp. salt. Stir in 3 Tbsp. water and 2 Tbsp. white vinegar until smooth.

ARTICHOKE PEPPERONCINI SANDWICH SPREAD — Process ⅓ cup rinsed and drained water-packed artichoke hearts with 2 whole pepperoncini peppers in a food processor until spreadable but not smooth.

CHIMICHURRI SANDWICH SPREAD — Whisk together 2 Tbsp. olive oil, 1 Tbsp. each red wine vinegar, minced onion and minced fresh cilantro, 1 minced garlic clove, ¼ tsp. dried oregano and ⅛ tsp. each salt and cayenne pepper.

SUN-DRIED TOMATO SPREAD — Mix 2 Tbsp. each mayonnaise and finely chopped oil-packed sun-dried tomatoes and 2 tsp. minced red onion.

THE EASIEST EGG SALAD SANDWICHES EVER!

Once you use a pressure cooker to hard-boil eggs for egg salad, you'll never want to go back!

- Place 1 cup of water in a pressure cooker. Place a steamer basket or trivet insert on top of the water and carefully place up to 12 eggs on top.

- Lock lid; close pressure-release valve. Adjust to pressure-cook on high (for large eggs), and set time for 5 minutes. Meanwhile, prepare an ice bath.

- When cooking is complete, allow pressure to naturally release for 5 minutes. Quick-release any remaining pressure. Open cooker; transfer the eggs to the ice bath to cool for 5 minutes. Peel eggs when ready to create your egg salad.

LAMB PITAS WITH YOGURT SAUCE

The spiced lamb in these stuffed pita pockets goes perfectly with cool cucumber and yogurt. It's like having your own Greek gyro stand in the kitchen!
—Angela Leinenbach, Mechanicsville, VA

Prep: 25 min.
Cook: 15 min. + releasing
Makes: 8 servings

  2 Tbsp. olive oil
  2 lbs. lamb stew meat
     (¾-in. pieces)
  ½ cup dry red wine
  1 large onion, chopped
  1 garlic clove, minced
1¼ tsp. salt, divided
  1 tsp. dried oregano
  ½ tsp. dried basil
  ⅓ cup tomato paste
  1 medium cucumber
  1 cup plain yogurt
16 pita pocket
     halves, warmed
  4 plum tomatoes, sliced

DID YOU KNOW?
You can buy lamb when it's on sale and freeze it for a later date. Allow at least 24 hours for lamb stew meat to defrost.

1. Select saute or browning setting on a 6-qt. electric pressure cooker. Adjust for medium heat; add the oil. When oil is hot, brown lamb in batches. Add wine to pressure cooker. Cook 30 seconds, stirring to loosen browned bits from pan. Press cancel. Add onion, garlic, 1 tsp. salt, oregano and basil. Return lamb to pressure cooker.

2. Lock lid; close pressure-release valve. Adjust to pressure-cook on high for 15 minutes. Let pressure release naturally for 10 minutes; quick-release any remaining pressure. Press cancel.

3. Select saute setting; adjust for low heat. Add the tomato paste; simmer, uncovered, until mixture is slightly thickened, 8-10 minutes, stirring occasionally. Press cancel.

4. To serve, dice enough cucumber to measure 1 cup; thinly slice remaining cucumber. Combine diced cucumber with yogurt and remaining salt. Fill pitas with the lamb mixture, tomatoes, sliced cucumbers and yogurt mixture.

FREEZE OPTION: Freeze the cooled lamb mixture in freezer containers. To use, partially thaw in refrigerator overnight. Heat through in a saucepan, stirring occasionally and adding a little broth or water if necessary.

2 FILLED PITA HALVES: 383 cal., 11g fat (3g sat. fat), 78mg chol., 766mg sod., 39g carb. (5g sugars, 3g fiber), 31g pro. **DIABETIC EXCHANGES:** 3 lean meat, 2½ starch, 1 fat.

VEGETABLE WILD RICE SOUP

This thick and hearty soup is packed with colorful vegetables. It's wonderful for lunch alongside a healthy salad or light sandwich.
—Thomas Faglon, Somerset, NJ

Prep: 25 min.
Cook: 20 min. + releasing
Makes: 12 servings (3 qt.)

- 6 cups reduced-sodium vegetable broth
- 2 cans (14½ oz. each) fire-roasted diced tomatoes, undrained
- 2 celery ribs, sliced
- 2 medium carrots, chopped
- 1¾ cups baby portobello mushrooms, sliced
- 1 medium onion, chopped
- 1 medium parsnip, peeled and chopped
- 1 medium sweet potato, peeled and cubed
- 1 medium green pepper, chopped
- 1 cup uncooked wild rice
- 2 garlic cloves, minced
- ¾ tsp. salt
- ¼ tsp. pepper
- 2 bay leaves
- 2 fresh thyme sprigs

1. Combine all ingredients in a 6-qt. electric pressure cooker. Lock lid; close pressure-release valve. Adjust to pressure-cook on high for 20 minutes. Let pressure release naturally for 10 minutes; quick-release any remaining pressure.

2. Discard the bay leaves and thyme sprigs before serving. If desired, serve with additional thyme.

FREEZE OPTION: Freeze the cooled soup in freezer containers. To use, partially thaw in refrigerator overnight. Heat through in a saucepan, stirring occasionally and adding a little broth if necessary.

1 CUP: 117 cal., 0 fat (0 sat. fat), 0 chol., 419mg sod., 25g carb. (7g sugars, 4g fiber), 4g pro. **DIABETIC EXCHANGES:** 2 vegetable, 1 starch.

MEXICAN SHREDDED BEEF WRAPS

The first time I served these wrap sandwiches was at the party after my son's baptism. Everyone liked them so much that it's become one of my go-to party recipes.
—Amy Lents, Grand Forks, ND

Prep: 20 min.
Cook: 50 min. + releasing
Makes: 6 servings

- 1 **boneless beef chuck roast (2 to 3 lbs.), halved**
- ½ **tsp. salt**
- ½ **tsp. pepper**
- 1 **small onion, finely chopped**
- 1 **jalapeno pepper, seeded and minced**
- 3 **garlic cloves, minced**
- 1 **can (8 oz.) tomato sauce**
- ½ **cup water**
- ¼ **cup lime juice**
- 1 **Tbsp. chili powder**
- 1 **tsp. ground cumin**
- ¼ **tsp. cayenne pepper**
- 6 **flour or whole wheat tortillas (8 in.)**
  Optional toppings:
    Torn romaine, chopped tomatoes, sliced avocado and sour cream

1. Sprinkle roast with salt and pepper; place in a 6-qt. electric pressure cooker. Top with onion, jalapeno pepper and garlic. In a small bowl, mix tomato sauce, water, lime juice, chili powder, cumin and cayenne; pour over roast. Lock lid; close pressure-release valve. Adjust to pressure-cook on high for 50 minutes. Let pressure release naturally. A thermometer inserted in beef should read at least 145°.

2. Remove roast; cool slightly. Shred meat with 2 forks; return to pressure cooker. Serve beef on tortillas with the toppings of your choice.

FREEZE OPTION: Freeze the cooled meat mixture and juices in freezer containers. To use, partially thaw in refrigerator overnight. Heat through in a saucepan, stirring occasionally and adding a little water if necessary.

1 WRAP: 440 cal., 18g fat (6g sat. fat), 98mg chol., 707mg sod., 33g carb. (2g sugars, 3g fiber), 35g pro. **DIABETIC EXCHANGES:** 5 lean meat, 2 starch.

BLACK BEAN SOUP

Life can get really crazy with young children, but I never want to compromise when it comes to cooking. This recipe is healthy and so easy thanks to my one-pot cooker!
—Angela Lemoine, Howell, NJ

Prep: 20 min.
Cook: 5 min. + releasing
Makes: 6 cups

- 1 tsp. olive oil
- 1 cup fresh or frozen corn
- 2 cans (15 oz. each) black beans, rinsed and drained
- 2 cans (14½ oz. each) vegetable broth
- 1 medium onion, finely chopped
- 1 medium sweet red pepper, finely chopped
- 4 garlic cloves, minced
- 2 tsp. ground cumin
  Dash pepper
  Minced fresh cilantro

1. Select saute or browning setting on a 6-qt. electric pressure cooker. Adjust for medium heat; add oil. When oil is hot, add corn. Cook and stir until golden brown, 4-6 minutes. Press cancel. Remove corn and keep warm. Add beans, vegetable broth, onion, red pepper, garlic and cumin to pressure cooker.

2. Lock lid; close pressure-release valve. Adjust to pressure-cook on high for 5 minutes. Let pressure release naturally for 10 minutes; quick-release any remaining pressure.

3. Puree soup using an immersion blender, or cool soup slightly and puree in batches in a blender. Return to pressure cooker; heat through. Sprinkle soup with pepper. Garnish with reserved corn and cilantro.

FREEZE OPTION: Freeze the cooled soup in freezer containers. To use, partially thaw in refrigerator overnight. Heat through in a saucepan, stirring occasionally and adding a little broth if necessary. Sprinkle with toppings.

¾ **CUP:** 125 cal., 1g fat (0 sat. fat), 0 chol., 517mg sod., 22g carb. (4g sugars, 5g fiber), 6g pro. **DIABETIC EXCHANGES:** 1½ starch.

BEEF & VEGGIE SLOPPY JOES

Because I'm always looking for new ways to serve my family healthy and delicious food, I started experimenting with my go-to veggies and ground beef. I came up with this favorite that my kids actually request!
—Megan Niebuhr, Yakima, WA

Prep: 35 min.
Cook: 5 min.
Makes: 10 servings

- 2 **lbs. lean ground beef (90% lean)**
- 4 **medium carrots, shredded**
- 1 **medium yellow summer squash, shredded**
- 1 **medium zucchini, shredded**
- 1 **medium sweet red pepper, finely chopped**
- 2 **medium tomatoes, seeded and chopped**
- 1 **small red onion, finely chopped**
- ½ **cup ketchup**
- ¼ **cup water**
- 3 **Tbsp. minced fresh basil or 3 tsp. dried basil**
- 2 **Tbsp. cider vinegar**
- 2 **garlic cloves, minced**
- ½ **tsp. salt**
- ½ **tsp. pepper**
- 3 **Tbsp. molasses**
- 10 **whole wheat hamburger buns, split**

1. Select saute or browning setting on a 6-qt. electric pressure cooker; adjust for medium heat. Cook beef until no longer pink, 8-10 minutes, breaking into crumbles; drain. Return to pressure cooker. Add carrots, summer squash, zucchini, red pepper, tomatoes, onion, ketchup, water, basil, vinegar, garlic, salt and pepper (do not stir).

2. Lock lid; close pressure-release valve. Adjust to pressure-cook on high for 5 minutes. Quick-release pressure. Stir in molasses. Using a slotted spoon, serve beef mixture on buns.

FREEZE OPTION: Freeze the cooled meat mixture and juices in freezer containers. To use, partially thaw in refrigerator overnight. Heat through in a saucepan, stirring occasionally and adding a little water if necessary.

1 SANDWICH: 316 cal., 10g fat (3g sat. fat), 57mg chol., 566mg sod., 36g carb. (15g sugars, 5g fiber), 22g pro. **DIABETIC EXCHANGES:** 3 lean meat, 2½ starch.

TEST KITCHEN TIP

This recipe is a great way to work more veggies into your family's mealtime lineup. For an extra nutrition and flavor boost, stir several tablespoons of canned pumpkin into the meat mixture just before serving.

GREEK-STYLE LENTIL SOUP

This is a nice warming soup on a chilly day. Lentils are so good for you, too!
—Mary E. Smith, Columbia, MO

Prep: 20 min.
Cook: 15 min. + releasing
Makes: 12 servings (3 qt.)

- 4 cups water
- 4 cups vegetable broth
- 2 cups dried lentils, rinsed
- 2 medium carrots, chopped
- 1 small onion, chopped
- 1 celery rib, chopped
- 2 garlic cloves, minced
- 1 tsp. dried oregano
- 1 cup chopped fresh spinach
- ½ cup tomato sauce
- 1 can (2¼ oz.) sliced ripe olives, drained
- 3 Tbsp. red wine vinegar
- ½ tsp. salt
- ¼ tsp. pepper
  Optional toppings:
  Chopped red onion,
  chopped parsley and
  lemon wedges

1. Place the water, broth, lentils, carrots, onion, celery, garlic and oregano in a 6-qt. electric pressure cooker. Lock lid; close pressure-release valve. Adjust to pressure cook on high for 15 minutes. Let pressure release naturally for 10 minutes; quick-release any remaining pressure.

2. Stir in spinach, tomato sauce, ripe olives, red wine vinegar, salt and pepper. If desired, serve with red onion, parsley and lemon wedges.

FREEZE OPTION: Freeze the cooled soup in freezer containers. To use, partially thaw in refrigerator overnight. Heat through in a saucepan, stirring occasionally and adding a little broth if necessary.

1 CUP: 134 cal., 1g fat (0 sat. fat), 0 chol., 420mg sod., 24g carb. (2g sugars, 4g fiber), 9g pro. **DIABETIC EXCHANGES:** 1½ starch, 1 lean meat.

ITALIAN BEEF SANDWICHES

With only a few ingredients, these roast beef sandwiches are a snap to throw together. The meat turns out wonderfully tender.
—Lauren Adamson, Layton, UT

Prep: 10 min.
Cook: 1 hour + releasing
Makes: 12 servings

- 1 jar (16 oz.) sliced pepperoncini, undrained
- 1 can (14½ oz.) diced tomatoes, undrained
- 1 medium onion, chopped
- ½ cup water
- 2 pkg. Italian salad dressing mix
- 1 tsp. dried oregano
- ½ tsp. garlic powder
- 1 beef rump roast or bottom round roast (3 to 4 lbs.)
- 12 Italian rolls, split

1. In a bowl, mix the first 7 ingredients. Halve beef roast; place in a 6-qt. electric pressure cooker. Pour pepperoncini mixture over the top. Lock lid; close pressure-release valve. Adjust to pressure-cook on high for 60 minutes. Let pressure release naturally. A thermometer inserted into beef should read at least 145°.

2. Remove roast; cool slightly. Skim fat from cooking juices. Shred beef with 2 forks. Return beef and cooking juices to pressure cooker; heat through. Serve on rolls.

TO MAKE AHEAD: In a large shallow freezer container, combine the first 7 ingredients. Add roast; cover and freeze. To use, place freezer container in refrigerator 48 hours or until roast is completely thawed. Cook and serve as directed.

FREEZE OPTION: Freeze cooled, cooked beef mixture in freezer containers. To use, partially thaw in refrigerator overnight. Heat through in a saucepan, stirring occasionally and adding a little water if necessary.

1 SANDWICH: 278 cal., 7g fat (2g sat. fat), 67mg chol., 735mg sod., 24g carb. (3g sugars, 2g fiber), 26g pro. **DIABETIC EXCHANGES:** 3 lean meat, 1½ starch.

TURKEY CHILI

I took my mother's milder recipe for chili and made it thicker and more robust. It's a favorite, especially in fall and winter.
—Celesta Zanger, Bloomfield Hills, MI

Prep: 20 min.
Cook: 5 min. + releasing
Makes: 12 servings (3 qt.)

- 1 **lb. lean ground turkey**
- 1½ **cups water**
- 2 **cans (14½ oz. each) no-salt-added diced tomatoes, undrained**
- 1 **jar (24 oz.) meatless pasta sauce**
- 1 **can (16 oz.) hot chili beans, undrained**
- 1 **can (16 oz.) kidney beans, rinsed and drained**
- 1 **can (15 oz.) pinto beans, rinsed and drained**
- ¾ **cup chopped celery**
- ¾ **cup chopped onion**
- ¾ **cup chopped green pepper**
- ½ **cup frozen corn**
- 2 **Tbsp. chili powder**
- 1 **tsp. ground cumin**
- ¼ **tsp. pepper**
- ⅛ **to ¼ tsp. cayenne pepper**
  Optional toppings: Sour cream, cubed avocado, diced jalapeno peppers

1. Select saute or browning setting on a 6-qt. electric pressure cooker; adjust for medium heat. Cook turkey until no longer pink, 6-8 minutes, breaking up turkey into crumbles; drain. Add the water to pressure cooker. Cook 1 minute, stirring to loosen browned bits from pan. Return turkey to pressure cooker. Stir in tomatoes, pasta sauce, beans, celery, onion, green pepper, corn and seasonings.

2. Lock lid; close pressure-release valve. Adjust to pressure-cook on high for 5 minutes. Let pressure release naturally for 10 minutes; quick-release any remaining pressure. If desired, serve with sour cream, avocado and jalapeno.

FREEZE OPTION: Freeze cooled chili in freezer containers. To use, partially thaw in refrigerator overnight. Heat through in a saucepan, stirring occasionally and adding a little water if necessary.

1 CUP: 200 cal., 4g fat (1g sat. fat), 26mg chol., 535mg sod., 29g carb. (8g sugars, 8g fiber), 15g pro. **DIABETIC EXCHANGES:** 2 lean meat, 2 vegetable, 1 starch.

TEST KITCHEN TIP
Want to trim down this recipe even more? Replace the ground turkey with vegetarian crumbles. Found in the frozen food aisle, these meat-free bits are ideal in robust dishes like chili and spaghetti sauce.

TANDOORI CHICKEN PANINI

Tandoori-style spices give this a bold flavor that's hard to resist. The shredded chicken tastes incredible tucked between pieces of naan, then grilled for an Indian-inspired panini.
—Yasmin Arif, Manassas, VA

Prep: 25 min.
Cook: 10 min.
Makes: 6 servings

1½ lbs. boneless skinless
    chicken breasts
½ cup reduced-sodium
    chicken broth
2 garlic cloves, minced
2 tsp. minced fresh
    gingerroot
1 tsp. paprika
¼ tsp. salt
¼ to ½ tsp. cayenne
    pepper
¼ tsp. ground turmeric
6 green onions, chopped
6 Tbsp. chutney
6 naan flatbreads

1. Place the first 8 ingredients in a 6-qt. electric pressure cooker. Lock lid; close pressure-release valve. Adjust to pressure-cook on high for 6 minutes. Quick-release pressure. A thermometer inserted in chicken should read at least 165°.

2. Remove chicken; shred with 2 forks. Return to pressure cooker. Stir in green onions; heat through.

3. Spread chutney over 1 side of each naan. Using a slotted spoon, top chutney side of 3 naan with chicken mixture; top with remaining naan, chutney side down.

4. Cook the sandwiches on a panini maker or indoor grill until golden brown, 6-8 minutes. To serve, cut each sandwich in half.

FREEZE OPTION: Freeze the cooled meat mixture and juices in freezer containers. To use, partially thaw in refrigerator overnight. Heat through in a saucepan, stirring occasionally and adding a little broth if necessary.

½ **SANDWICH:** 351 cal., 6g fat (2g sat. fat), 68mg chol., 853mg sod., 44g carb. (13g sugars, 2g fiber), 28g pro.

ENGLISH PUB SPLIT PEA SOUP

This family favorite is the same recipe my grandmother used. With the magic of today's appliances, I can put it together in just 15 minutes, walk away for a bit and then it's "soup's on!" Finish it with more milk if you like your soup a little thinner.
—Judy Batson, Tampa, FL

Prep: 15 min.
Cook: 15 min. + releasing
Makes: 8 servings (2 qt.)

- 1 meaty ham bone
- 4 cups water
- 1 bottle (12 oz.) light beer
- 1⅓ cups dried green split peas, rinsed
- 2 celery ribs, chopped
- 1 large carrot, chopped
- 1 sweet onion, chopped
- 1 Tbsp. prepared English mustard
- ½ cup 2% milk
- ¼ cup minced fresh parsley
- ½ tsp. salt
- ¼ tsp. pepper
- ¼ tsp. ground nutmeg

1. Place ham bone in a 6-qt. electric pressure cooker. Add water, beer, peas, celery, carrot, onion and mustard. Lock lid; close pressure-release valve. Adjust to pressure-cook on high for 15 minutes. Let pressure release naturally.

2. Remove bone from soup. Cool slightly, trim away fat and remove meat from bone; discard fat and bone. Cut meat into bite-sized pieces; return to pressure cooker. Stir in remaining ingredients. If desired, top with additional minced parsley.

1 CUP: 188 cal., 2g fat (1g sat. fat), 22mg chol., 622mg sod., 26g carb. (6g sugars, 9g fiber), 16g pro. **DIABETIC EXCHANGES:** 1½ starch, 1 lean meat.

ITALIAN PULLED PORK SANDWICHES

Enjoy all the flavors of Italian sausage sandwiches with this healthier alternative.
—Mike Dellario, Middleport, NY

Prep: 20 min.
Cook: 45 min. + releasing
Makes: 12 servings

- 1 Tbsp. fennel seed, crushed
- 1 Tbsp. steak seasoning
- 1 tsp. cayenne pepper, optional
- 1 boneless pork shoulder butt roast (3 lbs.)
- 1 Tbsp. olive oil
- 2 medium green or sweet red peppers, thinly sliced
- 2 medium onions, thinly sliced
- 1 can (14½ oz.) diced tomatoes, undrained
- ½ cup water
- 12 whole wheat hamburger buns, split

1. In a small bowl, combine fennel seed, steak seasoning and cayenne if desired. Cut roast in half. Rub seasoning mixture over pork. Select saute or browning setting on a 6-qt. electric pressure cooker. Adjust for medium heat; add oil. When oil is hot, brown a roast half on all sides. Remove; repeat with remaining pork. Press cancel.

2. Return all to pressure cooker. Add the peppers, onions, tomatoes and water. Lock lid; close pressure-release valve. Adjust to pressure-cook on high for 45 minutes. Let pressure release naturally. A thermometer inserted in pork should read at least 145°.

3. Remove pork roast; shred with 2 forks. Strain cooking juices; skim fat. Return cooking juices, vegetables and pork to pressure cooker; heat through. Using a slotted spoon, serve pork mixture on buns.

FREEZE OPTION: Freeze the cooled meat mixture and juices in freezer containers. To use, partially thaw in refrigerator overnight. Heat through in a saucepan, stirring occasionally and adding a little water if necessary.

1 SANDWICH: 285 cal., 9g fat (2g sat. fat), 57mg chol., 483mg sod., 27g carb. (6g sugars, 5g fiber), 26g pro. **DIABETIC EXCHANGES:** 3 lean meat, 2 starch, ½ fat.

TURKEY VEGETABLE SOUP

Our family is big on soup. This tasty favorite is quick to make, giving me plenty of time to have fun with the family before we dig in.
—Nancy Heishman, Las Vegas, NV

Prep: 30 min.
Cook: 5 min. + releasing
Makes: 10 servings (3½ qt.)

- 1 pkg. (19½ oz.) Italian turkey sausage links, casings removed
- 3 large tomatoes, chopped
- 1 can (15 oz.) garbanzo beans or chickpeas, rinsed and drained
- 3 medium carrots, thinly sliced
- 1½ cups cut fresh green beans (1-in. pieces)
- 1 medium zucchini, quartered lengthwise and sliced
- 1 large sweet red or green pepper, chopped
- 8 green onions, chopped
- 4 cups chicken stock
- 1 can (12 oz.) tomato paste
- ½ tsp. seasoned salt
- ⅓ cup minced fresh basil

1. Select saute or browning setting on a 6-qt. electric pressure cooker; adjust for medium heat. Cook sausage until no longer pink, 6-8 minutes, breaking into crumbles; drain. Return to pressure cooker. Press cancel.

2. Add tomatoes, beans, carrots, green beans, zucchini, pepper and onions. In a large bowl, whisk stock, tomato paste and seasoned salt; pour over the vegetables. Lock lid; close pressure-release valve. Adjust to pressure-cook on high for 5 minutes. Let pressure release naturally for 10 minutes; quick-release any remaining pressure. Just before serving, stir in basil.

FREEZE OPTION: Freeze cooled soup in freezer containers. To use, partially thaw in refrigerator overnight. Heat through in a saucepan, stirring occasionally and adding a little stock if necessary.

1⅓ **CUPS:** 167 cal., 5g fat (1g sat. fat), 20mg chol., 604mg sod., 21g carb. (9g sugars, 5g fiber), 13g pro. **DIABETIC EXCHANGES:** 2 lean meat, 2 vegetable, ½ starch.

SHREDDED CHICKEN GYROS

Our family has no ties of any kind to Greece, but we always have such a marvelous time at the annual Salt Lake City Greek Festival. One of my favorite parts is the awesome food. This meal is a good way to mix up our menu, and my kids are big fans.
—Camille Beckstrand, Layton, UT

Prep: 20 min.
Cook: 10 min.
Makes: 8 servings

- 2 **medium onions, chopped**
- 6 **garlic cloves, minced**
- 1 **tsp. lemon-pepper seasoning**
- 1 **tsp. dried oregano**
- ½ **tsp. ground allspice**
- ½ **cup lemon juice**
- ¼ **cup red wine vinegar**
- 2 **Tbsp. olive oil**
- 2 **lbs. boneless skinless chicken breasts**
- 8 **whole pita breads**
  Toppings: Tzatziki sauce, torn romaine and sliced tomato, cucumber and onion

1. In a 6-qt. electric pressure cooker, combine the first 8 ingredients; add chicken. Lock lid; close pressure-release valve. Adjust to pressure-cook on high for 6 minutes. Quick-release pressure. A thermometer inserted in chicken should read at least 165°.

2. Remove chicken; shred with 2 forks. Return to pressure cooker. Using tongs, place chicken mixture on pita breads. Serve with toppings.

FREEZE OPTION: Freeze the cooled meat mixture and juices in freezer containers. To use, partially thaw in refrigerator overnight. Heat through in a saucepan, stirring occasionally and adding a little water if necessary.

1 GYRO: 335 cal., 7g fat (1g sat. fat), 63mg chol., 418mg sod., 38g carb. (2g sugars, 2g fiber), 29g pro. **DIABETIC EXCHANGES:** 3 lean meat, 2½ starch, ½ fat.

CREAMY CAULIFLOWER SOUP

I love indulgent cream soups but not the fat that goes along with them. The velvety texture of this healthier cauliflower soup makes it feel so rich, and the spicy kick warms you from the inside out.
—Teri Rasey, Cadillac, MI

Prep: 20 min.
Cook: 5 min. + releasing
Makes: 14 servings (3½ qt.)

  6 cups water
1¾ lbs. Yukon Gold potatoes (about 4 medium), peeled and cut into 1-in. cubes
  1 medium head cauliflower (about 1½ lbs.), cut into 1-in. pieces
  1 small onion, chopped
  3 garlic cloves, minced
  1 large bay leaf
  3 tsp. dried celery flakes
1½ tsp. salt
1½ tsp. adobo seasoning
  ¾ tsp. ground mustard
  ¼ tsp. cayenne pepper
  ¾ cup nonfat dry milk powder
    Optional toppings: Shredded cheddar cheese, sliced green onions and croutons

1. Place water, vegetables and seasonings in a 6-qt. electric pressure cooker. Lock lid; close pressure-release valve. Adjust to pressure-cook on high for 5 minutes. Let pressure release naturally for 10 minutes; quick-release any remaining pressure.

2. Discard bay leaf. Stir in milk powder until dissolved. Puree soup using an immersion blender. Or, cool slightly and puree soup in batches in a blender; return to pressure cooker and heat through. If desired, serve with toppings.

1 CUP: 80 cal., 0 fat (0 sat. fat), 1mg chol., 434mg sod., 17g carb. (4g sugars, 2g fiber), 3g pro. **DIABETIC EXCHANGES:** 1 vegetable, ½ starch.

SWEETS & DESSERTS

If it's a treat you're craving, you've come to the right spot. High on flavor and low in calories, fat and sugar, these specialties satisfy everyone. Best of all, you don't have to be a baker. Your electric pressure cooker does the work for you!

MAKING ROOM FOR DESSERT

Eating right doesn't mean giving up on after-dinner treats that make meals special. When comes to light desserts that satisfy your cravings, you can't go wrong with fruit, a handful of kitchen staples and your electric pressure cooker. Review the tips and hints here, then see the delectable lineup of delightful treats that follows.

FRUIT	HOW TO BUY	HOW TO STORE	HOW TO PREP
APPLES	Deep colors indicate that an apple has absorbed lots of sunlight. Give apples a squeeze; they should be firm with no give. Also inspect them for blemishes or dents, as these can accelerate decay.	Store in a cool place. If storing in the refrigerator place apples, in a bag with holes in it, in the crisper bin. Remove any damaged apples so rot does not spread. Don't store other fruits or vegetables in the same drawer; apples give off ethylene gas, which causes produce to rot faster.	Always wash apples (especially nonorganic ones) before eating or prepping for use in a recipe. Use 1 tsp. of baking soda to 2 cups of water as a wash; this has been shown to remove the majority of trace pesticides from apple skin.
PEARS	Select pears that are plump. Avoid those with bruises, soft spots or cuts. For some varieties, the color of the skin will change as the pear ripens. Select firm pears for baking. For eating, select pears that give slightly when gently pressed.	Store unwashed ripe pears in the refrigerator for 3-5 days, away from other fruits and vegetables with strong aromas. To ripen firm pears, place them in a paper bag at room temperature for 2-3 days.	Wash before using. Peel if desired and eat whole, sliced or chopped. When preparing pears for a recipe, brush the cut flesh with lemon juice to prevent browning. For pressure cooking, choose pears that are slightly underripe.
BERRIES	Select berries that are plump; avoid those that are bruised, mushy or moldy. Avoid packages with juice-stained bottoms.	Fragile berries are highly perishable. Store the unwashed berries in their container for 1-2 days. To freeze, wash berries and drain well; arrange in a single layer on a parchment-lined baking sheet. Once frozen, transfer to a freezer container. Freeze berries for up to 1 year.	Gently wash berries before using. Eat them on their own or follow the recipe's directions for slicing, chopping or pureeing.
PEACHES	Select peaches and nectarines that are firm but yield a bit to gentle pressure. They should be bright with skin free of discoloration, soft spots or bruises. Choose fruits with defined clefts, as this indicates they are mature and sweeter.	Both peaches and nectarines can be stored unrefrigerated for up to 4 days, depending on how ripe they were when you bought them. Keeping your peaches at room temperature offers a fuller, more intense flavor.	Give the fruit a light rinse; scrubbing will remove its delicate skin. Fully slice the fruit lengthwise. Take the two halves and twist. A ripe peach will easily come apart in two halves, exposing the pit, which you can then pluck out.
PUMPKIN	Choose a pumpkin that has even color saturation. It should be firm and feel heavy for its size. Pie pumpkins are smaller than the "jack-o'-lantern" type and make flavorful puree for use in pies, cakes and other baked goods.	Pumpkin and other winter squash keeps very well; simply store it in a cool, dark place, such as the inside of a cabinet or kitchen pantry, and it will last for up to 1 month.	Rinse the pumpkin or other squash and cut it lengthwise, scooping out the fibrous section and seeds. If you like, microwave the squash for 3-4 minutes before cutting. This softens the skin and makes it easier to slice.

THE SPICE OF LIFE

Pumpkin pie spice is a wonderful way to add some heartwarming comfort to most any dessert--without adding fat or sugar. If you're out of the popular spice, it's easy to make your own. Simply mix 4 tsp. ground cinnamon, 2 tsp. ground ginger, 1 tsp. ground cloves and ½ tsp. ground nutmeg. Store in an airtight container in a cool, dry place up to 6 months.

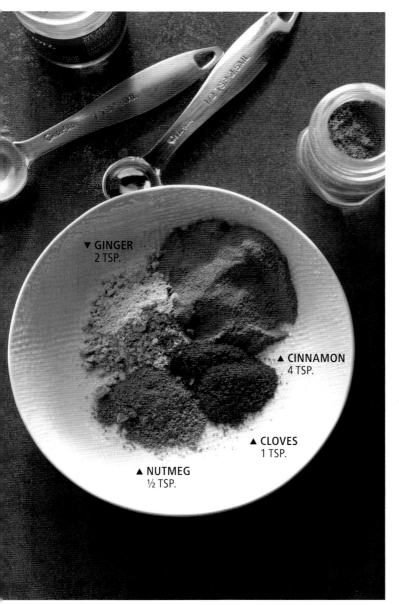

▼ GINGER
2 TSP.

▲ CINNAMON
4 TSP.

▲ CLOVES
1 TSP.

▲ NUTMEG
½ TSP.

CUT LIKE A PRO

Prepare the Peachy Summer Cheesecake on page 252, and serve it with ease. You'll need a sharp knife, some hot water and a towel. Dip the blade in water to heat, then wipe dry and cut. Repeat each time for pretty slices with a clean edge.

TEQUILA POACHED PEARS

Tequila may seem an unusual ingredient for a dessert, but give this one a try! The fresh pears and mint are so refreshing. Bring out this creative sweet when you want to impress guests.
—Nancy Heishman, Las Vegas, NV

Prep: 20 min. + simmering
Cook: 5 min.
Makes: 8 servings

- 2 **cups water**
- 1 **can (11.3 oz.) pear nectar**
- 1 **cup tequila**
- ½ **cup sugar**
- 2 **Tbsp. lime juice**
- 2 **tsp. grated lime zest**
- 1 **cinnamon stick (3 in.)**
- ¼ **tsp. ground nutmeg**
- 8 **whole Anjou pears, peeled**
  Sweetened whipped cream, optional
  Fresh mint leaves

1. Select saute setting on a 6-qt. pressure cooker and adjust for low heat. Add the first 8 ingredients; cook and stir until sugar is dissolved, about 3 minutes. Press cancel. Add pears. Lock lid; close pressure-release valve. Adjust to pressure-cook on high for 3 minutes. Quick-release pressure. Remove pears and keep warm. Press cancel.

2. Reserve 3 cups cooking juices; discard remaining juices and cinnamon stick. Return the reserved juices to pressure cooker. Select saute setting and adjust for medium heat. Simmer, uncovered, until liquid is reduced to 1 cup, about 30 minutes, stirring occasionally.

3. Halve pears lengthwise and core. Serve with the sauce, whipped cream if desired, and mint leaves.

1 PEAR WITH 2 TBSP. SAUCE: 155 cal., 0 fat (0 sat. fat), 0 chol., 3mg sod., 40g carb. (30g sugars, 6g fiber), 1g pro.

PUMPKIN FLANS

This silky, smooth dessert captures the essence and elegance of fall. I came up with the recipe myself, aiming to make something both luscious and light.
—Charles Insler, Silver Spring, MD

Prep: 45 min.
Cook: 15 min. + chilling
Makes: 6 servings

- 1 **cup sugar, divided**
- ¼ **cups water**
- 1½ **cups fat-free evaporated milk**
- 3 **large eggs**
- 1 **large egg white**
- ¼ **tsp. salt**
- ¼ **tsp. each ground ginger, cinnamon and cloves**
- 1 **cup canned pumpkin**
- 1 **tsp. vanilla extract**

TEST KITCHEN TIP
Flan is a sweet custard dessert that is often topped with a thin caramel sauce. Try making it with your own combination of spices and seasonings.

1. In a small heavy skillet over medium-low heat, combine ⅓ cup sugar and ¼ cup water. Cook, stirring occasionally, until sugar begins to melt. Cook without stirring until amber, about 20 minutes. Quickly pour into 6 ungreased 6-oz. ramekins or custard cups, tilting to coat bottoms of dishes. Let stand for 10 minutes.

2. In a small saucepan, heat milk until bubbles form around the sides of pan; remove from heat. In a large bowl, whisk eggs, egg white, salt, spices and remaining ⅔ cup sugar until blended but not foamy. Slowly stir in hot milk. Stir in pumpkin and vanilla. Slowly pour into prepared ramekins.

3. Cover each ramekin with foil. Place trivet insert and 1 cup water in pressure cooker. Set ramekins on trivet. Lock lid; close pressure-release valve. Adjust to pressure cook on high for 13 minutes. Quick-release pressure.

4. Centers should just be set (the mixture will jiggle) and a thermometer inserted in flan should read at least 160°. Carefully remove ramekins. Cool 10 minutes; refrigerate, covered, at least 4 hours. Carefully run a knife around the edges of ramekins to loosen; invert each dish onto a rimmed serving dish. If desired, sprinkle with additional cinnamon. Serve immediately.

1 SERVING: 235 cal., 3g fat (1g sat. fat), 96mg chol., 219mg sod., 45g carb. (42g sugars, 1g fiber), 9g pro.

LAVA CAKE

I love chocolate, and this decadent cake has long been a family favorite. It's even great cold the next day—assuming you have any leftovers!
—Elizabeth Farrell, Hamilton, MT

Prep: 15 min.
Cook: 20 min. + standing
Makes: 8 servings

1 cup all-purpose flour
1 cup packed brown sugar, divided
5 Tbsp. baking cocoa, divided
2 tsp. baking powder
¼ tsp. salt
½ cup fat-free milk
2 Tbsp. canola oil
½ tsp. vanilla extract
⅛ tsp. ground cinnamon
1¼ cups hot water
   Optional toppings:
     Fresh raspberries and ice cream

1. In a large bowl, whisk the flour, ½ cup brown sugar, 3 Tbsp. cocoa, baking powder and salt. In another bowl, whisk milk, oil and vanilla until blended. Add to flour mixture; stir just until moistened.

2. Spread into a 1½-qt. baking dish coated with cooking spray. In a small bowl, mix cinnamon and remaining ½ cup brown sugar and 2 Tbsp. cocoa; stir in hot water. Pour over batter (do not stir).

3. Place trivet insert and 1 cup water in a 6-qt. electric pressure cooker. Cover the baking dish with foil. Fold an 18x12-in. piece of foil lengthwise into thirds, making a sling. Use the sling to lower the dish onto the trivet. Lock lid; close pressure-release valve. Adjust to pressure-cook on high for 20 minutes. Quick-release pressure.

4. Using the foil sling, carefully remove baking dish. Let stand 15 minutes. A toothpick inserted in cake portion should come out clean.

1 SERVING: 208 cal., 4g fat (0 sat. fat), 0 chol., 208mg sod., 42g carb. (28g sugars, 1g fiber), 3g pro.

CRANBERRY STUFFED APPLES

Cinnamon, nutmeg and walnuts add to the homey flavor of these stuffed apples. What a lovely old-fashioned treat!
—Grace Sandvigen, Rochester, NY

Prep: 10 min.
Cook: 5 min.
Makes: 5 servings

5 medium apples
⅓ cup fresh or frozen cranberries, thawed and chopped
¼ cup packed brown sugar
2 Tbsp. chopped walnuts
¼ tsp. ground cinnamon
⅛ tsp. ground nutmeg
Optional toppings: Whipped cream or vanilla ice cream

1. Core apples, leaving bottoms intact. Peel top third of each apple. Place trivet insert and 1 cup water in a 6-qt. electric pressure cooker. Combine the cranberries, brown sugar, walnuts, cinnamon and nutmeg; spoon into apples. Place apples on trivet.

2. Lock lid; close pressure-release valve. Adjust to pressure-cook on high for 3 minutes. Quick-release pressure. Serve with whipped cream or ice cream if desired.

1 STUFFED APPLE: 142 cal., 2g fat (0 sat. fat), 0 chol., 5mg sod., 33g carb. (27g sugars, 4g fiber), 1g pro. **DIABETIC EXCHANGES:** 1 starch, 1 fruit.

TEST KITCHEN TIP
The moisture in brown sugar tends to trap air between the crystals, so the sugar should be firmly packed when measuring, particularly when recipes specify "packed brown sugar" in the ingredient list.

PEACHY SUMMER CHEESECAKE

This is a cool, creamy, refreshing dessert that is special enough to take to a gathering. You can even prepare this ahead of time and freeze it. Just make sure you wrap it well so it's airtight, and add the peaches only after it thaws.
—Joan Engelhardt, Latrobe, PA

Prep: 25 min.
Cook: 30 min. + chilling
Makes: 6 servings

- 1 pkg. (8 oz.) reduced-fat cream cheese
- 4 oz. fat-free cream cheese
- ½ cup sugar
- ½ cup reduced-fat sour cream
- 2 Tbsp. unsweetened apple juice
- 1 Tbsp. all-purpose flour
- ½ tsp. vanilla
- 3 large eggs, room temperature, lightly beaten
- 2 medium ripe peaches, peeled and thinly sliced

1. Place the trivet insert and 1 cup water in a 6-qt. electric pressure cooker. Grease a 6-in. springform pan; place on a double thickness of heavy-duty foil (about 12 in. square). Wrap securely around pan.

2. In a large bowl, beat cream cheeses and sugar until smooth. Beat in sour cream, apple juice, flour and vanilla. Add eggs; beat on low speed just until blended. Pour into the prepared pan. Cover pan with foil. Fold an 18x12-in. piece of foil lengthwise into thirds, making a sling. Use the sling to lower the pan onto trivet.

3. Lock lid; close pressure-release valve. Adjust to pressure-cook on high for 30 minutes. Let pressure release naturally for 10 minutes; quick-release any remaining pressure. Using foil sling, carefully remove springform pan. Let stand 10 minutes. Remove foil from pan. Cool cheesecake on a wire rack 1 hour.

4. Loosen sides from pan with a knife. Refrigerate overnight, covering when cooled. To serve, remove rim from springform pan. Serve with peaches.

1 SLICE: 262 cal., 12g fat (7g sat. fat), 124mg chol., 342mg sod., 27g carb. (25g sugars, 1g fiber), 12g pro.

INDEX

Spicy Pork & Squash Ragu, 117
Spring-Thyme Chicken Stew, 155
Steak Fajitas, 200
Steamed Mussels with Peppers, 87
Stuffed Peppers, 103
Summer Squash, 60
Sweet Onion & Cherry Pork Chops, 121
Swiss Steak, 203

T

Tandoori Chicken Panini, 228
Tequila Poached Pears, 244
Teriyaki Pork Roast, 125
Tomato-Poached Halibut, 99
Tropical Pulled Pork Sliders, 23
Turkey Chili, 227
Turkey Vegetable Soup, 235

V

Vegetable Wild Rice Soup, 215

Taste of Home®
SKINNY
SLOW COOKER

BOOK TWO

TASTE OF HOME BOOKS • RDA ENTHUSIAST BRANDS, LLC • MILWAUKEE, WI

Eat Right, *Save Time,* **Feel Great!**

With a hectic schedule, it's hard enough to sit the family down to a homemade meal, let alone one that cuts calories and satisfies everyone. The answer? Put your slow cooker to work with the healthy recipes in *Taste of Home Skinny Slow Cooker*!

Inside this handy book, you'll discover 278 recipes to help you set your table with the comforting foods your family craves...all big on flavor and short on fat, calories or sodium. With dishes like *Gone-All-Day Stew* (*p. 83*) and *Slow-Cooked Pork Tacos* (*p. 172*), a hot, hearty and healthy entree is always at your fingertips. Losing weight has never tasted so good!

Every recipe features nutrition facts and most contain diabetic exchanges so you know that you're feeding your family right. You'll also find prep/cook guidelines with each dish to make meal planning a snap. Plus, two bonus chapters offer low-calorie sides, breads, desserts and more.

Watch for the At-a-Glance icons that are scattered throughout the book, too. Only have a few ingredients on hand? Check for the ⑤ INGREDIENTS icon, which spotlights recipes that call for five or fewer items—not including any water, salt, pepper, oils and optional ingredients. Also, watch for the FREEZE IT icon when it comes to preplanning. These dishes go from the slow cooker to the freezer for nights when time is tight but a healthy meal is still your priority. Eating right has never been easier!

With these remarkable recipes at your fingertips, whipping up a family favorite is a snap—but so is cutting calories, losing weight and feeling great! Dig in to all the comfort, flavor and convenience your slow cooker offers, without an ounce of guilt. Let *Taste of Home Skinny Slow Cooker* show you how!

CONTENTS

PUMPKIN SPICE OVERNIGHT
OATMEAL, PAGE 8

BREAKFAST &
BRUNCH DISHES

8

10

12

CARROT CAKE OATMEAL

Set up this oatmeal in the slow cooker the night before so you can wake up to a healthy breakfast. For extra crunch, I garnish servings with ground nuts.
—DEBBIE KAIN
COLORADO SPRINGS, CO

PREP: 10 MIN. • **COOK:** 6 HOURS
MAKES: 8 SERVINGS

- 4½ cups water
- 1 can (20 ounces) crushed pineapple, undrained
- 2 cups shredded carrots
- 1 cup steel-cut oats
- 1 cup raisins
- 2 teaspoons ground cinnamon
- 1 teaspoon pumpkin pie spice
  Brown sugar, optional

In a 4-qt. slow cooker coated with cooking spray, combine the first seven ingredients. Cover and cook on low for 6-8 hours or until the oats are tender and the liquid is absorbed. Sprinkle with brown sugar if desired.
PER SERVING *1 cup (calculated without optional toppings) equals 197 cal., 2 g fat (trace sat. fat), 0 chol., 23 mg sodium, 46 g carb., 4 g fiber, 4 g pro.*

SLOW COOKER HAM & EGGS

This dish is great anytime, but I especially love to make it for Easter brunch. I like to serve the dish with hash browns or potato slices cooked up in the frying pan.
—ANDREA SCHAAK JORDAN, MN

PREP: 15 MIN. • **COOK:** 3 HOURS
MAKES: 6 SERVINGS

- 6 large eggs
- 1 cup biscuit/baking mix
- ⅔ cup 2% milk
- ⅓ cup sour cream
- 2 tablespoons minced fresh parsley
- 2 garlic cloves, minced
- ½ teaspoon salt
- ½ teaspoon pepper
- 1 cup cubed fully cooked ham
- 1 cup (4 ounces) shredded Swiss cheese
- 1 small onion, finely chopped
- ⅓ cup shredded Parmesan cheese

1. In a large bowl, whisk the first eight ingredients until blended; stir in remaining ingredients. Pour into a greased 3- or 4-qt. slow cooker.
2. Cook, covered, on low 3-4 hours or until the eggs are set. Cut into wedges.
PER SERVING *1 serving equals 315 cal., 18 g fat (9 g sat. fat), 256 mg chol., 942 mg sodium, 17 g carb., 1 g fiber, 21 g pro.*

PUMPKIN SPICE OVERNIGHT OATMEAL

There's nothing like a warm cup of oatmeal in the morning, and my spiced version comes from a slow cooker. Store leftovers in the fridge.
—JORDAN MASON BROOKVILLE, PA

PREP: 10 MIN. • **COOK:** 5 HOURS
MAKES: 6 SERVINGS

- 1 can (15 ounces) solid-pack pumpkin
- 1 cup steel-cut oats
- 3 tablespoons brown sugar
- 1½ teaspoons pumpkin pie spice
- 1 teaspoon ground cinnamon
- ¾ teaspoon salt
- 3 cups water
- 1½ cups 2% milk
  Optional toppings: toasted chopped pecans, ground cinnamon and additional brown sugar and milk

In a large bowl, combine the first six ingredients; stir in water and milk. Transfer to a greased 3-qt. slow cooker. Cook, covered, on low 5-6 hours or until oats are tender, stirring once. Serve with toppings as desired.
PER SERVING *1 cup (calculated without optional toppings) equals 183 cal., 3 g fat (1 g sat. fat), 5 mg chol., 329 mg sodium, 34 g carb., 5 g fiber, 6 g pro.* **Diabetic Exchanges:** *2 starch, ½ fat.*

HOW-TO

SERVE A STUNNING BRUNCH
- Measure, chop, cube or mix anything you can the night before to save time in the morning.
- Once you have your slow cooker going, move on to any last-minute details or recipes.
- Don't forget the coffee! Borrow a thermal carafe from a friend or local business, if you can, to keep it warm all morning long.

CARROT CAKE OATMEAL

SLOW COOKER HAM & EGGS

PUMPKIN SPICE OVERNIGHT OATMEAL

OVERNIGHT VEGETABLE & EGG BREAKFAST

My eggs and veggies cook while you sleep and make a hearty breakfast for those who have to rush out the door. I use sliced potatoes, but frozen potatoes work, too.

—KIMBERLY CLARK-THIRY
ANCHOR POINT, AK

PREP: 15 MIN. • **COOK:** 7 HOURS
MAKES: 8 SERVINGS

- 4 pounds potatoes, peeled and thinly sliced (about 8 cups)
- 1 medium green pepper, finely chopped
- 1 package (10 ounces) frozen chopped spinach, thawed and squeezed dry
- 1 cup sliced fresh mushrooms
- 1 medium onion, finely chopped
- 8 large eggs
- 1 cup water
- 1 cup 2% milk
- 1¼ teaspoons salt
- ¼ teaspoon pepper
- 2 cups (8 ounces) shredded cheddar cheese

1. In a greased 6-qt. slow cooker, layer first five ingredients. In a large bowl, whisk eggs, water, milk, salt and pepper; pour over top. Sprinkle with cheese.

2. Cook, covered, on low 7-9 hours or until potatoes are tender and eggs are set.

PER SERVING 1½ cups equals 354 cal., 15 g fat (7 g sat. fat), 217 mg chol., 668 mg sodium, 37 g carb., 4 g fiber, 19 g pro.

OVERNIGHT VEGETABLE & EGG BREAKFAST

APPLE-CRANBERRY GRAINS

I made some changes to my diet in order to lose weight. My kids are skeptical when it comes to healthy food, but they certainly go for these wholesome grains.

—SHERISSE DAWE
BLACK DIAMOND, AB

PREP: 10 MIN. • **COOK:** 4 HOURS
MAKES: 10 SERVINGS

- 2 medium apples, peeled and chopped
- 1 cup sugar
- 1 cup fresh cranberries
- ½ cup wheat berries
- ½ cup quinoa, rinsed
- ½ cup oat bran
- ½ cup medium pearl barley
- ½ cup chopped walnuts
- ½ cup packed brown sugar
- 1½ to 2 teaspoons ground cinnamon
- 6 cups water
  - Milk
  - Sliced apples, optional

In a 3-qt. slow cooker, combine the first 11 ingredients. Cook, covered, on low 4-5 hours or until grains are tender. Serve with milk. If desired, top with apple slices.

NOTE *Look for oat bran cereal near the hot cereals or in the natural foods section. Look for quinoa in the cereal, rice or organic food aisle.*

PER SERVING ¾ cup (calculated without milk) equals 286 cal., 5 g fat (1 g sat. fat), 0 chol., 8 mg sodium, 60 g carb., 5 g fiber, 5 g pro.

THE SKINNY

GO FOR SKIM MILK

By serving Apple-Cranberry Grains with ½ cup skim milk instead of 2%, you'd save yourself about 20 calories and 2 grams of fat—and keep the protein!

APPLE-CRANBERRY
GRAINS

SLOW COOKER FRITTATA PROVENCAL

This meatless slow cooker meal makes an elegant brunch dish or a breakfast-for-supper option.

—**CONNIE EATON** PITTSBURGH, PA

PREP: 30 MIN. • **COOK:** 3 HOURS
MAKES: 6 SERVINGS

- ½ cup water
- 1 tablespoon olive oil
- 1 medium Yukon Gold potato, peeled and sliced
- 1 small onion, thinly sliced
- ½ teaspoon smoked paprika
- 12 large eggs
- 1 teaspoon minced fresh thyme or ¼ teaspoon dried thyme
- 1 teaspoon hot pepper sauce
- ½ teaspoon salt
- ¼ teaspoon pepper
- 1 log (4 ounces) fresh goat cheese, coarsely crumbled, divided
- ½ cup chopped soft sun-dried tomatoes (not packed in oil)

1. Layer two 24-in. pieces of aluminum foil; starting with a long side, fold up the foil to create a 1-in.-wide strip. Shape strip into a coil to make a rack for bottom of a 6-qt. oval slow cooker. Add water to slow cooker; set foil rack in water.

2. In a large skillet, heat oil over medium-high heat. Add potato and onion; cook and stir 5-7 minutes or until potato is lightly browned. Stir in the paprika. Transfer to a greased 1½-qt. baking dish (dish must fit in slow cooker).

3. In a large bowl, whisk the eggs, thyme, pepper sauce, salt and pepper; stir in 2 ounces cheese. Pour over the potato mixture. Top with remaining goat cheese. Place dish on foil rack.

4. Cook, covered, on low 3 hours or until eggs are set and a knife inserted near the center comes out clean.

NOTE *This recipe was tested with sun-dried tomatoes that are ready to use without soaking. When using other sun-dried tomatoes that are not oil-packed, cover with boiling water and let stand until soft. Drain before using.*

PER SERVING *1 wedge equals 245 calories, 14 g fat (5 g sat. fat), 385 mg chol., 338 mg sodium, 12 g carb., 2 g fiber, 15 g pro.* **Diabetic Exchanges:** *2 medium-fat meat, 1 starch, ½ fat.*

SLOW COOKER FRITTATA PROVENCAL

PEAR-BLUEBERRY GRANOLA

Oatmeal fans will love this dish. Enjoy it as a delicious dessert when served with vanilla ice cream, but the pears, blueberries and granola also make a beautiful breakfast item.

—**LISA WORKMAN** BOONES MILL, VA

PREP: 15 MIN. • **COOK:** 3 HOURS
MAKES: 10 SERVINGS

- 5 medium pears, peeled and thinly sliced
- 2 cups fresh or frozen unsweetened blueberries
- ½ cup packed brown sugar
- ⅓ cup apple cider or unsweetened apple juice
- 1 tablespoon all-purpoon flour
- 1 tablespoon lemon juice
- 2 teaspoons ground cinnamon
- 2 tablespoons butter
- 3 cups granola without raisins

In a 4-qt. slow cooker, combine the first seven ingredients. Dot with butter. Sprinkle granola over top. Cover and cook on low for 3-4 hours or until fruit is tender.
PER SERVING *¾ cup equals 267 cal., 7 g fat (1 g sat. fat), 6 mg chol., 35 mg sodium, 51 g carb., 10 g fiber, 7 g pro.*

HOT FRUIT SALAD

Round out a brunch easily with my spiced fruit compote. With its pretty color, this salad is nice around the holidays or for any special occasion.

—**BARB VANDE VOORT**
NEW SHARON, IA

PREP: 5 MIN. • **COOK:** 3 HOURS
MAKES: 16 SERVINGS

- 1 jar (25 ounces) unsweetened applesauce
- 1 can (21 ounces) cherry pie filling
- 1 can (20 ounces) unsweetened pineapple chunks, undrained
- 1 can (15 ounces) sliced peaches in juice, undrained
- 1 can (15 ounces) reduced-sugar apricot halves, undrained
- 1 can (15 ounces) mandarin oranges, undrained
- ¼ cup packed brown sugar
- 1 teaspoon ground cinnamon

Place the first six ingredients in a 5-qt. slow cooker; stir gently. Mix brown sugar and cinnamon; sprinkle over fruit mixture. Cook, covered, on low until heated through, 3-4 hours.
PER SERVING *¾ cup equals 141 cal., trace fat (trace sat. fat), 0 chol., 13 mg sodium, 35 g carb., 2 g fiber, 1 g pro.*

TOP TIP

BROWN SUGAR 101

Dark brown sugar contains more molasses than light or golden brown sugar. The types are generally interchangeable in recipes. But if you prefer a bolder flavor, go for the dark brown sugar.

HOT FRUIT SALAD

RED BEAN VEGETABLE
SOUP, PAGE 31

SOUPS

32

16

29

HOME-STYLE
CHICKEN SOUP

2 teaspoons Italian seasoning
6 lasagna noodles, broken into
   1-inch pieces
2 cups coarsely chopped fresh
   spinach
1 cup cubed or shredded
   part-skim mozzarella cheese
   Shredded Parmesan cheese and
   minced fresh basil, optional

1. In a large skillet, cook the sausage over medium-high heat 8-10 minutes or until no longer pink, breaking into crumbles; drain. Transfer to a 5- or 6-qt. slow cooker.
2. Add the onion and carrots to the same skillet; cook and stir 2-4 minutes or until softened. Stir in the mushrooms and garlic; cook and stir 2-4 minutes or until the mushrooms are softened. Transfer to slow cooker. Stir in the broth, tomatoes, tomato sauce and Italian seasoning. Cook, covered, on low 4-6 hours or until the vegetables are tender.
3. Add the lasagna noodles; cook 1 hour longer or until tender. Stir in spinach. Remove insert; let stand 10 minutes. Divide mozzarella cheese among serving bowls; ladle soup over cheese. If desired, sprinkle with the Parmesan cheese and basil.
PER SERVING *1⅓ cups equals 266 cal., 8 g fat (3 g sat. fat), 36 mg chol., 725 mg sodium, 30 g carb., 5 g fiber, 18 g pro.* **Diabetic Exchanges:** *2 lean meat, 2 vegetable, 1½ starch.*

HOME-STYLE CHICKEN SOUP

I've used this easy soup recipe on many occasions. Mom shared it with me, and we love it.
—**KATHY RAIRIGH** MILFORD, IN

PREP: 15 MIN. • **COOK:** 6¼ HOURS
MAKES: 4 SERVINGS

1 can (14½ ounces) reduced-sodium chicken broth
1 can (14½ ounces) diced tomatoes, undrained
1 cup cubed cooked chicken
1 can (8 ounces) mushroom stems and pieces, drained
¼ cup sliced fresh carrot
¼ cup sliced celery
1 bay leaf
⅛ teaspoon dried thyme
¾ cup uncooked egg noodles

In a 1½-qt. slow cooker, combine the first eight ingredients. Cover and cook on low for 6 hours. Stir in noodles; cover and cook on high for 15-20 minutes or until tender. Discard bay leaf.

PER SERVING *1 cup equals 137 cal., 3 g fat (1 g sat. fat), 37 mg chol., 671 mg sodium, 13 g carb., 3 g fiber, 14 g pro.* **Diabetic Exchanges:** *2 lean meat, 1 vegetable, ½ starch.*

SLOW-COOKED LASAGNA SOUP

Every fall and winter, our staff has a soup rotation, so this is my usual contribution. My co-workers love it.
—**SHARON GERST** NORTH LIBERTY, IA

PREP: 35 MIN.
COOK: 5 HOURS + STANDING
MAKES: 8 SERVINGS (2½ QUARTS)

1 package (19½ ounces) Italian turkey sausage links
1 large onion, chopped
2 medium carrots, chopped
2 cups sliced fresh mushrooms
3 garlic cloves, minced
1 carton (32 ounces) reduced-sodium chicken broth
2 cans (14½ ounces each) no-salt-added stewed tomatoes
2 cans (8 ounces each) no-salt-added tomato sauce

THE SKINNY

SCALE BACK SALT
Switching to no-salt-added ingredients can really make a big difference. By subbing no-salt-added stewed tomatoes and tomato sauce in this soup, we cut out more than 400 mg of sodium per serving.

HOME-STYLE
CHICKEN SOUP

**SLOW-COOKED
LASAGNA SOUP**

SOUTHWESTERN CHICKEN SOUP

Here's the perfect recipe for a busy week, because the slow cooker does most of the work for you!

—HAROLD TARTAR
WEST PALM BEACH, FL

PREP: 10 MIN. • **COOK:** 7 HOURS
MAKES: 10 SERVINGS (2½ QUARTS)

- 1¼ pounds boneless skinless chicken breasts, cut into thin strips
- 1 tablespoon canola oil
- 2 cans (14½ ounces each) reduced-sodium chicken broth
- 1 package (16 ounces) frozen corn, thawed
- 1 can (14½ ounces) diced tomatoes, undrained
- 1 medium onion, chopped
- 1 medium green pepper, chopped
- 1 medium sweet red pepper, chopped
- 1 can (4 ounces) chopped green chilies
- 1½ teaspoons seasoned salt, optional
- 1 teaspoon ground cumin
- ½ teaspoon garlic powder

1. In a large skillet, saute the chicken in oil until lightly browned. Transfer to a 5-qt. slow cooker. Stir in the remaining ingredients.
2. Cover and cook on low for 7-8 hours or until the chicken and vegetables are tender. Stir before serving.
PER SERVING *1 cup equals 143 cal., 3 g fat (1 g sat. fat), 31 mg chol., 364 mg sodium, 15 g carb., 3 g fiber, 15 g pro.* **Diabetic Exchanges:** *2 lean meat, 1 starch.*

FAMILY-PLEASING TURKEY CHILI

My children really love this chili. The leftovers are wonderful, too.

—SHEILA CHRISTENSEN
SAN MARCOS, CA

PREP: 25 MIN. • **COOK:** 4 HOURS
MAKES: 6 SERVINGS (2¼ QUARTS)

- 1 pound lean ground turkey
- 1 medium green pepper, finely chopped
- 1 small red onion, finely chopped
- 2 garlic cloves, minced
- 1 can (28 ounces) diced tomatoes, undrained
- 1 can (16 ounces) kidney beans, rinsed and drained
- 1 can (15 ounces) black beans, rinsed and drained
- 1 can (14½ ounces) reduced-sodium chicken broth
- 1¾ cups frozen corn, thawed
- 1 can (6 ounces) tomato paste
- 1 tablespoon chili powder
- ½ teaspoon pepper
- ¼ teaspoon ground cumin
- ¼ teaspoon garlic powder
  Optional toppings: reduced-fat sour cream and minced fresh cilantro

1. In a large nonstick skillet, cook the turkey, green pepper and onion over medium heat until meat is no longer pink. Add the garlic; cook 1 minute longer. Drain.
2. Transfer to a 4-qt. slow cooker. Stir in the tomatoes, kidney beans, black beans, broth, corn, tomato paste, chili powder, pepper, cumin and garlic powder.
3. Cover and cook on low for 4-5 hours or until heated through. Serve with optional toppings if desired.
PER SERVING *1½ cups (calculated without optional toppings) equals 349 cal., 7 g fat (2 g sat. fat), 60 mg chol., 725 mg sodium, 47 g carb., 12 g fiber, 27 g pro.* **Diabetic Exchanges:** *3 lean meat, 2 starch, 2 vegetable.*

BUTTERNUT SQUASH SOUP

The golden color, smooth and creamy texture and comforting taste of this soup make it ideal for a chilly fall day. It has a slightly tangy taste from the cream cheese, and the cinnamon really comes through.

—JACKIE CAMPBELL STANHOPE, NJ

PREP: 30 MIN. • **COOK:** 6¼ HOURS
MAKES: 14 SERVINGS (2½ QUARTS)

- 1 medium onion, chopped
- 2 tablespoons butter
- 1 medium butternut squash (about 4 pounds), peeled and cubed
- 3 cans (14½ ounces each) vegetable broth
- 1 tablespoon brown sugar
- 1 tablespoon minced fresh gingerroot
- 1 garlic clove, minced
- 1 cinnamon stick (3 inches)
- 1 package (8 ounces) cream cheese, softened and cubed

1. In a small skillet, saute onion in butter until tender. Transfer to a 5- or 6-qt. slow cooker; add squash. Combine the broth, brown sugar, ginger, garlic and cinnamon; pour over squash. Cover and cook on low for 6-8 hours or until the squash is tender.
2. Cool slightly. Discard cinnamon stick. In a blender, process the soup in batches until smooth. Return all to slow cooker. Whisk in cream cheese; cover and cook 15 minutes longer or until cheese is melted.
PER SERVING *¾ cup equals 135 cal., 7 g fat (5 g sat. fat), 22 mg chol., 483 mg sodium, 17 g carb., 4 g fiber, 2 g pro.* **Diabetic Exchanges:** *1½ fat, 1 starch.*

SOUTHWESTERN
CHICKEN SOUP

FAMILY-PLEASING
TURKEY CHILI

BUTTERNUT
SQUASH SOUP

LOADED POTATO-LEEK SOUP

LOADED POTATO-LEEK SOUP

Growing up, my mother made potato and onion soup because it was affordable and fast. I've since trimmed the calories, and it's still a comforting family favorite.

—**COURTNEY STULTZ** WEIR, KS

PREP: 20 MIN. • **COOK:** 6 HOURS
MAKES: 6 SERVINGS (ABOUT 1½ QUARTS)

- 1 medium leek
- 1½ pounds potatoes (about 2 large), peeled and finely chopped
- 2 cups fresh cauliflowerets
- ¾ teaspoon rubbed sage
- ½ teaspoon salt
- ¼ teaspoon pepper
- 4 cups reduced-sodium chicken or vegetable broth
- 2 teaspoons olive oil
- 2 teaspoons lemon juice
  Sour cream, optional

1. Finely chop the white portion of leek. Cut leek greens into thin strips; reserve for the topping. In a 3- or 4-qt. slow cooker, combine the potatoes, cauliflower, seasonings, broth and chopped leek. Cook, covered, on low 6-8 hours or until vegetables are tender.
2. In a small skillet, heat oil over medium-high heat. Add reserved leek greens; cook 3-5 minutes or until light golden. Puree soup using an immersion blender. Or, cool soup slightly and puree in batches in a blender. Stir in lemon juice. Top with the leek greens and, if desired, sour cream.
PER SERVING *1 cup (calculated without sour cream) equals 108 cal., 2 g fat (trace sat. fat), 0 chol., 593 mg sodium, 20 g carb., 2 g fiber, 4 g pro.* **Diabetic Exchanges:** *1 starch, ½ fat.*

CHICKEN WILD RICE SOUP WITH SPINACH

I stir together this creamy chicken soup whenever we're craving something warm. Reduced-fat and reduced-sodium ingredients make it a healthier option.

—**DEBORAH WILLIAMS** PEORIA, AZ

PREP: 10 MIN. • **COOK:** 5¼ HOURS
MAKES: 6 SERVINGS (ABOUT 2 QUARTS)

- 3 cups water
- 1 can (14½ ounces) reduced-sodium chicken broth
- 1 can (10¾ ounces) reduced-fat reduced-sodium condensed cream of chicken soup, undiluted
- ⅔ cup uncooked wild rice
- 1 garlic clove, minced
- ½ teaspoon dried thyme
- ½ teaspoon pepper
- ¼ teaspoon salt
- 3 cups cubed cooked chicken breast
- 2 cups fresh baby spinach

1. In a 3-qt. slow cooker, mix the first eight ingredients until blended. Cook, covered, on low 5-7 hours or until rice is tender.
2. Stir in chicken and spinach. Cook, covered, on low 15 minutes longer or until heated through.
PER SERVING *1¼ cups equals 212 cal., 3 g fat (1 g sat. fat), 56 mg chol., 523 mg sodium, 19 g carb., 2 g fiber, 25 g pro.* **Diabetic Exchanges:** *3 lean meat, 1 starch.*

HEARTY BLACK BEAN SOUP

Cumin and chili powder give spark to this thick and hearty soup. If you have leftover meat—smoked sausage, browned ground beef or roast—toss it in during the last 30 minutes of cooking.

—**AMY CHOP** OAK GROVE, LA

PREP: 10 MIN. • **COOK:** 9 HOURS
MAKES: 8 SERVINGS

- 3 medium carrots, halved and thinly sliced
- 2 celery ribs, thinly sliced
- 1 medium onion, chopped
- 4 garlic cloves, minced
- 1 can (30 ounces) black beans, rinsed and drained
- 2 cans (14½ ounces each) reduced-sodium chicken broth or vegetable broth
- 1 can (15 ounces) crushed tomatoes
- 1½ teaspoons dried basil
- ½ teaspoon dried oregano
- ½ teaspoon ground cumin
- ½ teaspoon chili powder
- ½ teaspoon hot pepper sauce
  Hot cooked rice

In a 3-qt. slow cooker, combine the first 12 ingredients. Cover and cook on low for 9-11 hours or until the vegetables are tender. Serve with the rice.
PER SERVING *1 cup (calculated without rice) equals 129 cal., 0 fat (0 sat. fat), 0 chol., 627 mg sodium, 24 g carb., 6 g fiber, 8 g pro.* **Diabetic Exchanges:** *1½ starch, 1 lean meat.*

HOW-TO

PREPARING LEEKS

To prepare leeks, cut off the root end and tough green tops. Split the white portion in half and swish the pieces in a bowl of water to rinse away the sand between the layers. Then chop or slice. While leek tops aren't typically used in recipes, well-rinsed tops can be used to flavor homemade stock. Cut them into large pieces so they'll be easy to discard.

LEMON CHICKEN
& RICE SOUP

LEMON CHICKEN & RICE SOUP

When buying chicken for this soup, ask the butcher to cube it for you. It'll save you some prep time, and no mess!

—**KRISTIN CHERRY** BOTHELL, WA

PREP: 35 MIN. • **COOK:** 4¼ HOURS
MAKES: 12 SERVINGS (4 QUARTS)

- 2 **tablespoons olive oil**
- 2 **pounds boneless skinless chicken breasts, cut into ½-inch pieces**
- 5 **cans (14½ ounces each) reduced-sodium chicken broth**
- 8 **cups coarsely chopped Swiss chard, kale or spinach**
- 2 **large carrots, finely chopped**
- 1 **small onion, chopped**
- 1 **medium lemon, halved and thinly sliced**
- ¼ **cup lemon juice**
- 4 **teaspoons grated lemon peel**
- ½ **teaspoon pepper**
- 4 **cups cooked brown rice**

1. In a skillet, heat 1 tablespoon oil over medium-high heat. Add half of the chicken; cook and stir until browned. Transfer to a 6-qt. slow cooker. Repeat with remaining oil and chicken.

2. Stir broth, vegetables, lemon slices, lemon juice, peel and pepper into chicken. Cook, covered, on low 4-5 hours or until chicken is tender. Stir in rice; heat through.

PER SERVING *1⅓ cups equals 203 cal., 5 g fat (1 g sat. fat), 42 mg chol., 612 mg sodium, 20 g carb., 2 g fiber, 20 g pro.* **Diabetic Exchanges:** *2 lean meat, 1 starch, 1 vegetable, ½ fat.*

COLORFUL MINESTRONE

What makes my minestrone different from others? Butternut squash, a leek and fresh kale!

—**TIFFANY ANDERSON-TAYLOR** GULFPORT, FL

PREP: 40 MIN. • **COOK:** 7½ HOURS
MAKES: 10 SERVINGS (3½ QUARTS)

- 1 **medium leek (white portion only), thinly sliced**
- 1 **small onion, chopped**
- 1 **tablespoon olive oil**
- 3 **slices deli ham, chopped**
- 2 **garlic cloves, minced**
- 2 **quarts water**
- 1 **can (28 ounces) diced tomatoes, undrained**
- 1 **medium butternut squash, peeled, seeded and cubed**
- 2 **medium carrots, coarsely chopped**
- 2 **celery ribs, chopped**
- 2 **cups fresh baby spinach, cut into thin strips**
- 1 **cup thinly sliced fresh kale**
- 1 **medium potato, peeled and cubed**
- 1 **tablespoon minced fresh rosemary**
- 1 **teaspoon salt**
  Pepper to taste
- 1 **can (15 ounces) cannellini beans, rinsed and drained**

1. In a small skillet, saute leek and onion in oil for 2 minutes or until vegetables are tender. Add ham and garlic; cook 1 minute longer.

2. Transfer ham mixture to a 5-qt. slow cooker. Stir in the water, vegetables, rosemary, salt and pepper. Cover and cook on low for 7-8 hours or until vegetables are tender.

3. Stir in beans; cover and cook 30 minutes longer.

PER SERVING *1½ cups equals 134 cal., 2 g fat (trace sat. fat), 3 mg chol., 477 mg sodium, 26 g carb., 7 g fiber, 5 g pro.* **Diabetic Exchanges:** *2 vegetable, 1 starch.*

BEAN SOUP WITH CORNMEAL DUMPLINGS

This soup's great Southwestern flavor is a real winner with my family. I love it because I can have the soup already cooking when I get home from work. Then I simply make the dumplings and dinner is almost ready.

—JOAN HALLFORD
NORTH RICHLAND HILLS, TX

PREP: 15 MIN. • **COOK:** 6½ HOURS
MAKES: 6 SERVINGS

- 2 cans (14½ ounces each) chicken broth
- 1 package (16 ounces) frozen mixed vegetables
- 1 can (15 ounces) black beans, rinsed and drained
- 1 can (15 ounces) pinto beans, rinsed and drained
- 1 can (14½ ounces) diced tomatoes, undrained
- 1 medium onion, chopped
- 1 tablespoon chili powder
- 1 tablespoon minced fresh cilantro
- 4 garlic cloves, minced
- ¼ teaspoon pepper

CORNMEAL DUMPLINGS

- ½ cup all-purpose flour
- ½ cup shredded cheddar cheese
- ⅓ cup cornmeal
- 1 tablespoon sugar
- 1 teaspoon baking powder
- 1 large egg
- 2 tablespoons milk
- 2 teaspoons canola oil

1. In a 5-qt. slow cooker, combine the first 10 ingredients. Cover and cook on low for 6-8 hours or until vegetables are tender.

2. For dumplings, combine the flour, cheese, cornmeal, sugar and baking powder in a large bowl. In another bowl, combine the egg, milk and oil; add to dry ingredients just until moistened (batter will be stiff).

3. Drop by heaping tablespoons onto soup. Cover and cook on high for 30 minutes (without lifting cover) or until a toothpick inserted into a dumpling comes out clean. **PER SERVING** *1 serving (1 cup) equals 334 cal., 6 g fat (3 g sat. fat), 46 mg chol., 774 mg sodium, 55 g carb., 12 g fiber, 16 g pro.*

VEGGIE MEATBALL SOUP FOR 3

It's a snap to put together this hearty soup before I leave for work. I just add uncooked pasta when I get home, and I have a few minutes to relax before supper is ready.

—CHARLA TINNEY TYRONE, OK

PREP: 10 MIN. • **COOK:** 4¼ HOURS
MAKES: 3 CUPS

- 1½ cups reduced-sodium beef broth
- 1 cup frozen mixed vegetables, thawed
- ¾ cup canned stewed tomatoes
- 9 frozen fully cooked homestyle meatballs (½ ounce each), thawed
- 2 bay leaves
- ⅛ teaspoon pepper
- ½ cup uncooked spiral pasta

In a 1½-qt. slow cooker, combine the first six ingredients. Cover and cook on low for 4-5 hours or until heated through. Stir in pasta; cover and cook 20-30 minutes longer or until tender. Discard bay leaves.
PER SERVING *1 cup equals 250 cal., 11 g fat (5 g sat. fat), 35 mg chol., 671 mg sodium, 26 g carb., 5 g fiber, 11 g pro.* **Diabetic Exchanges:** *1½ starch, 1½ fat, 1 lean meat, 1 vegetable.*

THE SKINNY

BRING ON THE BEANS

Beans are packed with protein and fiber, making recipes such as Bean Soup with Cornmeal Dumplings a smart choice. The nutritional one-two punch of fiber and protein means you'll stay fuller longer, which can save you from snacking between meals and adding more calories.

VEGGIE MEATBALL
SOUP FOR 3

FORGOTTEN
MINESTRONE

SLOW-COOKED
CHILI

VEGETABLE
PORK SOUP

FORGOTTEN MINESTRONE

This soup gets its name because the broth simmers for hours, allowing me to work on other things. But after one taste, you and your family will agree this full-flavored soup is truly unforgettable!

—MARSHA RANSOM
SOUTH HAVEN, MI

PREP: 15 MIN. • **COOK:** 8½ HOURS
MAKES: 8 SERVINGS (2 QUARTS)

- 1 pound beef stew meat, cut into ½-inch cubes
- 1 can (28 ounces) diced tomatoes, undrained
- 1 medium onion, chopped
- 2 tablespoons minced dried parsley
- 1 teaspoon salt
- 1½ teaspoons ground thyme
- 1 beef bouillon cube
- ½ teaspoon pepper
- 6 cups water
- 1 medium zucchini, halved and thinly sliced
- 2 cups chopped cabbage
- 1 can (15 ounces) garbanzo beans or chickpeas, rinsed and drained
- 1 cup uncooked elbow macaroni
  Grated Parmesan cheese, optional

1. In a 5-qt. slow cooker, combine the first nine ingredients. Cover and cook on low for 8-10 hours or until meat is tender.
2. Add the zucchini, cabbage, beans and macaroni; cover and cook on high for 30-45 minutes or until the macaroni and vegetables are tender. Sprinkle servings with cheese, if desired.
PER SERVING 1 cup (calculated without cheese) equals 202 cal., 5 g fat (2 g sat. fat), 35 mg chol., 661 mg sodium, 24 g carb., 5 g fiber, 16 g pro. **Diabetic Exchanges:** 2 lean meat, 2 vegetable, 1 starch.

SLOW-COOKED CHILI

This hearty chili can cook for up to 10 hours on low in the slow cooker. It's so good to come home to its wonderful aroma after a long day.

—SUE CALL BEECH GROVE, IN

PREP: 20 MIN. • **COOK:** 8 HOURS
MAKES: 10 SERVINGS (2½ QUARTS)

- 2 pounds lean ground beef (90% lean)
- 2 cans (16 ounces each) kidney beans, rinsed and drained
- 2 cans (14½ ounces each) diced tomatoes, undrained
- 1 can (8 ounces) tomato sauce
- 2 medium onions, chopped
- 1 green pepper, chopped
- 2 garlic cloves, minced
- 2 tablespoons chili powder
- 1 teaspoon salt
- 1 teaspoon pepper
  Shredded cheddar cheese, optional

1. In a large skillet, cook the beef over medium heat until no longer pink; drain.
2. Transfer to a 5-qt. slow cooker. Add next nine ingredients. Cover and cook on low for 8-10 hours. Garnish individual servings with cheese, if desired.
PER SERVING 1 cup (calculated without cheese) equals 260 cal., 8 g fat (3 g sat. fat), 57 mg chol., 476 mg sodium, 23 g carb., 7 g fiber, 25 g pro. **Diabetic Exchanges:** 3 lean meat, 1½ starch, 1 vegetable.

VEGETABLE PORK SOUP

Packed with nutritious veggies, tender pork and savory flavor, this healthy soup fills the house with a tantalizing aroma as it cooks.

—DEB HALL HUNTINGTON, IN

PREP: 20 MIN. • **COOK:** 7 HOURS
MAKES: 6 SERVINGS (2 QUARTS)

- 1 pound pork tenderloin, cut into 1-inch pieces
- 1 teaspoon garlic powder
- 2 teaspoons canola oil
- 1 can (28 ounces) diced tomatoes
- 4 medium carrots, cut into ½-inch pieces
- 2 medium potatoes, cubed
- 1 can (12 ounces) light or nonalcoholic beer
- ¼ cup quick-cooking tapioca
- 2 bay leaves
- 1 tablespoon Worcestershire sauce
- 1 tablespoon honey
- 1 teaspoon dried thyme
- ¼ teaspoon salt
- ¼ teaspoon pepper
- ⅛ teaspoon ground nutmeg

1. Sprinkle pork with garlic powder. In a large skillet, brown pork in oil; drain.
2. Transfer to a 4-qt. slow cooker. Add the remaining ingredients. Cover and cook on low for 7-8 hours or until the meat is tender. Discard bay leaves.
PER SERVING 1⅓ cups equals 258 cal., 4 g fat (1 g sat. fat), 42 mg chol., 357 mg sodium, 34 g carb., 5 g fiber, 18 g pro. **Diabetic Exchanges:** 2 lean meat, 2 vegetable, 1½ starch.

TOP TIP

FREEZE INDIVIDUAL SOUP PORTIONS

To freeze soup or chili in handy single-serving packets, line a measuring cup with a small freezer bag to hold the bag upright, then fill with soup. Freeze the bags flat, then stack them for efficient storage.

BROCCOLI
POTATO SOUP

BROCCOLI POTATO SOUP

For a soothing soup with nice texture, try this one with broccoli and chunks of potato. The red pepper flakes add a hint of spice, and the fresh herbs make it a truly delicious soup.

—**CRYSTAL KELSO** SANDY, OR

PREP: 25 MIN. • **COOK:** 4½ HOURS
MAKES: 8 CUPS (2 QUARTS)

- 1 **pound small red potatoes, cubed**
- 1 **large onion, chopped**
- 1 **large carrot, coarsely chopped**
- 7 **garlic cloves, minced**
- 3 **cups water**
- 1 **can (14½ ounces) condensed cream of broccoli soup, undiluted**
- 1 **teaspoon each minced fresh thyme, basil and parsley**
- 1 **teaspoon garlic powder**
- ½ **teaspoon salt**
- ½ **teaspoon crushed red pepper flakes**
- ¼ **teaspoon pepper**
- 2 **cups frozen chopped broccoli, thawed and drained**
- 1 **cup (4 ounces) shredded Havarti cheese**

1. Place potatoes, onion, carrot and garlic in a 4- or 5-qt. slow cooker. Add the water, soup and seasonings. Cover and cook on low for 4-5 hours or until heated through.

2. Stir in the broccoli and cheese. Cover and cook for 30 minutes or until broccoli is tender.

PER SERVING *1 cup equals 158 cal., 6 g fat (3 g sat. fat), 15 mg chol., 563 mg sodium, 20 g carb., 3 g fiber, 7 g pro.* **Diabetic Exchanges:** *1½ starch, 1 fat.*

BLACK BEAN 'N' PUMPKIN CHILI

My family is crazy about this slow cooker recipe because it uses ingredients you don't usually find in chili. Believe it or not, I discovered that pumpkin is what makes this dish so special. Cook up a big batch and freeze some for later; it tastes even better reheated.

—**DEBORAH VLIET** HOLLAND, MI

PREP: 20 MIN. • **COOK:** 4 HOURS
MAKES: 10 SERVINGS (2½ QUARTS)

- 2 tablespoons olive oil
- 1 medium onion, chopped
- 1 medium sweet yellow pepper, chopped
- 3 garlic cloves, minced
- 2 cans (15 ounces each) black beans, rinsed and drained
- 1 can (15 ounces) solid-pack pumpkin
- 1 can (14½ ounces) diced tomatoes, undrained
- 3 cups chicken broth
- 2½ cups cubed cooked turkey
- 2 teaspoons dried parsley flakes
- 2 teaspoons chili powder
- 1½ teaspoons ground cumin
- 1½ teaspoons dried oregano
- ½ teaspoon salt
  Cubed avocado and thinly sliced green onions, optional

1. In a large skillet, heat oil over medium-high heat. Add onion and pepper; cook and stir until tender. Add garlic; cook 1 minute longer.
2. Transfer to a 5-qt. slow cooker; stir in the next 10 ingredients. Cook, covered, on low 4-5 hours. If desired, top with avocado and green onions.

PER SERVING *1 cup equals 192 cal., 5 g fat (1 g sat. fat), 28 mg chol., 658 mg sodium, 21 g carb., 7 g fiber, 16 g pro.* **Diabetic Exchanges:** *2 lean meat, 1½ starch, ½ fat.*

BLACK BEAN 'N' PUMPKIN CHILI

RED BEAN
VEGETABLE SOUP

RED BEAN VEGETABLE SOUP

Cajun seasoning boosts my bean soup that's loaded with fresh vegetables. Yum!
—**RONNIE LAPPE** BROWNWOOD, TX

PREP: 15 MIN. • **COOK:** 6 HOURS
MAKES: 12 SERVINGS (3 QUARTS)

- 3 large sweet red peppers, chopped
- 3 celery ribs, chopped
- 2 medium onions, chopped
- 4 cans (16 ounces each) kidney beans, rinsed and drained
- 4 cups chicken broth
- 2 bay leaves
- ½ to 1 teaspoon salt
- ½ to 1 teaspoon Cajun seasoning
- ½ teaspoon pepper
- ¼ to ½ teaspoon hot pepper sauce

In a 5-qt. slow cooker, combine the peppers, celery, onions and beans. Stir in the remaining ingredients. Cover and cook on low for 6 hours or until the vegetables are tender. Discard bay leaves before serving.
PER SERVING *1 cup equals 158 cal., trace fat (trace sat. fat), 2 mg chol., 701 mg sodium, 29 g carb., 8 g fiber, 11 g pro.* **Diabetic Exchanges:** *2 starch, 1 lean meat.*

MANHATTAN CLAM CHOWDER

I came up with this simple, delicious soup years ago when my husband and I both worked. It's easy to dump all the ingredients into the slow cooker in the morning and come home to a prepared meal.
—**MARY DIXON** NORTHVILLE, MI

PREP: 10 MIN. • **COOK:** 8 HOURS
MAKES: 9 SERVINGS

- 3 celery ribs, sliced
- 1 large onion, chopped
- 1 can (14½ ounces) sliced potatoes, drained
- 1 can (14½ ounces) sliced carrots, drained
- 2 cans (6½ ounces each) chopped clams
- 2 cups reduced-sodium tomato juice
- 1½ cups water
- ½ cup tomato puree
- 1 tablespoon dried parsley flakes
- 1½ teaspoons dried thyme
- ½ teaspoon salt
- 1 bay leaf
- 2 whole black peppercorns

In a 3-qt. slow cooker, combine all ingredients. Cover and cook on low for 8-10 hours or until vegetables are tender. Discard bay leaf and peppercorns.
PER SERVING *1 cup equals 80 cal., trace fat (trace sat. fat), 14 mg chol., 612 mg sodium, 13 g carb., 3 g fiber, 4 g pro.* **Diabetic Exchanges:** *1 starch, 1 lean meat.*

SLOW-COOKED HAMBURGER SOUP

I work full time but my family sits down to a home-cooked meal just about every night, thanks in part to simple recipes like this. I love that I can make it in the slow cooker.
—**THERESA JACKSON** CICERO, NY

PREP: 15 MIN. • **COOK:** 8 HOURS
MAKES: 10 SERVINGS (2½ QUARTS)

- 1 pound lean ground beef (90% lean)
- 1 medium onion, chopped
- 2 garlic cloves, minced
- 4 cups V8 juice
- 1 can (14½ ounces) stewed tomatoes
- 2 cups coleslaw mix
- 2 cups frozen green beans
- 2 cups frozen corn
- 2 tablespoons Worcestershire sauce
- 1 teaspoon dried basil
- ½ teaspoon salt
- ¼ teaspoon pepper

In a large saucepan, cook the beef and onion over medium heat until meat is no longer pink. Add garlic; cook 1 minute longer. Drain. In a 5-qt. slow cooker, combine the remaining ingredients. Stir in beef mixture. Cover and cook on low for 8-10 hours or until the vegetables are tender.
PER SERVING *1 cup equals 145 cal., 4 g fat (2 g sat. fat), 28 mg chol., 507 mg sodium, 17 g carb., 3 g fiber, 11 g pro.* **Diabetic Exchanges:** *1 lean meat, 1 vegetable, ½ starch.*

HOW-TO

MAKE YOUR OWN CAJUN SEASONING

Can't find Cajun seasoning in the spice section of your grocery store? Go the DIY route! There are many different blends, but a typical mix includes salt, onion powder, garlic powder, cayenne pepper, ground mustard, celery seed and pepper.

SLOW COOKER
SPLIT PEA SOUP

FREEZE IT

SLOW COOKER SPLIT PEA SOUP

When I have leftover ham in the fridge, I always like to make this soup. Just throw the ingredients into the slow cooker, turn it on and dinner is set.

—PAMELA CHAMBERS
WEST COLUMBIA, SC

PREP: 15 MIN. • **COOK:** 8 HOURS
MAKES: 8 SERVINGS

- 1 package (16 ounces) dried green split peas, rinsed
- 2 cups cubed fully cooked ham
- 1 large onion, chopped
- 1 cup julienned or chopped carrots
- 3 garlic cloves, minced
- ½ teaspoon dried rosemary, crushed
- ½ teaspoon dried thyme
- 1 carton (32 ounces) reduced-sodium chicken broth
- 2 cups water

In a 4- or 5-qt. slow cooker, combine all ingredients. Cover and cook on low for 8-10 hours or until the peas are tender.

FREEZE OPTION *Freeze cooled soup in freezer containers. To use, thaw overnight in the refrigerator. Heat through in a saucepan over medium heat, stirring occasionally.*
PER SERVING *1 cup equals 260 cal., 2 g fat (1 g sat. fat), 21 mg chol., 728 mg sodium, 39 g carb., 15 g fiber, 23 g pro.* **Diabetic Exchanges:** *2½ starch, 2 lean meat.*

TOP TIP

SOUP-ER TOPPINGS

Make your split pea soup even more filling by topping the servings with diced vegetables of your choice. Be creative and discover a new combination you like!

FRESH
PUMPKIN SOUP

LIME NAVY BEAN CHILI

I love using my slow cooker for tasty soups like this one. Just fill it in the morning and come home to a warm, wonderful meal—no matter how busy the day!

—**CONNIE THOMAS** JENSEN, UT

PREP: 15 MIN. + SOAKING
COOK: 5 HOURS • **MAKES:** 6 SERVINGS

- 1¼ cups dried navy beans
- 3 cups water
- 2 bone-in chicken breast halves (7 ounces each), skin removed
- 1 cup frozen corn
- 1 medium onion, chopped
- 1 can (4 ounces) chopped green chilies
- 4 garlic cloves, minced
- 1 tablespoon chicken bouillon granules
- 1 teaspoon ground cumin
- ½ teaspoon chili powder
- 2 tablespoons lime juice

1. Sort the beans and rinse with cold water. Place the beans in a large saucepan; add enough water to cover by 2 in. Bring to a boil; boil for 2 minutes. Remove from heat; cover and let soak for 1-4 hours or until beans are softened. Drain and rinse beans, discarding liquid.

2. In a 3-qt. slow cooker, combine the beans, 3 cups of water, chicken, corn, onion, chilies, garlic, bouillon, cumin and chili powder. Cover and cook on low for 5-6 hours or until a thermometer reads 170° and beans are tender.

3. Remove chicken breasts; set aside until cool enough to handle. Remove meat from bones; discard bones and cut meat into bite-size pieces. Return chicken to pot. Stir in lime juice just before serving.

PER SERVING *1 cup equals 250 cal., 2 g fat (1 g sat. fat), 30 mg chol., 532 mg sodium, 37 g carb., 12 g fiber, 22 g pro.* **Diabetic Exchanges:** *2 starch, 3 lean meat, 1 vegetable.*

FRESH PUMPKIN SOUP

This appealing soup harvests the fall flavors of just-picked pumpkins and tart apples, and is sure to warm you up on a crisp autumn day. I top the creamy puree with a sprinkling of toasted pumpkin seeds.

—**JANE SHAPTON** IRVINE, CA

PREP: 50 MIN. • **COOK:** 8 HOURS
MAKES: 9 SERVINGS (ABOUT 2 QUARTS)

- 8 cups chopped fresh pumpkin (about 3 pounds)
- 4 cups chicken broth
- 3 small tart apples, peeled and chopped
- 1 medium onion, chopped
- 2 tablespoons lemon juice
- 2 teaspoons minced fresh gingerroot
- 2 garlic cloves, minced
- ½ teaspoon salt

TOASTED PUMPKIN SEEDS

- ½ cup fresh pumpkin seeds
- 1 teaspoon canola oil
- ⅛ teaspoon salt

1. In a 5-qt. slow cooker, combine the first eight ingredients. Cover and cook on low for 8-10 hours or until the pumpkin and apples are tender.

2. Meanwhile, toss pumpkin seeds with oil and salt. Spread onto an ungreased 15x10x1-in. baking pan. Bake at 250° for 45-50 minutes or until golden brown. Set aside.

3. Cool soup slightly; process in batches in a blender. Transfer to a large saucepan; heat through. Garnish servings with toasted pumpkin seeds.

PER SERVING *1 cup soup with 1 tablespoon seeds equals 102 cal., 2 g fat (0.55 g sat. fat), 0 chol., 567 mg sodium, 22 g carb., 3 g fiber, 3 g pro.* **Diabetic Exchanges:** *1 starch, ½ fruit.*

SUMMER'S BOUNTY SOUP

This chunky soup, packed with garden-fresh veggies, is so versatile. You can add or omit just about any vegetable to make the most of what you have.

—VICTORIA HAHN
NORTHAMPTON, PA

PREP: 5 MIN. • **COOK:** 7 HOURS
MAKES: 14 SERVINGS
(ABOUT 3½ QUARTS)

- 4 medium tomatoes, chopped
- 2 medium potatoes, peeled and cubed
- 2 cups halved fresh green beans
- 2 small zucchini, cubed
- 1 medium yellow summer squash, cubed
- 4 small carrots, thinly sliced
- 2 celery ribs, thinly sliced
- 1 cup cubed peeled eggplant
- 1 cup sliced fresh mushrooms
- 1 small onion, chopped
- 1 tablespoon minced fresh parsley
- 1 tablespoon salt-free garlic and herb seasoning
- 4 cups reduced-sodium V8 juice

Combine all ingredients in a 5-qt. slow cooker. Cook, covered, on low 7-8 hours or until vegetables are tender.

PER SERVING *1 cup equals 67 cal., trace fat (trace sat. fat), 0 chol., 62 mg sodium, 15 g carb., 3 g fiber, 2 g pro. Diabetic Exchange: 2 vegetable.*

SPICY COWBOY CHILI

Toasting the peppers for this chili releases their earthy flavors, but wear gloves when handling dried peppers and seeds, as they can burn the skin.

—RACHEL SPRINKEL HILO, HI

PREP: 45 MIN. • **COOK:** 7 HOURS
MAKES: 14 SERVINGS (3½ QUARTS)

- 1 whole garlic bulb
- 2 to 3 tablespoons olive oil, divided
- 2 dried ancho chilies
- 2 dried chipotle chilies
- 1 bottle (12 ounces) dark beer
- 3 pounds beef stew meat, cut into ¾-inch pieces
- 2 large onions, chopped
- 3 cans (16 ounces each) kidney beans, rinsed and drained
- 3 cans (14½ ounces each) diced tomatoes, undrained
- 2 cans (8 ounces each) tomato sauce
- 2 tablespoons Worcestershire sauce
- 1 tablespoon chili powder
- 1 teaspoon pepper
- ½ teaspoon salt
  Shredded cheddar cheese, optional

1. Preheat oven to 425°. Remove papery outer skin from garlic bulb, but do not peel or separate the cloves. Cut off top of garlic bulb, exposing individual cloves. Brush cut cloves with 1 teaspoon oil. Wrap in foil. Bake 30-35 minutes or until cloves are soft. Unwrap and cool slightly. Squeeze garlic from skins; mash with a fork.

2. Meanwhile, in a large dry skillet over medium-high heat, toast chilies on both sides until puffy, about 3-6 minutes. (Do not blacken.) Cool. Remove stems and seeds; coarsely chop chilies. Place in a small bowl; cover with beer. Let stand to soften, about 30 minutes.

3. In the same skillet, heat 1 tablespoon oil over medium-high heat. Brown beef in batches, adding more oil if needed; transfer to a 6-qt. slow cooker. In the skillet, heat 2 teaspoons oil over medium heat. Add onions; cook and stir until tender. Add to beef.

4. Stir in the remaining ingredients, mashed garlic and beer-chilies mixture. Cover and cook on low 7-9 hours or until meat is tender. If desired, serve with cheese.

NOTE *You may substitute 1/2 teaspoon ground chipotle pepper for dried chipotle chilies; add ground chipotle to slow cooker along with mashed garlic and beer mixture.*

PER SERVING *1 cup equals 301 cal., 9 g fat (3 g sat. fat), 60 mg chol., 588 mg sodium, 27 g carb., 8 g fiber, 27 g pro. Diabetic Exchanges: 4 lean meat, 1½ starch, 1 vegetable.*

SUMMER'S BOUNTY SOUP

SPICY COWBOY
CHILI

CIOPPINO

CIOPPINO

If you're looking for a great seafood recipe to create in your slow cooker, this classic fish stew is just the ticket. It's full to the brim with clams, crab, fish and shrimp.

—LISA MORIARTY WILTON, NH

PREP: 20 MIN. • **COOK:** 4½ HOURS
MAKES: 8 SERVINGS (2½ QUARTS)

- 1 can (28 ounces) diced tomatoes, undrained
- 2 medium onions, chopped
- 3 celery ribs, chopped
- 1 bottle (8 ounces) clam juice
- 1 can (6 ounces) tomato paste
- ½ cup white wine or ½ cup vegetable broth
- 5 garlic cloves, minced
- 1 tablespoon red wine vinegar
- 1 tablespoon olive oil
- 1 to 2 teaspoons Italian seasoning
- 1 bay leaf
- ½ teaspoon sugar
- 1 pound haddock fillets, cut into 1-inch pieces
- 1 pound uncooked shrimp (41-50 per pound), peeled and deveined
- 1 can (6 ounces) chopped clams, undrained
- 1 can (6 ounces) lump crabmeat, drained
- 2 tablespoons minced fresh parsley

1. In a 4- or 5-qt. slow cooker, combine the first 12 ingredients. Cook, covered, on low 4-5 hours.
2. Stir in seafood. Cook, covered, 20-30 minutes longer or until fish just begins to flake easily with a fork and shrimp turn pink.
3. Remove bay leaf. Stir in parsley.
PER SERVING 1¼ cups equals 205 cal., 3 g fat (1 g sat. fat), 125 mg chol., 483 mg sodium, 15 g carb., 3 g fiber, 29 g pro. *Diabetic Exchanges: 3 lean meat, 2 vegetable.*

SLOW-COOKED HALIBUT CHOWDER

Mashed potato flakes are a great hands-free way to thicken the chowder as it simmers. When we lived in Alaska, we were spoiled with abundant fresh halibut, but feel free to substitute whatever fish you like.

—DONNA GOUTERMONT SEQUIM, WA

PREP: 20 MIN. • **COOK:** 5½ HOURS
MAKES: 6 SERVINGS

- 2 cups water
- 2 cups 2% milk
- 2 medium potatoes, cubed
- 1 large onion, chopped
- 1 cup mashed potato flakes
- 1 can (8 ounces) tomato sauce
- 2 garlic cloves, minced
- 1 teaspoon celery salt
- 1 teaspoon dried parsley flakes
- ½ teaspoon ground mustard
- ¼ teaspoon chili powder
- ¼ teaspoon cayenne pepper
- 1 pound halibut fillets, cut into chunks
- 1 tablespoon butter

1. In a 3-qt. slow cooker, combine the first 12 ingredients. Cover and cook on low for 5 hours or until potatoes are tender.
2. Add halibut and butter. Cover and cook 30-45 minutes longer or until fish flakes easily with a fork.
PER SERVING 1¼ cups equals 254 cal., 6 g fat (3 g sat. fat), 37 mg chol., 534 mg sodium, 27 g carb., 2 g fiber, 21 g pro. *Diabetic Exchanges: 2 lean meat, 2 starch.*

VERMICELLI BEEF STEW

I love to try new recipes for my husband and myself, and also when we entertain friends and relatives. This stew is a little different from most because of the vermicelli.

—SHARON DELANEY-CHRONIS SOUTH MILWAUKEE, WI

PREP: 20 MIN. • **COOK:** 8½ HOURS
MAKES: 8 SERVINGS (2 QUARTS)

- 1½ pounds beef stew meat, cut into 1-inch cubes
- 1 medium onion, chopped
- 2 tablespoons canola oil
- 3 cups water
- 1 can (14½ ounces) diced tomatoes
- 1 package (16 ounces) frozen mixed vegetables, thawed
- 1 tablespoon dried basil
- 1 teaspoon salt
- 1 teaspoon dried oregano
- 6 ounces uncooked vermicelli, broken into 2-inch pieces
- ¼ cup grated Parmesan cheese

1. In a large skillet, brown meat and onion in oil; drain. Transfer to a 5-qt. slow cooker. Stir in the water, tomatoes, vegetables, basil, salt and oregano. Cover and cook on low for 8-10 hours or until the meat and vegetables are tender.
2. Stir in vermicelli. Cover and cook for 30 minutes or until pasta is tender. Sprinkle with cheese.
PER SERVING 1 cup equals 294 cal., 10 g fat (3 g sat. fat), 55 mg chol., 455 mg sodium, 28 g carb., 5 g fiber, 22 g pro. *Diabetic Exchanges: 2 lean meat, 2 vegetable, 1 starch, 1 fat.*

TOP TIP

WHICH FISH?

If you'd like to swap out the halibut in Slow-Cooked Halibut Chowder, you can try one of these fish with similar textures: red snapper, catfish, sea bass, trout or salmon.

BROWN SUGAR-GLAZED
BABY CARROTS, PAGE 44

SLOW &
EASY SIDES

PARSLEY SMASHED POTATOES

I love potatoes but hate the work involved in making mashed potatoes from scratch. So I came up with a simple side dish made even easier thanks to my slow cooker. You can save the leftover broth to make soup the next day!

—**KATIE HAGY** BLACKSBURG, SC

PREP: 20 MIN. • **COOK:** 6 HOURS
MAKES: 8 SERVINGS

- 16 small red potatoes (about 2 pounds)
- 1 celery rib, sliced
- 1 medium carrot, sliced
- ¼ cup finely chopped onion
- 2 cups chicken broth
- 1 tablespoon minced fresh parsley
- 1½ teaspoons salt, divided
- 1 teaspoon pepper, divided
- 1 garlic clove, minced
- 2 tablespoons butter, melted
  Additional minced fresh parsley

1. Place potatoes, celery, carrot and onion in a 4-qt. slow cooker. In a small bowl, mix broth, parsley, 1 teaspoon salt, ½ teaspoon pepper and garlic; pour over vegetables. Cook, covered, on low 6-8 hours or until potatoes are tender.

2. Transfer potatoes from slow cooker to a 15x10x1-in. pan; discard cooking liquid and vegetables or save for other use. Using bottom of a measuring cup, flatten the potatoes slightly. Transfer to a large bowl; drizzle with butter. Sprinkle with the remaining salt and pepper; toss to coat. Sprinkle with additional parsley.

PER SERVING *2 smashed potatoes equals 114 cal., 3 g fat (2 g sat. fat), 8 mg chol., 190 mg sodium, 20 g carb., 2 g fiber, 2 g pro.* **Diabetic Exchanges:** *1 starch, ½ fat.*

HONEY-BUTTER PEAS AND CARROTS

The classic combination of peas and carrots is made even better with a few flavor enhancers. Slow cooking allows the ingredients to meld for maximum richness.

—**THERESA KREYCHE** TUSTIN, CA

PREP: 15 MIN. • **COOK:** 5¼ HOURS
MAKES: 12 SERVINGS (½ CUP EACH)

- 1 pound carrots, sliced
- 1 large onion, chopped
- ¼ cup water
- ¼ cup butter, cubed
- ¼ cup honey
- 4 garlic cloves, minced
- 1 teaspoon salt
- 1 teaspoon dried marjoram
- ⅛ teaspoon white pepper
- 1 package (16 ounces) frozen peas

In a 3-qt. slow cooker, combine the first nine ingredients. Cook, covered, on low 5 hours. Stir in peas. Cook, covered, on high for 15-25 minutes longer or until vegetables are tender.

PER SERVING *½ cup equals 106 cal., 4 g fat (2 g sat. fat), 10 mg chol., 293 mg sodium, 16 g carb., 3 g fiber, 3 g pro.* **Diabetic Exchanges:** *1 starch, 1 fat.*

TOP TIP

SERVE, THEN STORE

When food is finished cooking, remove it from the slow cooker within an hour. Promptly refrigerate any leftovers.

PARSLEY SMASHED POTATOES

HONEY-BUTTER PEAS AND CARROTS

SIMPLE VEGETARIAN
SLOW-COOKED BEANS

SIMPLE VEGETARIAN SLOW-COOKED BEANS

When I have a hungry family to feed, I often go to these tasty beans with spinach, tomatoes and carrots. It's a veggie delight worth having on the menu frequently.

—JENNIFER REID FARMINGTON, ME

PREP: 15 MIN. • **COOK:** 4 HOURS
MAKES: 8 SERVINGS

- 4   cans (15½ ounces each) great northern beans, rinsed and drained
- 4   medium carrots, finely chopped (about 2 cups)
- 1   cup vegetable stock
- 6   garlic cloves, minced
- 2   teaspoons ground cumin
- ¾   teaspoon salt
- ⅛   teaspoon chili powder
- 4   cups fresh baby spinach, coarsely chopped
- 1   cup oil-packed sun-dried tomatoes, patted dry and chopped
- ⅓   cup minced fresh cilantro
- ⅓   cup minced fresh parsley

In a 3-qt. slow cooker, combine the first seven ingredients. Cook, covered, on low for 4-5 hours or until the carrots are tender, adding spinach and tomatoes during the last 10 minutes of cooking. Stir in cilantro and parsley.

PER SERVING ¾ cup equals 229 cal., 3 g fat (trace sat. fat), 0 chol., 672 mg sodium, 40 g carb., 13 g fiber, 12 g pro.

⑤INGREDIENTS
EASY BEANS & POTATOES WITH BACON

Green beans and bacon are a combination I don't think you can beat, so I used them to crank up everyday potatoes .

—BARBARA BRITTAIN SANTEE, CA

PREP: 15 MIN. • **COOK:** 6 HOURS
MAKES: 10 SERVINGS

- **8** bacon strips, chopped
- **1½** pounds fresh green beans, trimmed and cut into 2-inch pieces (about 4 cups)
- **4** medium potatoes, peeled and cut into ½-inch cubes
- **1** small onion, halved and sliced
- **¼** cup reduced-sodium chicken broth
- **½** teaspoon salt
- **¼** teaspoon pepper

1. In a skillet, cook the bacon over medium heat until crisp, stirring occasionally. Remove to paper towels with a slotted spoon; drain, reserving 1 tablespoon drippings. Cover and refrigerate until serving.
2. In a 5-qt. slow cooker, combine the remaining ingredients; stir in reserved drippings. Cover and cook on low for 6-8 hours or until the potatoes are tender. Stir in bacon; heat through.

PER SERVING *¾ cup equals 116 cal., 4 g fat (1 g sat. fat), 8 mg chol., 256 mg sodium, 17 g carb., 3 g fiber, 5 g pro.* **Diabetic Exchanges:** *1 starch, 1 fat.*

**EASY BEANS &
POTATOES WITH BACON**

BLACK-EYED PEAS & HAM

We have slow-cooked black-eyed peas regularly at our house—they are just so good.
—**DAWN FRIHAUF** FORT MORGAN, CO

PREP: 20 MIN. + SOAKING
COOK: 5 HOURS
MAKES: 12 SERVINGS (¾ CUP EACH)

- 1 package (16 ounces) dried black-eyed peas, rinsed and sorted
- ½ pound fully cooked boneless ham, finely chopped
- 1 medium onion, finely chopped
- 1 medium sweet red pepper, finely chopped
- 5 bacon strips, cooked and crumbled
- 1 large jalapeno pepper, seeded and finely chopped
- 2 garlic cloves, minced
- 1½ teaspoons ground cumin
- 1 teaspoon reduced-sodium chicken bouillon granules
- ½ teaspoon salt
- ½ teaspoon cayenne pepper
- ¼ teaspoon pepper
- 6 cups water
   Minced fresh cilantro, optional
   Hot cooked rice

1. Rinse and sort the peas; soak according to package directions.
2. Transfer peas to a 6-qt. slow cooker; add the next 12 ingredients. Cover and cook on low for 5-7 hours or until peas are tender. Sprinkle with cilantro if desired. Serve with the rice.
NOTE *Wear disposable gloves when cutting hot peppers; the oils can burn skin. Avoid touching your face.*
PER SERVING *¾ cup (calculated without rice) equals 170 cal., 3 g fat (1 g sat. fat), 13 mg chol., 386 mg sodium, 24 g carb., 7 g fiber, 13 g pro.* **Diabetic Exchanges:** *1½ starch, 1 lean meat.*

FALL GARDEN MEDLEY

Here's a very colorful, tasty and healthy recipe to make for special occasions or anytime, especially in the fall and winter. It complements so many different meat dishes.
—**KRYSTINE KERCHER** LINCOLN, NE

PREP: 20 MIN. • **COOK:** 5 HOURS
MAKES: 8 SERVINGS

- 4 large carrots, cut into 1½-inch pieces
- 3 fresh beets, peeled and cut into 1½-inch pieces.
- 2 medium sweet potatoes, peeled and cut into 1½-inch pieces
- 2 medium onions, peeled and quartered
- ½ cup water
- 2 teaspoons salt
- ½ teaspoon pepper
- ¼ teaspoon dried thyme
- 1 tablespoon olive oil
   Fresh parsley or dried parsley flakes, optional

1. Place the carrots, beets, sweet potatoes, onions and water in a greased 3-qt. slow cooker. Sprinkle with salt, pepper and thyme. Drizzle with olive oil. Cover and cook on low for 5-6 hours or until tender.
2. Stir the vegetables and sprinkle with parsley if desired.
PER SERVING *¾ cup equals 83 cal., 2 g fat (trace sat. fat), 0 chol., 633 mg sodium, 16 g carb., 3 g fiber, 2 g pro.* **Diabetic Exchanges:** *1 vegetable, ½ starch.*

BROWN SUGAR-GLAZED BABY CARROTS

When things get busy during the holidays, delicious glazed carrots come to the rescue. They cook while I'm preparing other parts of the meal, and I'm able to use my oven for other dishes, especially the turkey.
—**ANNDREA BAILEY**
HUNTINGTON BEACH, CA

PREP: 10 MIN. • **COOK:** 6 HOURS
MAKES: 6 SERVINGS

- 2 pounds fresh baby carrots
- 1 celery rib, finely chopped
- 1 small onion, finely chopped
- ¼ cup packed brown sugar
- 3 tablespoons butter, cubed
- ½ teaspoon salt
- ½ teaspoon pepper

In a 3-qt. slow cooker, combine all the ingredients. Cover and cook on low for 6-8 hours or until the carrots are tender.
PER SERVING *¾ cup equals 144 cal., 6 g fat (4 g sat. fat), 15 mg chol., 364 mg sodium, 23 g carb., 3 g fiber, 1 g pro.*

HOW-TO

CHOP AN ONION

1. To quickly chop an onion, peel and cut in half from the root to the top. Leaving the root attached, place flat side down on work surface.
2. Cut vertically through the onion, leaving the root end uncut.
3. Cut across the onion, discarding root end. The closer the cuts, the more finely the onion will be chopped.

BLACK-EYED
PEAS & HAM

FALL GARDEN
MEDLEY

BROWN SUGAR-
GLAZED BABY CARROTS

FIESTA CORN
AND BEANS

FIESTA CORN AND BEANS

Bursting with Southwestern flavors, this zesty veggie medley can serve as a side dish or a meatless meal. Add a dollop of yogurt for a cool, creamy finishing touch.
—**GERALD HETRICK** ERIE, PA

PREP: 25 MIN. • **COOK:** 3 HOURS
MAKES: 10 SERVINGS

- 1 **large onion, chopped**
- 1 **medium green pepper, cut into 1-inch pieces**
- 1 **to 2 jalapeno peppers, seeded and sliced**
- 1 **tablespoon olive oil**
- 1 **garlic clove, minced**
- 2 **cans (16 ounces each) kidney beans, rinsed and drained**
- 1 **package (16 ounces) frozen corn**
- 1 **can (14½ ounces) diced tomatoes, undrained**
- 1 **teaspoon chili powder**
- ¾ **teaspoon salt**
- ½ **teaspoon ground cumin**
- ½ **teaspoon pepper**
  Optional toppings: plain yogurt and sliced ripe olives

1. In a large skillet, saute the onion and peppers in oil until tender. Add the garlic; cook for 1 minute longer. Transfer to a 4-qt. slow cooker. Stir in the beans, corn, tomatoes and the seasonings.
2. Cover and cook on low for 3-4 hours or until heated through. Serve corn and beans with yogurt and olives if desired.
NOTE *Wear disposable gloves when cutting hot peppers; the oils can burn skin. Avoid touching your face.*
PER SERVING ¾ *cup (calculated without optional toppings) equals 149 cal., 2 g fat (trace sat. fat), 0 chol., 380 mg sodium, 28 g carb., 7 g fiber, 8 g pro.* **Diabetic Exchanges:** *1 starch, 1 lean meat, 1 vegetable.*

SLOW-COOKED SAUSAGE DRESSING

Dressings are delicious but often are not the healthiest side. I've cut some of the fat but none of the good flavor. No one will mind.
—**RAQUEL HAGGARD** EDMOND, OK

PREP: 20 MIN. • **COOK:** 3 HOURS
MAKES: 12 SERVINGS (⅔ CUP EACH)

- ½ **pound reduced-fat bulk pork sausage**
- 2 **celery ribs, chopped**
- 1 **large onion, chopped**
- 7 **cups seasoned stuffing cubes**
- 1 **can (14½ ounces) reduced-sodium chicken broth**
- 1 **medium tart apple, chopped**
- ⅓ **cup chopped pecans**
- 2 **tablespoons reduced-fat butter, melted**
- 1½ **teaspoons rubbed sage**
- ½ **teaspoon pepper**

1. In a large nonstick skillet, cook the sausage, celery and onion over medium heat until the meat is no longer pink; drain. Transfer the mixture to a large bowl; stir in the remaining ingredients.
2. Place in a 5-qt. slow cooker coated with cooking spray. Cover and cook on low for 3-4 hours or until heated through and apple is tender, stirring once.
NOTE *This recipe was tested with Land O'Lakes light stick butter.*
PER SERVING ⅔ *cup equals 201 cal., 8 g fat (2 g sat. fat), 17 mg chol., 640 mg sodium, 26 g carb., 3 g fiber, 7 g pro.*

COCONUT-PECAN SWEET POTATOES

Let sweet potatoes cook effortlessly while you tend to other things. A little coconut gives the classic dish a new twist.
—**RAQUEL HAGGARD** EDMOND, OK

PREP: 15 MIN. • **COOK:** 4 HOURS
MAKES: 12 SERVINGS (⅔ CUP EACH)

- ½ **cup chopped pecans**
- ½ **cup flaked coconut**
- ⅓ **cup sugar**
- ⅓ **cup packed brown sugar**
- ½ **teaspoon ground cinnamon**
- ¼ **teaspoon salt**
- ¼ **cup reduced-fat butter, melted**
- 4 **pounds sweet potatoes (about 6 medium), peeled and cut into 1-inch pieces**
- ½ **teaspoon coconut extract**
- ½ **teaspoon vanilla extract**

1. In a small bowl, combine the first six ingredients; stir in melted butter. Place the sweet potatoes in a 5-qt. slow cooker coated with cooking spray. Sprinkle with the pecan mixture.
2. Cook, covered, on low 4 to 4½ hours or until potatoes are tender. Stir in extracts.
NOTE *This recipe was tested with Land O'Lakes light stick butter.*
PER SERVING ⅔ *cup equals 211 cal., 7 g fat (3 g sat. fat), 5 mg chol., 103 mg sodium, 37 g carb., 3 g fiber, 2 g pro.*

THE SKINNY

GREEK YOGURT IS THE PERFECT TOPPING
Add a tablespoon or two of low-fat plain Greek yogurt to Fiesta Corn and Beans servings—with no guilt attached! It's low in calories while providing calcium and other nutrients.

SPICED CARROTS & BUTTERNUT SQUASH

When I've got a lot going on, the slow cooker is my go-to tool for cooking veggies. Spicy seasonings complement the sweetness of squash and carrots beautifully.
—**COURTNEY STULTZ** WEIR, KS

PREP: 15 MIN. • **COOK:** 4 HOURS
MAKES: 6 SERVINGS

- **5** large carrots, cut into ½-inch pieces (about 3 cups)
- **2** cups cubed peeled butternut squash (1-inch pieces)
- **1** tablespoon balsamic vinegar
- **1** tablespoon olive oil
- **1** tablespoon honey
- **1** teaspoon ground cinnamon
- **½** teaspoon salt
- **½** teaspoon ground cumin
- **¼** teaspoon chili powder

Place carrots and squash in a 3-qt. slow cooker. In a small bowl, mix remaining ingredients; drizzle over vegetables and toss to coat. Cook, covered, on low 4-5 hours or until vegetables are tender. Gently stir before serving.

PER SERVING *⅔ cup equals 85 cal., 3 g fat (trace sat. fat), 0 chol., 245 mg sodium, 16 g carb., 3 g fiber, 1 g pro.* **Diabetic Exchanges:** *1 vegetable, ½ starch, ½ fat.*

TOP TIP

THE BEST SQUASH

Look for butternut squash with hard, deep-colored rinds and no blemishes. Store unwashed squash in a dry, cool place for up to 1 month.

SWEET POTATO STUFFING

Mom likes to make sure there will be enough stuffing to satisfy our large family. For holiday gatherings, she slow-cooks this tasty sweet potato dressing in addition to the traditional stuffing cooked inside the turkey.
—**KELLY POLLOCK** LONDON, ON

PREP: 15 MIN. • **COOK:** 4 HOURS
MAKES: 10 SERVINGS

- **¼** cup butter, cubed
- **½** cup chopped celery
- **½** cup chopped onion
- **½** cup chicken broth
- **½** teaspoon salt
- **½** teaspoon rubbed sage
- **½** teaspoon poultry seasoning
- **½** teaspoon pepper
- **6** cups dry bread cubes
- **1** large sweet potato, cooked, peeled and finely chopped
- **¼** cup chopped pecans

1. In a Dutch oven, heat the butter over medium-high heat. Add the celery and onion; cook and stir until tender. Stir in broth and seasonings. Add remaining ingredients; toss to combine.

2. Transfer to a greased 3-qt. slow cooker. Cook, covered, on low 4 hours or until heated through.

PER SERVING *1 cup equals 212 cal., 8 g fat (3 g sat. fat), 12 mg chol., 459 mg sodium, 33 g carb., 3 g fiber, 5 g pro.* **Diabetic Exchanges:** *2 starch, 1½ fat.*

SPICED CARROTS & BUTTERNUT SQUASH

**SWEET POTATO
STUFFING**

CHIPOTLE SHREDDED
BEEF, PAGE 91

BEEF

56

67

92

SPICY BEEF VEGETABLE STEW

This zesty beef stew is packed with richness and goes together quickly. Try pairing it with warm corn bread, sourdough or some French bread for a memorable meal.

—LYNNETTE DAVIS TULLAHOMA, TN

PREP: 10 MIN. • **COOK:** 8 HOURS
MAKES: 8 SERVINGS (3 QUARTS)

- 1 **pound lean ground beef (90% lean)**
- 1 **cup chopped onion**
- 1 **jar (24 ounces) meatless pasta sauce**
- 3½ **cups water**
- 1 **package (16 ounces) frozen mixed vegetables**
- 1 **can (10 ounces) diced tomatoes and green chilies**
- 1 **cup sliced celery**
- 1 **teaspoon beef bouillon granules**
- 1 **teaspoon pepper**

1. In a large skillet, cook beef and onion over medium heat until meat is no longer pink; drain.

2. Transfer to a 5-qt. slow cooker. Stir in the remaining ingredients. Cover and cook on low for 8 hours or until the vegetables are tender.

PER SERVING *1½ cup equals 177 cal., 5 g fat (2 g sat. fat), 35 mg chol., 675 mg sodium, 19 g carb., 5 g fiber, 15 g pro.* **Diabetic Exchanges:** *2 meat, 1 starch.*

SPICY BEEF VEGETABLE STEW

SHREDDED BEEF SANDWICHES

Coated with a tasty, cola-flavored sauce, the meat gets its zip from chili powder and cayenne pepper.

—MARIE ELAINE BASINGER
CONNELLSVILLE, PA

PREP: 30 MIN. • **COOK:** 8¼ HOURS
MAKES: 8 SERVINGS

- ¾ **cup cola**
- ¼ **cup Worcestershire sauce**
- 2 **garlic cloves, minced**
- 1 **tablespoon white vinegar**
- 1 **teaspoon reduced-sodium beef bouillon granules**
- ½ **teaspoon chili powder**
- ½ **teaspoon ground mustard**
- ¼ **teaspoon cayenne pepper**
- 1 **beef rump roast or bottom round roast (2 pounds)**
- 2 **teaspoons canola oil**
- 2 **medium onions, chopped**
- ½ **cup ketchup**
- 8 **hoagie buns, split**

1. In a measuring cup, combine the cola, Worcestershire sauce, garlic, vinegar, bouillon and the seasonings; set aside. Cut roast in half. In a nonstick skillet, brown meat in oil on all sides.

2. Place onions in a 3-qt. slow cooker. Top with meat. Pour half the cola mixture over meat. Cover and cook on low for 8-10 hours or until meat is tender. Cover and refrigerate remaining cola mixture.

3. Remove meat from cooking liquid and cool. Strain cooking liquid, reserving the onions and discarding the liquid. When meat is cool enough to handle, shred with two forks. Return meat and onions to slow cooker.

4. Combine ketchup and reserved cola mixture; pour over meat and heat through. Serve on buns.

PER SERVING *1 sandwich equals 354 cal., 10 g fat (2 g sat. fat), 59 mg chol., 714 mg sodium, 40 g carb., 2 g fiber, 26 g pro.* **Diabetic Exchanges:** *3 lean meat, 2½ starch.*

SHREDDED
BEEF SANDWICHES

MUSHROOM POT ROAST

Between wholesome veggies and tender beef, this is one special entree that all ages will like. Serve mashed potatoes alongside to soak up every last drop of the beefy gravy.

—ANGIE STEWART TOPEKA, KS

PREP: 25 MIN. • **COOK:** 6 HOURS
MAKES: 10 SERVINGS

- 1 **boneless beef chuck roast (3 to 4 pounds)**
- ½ **teaspoon salt**
- ¼ **teaspoon pepper**
- 1 **tablespoon canola oil**
- 1½ **pounds sliced fresh shiitake mushrooms**
- 2½ **cups thinly sliced onions**
- 1½ **cups reduced-sodium beef broth**
- 1½ **cups dry red wine or additional reduced-sodium beef broth**
- 1 **can (8 ounces) tomato sauce**
- ¾ **cup chopped peeled parsnips**
- ¾ **cup chopped celery**
- ¾ **cup chopped carrots**
- 8 **garlic cloves, minced**
- 2 **bay leaves**
- 1½ **teaspoons dried thyme**
- 1 **teaspoon chili powder**
- ¼ **cup cornstarch**
- ¼ **cup water**
    Mashed potatoes

1. Sprinkle the roast with salt and pepper. In a Dutch oven, brown the roast in oil on all sides. Transfer to a 6-qt. slow cooker. Add mushrooms, onions, broth, wine, tomato sauce, parsnips, celery, carrots, garlic, bay leaves, thyme and chili powder.

Cover and cook on low for 6-8 hours or until meat is tender.

2. Remove meat and vegetables to a serving platter; keep warm. Discard bay leaves. Skim fat from cooking juices; transfer to a small saucepan. Bring liquid to a boil. Combine cornstarch and water until smooth; gradually stir into the pan. Bring to a boil; cook, stir for 2 minutes or until thickened. Serve with mashed potatoes, meat and vegetables.

PER SERVING *4 ounces cooked beef with ⅔ cup vegetables and ½ cup gravy (calculated without the potatoes) equals 310 cal., 14 g fat (5 g sat. fat), 89 mg chol., 363 mg sodium, 14 g carb., 3 g fiber, 30 g pro.* **Diabetic Exchanges:** *4 lean meat, 2 vegetable, 1½ fat.*

MUSHROOM POT ROAST

FLANK STEAK
FAJITAS

MUSHROOM-BEEF SPAGHETTI SAUCE

I got the recipe for this sauce in a recipe exchange and wish I could credit the person who gave it to me. My children love it! I added the mushrooms, but if you'd like it even chunkier, add some bell pepper and other veggies, too.

—**MEG FISHER** MARIETTA, GA

PREP: 20 MIN. • **COOK:** 6 HOURS
MAKES: 12 SERVINGS (1½ QUARTS)

- 1 **pound lean ground beef (90% lean)**
- ½ **pound sliced fresh mushrooms**
- 1 **small onion, chopped**
- 2 **cans (14½ ounces each) diced tomatoes, undrained**
- 1 **can (12 ounces) tomato paste**
- 1 **can (8 ounces) tomato sauce**
- 1 **cup reduced-sodium beef broth**
- 2 **tablespoons dried parsley flakes**
- 1 **tablespoon brown sugar**
- 1 **teaspoon dried basil**
- 1 **teaspoon dried oregano**
- 1 **teaspoon salt**
- ¼ **teaspoon pepper**
  Hot cooked spaghetti
  Shredded Parmesan cheese, optional

1. In a large nonstick skillet, cook the beef, mushrooms and onion over medium heat until meat is no longer pink; drain. Transfer to a 3-qt. slow cooker.
2. Stir in the tomatoes, tomato paste, tomato sauce, broth, parsley, brown sugar, basil, oregano, salt and pepper. Cover and cook on low for 6-8 hours. Serve with spaghetti. Sprinkle with cheese if desired.
PER SERVING *½ cup sauce (calculated without spaghetti) equals 115 cal., 3 g fat (1 g sat. fat), 19 mg chol., 493 mg sodium, 12 g carb., 3 g fiber, 10 g pro.* **Diabetic Exchanges:** *2 vegetable, 1 lean meat.*

FLANK STEAK FAJITAS

Flank steak turns out tender, juicy and delicious in the slow cooker to create these tempting fajitas. I like to serve them with a side of Spanish rice.

—**TWILA BURKHOLDER**
MIDDLEBURG, PA

PREP: 20 MIN. • **COOK:** 6 HOURS
MAKES: 6 SERVINGS

- 1 **beef flank steak (1½ pounds)**
- 1 **medium onion, sliced**
- 1 **cup tomato juice**
- 1 **jalapeno pepper, seeded and chopped**
- 2 **garlic cloves, minced**
- 1 **tablespoon minced fresh cilantro**
- 1 **teaspoon ground cumin**
- 1 **teaspoon chili powder**
- ¼ **teaspoon salt**
- 1 **medium green pepper, julienned**
- 1 **medium sweet red pepper, julienned**
- 6 **flour tortillas (8 inches), warmed**
  Shredded cheddar cheese, sour cream and guacamole, optional

1. Thinly slice steak across the grain into strips; place in a 5-qt. slow cooker. Add onion, tomato juice, jalapeno, garlic, cilantro, cumin, chili powder and salt. Cover, cook on low for 5 hours.
2. Add green and red peppers. Cover and cook 1 hour longer or until the meat and vegetables are tender.
3. Using a slotted spoon, spoon meat mixture down the center of each tortilla. Sprinkle with cheese if desired. Fold sides of tortilla over filling. Serve with cheese, sour cream and guacamole if desired.
NOTE *Wear disposable gloves when cutting hot peppers; the oils can burn skin. Avoid touching your face.*
PER SERVING *1 fajita (calculated without optional ingredients) equals 340 cal., 12 g fat (4 g sat. fat), 48 mg chol., 549 mg sodium, 33 g carb., 2 g fiber, 25 g pro.* **Diabetic Exchanges:** *3 lean meat, 2 starch, 1 vegetable.*

MEAT LOAF FROM THE SLOW COOKER

I'm often asked for the recipe when I serve this easy-to-make meat loaf.

—LAURA BURGESS
MOUNT VERNON, SD

PREP: 25 MIN. • **COOK:** 3 HOURS
MAKES: 8 SERVINGS

- ½ cup tomato sauce
- 2 large eggs, lightly beaten
- ¼ cup ketchup
- 1 teaspoon Worcestershire sauce
- 1 small onion, chopped
- ⅓ cup crushed saltines (about 10 crackers)
- ¾ teaspoon minced garlic
- ¼ teaspoon seasoned salt
- ⅛ teaspoon seasoned pepper
- 1½ pounds lean ground beef (90% lean)
- ½ pound reduced-fat bulk pork sausage

SAUCE

- ½ cup ketchup
- 3 tablespoons brown sugar
- ¾ teaspoon ground mustard
- ¼ teaspoon ground nutmeg

1. Cut three 25x3-in. strips of heavy-duty foil; crisscross so they resemble spokes of a wheel. Place strips on the bottom and up the sides of a 4- or 5-qt. slow cooker. Coat strips with cooking spray.
2. In a large bowl, combine the first nine ingredients. Crumble beef and sausage over mixture and mix well (mixture will be moist). Shape into a loaf. Place meat loaf in the center of the strips.
3. In a small bowl, combine sauce ingredients. Spoon over meat loaf. Cover and cook on low 3-4 hours or until no pink remains and a thermometer reads 160°. Using foil strips as handles, remove the meat loaf to a platter.
PER SERVING *1 slice equals 284 cal., 14 g fat (5 g sat. fat), 119 mg chol., 681 mg sodium, 16 g carb., 1 g fiber, 24 g pro.* **Diabetic Exchanges:** *3 lean meat, 1 starch.*

FRENCH DIP SANDWICHES

I found this recipe in one of our local publications. The meat cooks for 10 to 12 hours, so come home to a dinner that's ready to go!

—DIANNE JOY RICHARDSON
COLORADO SPRINGS, CO

PREP: 15 MIN. • **COOK:** 10 HOURS
MAKES: 12 SANDWICHES

- 1 beef sirloin tip roast (3 to 4 pounds)
- ½ cup reduced-sodium soy sauce
- 1 teaspoon beef bouillon granules
- 1 bay leaf
- 3 to 4 whole peppercorns
- 1 teaspoon dried crushed rosemary
- 1 teaspoon dried thyme
- 1 teaspoon garlic powder
- 12 French rolls, split

1. Cut the roast in half. Place in a 5-qt. slow cooker. Combine the soy sauce, bouillon, seasonings; pour over roast. Add water to almost cover the roast, about 5 cups. Cover and cook on low 10-12 hours or until meat is tender.
2. Remove roast; cool slightly. Discard bay leaf. Shred the meat with two forks and return to slow cooker; heat through. Serve on rolls with broth.
PER SERVING *1 sandwich equals 318 cal., 8 g fat (2 g sat. fat), 72 mg chol., 792 mg sodium, 31 g carb., 1 g fiber, 29 g pro.* **Diabetic Exchanges:** *3 lean meat, 2 starch.*

TOP TIP

GET YOUR PROTEIN

Here's a hint for calculating your daily protein need: Multiply your body weight in pounds by .4 grams. For example, a 150-pound person needs about 60 grams of protein daily.

FRENCH DIP
SANDWICHES

ZESTY
BEEF STEW

ZESTY BEEF STEW

Preparation couldn't be simpler for this hearty stew. I created the dish when I didn't have some of my usual ingredients for vegetable beef soup. My husband told me it was the best stew I had ever made!

—**MARGARET TURZA** SOUTH BEND, IN

PREP: 10 MIN. • **COOK:** 3½ HOURS
MAKES: 6 SERVINGS

- 1 **pound beef stew meat, cut into 1-inch cubes**
- 1 **package (16 ounces) frozen mixed vegetables, thawed**
- 1 **can (15 ounces) pinto beans, rinsed and drained**
- 1½ **cups water**
- 1 **can (8 ounces) pizza sauce**
- 2 **tablespoons medium pearl barley**
- 1 **tablespoon dried minced onion**
- 2 **teaspoons beef bouillon granules**
- ¼ **teaspoon crushed red pepper flakes**

In a 3-qt. slow cooker, combine all ingredients. Cover and cook on low for 3½-4½ hours or until the meat is tender.

PER SERVING *1 serving (1 cup) equals 251 cal., 6 g fat (2 g sat. fat), 47 mg chol., 526 mg sodium, 28 g carb., 8 g fiber, 21 g pro.*

TOP TIP

MINCE IT YOURSELF

If you don't have or are out of dried minced onion, don't worry! Grab a raw onion and start chopping. A ¼ cup of minced raw onion equals 1 tablespoon of dried minced onion.

---

⑤INGREDIENTS

BRISKET WITH CRANBERRY GRAVY

With just a few minutes of work, this delectable beef brisket simmers into a comforting entree. The meat and gravy are great for sandwiches the next day.

—**NOELLE LABRECQUE**
ROUND ROCK, TX

PREP: 15 MIN. • **COOK:** 5½ HOURS
MAKES: 12 SERVINGS

- 1 **medium onion, sliced**
- 1 **fresh beef brisket (3 pounds), halved**
- 1 **can (14 ounces) jellied cranberry sauce**
- ½ **cup thawed cranberry juice concentrate**
- 2 **tablespoons cornstarch**
- ¼ **cup cold water**

1. Place the onion in a 5-qt. slow cooker; top with brisket. Combine the cranberry sauce and the juice concentrate; pour over beef. Cover and cook on low for 5½-6 hours or until meat is tender.

2. Remove the brisket and keep warm. Strain the cooking juices, discarding onion; skim fat. Place in a small saucepan and bring to a boil. Combine cornstarch and cold water until smooth; gradually stir into the pan. Cook and stir for 2 minutes or until thickened. Thinly slice brisket across the grain; serve with gravy.

NOTE *This is a fresh beef brisket, not corned beef.*

PER SERVING *3 ounces cooked beef with 3 tablespoons gravy equals 225 cal., 5 g fat (2 g sat. fat), 48 mg chol., 46 mg sodium, 21 g carb., 1 g fiber, 23 g pro.* **Diabetic Exchanges:** *3 lean meat, 1½ starch.*

BRISKET WITH
CRANBERRY GRAVY

SLOW-COOKED SIRLOIN

My family of five likes to eat beef, so this recipe is popular. I usually serve it with homemade bread or rolls to soak up the gravy.

—VICKI TORMASCHY DICKINSON, ND

PREP: 20 MIN. • **COOK:** 3½ HOURS
MAKES: 6 SERVINGS

- 1 beef top sirloin steak (1½ pounds)
- 1 medium onion, cut into 1-inch chunks
- 1 medium green pepper, cut into 1-inch chunks
- 1 can (14½ ounces) reduced-sodium beef broth
- ¼ cup Worcestershire sauce
- ¼ teaspoon dill weed
- ¼ teaspoon dried thyme
- ¼ teaspoon pepper
  Dash crushed red pepper flakes
- 2 tablespoons cornstarch
- 2 tablespoons cold water

1. In a large nonstick skillet coated with cooking spray, brown beef on both sides. Place onion and green pepper in a 3-qt. slow cooker. Top with beef. Combine the broth, Worcestershire sauce, dill, thyme, pepper and pepper flakes; pour over beef. Cover and cook on high for 3-4 hours or until meat reaches desired doneness and vegetables are crisp-tender.

2. Remove beef and keep warm. Combine cornstarch and water until smooth; gradually stir into cooking juices. Cover and cook on high for 30 minutes or until slightly thickened. Return beef to the slow cooker; heat through.

PER SERVING *1 serving equals 199 cal., 6 g fat (2 g sat. fat), 68 mg chol., 305 mg sodium, 8 g carb., 1 g fiber, 26 g pro.* **Diabetic Exchanges: 3 lean meat, 1 vegetable.**

BEEF AND BEANS

Serve this spicy steak and beans dish over rice. Family and friends will ask for more! It's a favorite in my recipe collection.

—MARIE LEAMON BETHESDA, MD

PREP: 10 MIN. • **COOK:** 1½ HOURS
MAKES: 8 SERVINGS

- 1½ pounds boneless round steak
- 1 tablespoon prepared mustard
- 1 tablespoon chili powder
- ½ teaspoon salt, optional
- ¼ teaspoon pepper
- 1 garlic clove, minced
- 2 cans (14½ ounces each) diced tomatoes, undrained
- 1 medium onion, chopped
- 1 beef bouillon cube, crushed
- 1 can (16 ounces) kidney beans, rinsed and drained
  Hot cooked rice

Cut steak into thin strips. Combine the mustard, chili powder, salt if desired, pepper and garlic in a bowl; add steak and toss to coat. Transfer to a 3-qt. slow cooker; add tomatoes, onion and bouillon. Cover and cook on low for 6-8 hours. Stir in beans; cook 30 minutes longer. Serve over the rice.

PER SERVING *1 cup (calculated without rice) equals 185 cal., 3 g fat (1 g sat. fat), 47 mg chol., 584 mg sodium, 16 g carb., 5 g fiber, 24 g pro.* **Diabetic Exchanges: 2 lean meat, 1 starch, 1 vegetable.**

SLOW-COOKED SIRLOIN

TOP TIP

RINSE BEANS

Wondering why it says to rinse and drain canned beans before including them in a recipe? The answer: salt! Canned beans contain extra salt because of the canning process, so rinsing and draining will cut back on sodium.

BEEF AND
BEANS

CHILI MAC

CHILI MAC

This recipe has regularly appeared on my family menus for more than 40 years, and it's never failed to please at potlucks and bring-a-dish gatherings. Sometimes I turn it into soup by adding a can of beef broth.
—**MARIE POSAVEC** BERWYN, IL

PREP: 15 MIN. • **COOK:** 6 HOURS
MAKES: 6 SERVINGS

- 1 **pound lean ground beef (90% lean), cooked and drained**
- 2 **cans (16 ounces each) hot chili beans, undrained**
- 2 **large green peppers, chopped**
- 1 **large onion, chopped**
- 4 **celery ribs, chopped**
- 1 **can (8 ounces) no-salt-added tomato sauce**
- 2 **tablespoons chili seasoning mix**
- 2 **garlic cloves, minced**
- 1 **package (7 ounces) elbow macaroni, cooked and drained Salt and pepper to taste**

In a 5-qt. slow cooker, combine the first eight ingredients. Cover and cook on low for 6 hours or until heated through. Stir in macaroni. Season with salt and pepper.
PER SERVING *1 serving equals 348 cal., 8 g fat (3 g sat. fat), 47 mg chol., 713 mg sodium, 49 g carb., 12 g fiber, 27 g pro. **Diabetic Exchanges:** 3 starch, 3 lean meat.*

TERIYAKI BEEF STEW

In the spirit of the saying "Invention is the mother of necessity," I created this sweet-tangy beef stew because I had a package of stew meat that needed to be used. After spotting the ginger beer in the fridge, the rest is history.
—**LESLIE SIMMS** SHERMAN OAKS, CA

PREP: 20 MIN. • **COOK:** 6½ HOURS
MAKES: 8 SERVINGS

- 2 **pounds beef stew meat**
- 1 **bottle (12 ounces) ginger beer or ginger ale**
- ¼ **cup teriyaki sauce**
- 2 **garlic cloves, minced**
- 2 **tablespoons sesame seeds**
- 2 **tablespoons cornstarch**
- 2 **tablespoons cold water**
- 2 **cups frozen peas, thawed Hot cooked rice, optional**

1. In a large nonstick skillet, brown beef in batches. Transfer to a 3-qt. slow cooker.
2. In a small bowl, combine the ginger beer, teriyaki sauce, garlic and sesame seeds; pour over beef. Cover and cook on low for 6-8 hours or until meat is tender.
3. Combine the cornstarch and cold water until smooth; gradually stir into the stew. Stir in peas. Cover and cook on high for 30 minutes or until thickened. Serve with rice if desired.
PER SERVING *1 cup stew (calculated without rice) equals 310 cal., 12 g fat (4 g sat. fat), 94 mg chol., 528 mg sodium, 17 g carb., 2 g fiber, 33 g pro. **Diabetic Exchanges:** 4 lean meat, 1 starch.*

SLOW COOKER FAJITAS

I love fajitas from Mexican restaurants, but when I tried to make them at home, the meat always seemed too chewy. Then I tried this recipe in my slow cooker, and my husband and I enjoyed every bite.
—**KATIE URSO** SENECA, IL

PREP: 25 MIN. • **COOK:** 8 HOURS
MAKES: 8 SERVINGS

- 1 **each medium green, sweet red and yellow peppers, cut into ½-inch strips**
- 1 **sweet onion, cut into ½-inch strips**
- 2 **pounds beef top sirloin steaks, cut into thin strips**
- ¾ **cup water**
- 2 **tablespoons red wine vinegar**
- 1 **tablespoon lime juice**
- 1 **teaspoon ground cumin**
- 1 **teaspoon chili powder**
- ½ **teaspoon salt**
- ½ **teaspoon garlic powder**
- ½ **teaspoon pepper**
- ½ **teaspoon cayenne pepper**
- 8 **flour tortillas (8 inches), warmed**
- ½ **cup salsa**
- ½ **cup shredded reduced-fat cheddar cheese**
- 8 **teaspoons minced fresh cilantro**

1. Place peppers and onion in a 5-qt. slow cooker. Top with beef. Combine the water, vinegar, lime juice and seasonings; pour over meat. Cover and cook on low for 8-10 hours or until meat is tender.
2. Using a slotted spoon, place about ¾ cup meat mixture down the center of each tortilla. Top with salsa, cheese and cilantro; roll up.
PER SERVING *1 fajita equals 335 cal., 10 g fat (3 g sat. fat), 69 mg chol., 564 mg sodium, 32 g carb., 2 g fiber, 29 g pro. **Diabetic Exchanges:** 3 lean meat, 2 starch, 1 vegetable.*

TOP TIP

PERK UP CELERY

Give limp celery a second chance to season dishes such as Chili Mac. Cut ends from limp celery stalks and place the stalks in a glass of cold water in the refrigerator for several hours or overnight. You'll be surprised how refreshed the celery will be.

ROUND STEAK SAUERBRATEN

My easy version of an old-world classic takes just minutes to prepare for the slow cooker. If you prefer, serve the meat with rice.

—**LINDA BLOOM** MCHENRY, IL

PREP: 20 MIN. • **COOK:** 6½ HOURS
MAKES: 10 SERVINGS

- 1 envelope brown gravy mix
- 2 tablespoons plus 1½ teaspoons brown sugar
- 2½ cups cold water, divided
- 1 cup chopped onion
- 2 teaspoons Worcestershire sauce
- 2 tablespoons white vinegar
- 2 bay leaves
- 2½ pounds beef top round steak, cut into 3x½-inch strips
- 2 teaspoons salt
- 1 teaspoon pepper
- ¼ cup cornstarch
- 10 cups hot cooked egg noodles

1. In a 5-qt. slow cooker, combine the gravy mix, brown sugar, 2 cups water, onion, Worcestershire sauce vinegar and bay leaves.
2. Sprinkle the beef with salt and pepper; stir into the gravy mixture. Cover and cook on low for 6-8 hours or until meat is tender.
3. Combine the cornstarch and remaining water until smooth; stir into beef mixture. Cover and cook on high for 30 minutes or until thickened. Discard bay leaves. Serve with noodles.
PER SERVING *¾ cup beef mixture with 1 cup noodles equals 331 cal., 6 g fat (2 g sat. fat), 96 mg chol., 741 mg sodium, 37 g carb., 2 g fiber, 32 g pro.* **Diabetic Exchanges:** *3 lean meat, 2½ starch.*

SLOW COOKER VEGETABLE BEEF STEW

Here's a fun variation of beef stew that I came across. With some sweetness from apricots and butternut squash, the dish has a bit of a South American or Cuban flair.

—**RUTH RODRIGUEZ** FORT MYERS BEACH, FL

PREP: 15 MIN. • **COOK:** 5½ HOURS
MAKES: 4 SERVINGS

- ¾ pound beef stew meat, cut into ½-inch cubes
- 2 teaspoons canola oil
- 1 can (14½ ounces) beef broth
- 1 can (14½ ounces) stewed tomatoes, cut up
- 1½ cups cubed peeled butternut squash
- 1 cup frozen corn, thawed
- 6 dried apricots or peaches, quartered
- ½ cup chopped carrot
- 1 teaspoon dried oregano
- ¼ teaspoon salt
- ¼ teaspoon pepper
- 2 tablespoons cornstarch
- ¼ cup cold water
- 2 tablespoons minced fresh parsley

1. In a nonstick skillet, brown beef in oil over medium heat. Transfer to a 3-qt. slow cooker. Add broth, tomatoes, squash, corn, apricots, carrot, oregano, salt and pepper.
2. Cover and cook on high for 5-6 hours or until vegetables and meat are tender.
3. Combine the cornstarch and water until smooth; gradually stir into stew. Cover and cook on high for 30 minutes or until thickened. Stir in parsley.
PER SERVING *1 serving (1½ cups) equals 278 cal., 9 g fat (3 g sat. fat), 53 mg chol., 717 mg sodium, 32 g carb., 5 g fiber, 21 g pro.*

STUFFED FLANK STEAK

This recipe came with my first slow cooker. Now on my fourth slow cooker, I still use the recipe!

—**KATHY CLARK** BYRON, MN

PREP: 20 MIN. • **COOK:** 8 HOURS + 10 MIN.
MAKES: 8 SERVINGS

- 1 beef flank steak (2 pounds)
- 1 medium onion, chopped
- 1 garlic clove, minced
- 1 tablespoon butter
- 1½ cups soft bread crumbs (about 3 slices)
- ½ cup chopped fresh mushrooms
- ¼ cup minced fresh parsley
- ¼ cup egg substitute
- ¾ teaspoon poultry seasoning
- ½ teaspoon salt
- ⅛ teaspoon pepper
- ½ cup beef broth
- 2 teaspoons cornstarch
- 4 teaspoons water

1. Flatten steak to ½-in. thickness; set aside.
2. In a skillet, saute the onion and garlic in butter until tender. Add bread crumbs, mushrooms, parsley, egg substitute, poultry seasoning, salt and pepper; mix well.
3. Spread over steak to within 1 in. of edge. Roll up jelly-roll style, starting with a long side; tie with kitchen string. Place in a 5-qt. slow cooker; add broth. Cover and cook on low for 8-10 hours.
4. Remove meat to a platter and keep warm. Skim fat from cooking juices; pour into a small saucepan.
5. Combine the cornstarch and water until smooth; stir into juices. Bring to a boil; cook and stir for 1-2 minutes or until thickened. Remove string before slicing the steak; serve with gravy.
PER SERVING *1 serving equals 230 cal., 11 g fat (5 g sat. fat), 62 mg chol., 348 mg sodium, 6 g carb., trace fiber, 26 g pro.* **Diabetic Exchanges:** *3 lean meat, ½ starch, ½ fat.*

STUFFED
FLANK STEAK

**PUMPKIN HARVEST
BEEF STEW**

**STEAK
BURRITOS**

**GERMAN-STYLE
SHORT RIBS**

PUMPKIN HARVEST BEEF STEW

With this simmering and a batch of bread baking, your house will smell absolutely wonderful.

—**MARCIA O'NEIL** CEDAR CREST, NM

PREP: 25 MIN. • **COOK:** 6½ HOURS
MAKES: 6 SERVINGS

- 1 tablespoon canola oil
- 1 beef top round steak (1½ pounds), cut into 1-inch cubes
- 1½ cups cubed peeled pie pumpkin or sweet potatoes
- 3 small red potatoes, peeled and cubed
- 1 cup cubed acorn squash
- 1 medium onion, chopped
- 2 cans (14½ ounces each) reduced-sodium beef broth
- 1 can (14½ ounces) diced tomatoes, undrained
- 2 bay leaves
- 2 garlic cloves, minced
- 2 teaspoons reduced-sodium beef bouillon granules
- ½ teaspoon chili powder
- ½ teaspoon pepper
- ¼ teaspoon ground allspice
- ¼ teaspoon ground cloves
- ¼ cup water
- 3 tablespoons all-purpose flour

1. In a large skillet, heat oil over medium-high heat. Brown beef in batches; remove with a slotted spoon to a 4- or 5-qt. slow cooker. Add pumpkin, potatoes, squash and onion. Stir in broth, tomatoes and seasonings. Cover and cook on low for 6-8 hours or until meat is tender.
2. Remove bay leaves. In a small bowl, mix water and flour until smooth; gradually stir into stew. Cover and cook on high for 30 minutes or until liquid is thickened.
PER SERVING 1⅔ cups equals 258 cal., 6 g fat (1 g sat. fat), 67 mg chol., 479 mg sodium, 21 g carb., 4 g fiber, 29 g pro. **Diabetic Exchanges:** 3 lean meat, 1 starch, 1 vegetable, ½ fat.

STEAK BURRITOS

Your slow cooker does all the hard work, so just fill flour tortillas and add toppings for a tasty meal.

—**VALERIE JONES** PORTLAND, ME

PREP: 15 MIN. • **COOK:** 8 HOURS
MAKES: 10 SERVINGS

- 2 beef flank steaks (about 1 pound each)
- 2 envelopes reduced-sodium taco seasoning
- 1 medium onion, chopped
- 1 can (4 ounces) chopped green chilies
- 1 tablespoon white vinegar
- 10 flour tortillas (8 inches), warmed
- 1 cup (4 ounces) shredded Monterey Jack cheese
- 1½ cups chopped seeded plum tomatoes
- ¾ cup reduced-fat sour cream

1. Cut steaks in half; rub with taco seasoning. Place in a 3-qt. slow cooker coated with cooking spray. Top with onion, chilies and vinegar. Cover and cook on low for 8-9 hours or until meat is tender.
2. Remove steaks and cool slightly; shred meat with two forks. Return to slow cooker; heat through.
3. Spoon about ½ cup meat mixture near the center of each tortilla. Top with cheese, tomato and sour cream. Fold bottom and sides of tortilla over filling and roll up.
PER SERVING 1 burrito equals 339 cal., 12 g fat (6 g sat. fat), 59 mg chol., 816 mg sodium, 33 g carb., 2 g fiber, 25 g pro. **Diabetic Exchanges:** 3 lean meat, 2 starch.

GERMAN-STYLE SHORT RIBS

Our whole family is excited when I plug in the slow cooker to make these amazing ribs. We like them served over rice or egg noodles.

—**BREGITTE RUGMAN**
SHANTY BAY, ON

PREP: 15 MIN. • **COOK:** 8 HOURS
MAKES: 8 SERVINGS

- ¾ cup dry red wine or beef broth
- ½ cup mango chutney
- 3 tablespoons quick-cooking tapioca
- ¼ cup water
- 3 tablespoons brown sugar
- 3 tablespoons cider vinegar
- 1 tablespoon Worcestershire sauce
- ½ teaspoon salt
- ½ teaspoon ground mustard
- ½ teaspoon chili powder
- ½ teaspoon pepper
- 4 pounds bone-in beef short ribs
- 2 medium onions, sliced
  Hot cooked egg noodles

1. In a 5-qt. slow cooker, combine the first 11 ingredients. Add ribs and turn to coat. Top with onions.
2. Cover and cook on low for 8-10 hours or until meat is tender. Remove ribs from slow cooker. Skim fat from cooking juices; serve with ribs and noodles.
PER SERVING 1 serving (calculated without noodles) equals 302 cal., 11 g fat (5 g sat. fat), 55 mg chol., 378 mg sodium, 28 g carb., 1 g fiber, 19 g pro.

SLOW-COOKED
PEPPER STEAK

COFFEE BEEF ROAST

Coffee is the key to this tasty beef roast that cooks until it's fall-apart tender. Try it once, and I'm sure you'll make it again and again.
—**CHARLES TRAHAN** SAN DIMAS, CA

PREP: 15 MIN. • **COOK:** 8 HOURS
MAKES: 6 SERVINGS

- 1 beef sirloin tip roast (2½ pounds), cut in half
- 2 teaspoons canola oil
- 1½ cups sliced fresh mushrooms
- ⅓ cup sliced green onions
- 2 garlic cloves, minced
- 1½ cups brewed coffee
- 1 teaspoon liquid smoke, optional
- ½ teaspoon salt
- ½ teaspoon chili powder
- ¼ teaspoon pepper
- ¼ cup cornstarch
- ⅓ cup cold water

1. In a large nonstick skillet, brown roast on all sides in oil over medium-high heat. Place in a 5-qt. slow cooker. In the same skillet, saute mushrooms, onions and garlic until tender; stir in the coffee, liquid smoke if desired, salt, chili powder and pepper. Pour over roast.

2. Cover and cook on low for 8-10 hours or until the meat is tender. Remove roast and keep warm. Pour cooking juices into a 2-cup measuring cup; skim fat.

3. In a small saucepan, combine cornstarch and water until smooth. Gradually stir in 2 cups cooking juices. Bring to a boil; cook and stir for 2 minutes or until thickened. Serve with beef.

PER SERVING *1 serving (3 ounces cooked beef with ⅓ cup gravy) equals 209 cal., 7 g fat (2 g sat. fat), 82 mg chol., 244 mg sodium, 6 g carb., trace fiber, 28 g pro.* **Diabetic Exchanges:** *3 lean meat, ½ starch.*

FREEZE IT
SLOW-COOKED PEPPER STEAK

After a long day working in our greenhouse raising bedding plants, I enjoy coming in to this hearty beef dish for supper. It's one of my favorite meals.
—**SUE GRONHOLZ** BEAVER DAM, WI

PREP: 10 MIN. • **COOK:** 6½ HOURS
MAKES: 6 SERVINGS

- 1½ pounds beef top round steak
- 2 tablespoons canola oil
- 1 cup chopped onion
- ¼ cup reduced-sodium soy sauce
- 1 garlic clove, minced
- 1 teaspoon sugar
- ½ teaspoon salt
- ¼ teaspoon ground ginger
- ¼ teaspoon pepper
- 4 medium tomatoes, cut into wedges or 1 can (14½ ounces) diced tomatoes, undrained
- 1 large green pepper, cut into strips
- 1 tablespoon cornstarch
- ½ cup cold water
   Hot cooked noodles or rice

1. Cut beef into 3x1-in. strips. In a large skillet, brown beef in oil. Transfer to a 3-qt. slow cooker. Combine the onion, soy sauce, garlic, sugar, salt, ginger and pepper; pour over beef. Cover and cook on low for 5-6 hours or until meat is tender. Add tomatoes and green pepper; cook on low 1 hour longer or until vegetables are tender.

2. Combine cornstarch and cold water until smooth; gradually stir into slow cooker. Cover and cook on high for 20-30 minutes until thickened. Serve with noodles or rice.

FREEZE OPTION *Freeze cooled beef mixture in freezer containers. To use, partially thaw in the refrigerator overnight. Heat through in a covered saucepan, gently stirring and adding a little broth or water if necessary.*

PER SERVING *1 cup (calculated without noodles) equals 176 cal., 6 g fat (1 g sat. fat), 48 mg chol., 639 mg sodium, 8 g carb., 2 g fiber, 21 g pro.*

COFFEE BEEF
ROAST

BIG BATCH HUNGARIAN GOULASH

My grandmother used to make this goulash for my mother. Paprika and caraway add wonderful flavor, and the sour cream gives it a traditional creamy richness. It's scrumptious!
—MARCIA DOYLE POMPANO, FL

PREP: 20 MIN. • **COOK:** 7 HOURS
MAKES: 12 SERVINGS

BIG BATCH
HUNGARIAN
GOULASH

- 3 medium onions, chopped
- 2 medium carrots, chopped
- 2 medium green peppers, chopped
- 3 pounds beef stew meat
- ¾ teaspoon salt, divided
- ¾ teaspoon pepper, divided
- 2 tablespoons olive oil
- 1½ cups reduced-sodium beef broth
- ¼ cup all-purpose flour
- 3 tablespoons paprika
- 2 tablespoons tomato paste
- 1 teaspoon caraway seeds
- 1 garlic clove, minced
  Dash sugar
- 12 cups uncooked whole wheat egg noodles
- 1 cup (8 ounces) reduced-fat sour cream

1. Place the onions, carrots and green peppers in a 5-qt. slow cooker. Sprinkle meat with ½ teaspoon salt and ½ teaspoon pepper. In a large skillet, brown meat in oil in batches. Transfer to slow cooker.

2. Add broth to skillet, stirring to loosen browned bits from the pan. Combine the flour, paprika, tomato paste, caraway seeds, garlic, sugar and remaining salt and pepper; stir into skillet. Bring to a boil; cook and stir for 2 minutes or until thickened. Pour over meat. Cover and cook on low for 7-9 hours or until meat is tender.

3. Cook noodles according to package directions. Stir sour cream into slow cooker. Drain noodles; serve with goulash.

PER SERVING *⅔ cup goulash with 1 cup noodles equals 388 cal., 13 g fat (4 g sat. fat), 78 mg chol., 285 mg sodium, 41 g carb., 7 g fiber, 31 g pro.* **Diabetic Exchanges:** *3 lean meat, 2 starch, 1 vegetable, 1 fat.*

TOP TIP

GOULASH HISTORY

Goulash is actually a type of stew, with origins traced back to Hungary. And the key ingredient? Paprika!

BEEF ROAST DINNER

Because this healthy dish is slow-cooked, you can use less expensive beef roasts and have the same mouthwatering results you would get with more costly cuts. Change up the veggies for variety, nutrition or just to suit your tastes.

—SANDRA DUDLEY BEMIDJI, MN

PREP: 20 MIN. • **COOK:** 8 HOURS
MAKES: 10 SERVINGS

- 1 **pound red potatoes (about 4 medium), cubed**
- ¼ **pound small fresh mushrooms**
- 1½ **cups fresh baby carrots**
- 1 **medium green pepper, chopped**
- 1 **medium parsnip, chopped**
- 1 **small red onion, chopped**
- 1 **beef rump roast or bottom round roast (3 pounds)**
- 1 **can (14½ ounces) beef broth**
- ¾ **teaspoon salt**
- ¾ **teaspoon dried oregano**
- ¼ **teaspoon pepper**
- 3 **tablespoons cornstarch**
- ¼ **cup cold water**

1. Place vegetables in a 5-qt. slow cooker. Cut roast in half; place in slow cooker. Combine the broth, salt, oregano and pepper; pour over meat. Cover and cook on low for 8 hours or until meat is tender.
2. Remove meat and vegetables to a serving platter; keep warm. Skim the fat from cooking juices; transfer to a small saucepan. Bring liquid to a boil.
3. Combine cornstarch and water until smooth. Gradually stir into the pan. Bring to a boil; cook and stir for 2 minutes or until thickened. Serve with meat and vegetables.

PER SERVING *4 ounces cooked beef with ⅔ cup vegetables and ¼ cup gravy equals 245 cal., 7 g fat (2 g sat. fat), 82 mg chol., 427 mg sodium, 16 g carb., 2 g fiber, 29 g pro.* ***Diabetic Exchanges:*** *4 lean meat, 1 starch.*

ALL-DAY BRISKET
WITH POTATOES

ALL-DAY BRISKET WITH POTATOES

I think the slow cooker was invented with brisket in mind. This sweet and savory version just melts in your mouth. I always buy "first-cut" or "flat-cut" brisket, which has far less fat than other cuts.

—LANA GRYGA GLEN FLORA, WI

PREP: 30 MIN. • **COOK:** 8 HOURS
MAKES: 8 SERVINGS

- 2 **medium potatoes, peeled and cut into ¼-inch slices**
- 2 **celery ribs, sliced**
- 1 **fresh beef brisket (3 pounds)**
- 1 **tablespoon canola oil**
- 1 **large onion, sliced**
- 2 **garlic cloves, minced**
- 1 **can (12 ounces) beer**
- ½ **teaspoon beef bouillon granules**
- ¾ **cup stewed tomatoes**
- ⅓ **cup tomato paste**
- ¼ **cup red wine vinegar**
- 3 **tablespoons brown sugar**
- 3 **tablespoons Dijon mustard**
- 3 **tablespoons soy sauce**
- 2 **tablespoons molasses**
- ½ **teaspoon paprika**
- ¼ **teaspoon salt**
- ⅛ **teaspoon pepper**
- 1 **bay leaf**

1. Place potatoes and celery in a 5-qt. slow cooker. Cut brisket in half. In a large skillet, brown beef in oil on all sides; transfer to slow cooker. In the same pan, saute the onion until tender. Add garlic; cook 1 minute longer. Add to slow cooker.
2. Add beer and bouillon granules to skillet, stirring to loosen browned bits from pan; pour over meat. In a large bowl, combine remaining ingredients; add to slow cooker.
3. Cover and cook on low for 8-10 hours or until vegetables and meat are tender. Discard bay leaf. To serve, thinly slice across grain.
NOTE *This is a fresh beef brisket, not corned beef.*
PER SERVING *1 serving equals 352 cal., 9 g fat (3 g sat. fat), 72 mg chol., 722 mg sodium, 25 g carb., 2 g fiber, 38 g pro.* ***Diabetic Exchanges:*** *5 lean meat, 1 starch, 1 vegetable, ½ fat.*

HEALTHY SLOW-COOKED MEAT LOAF

What could be easier than an Italian-inspired meat loaf made in the slow cooker? No fuss, easy cleanup and great taste; it's all right here!

—SHARON DELANEY-CHRONIS
SOUTH MILWAUKEE, WI

PREP: 15 MIN. • **COOK:** 3 HOURS
MAKES: 8 SERVINGS

- 1 cup soft bread crumbs
- 1½ cups spaghetti sauce, divided
- 1 large egg, lightly beaten
- 2 tablespoons dried minced onion
- 1 teaspoon salt
- ½ teaspoon garlic powder
- ½ teaspoon Italian seasoning
- ¼ teaspoon pepper
- 2 pounds lean ground beef (90% lean)

1. Cut four 20x3-in. strips of heavy-duty foil; crisscross so they resemble spokes of a wheel. Place strips on the bottom and up the sides of a 3-qt. slow cooker. Coat strips with cooking spray.
2. In a large bowl, combine bread crumbs, 1 cup spaghetti sauce, egg, onion, and seasonings. Crumble beef over mixture and mix well. Shape into a loaf; place in the center of the strips.
3. Spoon remaining spaghetti sauce over meat loaf. Cover and cook on low for 3-4 hours or until a thermometer reads 160°. Using foil strips as handles, remove meat loaf to a platter.
PER SERVING *1 slice equals 243 cal., 12 g fat (4 g sat. fat), 98 mg chol., 635 mg sodium, 8 g carb., 1 g fiber, 24 g pro.* **Diabetic Exchanges:** *3 lean meat, 1 fat, ½ starch.*

SOUTHWEST BLACK BEAN & BEEF STEW

I made this stew for my ladies' group at church, and everyone loved it! Best of all, I started the dish before I left for work and had it ready to go when I got home.

—ANITA ROBERSON
WILLIAMSTON, NC

PREP: 30 MIN. • **COOK:** 7 HOURS
MAKES: 11 SERVINGS (2¾ QUARTS)

- 1½ pounds lean ground beef (90% lean)
- 1 large onion, chopped
- 2 cans (14½ ounces each) diced tomatoes, undrained
- 1 package (16 ounces) frozen corn
- 1 can (15 ounces) black beans, rinsed and drained
- 1 can (14½ ounces) chicken broth
- 1 can (10 ounces) diced tomatoes and green chilies, undrained
- 1 teaspoon garlic powder
- 1½ teaspoons salt-free Southwest chipotle seasoning blend
- 1½ cups cooked rice
- ¼ cup shredded cheddar cheese

1. In a large skillet, cook beef and onion over medium heat until meat is no longer pink; drain.
2. Transfer to a 5-qt. slow cooker. Stir in the tomatoes, corn, black beans, broth, tomatoes, garlic powder and seasoning blend. Cover and cook on low 6-8 hours or until heated through.
3. Stir in the rice; heat through. Sprinkle each serving with cheese.
PER SERVING *1 cup equals 228 cal., 6 g fat (3 g sat. fat), 42 mg chol., 482 mg sodium, 26 g carb., 4 g fiber, 17 g pro.* **Diabetic Exchanges:** *2 lean meat, 1½ starch, 1 vegetable.*

⑤ INGREDIENTS

CIDER MUSHROOM BRISKET

Apple juice and gingersnaps give an autumn feel to this tender brisket. It's quick to prep, and the pleasing aroma will linger for hours.

—COLLEEN WESTON DENVER, CO

PREP: 10 MIN. • **COOK:** 6 HOURS
MAKES: 12 SERVINGS

- 1 fresh beef brisket (6 pounds)
- 2 jars (12 ounces each) mushroom gravy
- 1 cup apple cider or juice
- 1 envelope onion mushroom soup mix
- ⅓ cup crushed gingersnap cookies

1. Cut brisket into thirds; place in a 5- or 6-qt. slow cooker. In a large bowl, combine gravy, cider, soup mix and cookie crumbs; pour over the beef. Cover and cook on low for 6-8 hours or until meat is tender.
2. Thinly slice meat across grain. Skim the fat from cooking juices; thicken if desired.
NOTE *This is a fresh beef brisket, not corned beef.*
PER SERVING *6 ounces cooked meat with ½ cup cooking juices equals 336 cal., 11 g fat (4 g sat. fat), 101 mg chol., 566 mg sodium, 9 g carb., trace fiber, 47 g pro.* **Diabetic Exchanges:** *6 lean meat, ½ starch, ½ fat.*

THE SKINNY

KEEP IT LEAN
Using lean ground beef in Healthy Slow-Cooked Meat Loaf instead of beef that's 80% lean saves 45 calories per 4-ounce serving of beef. Lean ground beef also is 29% lower in saturated fat.

HEALTHY SLOW-COOKED
MEAT LOAF

SOUTHWEST BLACK
BEAN & BEEF STEW

CIDER MUSHROOM
BRISKET

MEATBALL
CABBAGE ROLLS

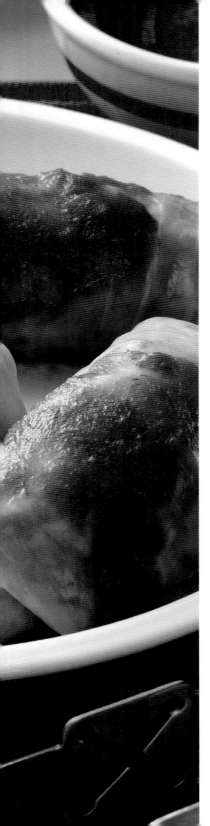

MEATBALL CABBAGE ROLLS

My mother often would have these cabbage rolls waiting in her slow cooker when my family and I arrived home for visits. The mouthwatering meatballs tucked inside set the rolls apart from others.
—BETTY BUCKMASTER MUSKOGEE, OK

PREP: 25 MIN. • **COOK:** 8 HOURS
MAKES: 4 SERVINGS

- 1 **large head cabbage**
- 1 **can (8 ounces) no-salt-added tomato sauce**
- 1 **small onion, chopped**
- ⅓ **cup uncooked long grain rice**
- 2 **tablespoons chili powder**
- ¼ **teaspoon garlic powder**
- ⅛ **teaspoon salt**
- 1 **pound lean ground beef (90% lean)**
- 1 **can (15 ounces) tomato sauce**

1. In a Dutch oven, cook cabbage in boiling water just until the leaves fall off head. Set aside 12 large leaves for rolls. (Refrigerate the rest of the cabbage for another use.) Cut out thick vein from the bottom of each reserved leaf, making V-shaped cut.
2. In a large bowl, combine the no-salt-added tomato sauce, onion, rice, chili powder, garlic powder and salt. Crumble beef over mixture; mix well. Shape into 12 balls. Place one meatball on each cabbage leaf; overlap cut ends of leaf. Fold in sides, beginning from the cut end. Roll up completely to enclose meatball. Secure with toothpicks.
3. Place in a 5-qt. slow cooker. Pour the remaining tomato sauce over cabbage rolls. Cover and cook on low for 8 hours or until meat is no longer pink and the cabbage is tender. Discard toothpicks.
PER SERVING *3 rolls equals 323 cal., 11 g fat (4 g sat. fat), 71 mg chol., 762 mg sodium, 31 g carb., 7 g fiber, 28 g pro.* **Diabetic Exchanges:** *3 lean meat, 1½ starch, 1 vegetable.*

SATISFYING BEEF STEW

This stew is so hearty and tastes even better the next day—if there are leftovers! It goes great with corn bread or any bakery bread.
—ABBEY MUELLER ENID, OK

PREP: 30 MIN. • **COOK:** 6 HOURS
MAKES: 8 SERVINGS

- 2 **pounds beef stew meat**
- 1 **medium onion, chopped**
- 2 **tablespoons canola oil**
- 2 **cups water**
- ¼ **cup all-purpose flour**
- 3 **medium carrots, sliced**
- 3 **medium potatoes, peeled and cubed**
- 2 **cups frozen corn**
- 1½ **cups frozen cut green beans**
- 1 **can (15 ounces) Italian tomato sauce**
- 2 **teaspoons Worcestershire sauce**
- 1 **teaspoon salt**
- 1 **teaspoon paprika**
- 1 **teaspoon pepper**
  Dash ground cloves
- 2 **bay leaves**

1. In a large skillet, brown beef and onion in oil; drain. Transfer to a 5-qt. slow cooker. Combine water and flour; pour over beef. Stir in the remaining ingredients.
2. Cover and cook on low for 6-8 hours or until the meat and vegetables are tender. Discard bay leaves.
PER SERVING *1 cup equals 330 cal., 12 g fat (3 g sat. fat), 70 mg chol., 680 mg sodium, 32 g carb., 4 g fiber, 26 g pro.* **Diabetic Exchanges:** *3 lean meat, 1½ starch, 1 vegetable, 1 fat.*

BAVARIAN POT ROAST

I wasn't a fan of pot roast until I got this recipe at a church social and changed a few ingredients. My 7-year-old especially enjoys the seasoned apple gravy.

—PATRICIA GASMUND ROCKFORD, IL

PREP: 10 MIN. • **COOK:** 5 HOURS
MAKES: 12 SERVINGS

- 1   beef top round roast (4 pounds), halved
- 1½ cups apple juice
- 1   can (8 ounces) tomato sauce
- 1   small onion, chopped
- 2   tablespoons white vinegar
- 1   tablespoon salt
- 2   to 3 teaspoons ground cinnamon
- 1   tablespoon minced fresh gingerroot
- ¼   cup cornstarch
- ½   cup water

1. In a Dutch oven coated with cooking spray, brown the roast on all sides over medium-high heat. Transfer to a 5-qt. slow cooker. In a bowl, combine juice, tomato sauce, onion, vinegar, salt, cinnamon and ginger; pour over roast. Cover and cook on high for 5-7 hours.

2. In a small bowl, combine the cornstarch and water until smooth; stir into cooking juices until well combined. Cover and cook 1 hour longer or until the meat is tender and gravy begins to thicken.

PER SERVING *1 serving (4 ounces cooked beef with ½ cup gravy) equals 230 cal., 7 g fat (2 g sat. fat), 96 mg chol., 753 mg sodium, 8 g carb., 1 g fiber, 32 g pro.* **Diabetic Exchanges:** *4 lean meat, ½ fruit.*

BAVARIAN POT ROAST

BARBECUES FOR THE BUNCH

Serve a party-perfect meal right from your slow cooker. Just add chips and your best sides.

—LOUISE WATKINS LONG KEY, FL

PREP: 25 MIN. • **COOK:** 6 HOURS
MAKES: 16 SERVINGS

- 2 **pounds beef top sirloin steak, cubed**
- 1½ **pounds boneless pork loin roast, cubed**
- 2 **large onions, chopped**
- ¾ **cup chopped celery**
- 1 **can (6 ounces) tomato paste**
- ½ **cup packed brown sugar**
- ¼ **cup cider vinegar**
- ¼ **cup chili sauce**
- 2 **tablespoons Worcestershire sauce**
- 1 **tablespoon ground mustard**
- 16 **hamburger buns, split**

1. In a 5-qt. slow cooker, combine beef, pork, onions and celery. In a small bowl, combine the tomato paste, brown sugar, vinegar, chili sauce, Worcestershire sauce and mustard. Pour over meat mixture.
2. Cover and cook on high for 6-8 hours or until meat is very tender. Shred meat in the slow cooker with two forks. With a slotted spoon, serve ½ cup meat mixture on each bun.
PER SERVING *1 sandwich equals 297 cal., 7 g fat (2 g sat. fat), 53 mg chol., 336 mg sodium, 34 g carb., 2 g fiber, 24 g pro.* **Diabetic Exchanges:** *3 lean meat, 2 starch.*

TOP TIP

VINEGAR SWAP

Don't have cider vinegar on hand? Substitute balsamic vinegar or a mild red wine vinegar.

BARBECUES FOR
THE BUNCH

SLOW-COOKED STROGANOFF

SLOW-COOKED STROGANOFF

I've been preparing Stroganoff in the slow cooker for more than 30 years. Once you've done it this way, you'll never cook it on the stovetop again. It's great for family or company.

—KAREN HERBERT PLACERVILLE, CA

PREP: 20 MIN. • **COOK:** 5 HOURS
MAKES: 8-10 SERVINGS

- 3 pounds beef top round steaks
- ½ cup all-purpose flour
- 1½ teaspoons salt
- ½ teaspoon ground mustard
- ⅛ teaspoon pepper
- 1 medium onion, sliced and separated into rings
- 1 can (8 ounces) mushroom stems and pieces, drained
- 1 can (10½ ounces) condensed beef broth, undiluted
- 1½ cups (12 ounces) sour cream
  Hot cooked noodles

1. Cut beef into thin strips. In a shallow bowl, mix flour, salt, mustard and pepper. Add beef in batches; toss to coat.
2. In a 5-qt. slow cooker, layer the onion, mushrooms and beef. Pour the broth over top. Cook, covered, on low 5-7 hours or until meat is tender. Just before serving, stir in sour cream. Serve with noodles.
PER SERVING *4 ounces cooked beef (calculated without noodles) equals 275 cal., 10 g fat (5 g sat. fat), 99 mg chol., 680 mg sodium, 8 g carb., 1 g fiber, 34 g pro.*

HOW-TO

PREP MUSHROOMS

To clean mushrooms, gently remove the dirt by rubbing with a mushroom brush or a damp paper towel. Trim stems.

FREEZE IT
SWEET-AND-SOUR BEEF STEW

Combine meat and nutrient-packed vegetables into one delicious stew. Better yet, freeze some for later!

—FRANCES CONKLIN COTTONWOOD, ID

PREP: 25 MIN. • **COOK:** 8 HOURS
MAKES: 8 SERVINGS

- 2 pounds beef top round steak, cut into 1-inch cubes
- 2 tablespoons olive oil
- 1 can (15 ounces) tomato sauce
- 2 large onions, chopped
- 4 medium carrots, thinly sliced
- 1 large green pepper, cut into 1-inch pieces
- 1 cup canned pineapple chunks, drained
- ½ cup cider vinegar
- ¼ cup packed brown sugar
- ¼ cup light corn syrup
- 2 teaspoons chili powder
- 2 teaspoons paprika
- ½ teaspoon salt
  Hot cooked rice, optional

1. In a large skillet, brown beef in oil in batches; drain. Transfer to a 4- or 5-qt. slow cooker.
2. In a large bowl, combine the tomato sauce, onions, carrots, green pepper, pineapple, vinegar, brown sugar, corn syrup, chili powder, paprika and salt; pour over beef.
3. Cover and cook on low for 8-10 hours or until beef is tender. Serve with rice if desired.
FREEZE OPTION *Freeze cooled stew in freezer containers. To use, partially thaw in refrigerator overnight. Heat through in a saucepan, stirring occasionally and adding a little broth or water if necessary.*
PER SERVING *1 cup (calculated without rice) equals 290 cal., 7 g fat (2 g sat. fat), 64 mg chol., 465 mg sodium, 29 g carb., 3 g fiber, 28 g pro.* **Diabetic Exchanges:** *3 lean meat, 2 vegetable, 1 starch, ½ fat.*

SWISS STEAK SUPPER

Here is a satisfying dinner that is loaded with veggies. Save a step by seasoning the steak with peppered seasoned salt instead of using both pepper and seasoned salt.

—KATHLEEN ROMANIUK CHOMEDEY, QC

PREP: 20 MIN. • **COOK:** 5 HOURS
MAKES: 6 SERVINGS

- 1½ pounds beef top round steak
- ½ teaspoon seasoned salt
- ¼ teaspoon coarsely ground pepper
- 1 tablespoon canola oil
- 3 medium potatoes
- 1½ cups fresh baby carrots
- 1 medium onion, sliced
- 1 can (14½ ounces) Italian diced tomatoes
- 1 jar (12 ounces) home-style beef gravy
- 1 tablespoon minced fresh parsley

1. Cut steak into six serving-size pieces; flatten to ¼-in. thickness. Rub with seasoned salt and pepper. In a large skillet, brown beef in oil on both sides; drain.
2. Cut each potato into eight wedges. In a 5-qt. slow cooker, layer the potatoes, carrots, beef and onion. Combine tomatoes and gravy; pour over the top.
3. Cover and cook on low for 5-6 hours or until meat and vegetables are tender. Sprinkle with parsley.
PER SERVING *1 serving (1 each) equals 402 cal., 6 g fat (2 g sat. fat), 67 mg chol., 822 mg sodium, 53 g carb., 5 g fiber, 33 g pro.*

ROUND STEAK ITALIANO

My mom used to make this savory dish, and it's always been one that I've enjoyed. I especially like how the thick gravy drapes over the meat.

—DEANNE STEPHENS
MCMINNVILLE, OR

PREP: 15 MIN. ● **COOK:** 7 HOURS
MAKES: 8 SERVINGS

- 2 pounds beef top round steak
- 1 can (8 ounces) tomato sauce
- 2 tablespoons onion soup mix
- 2 tablespoons canola oil
- 2 tablespoons red wine vinegar
- 1 teaspoon ground oregano
- ½ teaspoon garlic powder
- ¼ teaspoon pepper
- 8 medium potatoes (7 to 8 ounces each)
- 1 tablespoon cornstarch
- 1 tablespoon cold water

1. Cut steak into serving-size pieces; place in a 5-qt. slow cooker. In a large bowl, combine the tomato sauce, soup mix, oil, vinegar, oregano, garlic powder and pepper; pour over the meat. Scrub and pierce potatoes; place over meat. Cover and cook on low for 7 to 8 hours or until the meat and potatoes are tender.
2. Remove the meat and potatoes; keep warm. For gravy, pour cooking juices into a small saucepan; skim fat. Combine cornstarch and water until smooth; gradually stir into juices. Bring to a boil; cook and stir for 2 minutes or until thickened. Serve with meat and potatoes.
PER SERVING *1 serving equals 357 cal., 7 g fat (2 g sat. fat), 64 mg chol., 329 mg sodium, 42 g carb., 4 g fiber, 31 g pro.* **Diabetic Exchanges:** *3 lean meat, 2½ starch, ½ fat.*

CREAMY SWISS STEAK

When I was working, I would put this Swiss steak in the slow cooker before I left for the day. A creamy mushroom sauce made with canned soup nicely complements the round steak. It's so simple to make.

—GLORIA CARPENTER BANCROFT, MI

PREP: 15 MIN. ● **COOK:** 8 HOURS
MAKES: 8 SERVINGS

- ¾ cup all-purpose flour
- 1 teaspoon salt
- ½ teaspoon pepper
- 2 pounds boneless beef round steak, cut into serving-size portions
- 2 tablespoons butter
- ½ cup chopped onion
- 2 cans (10¾ ounces each) condensed cream of mushroom soup, undiluted
- 1 cup water
  Hot cooked noodles

1. In a large resealable plastic bag, combine the flour, salt and pepper. Add beef, a few pieces at a time, and shake to coat.
2. In a large skillet, brown beef in butter on both sides. Transfer to a 3-qt. slow cooker; top with onion. Combine soup and water; pour over onion. Cover and cook on low for 8-10 hours or until meat is tender. Serve with noodles.
PER SERVING *1 serving (calculated without noodles) equals 243 cal., 8 g fat (4 g sat. fat), 73 mg chol., 624 mg sodium, 13 g carb., 1 g fiber, 28 g pro.*

SIRLOIN ROAST WITH GRAVY

My husband is a big fan of this recipe. The peppery fork-tender roast combines with rich gravy to create a tasty meal.

—RITA CLARK MONUMENT, CO

PREP: 15 MIN. ● **COOK:** 5½ HOURS
MAKES: 10 SERVINGS

- 1 beef sirloin tip roast (3 pounds)
- 1 to 2 tablespoons coarsely ground pepper
- 1½ teaspoons minced garlic
- ¼ cup reduced-sodium soy sauce
- 3 tablespoons balsamic vinegar
- 1 tablespoon Worcestershire sauce
- 2 teaspoons ground mustard
- 2 tablespoons cornstarch
- ¼ cup cold water

1. Rub roast with pepper and garlic; cut in half and place in a 3-qt. slow cooker. Combine soy sauce, vinegar, Worcestershire sauce and mustard; pour over the beef. Cover and cook on low for 5½-6 hours or until meat is tender.
2. Remove roast and keep warm. Strain cooking juices into a small saucepan; skim fat. Combine the cornstarch and water until smooth; gradually stir into cooking juices. Bring to a boil; cook and stir for 2 minutes or until thickened. Serve with beef.
PER SERVING *4 ounces cooked beef with 3 tablespoons gravy equals 185 cal., 6 g fat (2 g sat. fat), 72 mg chol., 318 mg sodium, 4 g carb., trace fiber, 26 g pro.* **Diabetic Exchange:** *4 lean meat.*

SIRLOIN ROAST
WITH GRAVY

SAUCY
ITALIAN ROAST

ROSEMARY POT ROAST

Come home to a comforting, ready-to-eat entree tonight. A neighbor shared this recipe with me. It always fills the house with a wonderful aroma.

—MARCIA SCHROEDER
RIVER EDGE, NJ

PREP: 15 MIN. • **COOK:** 8 HOURS
MAKES: 2 SERVINGS

- 1 **boneless beef chuck steak (¾ inch thick and ¾ pound)**
- 1 **to 2 teaspoons canola oil**
- ¼ **cup beef broth**
- ¼ **cup tomato sauce**
- ¼ **cup dry red wine or additional beef broth**
- 2 **tablespoons chopped onion**
- 1 **garlic clove, minced**
- 1½ **teaspoons dried parsley flakes**
- ¼ **teaspoon minced fresh rosemary**
- ⅛ **teaspoon salt**
- ⅛ **teaspoon pepper**
- 1½ **teaspoons cornstarch**
- 1 **tablespoon water**

1. In a large skillet, brown beef in oil on both sides. Transfer to a 1½-qt. slow cooker. In a small bowl, combine broth, tomato sauce, wine, onion, garlic, parsley, rosemary, salt and pepper; pour over beef. Cover and cook on low for 8 hours or until meat is tender.

2. Remove beef and keep warm. In a small saucepan, combine the cornstarch and water until smooth; stir in cooking juices. Bring to a boil; cook and stir for 2 minutes or until thickened. Serve with beef.

PER SERVING *1 serving (calculated with 1 teaspoon oil) equals 354 cal., 19 g fat (7 g sat. fat), 111 mg chol., 463 mg sodium, 6 g carb., 1 g fiber, 34 g pro.* **Diabetic Exchanges:** *5 lean meat, 2 fat, 1 vegetable.*

SAUCY ITALIAN ROAST

This roast is one of my favorite set-and-forget meals. I thicken the juices with a little flour and add ketchup, then serve the sauce and beef slices over pasta.

—JAN ROAT RED LODGE, MT

PREP: 10 MIN. • **COOK:** 8 HOURS
MAKES: 10 SERVINGS

- ½ **to 1 teaspoon salt**
- ½ **teaspoon garlic powder**
- ¼ **teaspoon pepper**
- 1 **beef rump roast or bottom round roast (3 to 3½ pounds)**
- 1 **jar (4½ ounces) sliced mushrooms, drained**
- 1 **medium onion, diced**
- 1 **jar (14 ounces) spaghetti sauce**
- ¼ **to ½ cup red wine or beef broth**
  Hot cooked pasta

1. Combine the salt, garlic powder and pepper; rub over roast. Place in a 5-qt. slow cooker. Top with mushrooms and onion. Combine the spaghetti sauce and wine; pour over meat and vegetables.

2. Cover and cook on low for 8-10 hours or until the meat is tender. Slice roast; serve with pasta and pan juices.

PER SERVING *4 ounces cooked beef (calculated without pasta) equals 218 cal., 8 g fat (3 g sat. fat), 82 mg chol., 415 mg sodium, 6 g carb., 1 g fiber, 28 g pro.*

GONE-ALL-DAY STEW

My whole family will dig into this healthy, hearty stew, but it's definitely one of my husband's favorites. I always use fresh mushrooms when possible.

—**PATRICIA KILE** ELIZABETHTOWN, PA

PREP: 25 MIN. • **COOK:** 4 HOURS
MAKES: 8 SERVINGS

- ¼ cup all-purpose flour
- 2 pounds boneless beef chuck roast, trimmed and cut into 1-inch cubes
- 2 tablespoons canola oil
- 1 can (10¾ ounces) condensed tomato soup, undiluted
- 1 cup water or red wine
- 2 teaspoons beef bouillon granules
- 3 teaspoons Italian seasoning
- 1 bay leaf
- ½ teaspoon coarsely ground pepper
- 6 white onions or yellow onions, quartered
- 4 medium potatoes, cut into 1½-inch slices
- 3 medium carrots, cut into 1-inch slices
- ½ cup sliced celery
- 12 large fresh mushrooms
  Hot cooked pasta or French bread, optional

1. Place flour in a large resealable plastic bag. Add beef, a few pieces at a time, and shake to coat.

2. In a large skillet, brown meat in oil in batches; drain. Transfer to a 5-qt. slow cooker. Combine the tomato soup, water or wine, bouillon and seasonings; pour over beef. Add onions, potatoes, carrots, celery and mushrooms.

3. Cover and cook on low for 4-5 hours or until meat is tender. Discard bay leaf. If desired, serve with pasta or French bread.

PER SERVING *1 serving equals 385 cal., 15 g fat (5 g sat. fat), 74 mg chol., 416 mg sodium, 36 g carb., 5 g fiber, 27 g pro.*

GONE-ALL-DAY STEW

HERBED BEEF WITH NOODLES

Just a handful of ingredients and a sprinkling of spices go into this down-home dish. Although it's very simple, it's full of subtle and creamy flavors.

—ROSLYN HURST BELMONT, CA

PREP: 25 MIN. • **COOK:** 5 HOURS
MAKES: 8 SERVINGS

- 2 pounds beef top round steak
- ½ teaspoon salt
- ½ teaspoon pepper, divided
- 2 teaspoons canola oil
- 1 can (10¾ ounces) reduced-fat reduced-sodium condensed cream of celery soup, undiluted
- 1 medium onion, chopped
- 1 tablespoon fat-free milk
- 1 teaspoon dried oregano
- ½ teaspoon dried thyme
- 6 cups cooked wide egg noodles
  Chopped celery leaves, optional

1. Cut steak into serving-size pieces; sprinkle with salt and ¼ teaspoon pepper. In a nonstick skillet coated with cooking spray, brown meat in oil on both sides. Transfer to a 3-qt. slow cooker.
2. In a small bowl, combine the soup, onion, milk, oregano, thyme and remaining pepper. Pour over meat. Cover and cook on low for 5-6 hours or until meat is tender.
3. Serve with noodles. Sprinkle with celery leaves if desired.
PER SERVING *3 ounces cooked beef with ¾ cup noodles equals 290 cal., 7 g fat (2 g sat. fat), 92 mg chol., 334 mg sodium, 26 g carb., 2 g fiber, 30 g pro.* **Diabetic Exchanges:** *3 lean meat, 1½ starch.*

CABBAGE PATCH STEW

I like to serve steaming helpings of this stew with slices of homemade bread. For a quicker prep, substitute coleslaw mix for the chopped cabbage.

—KAREN ANN BLAND GOVE, KS

PREP: 20 MIN. • **COOK:** 6 HOURS
MAKES: 8 SERVINGS (2 QUARTS)

- 1 pound lean ground beef (90% lean)
- 1 cup chopped onions
- 2 celery ribs, chopped
- 11 cups coarsely chopped cabbage (about 2 pounds)
- 2 cans (14½ ounces each) stewed tomatoes, undrained
- 1 can (15 ounces) pinto beans, rinsed and drained
- 1 can (10 ounces) diced tomatoes with green chilies, undrained
- ½ cup ketchup
- 1 to 1½ teaspoons chili powder
- ½ teaspoon dried oregano
- ½ teaspoon pepper
- ¼ teaspoon salt
  Sour cream and shredded cheddar cheese, optional

1. In a large skillet, cook the beef, onions and celery over medium heat until the meat is no longer pink; drain.
2. Transfer to a 5-qt. slow cooker. Stir in cabbage, stewed tomatoes, beans, diced tomatoes, ketchup, chili powder, oregano, pepper and the salt. Cover and cook on low for 6-8 hours or until cabbage is tender.
3. Serve with sour cream and cheese if desired.
PER SERVING *1½ cups (calculated without salt and optional toppings) equals 214 cal., 5 g fat (2 g sat. fat), 28 mg chol., 642 mg sodium, 29 g carb., 6 g fiber, 16 g pro.* **Diabetic Exchanges:** *2 lean meat, 2 vegetable, 1 starch.*

CABBAGE PATCH STEW

SLOW COOKER BOEUF BOURGUIGNON

I've wanted to make boeuf bourguignon ever since I got one of Julia Child's cookbooks. My slow-cooked version of the popular beef stew equals the taste without the need to watch on the stovetop or in the oven.

—CRYSTAL JO BRUNS ILIFF, CO

PREP: 30 MIN. + MARINATING
COOK: 8 HOURS
MAKES: 12 SERVINGS (⅔ CUP EACH)

- 3 **pounds beef stew meat**
- 1¾ **cups dry red wine**
- 3 **tablespoons olive oil**
- 3 **tablespoons dried minced onion**
- 2 **tablespoons dried parsley flakes**
- 1 **bay leaf**
- 1 **teaspoon dried thyme**
- ¼ **teaspoon pepper**
- 8 **bacon strips, chopped**
- 1 **pound whole fresh mushrooms, quartered**
- 24 **pearl onions, peeled (about 2 cups)**
- 2 **garlic cloves, minced**
- ⅓ **cup all-purpose flour**
- 1 **teaspoon salt**
  Hot cooked whole wheat egg noodles, optional

1. Place beef in a large resealable plastic bag; add the wine, oil and seasonings. Seal bag and turn to coat. Refrigerate overnight.

2. In a large skillet, cook bacon over medium heat until crisp, stirring occasionally. Remove with a slotted spoon; drain on paper towels. Discard drippings, reserving 1 tablespoon in pan.

3. Add mushrooms and onions to drippings; cook and stir over medium-high heat until tender. Add garlic; cook 1 minute longer.

4. Drain beef, reserving marinade; transfer beef to a 4- or 5-qt. slow cooker. Sprinkle beef with flour and salt; toss to coat. Top with bacon and mushroom mixture. Add reserved marinade.

5. Cook, covered, on low for 8-10 hours or until the beef is tender. Remove the bay leaf. If desired, serve stew with noodles.

PER SERVING ⅔ *cup beef mixture (calculated without noodles) equals 289 cal., 15 g fat (5 g sat. fat), 77 mg chol., 350 mg sodium, 8 g carb., 1 g fiber, 25 g pro.* **Diabetic Exchanges:** *3 lean meat, 1½ fat, 1 vegetable.*

SLOW COOKER BOEUF BOURGUIGNON

TOP TIP

PASTA OPTIONS

Don't like whole wheat pasta? Try multigrain. It looks and tastes like white pasta, but is better for you.

SLOW-COOKED
ROUND STEAK

SLOW-COOKED ROUND STEAK

Quick and easy slow cooker recipes like this are a real plus, especially around the holidays. Serve these saucy steaks over mashed potatoes, rice or noodles.

—DONA MCPHERSON SPRING, TX

PREP: 15 MIN. • **COOK:** 7 HOURS
MAKES: 6-8 SERVINGS

- ¼ cup all-purpose flour
- ½ teaspoon salt
- ⅛ teaspoon pepper
- 2 pounds boneless beef round steak, cut into serving-size pieces
- 6 teaspoons canola oil, divided
- 1 medium onion, thinly sliced
- 1 can (10¾ ounces) condensed cream of mushroom soup, undiluted
- ½ teaspoon dried oregano
- ¼ teaspoon dried thyme

1. In a large resealable plastic bag, combine the flour, salt and pepper. Add the beef, a few pieces at a time, and shake to coat. In a large skillet, brown the meat on both sides in 4 teaspoons oil. Place in a 5-qt. slow cooker.

2. In the same skillet, saute onion in the remaining oil until lightly browned; place over beef. Combine the soup, oregano and thyme; pour over onion. Cover and cook on low for 7-8 hours or until meat is tender.

PER SERVING *1 serving equals 224 cal., 9 g fat (2 g sat. fat), 65 mg chol., 447 mg sodium, 8 g carb., 1 g fiber, 27 g pro.*

FREEZE IT
SIMPLE HUNGARIAN GOULASH

You'll love how simply this slow-cooked version of a beloved dish comes together. My son shared the recipe with me years ago.

—JACKIE KOHN DULUTH, MN

PREP: 15 MIN. • **COOK:** 8 HOURS
MAKES: 6-8 SERVINGS

- 2 pounds beef top round steak, cut into 1-inch cubes
- 1 cup chopped onion
- 2 tablespoons all-purpose flour
- 1½ teaspoons paprika
- 1 teaspoon garlic salt
- ½ teaspoon pepper
- 1 can (14½ ounces) diced tomatoes, undrained
- 1 bay leaf
- 1 cup (8 ounces) sour cream
  Hot cooked egg noodles

1. Place the beef and onion in a 3-qt. slow cooker. Combine flour, paprika, garlic salt and pepper; sprinkle over beef and stir to coat. Stir in tomatoes; add bay leaf. Cover and cook on low for 8-10 hours or until meat is tender.

2. Discard bay leaf. Just before serving, stir in sour cream; heat through. Serve with noodles.

FREEZE OPTION *Before adding sour cream, cool the stew. Freeze the stew in freezer containers. To use, partially thaw in refrigerator overnight. Heat through in a saucepan, stirring occasionally and adding a little broth if necessary. Remove from the heat; stir in the sour cream.*

PER SERVING *1 cup equals 224 cal., 8 g fat (5 g sat. fat), 83 mg chol., 339 mg sodium, 7 g carb., 1 g fiber, 27 g pro.*

SIMPLE HUNGARIAN GOULASH

SO-EASY SPAGHETTI SAUCE

Let the slow cooker do all the work for this filling spaghetti sauce. All you need to do is cook the pasta and bake up some crusty garlic bread.

—CATHY JOHNSON SOMERSET, PA

PREP: 30 MIN. • **COOK:** 5 HOURS
MAKES: ABOUT 2¼ QUARTS

- 1 **pound lean ground beef (90% lean)**
- 1 **medium onion, finely chopped**
- ¼ **cup finely chopped celery**
- 1 **can (29 ounces) tomato sauce**
- 2½ **cups tomato juice**
- 1 **can (14½ ounces) diced tomatoes, undrained**
- 1 **can (12 ounces) tomato paste**
- 2 **teaspoons sugar**
- 2 **teaspoons chili powder**
- 1 **teaspoon salt**
- 1 **teaspoon garlic powder**
- 1 **teaspoon dried basil**
- 1 **teaspoon dried oregano**
- ½ **teaspoon pepper**
- 4 **bay leaves**
  Hot cooked spaghetti
  Grated Parmesan cheese, optional

1. In a large skillet, cook the beef, onion and celery over medium heat until meat is no longer pink; drain. In a 4- or 5-qt. slow cooker, combine the tomato sauce, tomato juice, tomatoes, tomato paste, sugar, seasonings and beef mixture.

2. Cover and cook on low for 5-6 hours or until heated through. Discard bay leaves. Serve with spaghetti; sprinkle with cheese if desired.

PER SERVING *¾ cup (calculated without spaghetti and cheese) equals 125 cal., 3 g fat (1 g sat. fat), 19 mg chol., 744 mg sodium, 16 g carb., 4 g fiber, 10 g pro.* **Diabetic Exchanges:** *1 lean meat, 1 vegetable, ½ starch, ½ fat.*

SO-EASY SPAGHETTI SAUCE

HEARTY BEANS WITH BEEF

My husband raved about this sweet bean dish after tasting it at a party, so I knew I had to get the recipe. It's perfect for get-togethers because you can mix it up a day early and toss it into the slow cooker a few hours before guests arrive.

—JAN BIEHL LEESBURG, IN

PREP: 15 MIN. • **COOK:** 3 HOURS
MAKES: 8-10 SERVINGS

- 1 **pound ground beef**
- 1 **medium onion, chopped**
- 1 **can (16 ounces) baked beans, undrained**
- 1 **can (15½ ounces) butter beans, rinsed and drained**
- ½ **cup ketchup**
- ⅓ **cup packed brown sugar**
- 1 **tablespoon barbecue sauce**
- ¼ **teaspoon Worcestershire sauce**

1. In a large skillet, cook the beef and onion over medium heat until the meat is no longer pink; drain. Transfer to a 5-qt. slow cooker. Stir in the remaining ingredients.

2. Cover and cook on high for 3-4 hours or until heated through.

PER SERVING *1 serving (1 cup) equals 209 cal., 6 g fat (2 g sat. fat), 33 mg chol., 525 mg sodium, 27 g carb., 5 g fiber, 14 g pro.*

TOP TIP

CINNAMON TWIST
Want to add another flavor layer to Hearty Beans with Beef for only a few extra calories? Once finished, sprinkle a teaspoon or two of cinnamon on top.

HEARTY BEANS
WITH BEEF

SLOW-COOKED
SWISS STEAK

SLOW-COOKED SWISS STEAK

Everyone raves about how tender and rich this dish is. I make it about every two weeks during the winter! I modified my mom's Swiss steak to cook the recipe hands-free.

—**KATHIE MORRIS** REDMOND, OR

PREP: 15 MIN. • **COOK:** 8 HOURS
MAKES: 6 SERVINGS

- ¾ **cup all-purpose flour**
- 1 **teaspoon pepper**
- ¼ **teaspoon salt**
- 2 **to 2½ pounds boneless beef top round steak**
- 1 **to 2 tablespoons butter**
- 1 **can (10¾ ounces) condensed cream of mushroom soup, undiluted**
- 1⅓ **cups water**
- 1 **cup sliced celery, optional**
- ½ **cup chopped onion**
- 1 **to 3 teaspoons beef bouillon granules**
- ½ **teaspoon minced garlic**

1. In a shallow bowl, combine the flour, pepper and salt. Cut steak into six serving-size pieces; dredge in flour mixture.
2. In a large skillet, brown steak in butter. Transfer to a 3-qt. slow cooker. Combine the remaining ingredients; pour over steak. Cover and cook on low for 8-9 hours or until meat is tender.
PER SERVING *1 steak with about ½ cup gravy equals 313 cal., 9 g fat (4 g sat. fat), 92 mg chol., 666 mg sodium, 18 g carb., 2 g fiber, 37 g pro.*

FREEZE IT
CHIPOTLE SHREDDED BEEF

My slow cooker beef is irresistible when rolled up in a tortilla, burrito-style. We also like it over mashed potatoes or in buns. Leftovers make awesome quesadillas.

—**DARCY WILLIAMS** OMAHA, NE

PREP: 25 MIN. • **COOK:** 8 HOURS
MAKES: 10 SERVINGS

- 1 **teaspoon canola oil**
- 1 **small onion, chopped**
- 1 **can (28 ounces) diced tomatoes, undrained**
- ¼ **cup cider vinegar**
- ¼ **cup chopped chipotle peppers in adobo sauce plus 2 teaspoons sauce**
- 6 **garlic cloves, minced**
- 2 **tablespoons brown sugar**
- 2 **bay leaves**
- ½ **teaspoon ground cumin**
- ½ **teaspoon paprika**
- ½ **teaspoon pepper**
- ¼ **teaspoon ground cinnamon**
- 1 **boneless beef chuck roast (2½ pounds)**
- 5 **cups cooked brown rice Shredded reduced-fat cheddar cheese and reduced-fat sour cream, optional**

1. In a large skillet coated with cooking spray, heat the oil over medium-high heat. Add onion; cook and stir 2-3 minutes. Stir in tomatoes, vinegar, peppers with sauce, garlic, brown sugar, bay leaves and spices. Bring to a boil. Reduce heat; simmer, uncovered, 4-6 minutes or until thickened.
2. Place the roast in a 5-qt. slow cooker; add tomato mixture. Cook, covered, on low 8-10 hours or until meat is tender.
3. Discard bay leaves. Remove roast; cool slightly. Skim fat from cooking juices. Shred beef with two forks. Return the beef and cooking juices to slow cooker; heat through. Serve with rice. If desired, top with cheese and sour cream.
FREEZE OPTION *Freeze cooled meat mixture and juices in freezer containers. To use, partially thaw in refrigerator overnight. Heat through in a saucepan, stirring occasionally and adding a little water if necessary.*
PER SERVING *⅔ cup beef mixture with ½ cup cooked rice (calculated without optional ingredients) equals 345 cal., 13 g fat (4 g sat. fat), 74 mg chol., 194 mg sodium, 31 g carb., 3 g fiber, 26 g pro.* **Diabetic Exchanges:** *3 lean meat, 2 starch.*

CHIPOTLE SHREDDED BEEF

SLOW COOKER BEEF TOSTADAS

I dedicate these slow-simmered tostadas to my husband, the only Italian man I know who can't get enough of Mexican flavors. Pile on your best toppings.
—TERESA DEVONO RED LION, PA

PREP: 20 MIN. • **COOK:** 6 HOURS
MAKES: 6 SERVINGS

- 1 large onion, chopped
- ¼ cup lime juice
- 1 jalapeno pepper, seeded and minced
- 1 serrano pepper, seeded and minced
- 1 tablespoon chili powder
- 3 garlic cloves, minced
- ½ teaspoon ground cumin
- 1 beef top round steak (about 1½ pounds)
- 1 teaspoon salt
- ½ teaspoon pepper
- ¼ cup chopped fresh cilantro
- 12 corn tortillas (6 inches)
  Cooking spray

TOPPINGS
- 1½ cups shredded lettuce
- 1 medium tomato, finely chopped
- ¾ cup shredded sharp cheddar cheese
- ¾ cup reduced-fat sour cream, optional

1. Place the first seven ingredients in a 3- or 4-qt. slow cooker. Cut the steak in half and sprinkle with salt and pepper; add to slow cooker. Cook, covered, on low 6-8 hours or until meat is tender.

2. Remove meat; cool slightly. Shred meat with two forks. Return beef to slow cooker and stir in the cilantro; heat through. Spritz both sides of tortillas with cooking spray. Place in a single layer on baking sheets; broil 1-2 minutes on each side or until crisp. Spoon beef mixture over tortillas; top with lettuce, tomato, cheese and, if desired, sour cream.

NOTE *Wear disposable gloves when cutting hot peppers; the oils can burn skin. Avoid touching your face.*
PER SERVING *2 tostadas equals 372 cal., 13 g fat (6 g sat. fat), 88 mg chol., 602 mg sodium, 30 g carb., 5 g fiber, 35 g pro.* **Diabetic Exchanges:** *4 lean meat, 2 starch, ½ fat.*

SLOW-COOKED CARIBBEAN POT ROAST

This dish is especially good in the fall and winter, but it's definitely an all-year-round recipe.
—JENN TIDWELL FAIR OAKS, CA

PREP: 30 MIN. • **COOK:** 6 HOURS
MAKES: 10 SERVINGS

- 2 medium sweet potatoes, cubed
- 2 large carrots, sliced
- ¼ cup chopped celery
- 1 boneless beef chuck roast (2½ pounds)
- 1 tablespoon canola oil
- 1 large onion, chopped
- 2 garlic cloves, minced
- 1 tablespoon all-purpose flour
- 1 tablespoon sugar
- 1 tablespoon brown sugar
- 1 teaspoon ground cumin
- ¾ teaspoon salt
- ¾ teaspoon ground coriander
- ¾ teaspoon chili powder
- ½ teaspoon dried oregano
- ⅛ teaspoon ground cinnamon
- ¾ teaspoon grated orange peel
- ¾ teaspoon baking cocoa
- 1 can (15 ounces) tomato sauce

1. Place the potatoes, carrots and the celery in a 5-qt. slow cooker. In a large skillet, brown meat in oil. Transfer meat to slow cooker.

2. In the same skillet, saute onion in the drippings until tender. Add the garlic; cook 1 minute longer. Combine the flour, sugar, brown sugar, seasonings, orange peel and cocoa. Stir in tomato sauce; add to skillet and heat through. Pour over the beef.

3. Cover and cook on low for 6-8 hours or until beef and vegetables are tender.

PER SERVING *3 ounces cooked beef with ½ cup vegetable mixture equals 278 cal., 12 g fat (4 g sat. fat), 74 mg chol., 453 mg sodium, 16 g carb., 3 g fiber, 25 g pro.* **Diabetic Exchanges:** *3 lean meat, 1 starch, 1 vegetable, ½ fat.*

MUSHROOM STEAK

When I knew in advance I wouldn't have time for this steak to bake one night, I let it simmer all day instead.
—SANDY PETTINGER LINCOLN, NE

PREP: 20 MIN. • **COOK:** 7 HOURS
MAKES: 6 SERVINGS

- ⅓ cup all-purpose flour
- ½ teaspoon salt
- ½ teaspoon pepper, divided
- 1 beef top round steak (2 pounds), cut into 1½-inch strips
- 2 cups sliced fresh mushrooms
- 1 small onion, cut into thin wedges
- 1 can (10¾ ounces) condensed golden mushroom soup, undiluted
- ¼ cup sherry or beef broth
- ½ teaspoon dried oregano
- ¼ teaspoon dried thyme
  Hot cooked egg noodles

1. In a large resealable plastic bag, combine flour, salt and ¼ teaspoon pepper. Add beef, a few pieces at a time, and shake to coat.

2. In a 3-qt. slow cooker, combine the mushrooms, onion and beef. Combine the soup, sherry, oregano, thyme and remaining pepper; pour over top. Cover and cook on low for 7-9 hours or until beef is tender. Serve with noodles.

PER SERVING *¾ cup (calculated without noodles) equals 265 cal., 6 g fat (2 g sat. fat), 87 mg chol., 612 mg sodium, 12 g carb., 1 g fiber, 36 g pro.* **Diabetic Exchanges:** *5 lean meat, 1 starch.*

SLOW COOKER
BEEF TOSTADAS

APPLE AND ONION BEEF POT ROAST

reduced to 2 cups, about 15 minutes. Combine cornstarch and cold water until smooth; stir in the browning sauce. Stir into cooking liquid. Bring to a boil; cook and stir for 2 minutes or until thickened. Serve with beef and onion.

PER SERVING *1 serving (3 ounces cooked beef with 3 tablespoons gravy) equals 173 cal., 6 g fat (2 g sat. fat), 69 mg chol., 262 mg sodium, 4 g carb., trace fiber, 25 g pro.* **Diabetic Exchanges:** *3 lean meat.*

BEEF BURGUNDY

I trim the meat, cut up the veggies and store them separately the night before. The next day, I toss all the ingredients into the slow cooker. Shortly before dinnertime, I cook the noodles and sometimes bake some cheesy garlic toast.

—MARY JO MILLER MANSFIELD, OH

PREP: 10 MIN. • **COOK:** 5 HOURS
MAKES: 6 SERVINGS

- 1½ **pounds beef stew meat, cut into 1-inch cubes**
- ½ **pound whole fresh mushrooms, halved**
- 4 **medium carrots, chopped**
- 1 **can (10¾ ounces) condensed golden mushroom soup, undiluted**
- 1 **large onion, cut into thin wedges**
- ½ **cup Burgundy wine or beef broth**
- ¼ **cup quick-cooking tapioca**
- ½ **teaspoon salt**
- ¼ **teaspoon dried thyme**
- ¼ **teaspoon pepper**
  Hot cooked egg noodles

1. In a 5-qt. slow cooker, combine the first 10 ingredients.
2. Cover and cook on low for 5-6 hours or until meat is tender. Serve with noodles.

PER SERVING *1 cup (calculated without noodles) equals 273 cal., 9 g fat (3 g sat. fat), 73 mg chol., 642 mg sodium, 19 g carb., 3 g fiber, 24 g pro.*

APPLE AND ONION BEEF POT ROAST

I thicken the cooking juices from this roast to make an apple gravy that's wonderful over the beef and onions.
—RACHEL KOISTINEN HAYTI, SD

PREP: 30 MIN.
COOK: 5 HOURS + STANDING
MAKES: 8 SERVINGS WITH LEFTOVERS

- 1 **beef sirloin tip roast (3 pounds), cut in half**
- 1 **cup water**
- 1 **teaspoon seasoned salt**
- ½ **teaspoon reduced-sodium soy sauce**
- ½ **teaspoon Worcestershire sauce**
- ¼ **teaspoon garlic powder**
- 1 **large tart apple, quartered**
- 1 **large onion, sliced**
- 2 **tablespoons cornstarch**
- 2 **tablespoons cold water**
- ⅛ **teaspoon browning sauce**

1. In a large nonstick skillet coated with cooking spray, brown roast on all sides. Transfer to a 5-qt. slow cooker. Add water to skillet, stirring to loosen any browned bits; pour over roast. Sprinkle with seasoned salt, soy sauce, Worcestershire sauce and garlic powder. Top with apple and onion.
2. Cover and cook on low for 5-6 hours or until meat is tender.
3. Remove roast and onion; let stand for 15 minutes before slicing. Strain the cooking liquid into a saucepan, discarding the apple. Bring liquid to a boil; cook until

TRADITIONAL BEEF STEW

The aroma of this classic beef stew is irresistible, making it impossible not to dig in almost immediately the moment after you walk in the door.

—**ROSANA PAPE** HAMILTON, IN

PREP: 15 MIN. • **COOK:** 8 HOURS
MAKES: 4 SERVINGS

- 1 **pound beef stew meat, cut into 1-inch cubes**
- 1 **pound fresh baby carrots**
- 2 **medium potatoes, cut into chunks**
- 2 **medium onions, cut into wedges**
- 1 **cup drained diced tomatoes**
- 1 **cup beef broth**
- 1 **celery rib, cut into ½-inch pieces**
- 2 **tablespoons quick-cooking tapioca**
- 1 **teaspoon Worcestershire sauce**
- ¼ **teaspoon salt**
- ¼ **teaspoon pepper**

1. In a 3-qt. slow cooker, combine all ingredients.

2. Cover and cook on low for 8-10 hours or until meat and vegetables are tender.

PER SERVING *1½ cups equals 334 cal., 8 g fat (3 g sat. fat), 70 mg chol., 611 mg sodium, 39 g carb., 6 g fiber, 26 g pro.* **Diabetic Exchanges:** *3 lean meat, 2 starch, 2 vegetable.*

TRADITIONAL BEEF STEW

SWEET 'N' TANGY
POT ROAST

SWEET 'N' TANGY POT ROAST

I fixed this roast the first time I cooked for my future husband more than 20 years ago. For the dessert, I made chocolate pudding spooned over marshmallows. He was absolutely impressed!

—CAROL MULLIGAN HONEOYE FALLS, NY

PREP: 10 MIN. • **COOK:** 9½ HOURS
MAKES: 8 SERVINGS

- 1 boneless beef chuck roast (3 pounds)
- ½ teaspoon salt
- ½ teaspoon pepper
- 1 cup water
- 1 cup ketchup
- ¼ cup red wine or beef broth
- 1 envelope brown gravy mix
- 2 teaspoons Dijon mustard
- 1 teaspoon Worcestershire sauce
- ⅛ teaspoon garlic powder
- 3 tablespoons cornstarch
- ¼ cup cold water

1. Cut the meat in half and place in a 5-qt. slow cooker. Sprinkle with salt and pepper. In a bowl, combine the water, ketchup, wine or broth, gravy mix, mustard, Worcestershire sauce and garlic powder; pour over the meat.
2. Cover and cook on low for 9-10 hours or until meat is tender.
3. Combine cornstarch and cold water until smooth. Stir into slow cooker. Cover and cook on high for 30 minutes or until gravy is thickened. Remove meat from slow cooker. Slice and serve with gravy.
PER SERVING *1 serving (3 ounces cooked beef with ½ cup gravy) equals 249 cal., 8 g fat (3 g sat. fat), 89 mg chol., 748 mg sodium, 13 g carb., 1 g fiber, 30 g pro.*

ITALIAN BEEF SANDWICHES

It takes very little effort to make these delicious sandwiches. Just set it and forget it for 8 hours!

—CHER SCHWARTZ ELLISVILLE, MO

PREP: 20 MIN. • **COOK:** 8 HOURS
MAKES: 12 SERVINGS

- 1 beef rump roast or bottom round roast (3 pounds)
- 3 cups reduced-sodium beef broth
- 1 envelope Italian salad dressing mix
- 1 teaspoon garlic powder
- 1 teaspoon onion powder
- 1 teaspoon dried parsley flakes
- 1 teaspoon dried basil
- 1 teaspoon dried oregano
- 1 teaspoon pepper
- 1 large onion, julienned
- 1 large green pepper, julienned
- 4½ teaspoons olive oil
- 12 hamburger buns, split
- 12 slices reduced-fat provolone cheese

1. Cut the roast in half; place in a 4-qt. slow cooker. Combine the broth, dressing mix and seasonings; pour over meat. Cover and cook on low for 8 hours or until tender.
2. Remove roast; cool slightly. Skim fat from cooking juices; reserve 1 cup juices. Shred the beef and return to slow cooker. Stir in reserved cooking juices; heat through.
3. Meanwhile, in a large skillet, saute onion and green pepper in oil until tender.
4. Using a slotted spoon, place beef on bun bottoms; layer with cheese and vegetables. Replace bun tops.
PER SERVING *1 sandwich equals 346 cal., 12 g fat (5 g sat. fat), 79 mg chol., 707 mg sodium, 25 g carb., 2 g fiber, 32 g pro.* **Diabetic Exchanges:** *4 lean meat, 1½ starch, 1 fat.*

FLAVORFUL BEEF STEW

One way to enjoy the thick gravy in this stew? Dunk a slice of bread in it! I find it much easier to prepare the stew in the slow cooker than on the stove or in the oven.

—JACKITT TASTEOFHOME.COM

PREP: 25 MIN. • **COOK:** 6 HOURS
MAKES: 6 SERVINGS

- ½ pound medium fresh mushrooms, quartered
- 2 medium red potatoes, cubed
- 3 medium carrots, sliced
- 1 medium onion, chopped
- 1 celery rib, thinly sliced
- ¼ cup all-purpose flour
- 1 tablespoon paprika
- ¾ teaspoon salt
- ¼ teaspoon pepper
- 1 pound beef stew meat
- 1 can (14½ ounces) beef broth
- 4½ teaspoons reduced-sodium teriyaki sauce
- 2 garlic cloves, minced
- 1 bay leaf

1. Place mushrooms, potatoes, carrots, onion and celery in a 3-qt. slow cooker. In a large resealable plastic bag, combine flour, paprika, salt and pepper. Add beef, a few pieces at a time, and shake to coat. Add to slow cooker.
2. Combine the broth, teriyaki sauce, garlic and bay leaf; pour over beef. Cover and cook on low for 6-8 hours or until meat and vegetables are tender. Discard bay leaf.
PER SERVING *1 cup equals 202 cal., 6 g fat (2 g sat. fat), 47 mg chol., 745 mg sodium, 19 g carb., 3 g fiber, 19 g pro.* **Diabetic Exchanges:** *2 lean meat, 1 starch, 1 vegetable.*

TENDER
SALSA BEEF

TENDER SALSA BEEF

This is my Mexican-style twist on comfort food. To keep it kid-friendly, use mild salsa.

—STACIE STAMPER NORTH WILKESBORO, NC

PREP: 15 MIN. • **COOK:** 8 HOURS
MAKES: 8 SERVINGS

- 1½ **pounds beef stew meat, cut into ¾-inch cubes**
- 2 **cups salsa**
- 1 **tablespoon brown sugar**
- 1 **tablespoon reduced-sodium soy sauce**
- 1 **garlic clove, minced**
- 4 **cups hot cooked brown rice**

In a 3-qt. slow cooker, combine the beef, salsa, brown sugar, soy sauce and garlic. Cover and cook on low for 8-10 hours or until the meat is tender. Using a slotted spoon, serve beef with rice.

FREEZE OPTION *Freeze individual portions of cooled stew in freezer containers. To use, partially thaw in refrigerator overnight. Heat through in a saucepan, stirring occasionally and adding water if necessary.*

PER SERVING *½ cup beef mixture with ½ cup rice equals 259 cal., 7 g fat (2 g sat. fat), 53 mg chol., 356 mg sodium, 28 g carb., 2 g fiber, 19 g pro.* **Diabetic Exchanges:** *2 starch, 2 lean meat.*

SUNDAY DINNER
BRISKET

SUNDAY DINNER BRISKET

We loved how tender this brisket turned out. The sauce has a robust taste with a slight tang from the balsamic vinegar, and caramelized onions complete the dish.

—*TASTE OF HOME* TEST KITCHEN

PREP: 45 MIN. • **COOK:** 8 HOURS
MAKES: 10 SERVINGS

- 3 tablespoons olive oil, divided
- 4 cups sliced onions (about 4 medium)
- 4 garlic cloves, minced
- 1 tablespoon brown sugar
- 1 fresh beef brisket (4 to 5 pounds)
- ⅓ cup all-purpose flour
- 1 teaspoon salt
- 1 teaspoon coarsely ground pepper
- ¼ cup balsamic vinegar
- 1 can (14½ ounces) reduced-sodium beef broth
- 2 tablespoons tomato paste
- 2 teaspoons Italian seasoning
- 1 teaspoon Worcestershire sauce
- ½ teaspoon paprika
- 1 tablespoon cornstarch
- 2 tablespoons cold water

1. In a skillet, heat 1 tablespoon oil over medium heat. Add the onions; cook and stir until softened. Sprinkle with the garlic and brown sugar. Reduce heat to medium-low; cook 10 minutes or until onions are golden brown, stirring occasionally. Transfer to an oval 6-qt. slow cooker.

2. If necessary to fit in the skillet, cut brisket in half. Sprinkle the brisket with flour and shake off excess. In skillet, heat remaining oil over medium heat. Brown both sides of brisket; sprinkle with salt and pepper. Place in slow cooker over onions.

3. Add vinegar to skillet; increase heat to medium-high. Cook, stirring to loosen browned bits from pan. Stir in broth, tomato paste, Italian seasoning, Worcestershire sauce and paprika until blended. Pour over brisket. Cook, covered, on low 8-10 hours or until meat is tender.

4. Remove brisket; keep warm. Transfer the cooking juices to a saucepan; skim fat and bring to a boil. In a small bowl, mix cornstarch and water until smooth; stir into cooking juices. Return to a boil; cook and stir 1-2 minutes or until thickened.

5. Cut brisket diagonally across the grain into thin slices. Serve with sauce.

NOTE *This is a fresh beef brisket, not corned beef.*

PER SERVING *5 ounces cooked beef with ⅓ cup sauce equals 319 cal., 12 g fat (4 g sat. fat), 78 mg chol., 381 mg sodium, 12 g carb., 1 g fiber, 39 g pro.* **Diabetic Exchanges:** *5 lean meat, 1 starch, 1 fat.*

TEXAS BEEF BARBECUE

We love these sandwiches! The beef simmers for hours in a slightly sweet sauce with plenty of spices.

—**JENNIFER BAUER** LANSING, MI

PREP: 15 MIN. • **COOK:** 8 HOURS
MAKES: 16 SERVINGS

- 1 beef sirloin tip roast (4 pounds)
- 1 can (5½ ounces) spicy hot V8 juice
- ½ cup water
- ¼ cup white vinegar
- ¼ cup ketchup
- 2 tablespoons Worcestershire sauce
- ½ cup packed brown sugar
- 1 teaspoon salt
- 1 teaspoon ground mustard
- 1 teaspoon paprika
- ¼ teaspoon chili powder
- ⅛ teaspoon pepper
- 16 kaiser rolls, split

1. Cut the roast in half; place in a 5-qt. slow cooker. Combine the V8 juice, water, vinegar, ketchup, Worcestershire sauce, brown sugar and seasonings; pour over roast. Cover and cook on low for 8-10 hours or until meat is tender.

2. Remove meat and shred with two forks; return to slow cooker and heat through. Spoon ½ cup meat mixture onto each roll.

PER SERVING *1 sandwich equals 339 cal., 8 g fat (2 g sat. fat), 60 mg chol., 606 mg sodium, 39 g carb., 1 g fiber, 27 g pro.* **Diabetic Exchanges:** *3 lean meat, 2½ starch.*

ITALIAN CHICKEN
CHARDONNAY, PAGE 105

CHICKEN & TURKEY

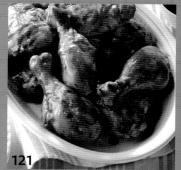

121

116

130

LEMON CHICKEN BREASTS

Dijon mustard, rosemary and lemon juice season the chicken breasts wonderfully in this fuss-free recipe. For an elegant finish, sprinkle on toasted almonds and fresh parsley.
—**KATHY EVANS** LACEY, WA

PREP: 20 MIN. • **COOK:** 4 HOURS
MAKES: 6 SERVINGS

- 6 boneless skinless chicken breast halves (5 ounces each)
- 1 cup chicken broth, divided
- ¼ cup lemon juice
- 3 tablespoons Dijon mustard
- 3 garlic cloves, minced
- 2 tablespoons butter, melted
- ¼ teaspoon dried rosemary, crushed
- 3 tablespoons cornstarch Hot cooked rice
- ½ cup slivered almonds, toasted
- 3 tablespoons minced fresh parsley

1. Place chicken in a 3-qt. slow cooker. In a small bowl, combine ¾ cup broth, lemon juice, mustard, garlic, butter and dried rosemary; pour over chicken. Cover and cook on low for 4-5 hours or until a thermometer reads 170°. Remove chicken; keep warm.
2. Skim fat from cooking juices; transfer to a small saucepan. Bring liquid to a boil. Combine cornstarch and remaining broth until smooth. Gradually stir into the pan. Bring to a boil; cook and stir for 2 minutes or until thickened.
3. Serve the chicken with rice and sauce. Sprinkle with the almonds and parsley.
PER SERVING *1 chicken breast half with ⅓ cup sauce equals 268 cal., 12 g fat (4 g sat. fat), 89 mg chol., 440 mg sodium, 9 g carb., 1 g fiber, 31 g pro.* **Diabetic Exchanges:** *4 lean meat, 2 fat, ½ starch.*

SWEET 'N' SOUR CURRY CHICKEN

A little mango chutney goes a long way in adding a zesty twist to this chicken. I also add some curry powder to give the dish flair.
—**CAROL CONRAD** EDMONTON, AB

PREP: 15 MIN. • **COOK:** 4½ HOURS
MAKES: 4 SERVINGS

- 1 pound boneless skinless chicken breasts, cut into 1-inch pieces
- 1 can (14½ ounces) stewed tomatoes, cut up
- 1 large green pepper, cut into 1-inch pieces
- 1 large onion, sliced
- ½ cup mango chutney
- 1½ teaspoons curry powder
- 2 tablespoons cornstarch
- ¼ cup cold water

1. In a 3-qt. slow cooker, combine chicken, tomatoes, green pepper, onion, chutney and curry powder. Cover and cook on low for 4-5 hours or until chicken is no longer pink.
2. Combine the cornstarch and water until smooth; stir into slow cooker. Cover and cook on high for 30 minutes or until thickened.
PER SERVING *1½ cups equals 314 cal., 3 g fat (1 g sat. fat), 63 mg chol., 583 mg sodium, 46 g carb., 3 g fiber, 25 g pro.*

LEMON CHICKEN BREASTS

SWEET 'N' SOUR
CURRY CHICKEN

CARIBBEAN
CHICKEN STEW

CARIBBEAN CHICKEN STEW

I lived with a family from the West Indies for a while and learned a lot from spending time in the kitchen with them. I lightened up this recipe by leaving out the oil and sugar, removing the skin from the chicken and using chicken sausage in place of pork.

—**JOANNE IOVINO** KINGS PARK, NY

PREP: 25 MIN. + MARINATING
COOK: 6 HOURS • **MAKES:** 8 SERVINGS

- ¼ cup ketchup
- 3 garlic cloves, minced
- 1 tablespoon sugar
- 1 tablespoon hot pepper sauce
- 1 teaspoon browning sauce, optional
- 1 teaspoon dried basil
- 1 teaspoon dried thyme
- 1 teaspoon paprika
- ½ teaspoon salt
- ½ teaspoon dried oregano
- ½ teaspoon ground allspice
- ½ teaspoon pepper
- 8 bone-in chicken thighs (about 3 pounds), skin removed
- 1 pound fully cooked andouille chicken sausage links, sliced
- 1 medium onion, finely chopped
- 2 medium carrots, finely chopped
- 2 celery ribs, finely chopped

1. In a large resealable plastic bag, combine ketchup, garlic, sugar, hot pepper sauce and, if desired, browning sauce; stir in seasonings. Add the chicken thighs, sausage and vegetables. Seal bag and turn to coat. Refrigerate 8 hours or overnight.

2. Transfer contents of bag to a 4- or 5-qt. slow cooker. Cook, covered, on low 6-8 hours or until chicken is tender.

PER SERVING *1 serving equals 309 cal., 14 g fat (4 g sat. fat), 131 mg chol., 666 mg sodium, 9 g carb., 1 g fiber, 35 g pro.* **Diabetic Exchanges:** *5 lean meat, ½ starch.*

ITALIAN CHICKEN CHARDONNAY

One day I needed to have dinner ready as soon as we walked in the door. So I altered a skillet dish that my family likes into this delicious slow cooker meal. It's perfect for just about any occasion.

—JUDY ARMSTRONG PRAIRIEVILLE, LA

PREP: 20 MIN. • **COOK:** 5 HOURS
MAKES: 6 SERVINGS

- 2 teaspoons paprika
- 1 teaspoon salt
- 1 teaspoon pepper
- ¼ teaspoon cayenne pepper
- 3 pounds bone-in chicken breast halves, skin removed
- ½ pound baby portobello mushrooms, quartered
- 1 medium sweet red pepper, chopped
- 1 medium onion, chopped
- 1 can (14 ounces) water-packed artichoke hearts, rinsed and drained
- 1½ cups chardonnay
- 1 can (6 ounces) tomato paste
- 3 garlic cloves, minced
- 2 tablespoons minced fresh thyme or 2 teaspoons dried thyme
- ¼ cup minced fresh parsley
  Hot cooked pasta
  Shredded Romano cheese

1. Combine the paprika, salt, pepper and cayenne; sprinkle over chicken. Place the chicken, mushrooms, red pepper, onion and artichokes in a 5-qt. slow cooker. In a small bowl, combine the chardonnay, tomato paste, garlic and thyme; pour over vegetables.

2. Cover and cook on low for 5-6 hours or until chicken is tender. Stir in parsley. Serve with pasta; sprinkle with cheese.

PER SERVING *1 serving (calculated without pasta and cheese) equals 282 cal., 5 g fat (2 g sat. fat), 103 mg chol., 550 mg sodium, 16 g carb., 5 g fiber, 43 g pro.* **Diabetic Exchanges:** *5 lean meat, 3 vegetable.*

ITALIAN CHICKEN CHARDONNAY

MOIST & TENDER
TURKEY BREAST

(5) INGREDIENTS
MOIST & TENDER TURKEY BREAST

The first time I slow-cooked turkey was on vacation. It simmered while we were out, and we came back to a spectacularly juicy finished meal.

—**HEIDI VAWDREY** RIVERTON, UT

PREP: 10 MIN. • **COOK:** 4 HOURS
MAKES: 12 SERVINGS

- 1 **bone-in turkey breast (6 to 7 pounds)**
- 4 **fresh rosemary sprigs**
- 4 **garlic cloves, peeled**
- ½ **cup water**
- 1 **tablespoon brown sugar**
- ½ **teaspoon coarsely ground pepper**
- ¼ **teaspoon salt**

Place turkey breast, rosemary, garlic and water in a 6-qt. slow cooker. Mix the brown sugar, pepper and salt; sprinkle over turkey. Cook, covered, on low 4-6 hours or until turkey is tender and a thermometer inserted in turkey reads at least 170°.

PER SERVING *5 ounces cooked turkey equals 318 cal., 12 g fat (3 g sat. fat), 122 mg chol., 154 mg sodium, 2 g carb., trace fiber, 47 g pro.*

TOP TIP
PEEL IN A FLASH
To quickly peel fresh garlic, gently crush the clove with the flat side of a large knife blade to loosen the peel. If you don't have a large knife, you can crush the garlic with a small can.

TANGY TROPICAL CHICKEN

Pineapple and mango complement the chicken beautifully in this colorful dish. They lend a pleasant hint of sweetness that's balanced by the salty zip of soy sauce.

—**CHRISTINA AHO** NAPLES, FL

PREP: 20 MIN. • **COOK:** 4 HOURS
MAKES: 4 SERVINGS

- 1 **pound boneless skinless chicken breasts, cut into 1-inch strips**
- 2 **cups chopped peeled mangoes**
- 1 **medium onion, chopped**
- 1 **medium green pepper, sliced**
- 1 **garlic clove, minced**
- 1 **cup unsweetened pineapple juice**
- 1 **cup orange juice**
- ¼ **cup reduced-sodium soy sauce**
- 2 **tablespoons Thai chili sauce**
- ¼ **teaspoon pepper**
- 2 **tablespoons cornstarch**
- 2 **tablespoons cold water**
  Hot cooked rice

1. Place chicken in a 3-qt. slow cooker. Top with mangoes, onion, green pepper and garlic. In a small bowl, combine the pineapple juice, orange juice, soy sauce, chili sauce and pepper; pour over the chicken. Cover and cook on low for 4-5 hours or until chicken is tender.
2. Remove the chicken mixture to a serving platter; keep warm. Transfer cooking juices to a small saucepan. Bring juices to a boil. Combine cornstarch and water until smooth; gradually stir into the pan. Bring to a boil; cook and stir for 2 minutes or until thickened. Serve with chicken mixture and rice.

PER SERVING *1 cup (calculated without rice) equals 299 cal., 3 g fat (1 g sat. fat), 63 mg chol., 760 mg sodium, 42 g carb., 3 g fiber, 26 g pro.*

TANGY ORANGE CHICKEN THIGHS

It takes only 20 minutes to get this recipe ready. You can easily double or triple the ingredients, depending on the size of your slow cooker and expected crowd.
—**DAHLIA ABRAMS** DETROIT, MI

PREP: 20 MIN. • **COOK:** 5 HOURS
MAKES: 8 SERVINGS

- 2 cups sliced fresh carrots
- 1 can (14½ ounces) diced tomatoes, undrained
- 1 medium onion, chopped
- 1 can (6 ounces) tomato paste
- ½ cup orange juice
- 2 garlic cloves, minced
- 2 teaspoons dried basil
- 1½ teaspoons sugar
- ½ teaspoon dried oregano
- ½ teaspoon dried thyme
- ½ teaspoon dried rosemary, crushed
- ½ teaspoon pepper
- 2 teaspoons grated orange peel, divided
- 8 boneless skinless chicken thighs (about 2 pounds)
- 2 tablespoons lemon juice
- 4 bacon strips, cooked and crumbled

1. In a 3-qt. slow cooker, combine the first 12 ingredients. Stir in 1 teaspoon orange peel. Add the chicken; spoon sauce over top. Cover and cook on low for 5-6 hours or until chicken is tender.
2. Remove to a serving platter. Stir lemon juice and remaining orange peel into sauce; pour over chicken. Sprinkle with bacon.
PER SERVING *1 chicken thigh with ½ cup sauce equals 248 cal., 10 g fat (3 g sat. fat), 80 mg chol., 236 mg sodium, 15 g carb., 3 g fiber, 25 g pro.* **Diabetic Exchanges:** *3 lean meat, 1 starch.*

CHICKEN WITH BEANS AND POTATOES

This all-in-one entree is ideal for when you know your day is going to be busy. The onion soup mix and veggies give the broth lots of flavor.
—**TASTE OF HOME** TEST KITCHEN

PREP: 20 MIN. • **COOK:** 4 HOURS
MAKES: 10 SERVINGS

- 2 pounds boneless skinless chicken breasts, cut into 1-inch cubes
- ½ teaspoon lemon-pepper seasoning
- 1 tablespoon canola oil
- 1 pound fresh green beans, trimmed
- 1 pound small red potatoes, quartered
- ½ pound medium fresh mushrooms, halved
- ½ cup thinly sliced sweet onion
- 2 cans (14½ ounces each) chicken broth
- 2 tablespoons onion soup mix
- 2 teaspoons Worcestershire sauce
- 1 teaspoon grated lemon peel
- ½ teaspoon salt
- ½ teaspoon pepper
- ¼ teaspoon garlic powder

1. Sprinkle chicken with lemon-pepper. In a large skillet, saute chicken in oil over medium heat for 4-5 minutes or until lightly browned.
2. In a 5- or 6-qt. slow cooker, layer the green beans, potatoes, mushrooms and onion. In a small bowl, combine the remaining ingredients; pour over vegetables. Top with chicken.
3. Cover and cook on low for 4-5 hours or until vegetables are tender. Serve with a slotted spoon.
PER SERVING *1¼ cups equals 209 cal., 5 g fat (1 g sat. fat), 63 mg chol., 324 mg sodium, 15 g carb., 3 g fiber, 26 g pro.* **Diabetic Exchanges:** *3 lean meat, 1 vegetable, ½ starch.*

FREEZE IT
SLOW-COOKED SOUTHWEST CHICKEN

This savory low-fat chicken gets even more delicious with a garnish of reduced-fat sour cream and some fresh cilantro. With just 15 minutes of prep to this dish, you'll be out of the kitchen in no time.
—**BRANDI CASTILLO** SANTA MARIA, CA

PREP: 15 MIN. • **COOK:** 6 HOURS
MAKES: 6 SERVINGS

- 2 cans (15 ounces each) black beans, rinsed and drained
- 1 can (14½ ounces) reduced-sodium chicken broth
- 1 can (14½ ounces) diced tomatoes with mild green chilies, undrained
- ½ pound boneless skinless chicken breast
- 1 jar (8 ounces) chunky salsa
- 1 cup frozen corn
- 1 tablespoon dried parsley flakes
- 1 teaspoon ground cumin
- ¼ teaspoon pepper
- 3 cups hot cooked rice

1. In a 2- or 3-qt. slow cooker, combine beans, broth, tomatoes, chicken, salsa, corn and seasonings. Cover and cook on low for 6-8 hours or until a thermometer reads 170°.
2. Shred chicken with two forks and return to the slow cooker; heat through. Serve with rice.
FREEZE OPTION *After shredding chicken, freeze cooled mixture in freezer containers. To use, partially thaw in refrigerator overnight. Heat the mixture through in a saucepan, stirring occasionally and adding a little broth or water if necessary.*
PER SERVING *1 cup chicken mixture with ½ cup rice equals 320 cal., 1 g fat (trace sat. fat), 21 mg chol., 873 mg sodium, 56 g carb., 8 g fiber, 19 g pro.*

TANGY ORANGE CHICKEN THIGHS

CHICKEN WITH BEANS AND POTATOES

SLOW-COOKED SOUTHWEST CHICKEN

CINCINNATI-STYLE
CHILI

CINCINNATI-STYLE CHILI

My husband had this type of chili when visiting a friend in Ohio and he was super thrilled when I made it at home. We like to plate it with spaghetti, cheese, onions and kidney beans.

—**TARI AMBLER** SHOREWOOD, IL

PREP: 35 MIN. • **COOK:** 6 HOURS
MAKES: 10 SERVINGS

- 2 **pounds extra-lean ground turkey**
- 2 **medium onions, finely chopped**
- 4 **garlic cloves, minced**
- 2 **cans (8 ounces each) no-salt-added tomato sauce**
- 1 **can (14½ ounces) reduced-sodium beef broth**
- 2 **tablespoons cider vinegar**
- ½ **ounce unsweetened chocolate, chopped**
- 3 **tablespoons chili powder**
- 1 **bay leaf**
- 2 **teaspoons Worcestershire sauce**
- 1 **teaspoon ground cumin**
- ¾ **teaspoon salt**
- ¾ **teaspoon ground cinnamon**
- ¼ **teaspoon ground allspice**
- ⅛ **teaspoon ground cloves**
- ⅛ **teaspoon cayenne pepper**
- 1 **package (16 ounces) whole wheat spaghetti**

TOPPINGS

- 1 **can (16 ounces) kidney beans, rinsed and drained**
- 1¼ **cups (5 ounces) shredded reduced-fat cheddar cheese**
- 1 **medium onion, chopped**

1. In a nonstick Dutch oven coated with cooking spray, cook turkey, onions and garlic until the turkey is no longer pink. Transfer to a 3-qt. slow cooker.
2. In a large bowl, combine tomato sauce, broth, vinegar, chocolate and seasonings; pour over turkey mixture. Cook, covered, on low 6-8 hours.

3. Cook the spaghetti according to package directions; drain. Remove the bay leaf from chili. For each serving, place ¾ cup spaghetti in a bowl. Top with about ⅔ cup chili, 3 tablespoons kidney beans, 2 tablespoons cheese and 1 tablespoon chopped onion.
PER SERVING *1 serving equals 388 cal., 6 g fat (3 g sat. fat), 47 mg chol., 523 mg sodium, 52 g carb., 10 g fiber, 37 g pro.*

TURKEY SLOPPY JOES

These tangy sandwiches go over well at gatherings large and small. I frequently take them to potlucks, and I'm always asked if there's a secret ingredient.

—**MARYLOU LARUE** FREELAND, MI

PREP: 15 MIN. • **COOK:** 4 HOURS
MAKES: 8 SERVINGS

- 1 **pound lean ground turkey**
- 1 **small onion, chopped**
- ½ **cup chopped celery**
- ¼ **cup chopped green pepper**
- 1 **can (10¾ ounces) reduced-sodium condensed tomato soup, undiluted**
- ½ **cup ketchup**
- 2 **tablespoons prepared mustard**
- 1 **tablespoon brown sugar**
- ¼ **teaspoon pepper**
- 8 **hamburger buns, split**

1. In a large skillet coated with cooking spray, cook the turkey, onion, celery and green pepper over medium heat until the meat is no longer pink; drain. Stir in the soup, ketchup, mustard, brown sugar and pepper.
2. Transfer to a 3-qt. slow cooker. Cover and cook on low for 4 hours. Serve on buns.
PER SERVING *1 serving equals 247 cal., 7 g fat (2 g sat. fat), 45 mg chol., 553 mg sodium, 32 g carb., 2 g fiber, 14 g pro.* **Diabetic Exchanges:** *2 starch, 1½ lean meat.*

ITALIAN SAUSAGE AND VEGETABLES

A complete meal in a pot is even better when it's also healthy and delicious! I found this recipe in a magazine and then made a few adjustments. I usually serve it with hot garlic bread.

—**GINNY STUBY** ALTOONA, PA

PREP: 20 MIN. • **COOK:** 5½ HOURS
MAKES: 6 SERVINGS

- 1¼ **pounds sweet or hot Italian turkey sausage links**
- 1 **can (28 ounces) diced tomatoes, undrained**
- 2 **medium potatoes, cut into 1-inch pieces**
- 4 **small zucchini, cut into 1-inch slices**
- 1 **medium onion, cut into wedges**
- ½ **teaspoon garlic powder**
- ¼ **teaspoon crushed red pepper flakes**
- ¼ **teaspoon dried oregano**
- ¼ **teaspoon dried basil**
- 1 **tablespoon dry bread crumbs**
- ¾ **cup shredded pepper jack cheese**

1. In a nonstick skillet, brown sausages over medium heat. Place in a 5-qt. slow cooker. Add the vegetables and seasonings. Cover and cook on low for 5½-6½ hours or until a thermometer reads 165°.
2. Remove sausages and cut into 1-in. pieces; return to slow cooker. Stir in bread crumbs. Serve in bowls; sprinkle with cheese.
PER SERVING *1 serving equals 304 cal., 13 g fat (4 g sat. fat), 71 mg chol., 838 mg sodium, 26 g carb., 5 g fiber, 22 g pro.*

CURRY
CHICKEN

SLOW-COOKED LEMON CHICKEN

A hint of lemon and fresh parsley brighten up everyday chicken. This is the perfect midwinter recipe for when you need a taste of spring.

—**WALTER POWELL** WILMINGTON, DE

PREP: 20 MIN. • **COOK:** 5¼ HOURS
MAKES: 6 SERVINGS

- 6 **bone-in chicken breast halves (12 ounces each), skin removed**
- 1 **teaspoon dried oregano**
- ½ **teaspoon seasoned salt**
- ¼ **teaspoon pepper**
- 2 **tablespoons butter**
- ¼ **cup water**
- 3 **tablespoons lemon juice**
- 2 **garlic cloves, minced**
- 1 **teaspoon chicken bouillon granules**
- 2 **teaspoons minced fresh parsley**
  Hot cooked rice

1. Pat chicken dry with paper towels. Combine the oregano, seasoned salt and pepper; rub over chicken. In a skillet over medium heat, brown the chicken in butter; transfer to a 5-qt. slow cooker. Add the water, lemon juice, garlic and bouillon to the skillet; bring to a boil, stirring to loosen browned bits. Pour over chicken.

2. Cover and cook on low for 5-6 hours. Baste chicken with cooking juices. Add parsley. Cover and cook 15-30 minutes longer or until meat juices run clear. Remove chicken to a platter and keep warm; if desired, thicken cooking juices. Serve over chicken and rice.

PER SERVING *1 chicken breast half equals 336 cal., 10 g fat (4 g sat. fat), 164 mg chol., 431 mg sodium, 1 g carb., 0 fiber, 56 g pro.*

CURRY CHICKEN

Our three children all love the spicy flavors found in this recipe. Add more or less curry depending on your preferences.

—**HELEN TOULANTIS** WANTAGH, NY

PREP: 25 MIN. • **COOK:** 4½ HOURS
MAKES: 6 SERVINGS

- 6 **boneless skinless chicken breast halves (6 ounces each)**
- 1¼ **teaspoons salt**
- 1 **can (13.66 ounces) light coconut milk**
- 1 **teaspoon curry powder**
- ½ **teaspoon ground turmeric**
- ½ **teaspoon cayenne pepper**
- 3 **green onions, sliced, divided**
- 2 **tablespoons cornstarch**
- 2 **tablespoons cold water**
- 1 **to 2 tablespoons lime juice**
- 3 **cups hot cooked rice**

1. Sprinkle the chicken with salt. In a large nonstick skillet coated with cooking spray, brown the chicken on both sides. Place in a 5-qt. slow cooker.

2. Combine coconut milk, curry, turmeric and cayenne; pour over chicken. Sprinkle with half of the onions. Cover and cook on low for 4-5 hours or until chicken is tender.

3. Combine cornstarch and water until smooth; stir into the slow cooker. Cover and cook on high for 30 minutes or until the sauce is thickened. Stir in the lime juice. Serve chicken with rice and sauce; sprinkle with remaining onions.

PER SERVING *1 serving equals 353 cal., 9 g fat (5 g sat. fat), 94 mg chol., 576 mg sodium, 27 g carb., 1 g fiber, 37 g pro.* **Diabetic Exchanges:** *5 lean meat, 1½ starch, 1 fat.*

SLOW-COOKED
LEMON CHICKEN

SOUTHWEST
TURKEY STEW

SOUTHWEST TURKEY STEW

I prefer main dishes that let me stay on my diet but still eat what the rest of the family is having. This stew is a constant hit with my husband and our young children.

—STEPHANIE HUTCHINSON
HELIX, OR

PREP: 15 MIN. • **COOK:** 5 HOURS
MAKES: 6 SERVINGS

1½	pounds turkey breast tenderloins, cubed
2	teaspoons canola oil
1	can (15 ounces) turkey chili with beans, undrained
1	can (14½ ounces) diced tomatoes, undrained
1	medium sweet red pepper, chopped
1	medium green pepper, chopped
¾	cup chopped onion
¾	cup salsa
3	garlic cloves, minced
1½	teaspoons chili powder
½	teaspoon salt
½	teaspoon ground cumin
1	tablespoon minced fresh cilantro, optional

1. In a nonstick skillet, brown turkey in oil; transfer to a 3-qt. slow cooker. Stir in the chili, tomatoes, peppers, onion, salsa, garlic, chili powder, salt and cumin.

2. Cover and cook on low 5-6 hours or until turkey is no longer pink and vegetables are tender. Garnish with cilantro if desired.

PER SERVING 1¼ cups equals 238 cal., 4 g fat (1 g sat. fat), 65 mg chol., 837 mg sodium, 17 g carb., 5 g fiber, 33 g pro. **Diabetic Exchanges:** 4 lean meat, 1 vegetable, ½ starch.

SLOW-COOKED CHICKEN CACCIATORE

Here's an all-time-favorite Italian dish made easy in the slow cooker! The herbs and garlic give it such a wonderful aroma as it cooks.

—DENISE HOLLEBEKE PENHOLD, AB

PREP: 20 MIN. • **COOK:** 4 HOURS
MAKES: 6 SERVINGS

- ⅓ cup all-purpose flour
- 1 broiler/fryer chicken (3 to 4 pounds), cut up
- 2 tablespoons canola oil
- 2 medium onions, cut into wedges
- 1 medium green pepper, cut into strips
- 1 jar (6 ounces) sliced mushrooms, drained
- 1 can (14½ ounces) diced tomatoes, undrained
- 2 garlic cloves, minced
- ½ teaspoon salt
- ½ teaspoon dried oregano
- ¼ teaspoon dried basil
- ½ cup shredded Parmesan cheese

1. Place flour in a large resealable plastic bag. Add the chicken, a few pieces at a time, and shake to coat. In a large skillet, brown chicken in oil on all sides.

2. Transfer to a 5-qt. slow cooker. Top with the onions, green pepper and mushrooms. In a small bowl, combine the tomatoes, garlic, salt, oregano and basil; pour over the vegetables. Cover and cook on low for 4-5 hours or until chicken juices run clear and vegetables are tender. Serve with cheese.

PER SERVING *1 serving (calculated without skin) equals 296 cal., 12 g fat (3 g sat. fat), 78 mg chol., 582 mg sodium, 16 g carb., 3 g fiber, 29 g pro. **Diabetic Exchanges:** 3 lean meat, 2 vegetable, 1 fat, ½ starch.*

⑤INGREDIENTS
SIMPLE SOUTHWEST CHICKEN

Chicken is cooked until tender and combined with corn, beans, cheese and salsa for a Southwestern-style meal. The garnishes really pull everything together.

—MADDYMOO TASTEOFHOME.COM

PREP: 15 MIN. • **COOK:** 4 HOURS
MAKES: 6 SERVINGS

- 1 can (15¼ ounces) whole kernel corn, drained
- 1 can (15 ounces) black beans, rinsed and drained
- 1 jar (16 ounces) mild salsa
- 4 boneless skinless chicken breast halves (5 ounces each)
  Sweet red and yellow pepper strips, sour cream, shredded cheddar cheese and sliced green onions, optional

1. In a 3-qt. slow cooker, layer three-fourths each of the corn and beans and half of the salsa. Arrange the chicken over the salsa; top with remaining corn, beans and salsa. Cover and cook on low for 4-5 hours or until chicken is tender.

2. Shred chicken with two forks and return to slow cooker; heat through. Top with the peppers, sour cream, cheese and onions if desired.

PER SERVING *1 cup (calculated without optional ingredients) equals 234 cal., 3 g fat (1 g sat. fat), 52 mg chol., 678 mg sodium, 23 g carb., 4 g fiber, 24 g pro. **Diabetic Exchanges:** 3 lean meat, 1 starch, 1 vegetable.*

SIMPLE SOUTHWEST CHICKEN

FREEZE IT
SIMPLE CHICKEN TAGINE

Flavored with cinnamon and a touch of sweetness from the apricots, this stew tastes as if you spent all day in the kitchen! I like to sprinkle it with toasted almonds or cashews and serve it with hot couscous.

—ANGELA BUCHANAN
LONGMONT, CO

PREP: 15 MIN. • **COOK:** 6 HOURS
MAKES: 6 SERVINGS

- 2¼ **pounds bone-in chicken thighs, skin removed**
- 1 **large onion, chopped**
- 2 **medium carrots, sliced**
- ¾ **cup unsweetened apple juice**
- 1 **garlic clove, minced**
- 1 **teaspoon salt**
- ½ **teaspoon ground cinnamon**
- ½ **teaspoon pepper**
- 1 **cup chopped dried apricots**
  Hot cooked couscous

1. Place the chicken, onion and carrots in a 3- or 4-qt. slow cooker coated with cooking spray. In a small bowl, combine the apple juice, garlic, salt, cinnamon and pepper; pour over vegetables.
2. Cover and cook on low for 6-8 hours or until chicken is tender.
3. Remove chicken from slow cooker; shred meat with two forks. Skim fat from cooking juices; stir in apricots. Return shredded chicken to slow cooker; heat though. Serve with couscous.

FREEZE OPTION *Freeze cooled stew in freezer containers. To use, partially thaw in the refrigerator overnight. Heat the stew through in a saucepan, stirring occasionally and, if necessary, adding a little water. Serve with couscous.*
PER SERVING *1⅓ cups (calculated without couscous) equals 279 cal., 10 g fat (3 g sat. fat), 87 mg chol., 497 mg sodium, 23 g carb., 3 g fiber, 25 g pro.* **Diabetic Exchanges:** *3 lean meat, 1 vegetable, 1 fruit.*

FREEZE IT
ITALIAN TURKEY SANDWICHES

I hope you enjoy these tasty turkey sandwiches as much as our family does. The recipe makes plenty, so it's great for potlucks. Leftovers are just as good reheated the next day.

—CAROL RILEY OSSIAN, IN

PREP: 10 MIN. • **COOK:** 5 HOURS
MAKES: 12 SERVINGS

- 1 **bone-in turkey breast (6 pounds), skin removed**
- 1 **medium onion, chopped**
- 1 **small green pepper, chopped**
- ¼ **cup chili sauce**
- 3 **tablespoons white vinegar**
- 2 **tablespoons dried oregano or Italian seasoning**
- 4 **teaspoons beef bouillon granules**
- 12 **kaiser or hard rolls, split**

1. Place turkey breast in a greased 5-qt. slow cooker. Add onion and green pepper.
2. Combine chili sauce, vinegar, oregano and bouillon; pour over turkey and vegetables. Cover and cook on low for 5-6 hours or until turkey is tender.
3. Shred turkey with two forks and return to slow cooker; heat through. Spoon ½ cup onto each roll.

FREEZE OPTION *Place the cooled meat and juice mixture in freezer containers. To use, partially thaw in refrigerator overnight. Microwave, covered, on high in a microwave-safe dish until heated through, gently stirring and adding a little water if necessary.*
PER SERVING *1 sandwich equals 374 cal., 4 g fat (1 g sat. fat), 118 mg chol., 724 mg sodium, 34 g carb., 2 g fiber, 49 g pro.* **Diabetic Exchanges:** *6 lean meat, 2 starch.*

SIMPLE CHICKEN TAGINE

**ITALIAN TURKEY
SANDWICHES**

ONE-DISH
MOROCCAN CHICKEN

ONE-DISH MOROCCAN CHICKEN

Spices really work their magic on the chicken here. Dried fruit and couscous add an exotic touch.

—KATHY MORGAN RIDGEFIELD, WA

PREP: 20 MIN. • **COOK:** 6 HOURS
MAKES: 4 SERVINGS

- 4 medium carrots, sliced
- 2 large onions, halved and sliced
- 1 broiler/fryer chicken (3 to 4 pounds), cut up, skin removed
- ½ teaspoon salt
- ½ cup chopped dried apricots
- ½ cup raisins
- 1 can (14½ ounces) reduced-sodium chicken broth
- ¼ cup tomato paste
- 2 tablespoons all-purpose flour
- 2 tablespoons lemon juice
- 2 garlic cloves, minced
- 1½ teaspoons ground ginger
- 1½ teaspoons ground cumin
- 1 teaspoon ground cinnamon
- ¾ teaspoon pepper
  Hot cooked couscous

1. Place carrots and onions in a greased 5-qt. slow cooker. Sprinkle chicken with salt; add to the slow cooker. Top with the apricots and raisins. In a small bowl, whisk the broth, tomato paste, flour, lemon juice, garlic and seasonings until blended; add to slow cooker.

2. Cook, covered, on low 6-7 hours or until chicken is tender. Serve with couscous.

PER SERVING *1 serving (calculated without couscous) equals 435 cal., 9 g fat (3 g sat. fat), 110 mg chol., 755 mg sodium, 47 g carb., 6 g fiber, 42 g pro.*

THE SKINNY

REDUCE SODIUM

Using reduced-sodium chicken broth in this recipe saves you about 145 mg sodium per serving.

CONTEST-WINNING CHICKEN CACCIATORE

My husband and I operate a very busy farm. There are days when there's just no time left for cooking, so it's really nice to be able to come into the house and smell this chicken cacciatore meal. Then I just have to cook the pasta for dinner to be set.

—AGGIE ARNOLD-NORMAN
LIBERTY, PA

PREP: 15 MIN. • **COOK:** 6 HOURS
MAKES: 6 SERVINGS

- 2 **medium onions, thinly sliced**
- 1 **broiler/fryer chicken (3 to 4 pounds), cut up and skin removed**
- 2 **garlic cloves, minced**
- 1 **to 2 teaspoons dried oregano**
- 1 **teaspoon salt**
- ½ **teaspoon dried basil**
- ¼ **teaspoon pepper**
- 1 **bay leaf**
- 1 **can (14½ ounces) diced tomatoes, undrained**
- 1 **can (8 ounces) tomato sauce**
- 1 **can (4 ounces) mushroom stems and pieces, drained, or 1 cup sliced fresh mushrooms**
- ¼ **cup white wine or water**
  Hot cooked pasta

1. Place onions in a 5-qt. slow cooker. Add the chicken, seasonings, tomatoes, tomato sauce, mushrooms and wine.

2. Cover and cook on low for 6-8 hours or until chicken is tender. Discard bay leaf. Serve chicken with sauce over pasta.

PER SERVING *1 serving (calculated without pasta) equals 207 calories, 6 g fat (2 g saturated fat), 73 mg cholesterol, 787 mg sodium, 11 g carbohydrate, 3 g fiber, 27 g protein. Diabetic Exchanges: 4 lean meat, 2 vegetable.*

CONTEST-WINNING
CHICKEN CACCIATORE

SLOW COOKER
BBQ CHICKEN

SLOW COOKER BBQ CHICKEN

Of all the recipes I make in a slow cooker, this is my favorite. If you like your barbecue sweet with a little spice, this'll be your new go-to, too.

—YVONNE MCKIM VANCOUVER, WA

PREP: 15 MIN. • **COOK:** 5 HOURS
MAKES: 12 SERVINGS

- 6 chicken leg quarters, skin removed
- ¾ cup ketchup
- ½ cup orange juice
- ¼ cup packed brown sugar
- ¼ cup red wine vinegar
- ¼ cup olive oil
- 4 teaspoons minced fresh parsley
- 2 teaspoons Worcestershire sauce
- 1 teaspoon garlic salt
- ½ teaspoon pepper
- 2 tablespoons plus 2 teaspoons cornstarch
- ¼ cup water

1. Using a sharp knife, cut through the joint of each leg quarter to separate into two pieces. Place the chicken in a 4-qt. slow cooker.
2. In a small bowl, mix ketchup, orange juice, brown sugar, vinegar, oil, parsley, Worcestershire sauce, garlic salt and pepper; pour over chicken. Cook, covered, on low for 5-6 hours or until meat is tender.
3. Remove chicken to a serving platter; keep warm. Skim the fat from cooking juices; pour juices into a measuring cup to measure 2 cups. Transfer to a saucepan; bring to a boil. In a small bowl, mix the cornstarch and water until smooth; stir into cooking juices. Return to a boil, stirring constantly; cook and stir 1-2 minutes or until thickened. Serve with chicken.
PER SERVING *1 serving equals 179 cal., 9 g fat (2 g sat. fat), 45 mg chol., 392 mg sodium, 12 g carb., trace fiber, 13 g pro.* **Diabetic Exchanges:** *2 lean meat, 1 starch, 1 fat.*

NACHO CHICKEN & RICE

Simmer up a delicious low-fat meal with just a few basic ingredients. Your family is sure to love this medley of tender chicken, veggies and a zippy cheese sauce.

—LINDA FOREMAN
LOCUST GROVE, OK

PREP: 20 MIN. • **COOK:** 5 HOURS
MAKES: 6 SERVINGS

- 2½ pounds boneless skinless chicken breast halves, cubed
- 1 each small green, sweet red and orange peppers, cut into thin strips
- 1 can (10¾ ounces) condensed nacho cheese soup, undiluted
- ½ cup chunky salsa
- ⅛ teaspoon chili powder
- 4½ cups hot cooked rice

In a 3-qt. slow cooker, combine the chicken, peppers, soup, salsa and chili powder. Cover and cook on low for 5-6 hours or until chicken is tender. Serve with rice.
PER SERVING *1 cup chicken mixture with ¾ cup rice equals 360 cal., 7 g fat (2 g sat. fat), 84 mg chol., 553 mg sodium, 41 g carb., 2 g fiber, 34 g pro.* **Diabetic Exchanges:** *4 lean meat, 2½ starch, ½ fat.*

SOUTHWESTERN CHICKEN & LIMA BEAN STEW

When I make this for supper, my daughter, son-in-law and grandchildren make me happy by saying, "That was so good!" or just by quickly filling up their bowls.

—PAM CORDER MONROE, LA

PREP: 20 MIN. • **COOK:** 6 HOURS
MAKES: 6 SERVINGS

- 4 bone-in chicken thighs (1½ pounds), skin removed
- 2 cups frozen lima beans
- 2 cups frozen corn
- 1 large green pepper, chopped
- 1 large onion, chopped
- 2 cans (14 ounces each) fire-roasted diced tomatoes, undrained
- ¼ cup tomato paste
- 3 tablespoons Worcestershire sauce
- 3 garlic cloves, minced
- 1½ teaspoons ground cumin
- 1½ teaspoons dried oregano
- ¼ teaspoon salt
- ¼ teaspoon pepper
  Chopped fresh cilantro or parsley

1. Place the first five ingredients in a 5-qt. slow cooker. In a large bowl, combine tomatoes, tomato paste, Worcestershire sauce, garlic and dry seasonings; pour over top.
2. Cook, covered, on low 6-8 hours or until chicken is tender. Remove chicken from slow cooker. When cool enough to handle, remove meat from bones; discard bones. Shred meat with two forks; return to slow cooker and heat through. If desired, sprinkle with cilantro.
PER SERVING 1½ cups equals 312 cal., 7 g fat (2 g sat. fat), 58 mg chol., 614 mg sodium, 39 g carb., 8 g fiber, 24 g pro. **Diabetic Exchanges:** 3 lean meat, 2 starch, 1 vegetable.

SLOW-COOKED ORANGE CHICKEN

I decided I wanted to make a flavorful chicken dish that's lower in calories and fat. Everyone likes the taste, including my grandkids. It travels well, and I often take it to potluck suppers.

—NANCY WIT FREMONT, NE

PREP: 15 MIN. • **COOK:** 4½ HOURS
MAKES: 4 SERVINGS

- 1 broiler/fryer chicken (3 pounds), cut up and skin removed
- 3 cups orange juice
- 1 cup chopped celery
- 1 cup chopped green pepper
- 1 can (4 ounces) mushroom stems and pieces, drained
- 4 teaspoons dried minced onion
- 1 tablespoon minced fresh parsley or 1 teaspoon dried parsley flakes
- ½ teaspoon salt
- ¼ teaspoon pepper
- 3 tablespoons cornstarch
- 3 tablespoons cold water
  Hot cooked rice, optional
  Additional minced fresh parsley, optional

1. In a 3-qt. slow cooker, combine the first nine ingredients. Cover and cook on low for 4-5 hours or until chicken juices run clear.
2. Combine cornstarch and water until smooth; gradually stir into cooking liquid. Cover and cook on high for 30-45 minutes or until thickened. If desired, serve with rice and sprinkle with parsley.
PER SERVING 1 serving (calculated without rice) equals 364 cal., 9 g fat (2 g sat. fat), 110 mg chol., 515 mg sodium, 30 g carb., 2 g fiber, 39 g pro.

COCONUT CURRY CHICKEN

My husband and I love this yummy dish! It's a breeze to prepare in the slow cooker, and it tastes just like a meal you'd have at your favorite Indian or Thai restaurant.

—ANDI KAUFFMAN BEAVERCREEK, OR

PREP: 20 MIN. • **COOK:** 5 HOURS
MAKES: 4 SERVINGS

- 2 medium potatoes, peeled and cubed
- 1 small onion, chopped
- 4 boneless skinless chicken breast halves (4 ounces each)
- 1 cup light coconut milk
- 4 teaspoons curry powder
- 1 garlic clove, minced
- 1 teaspoon reduced-sodium chicken bouillon granules
- ¼ teaspoon salt
- ¼ teaspoon pepper
- 2 cups hot cooked rice
- ¼ cup thinly sliced green onions
  Raisins, flaked coconut and chopped unsalted peanuts, optional

1. Place potatoes and onion in a 3- or 4-qt. slow cooker. In a large nonstick skillet coated with cooking spray, brown chicken on both sides.
2. Transfer to slow cooker. In a small bowl, combine the coconut milk, curry, garlic, bouillon, salt and pepper; pour over chicken. Cover and cook on low for 5-6 hours or until meat is tender.
3. Serve chicken and sauce with rice; sprinkle with green onions. Garnish with raisins, coconut and peanuts if desired.
PER SERVING 1 serving (calculated without optional ingredients) equals 396 cal., 11 g fat (7 g sat. fat), 63 mg chol., 309 mg sodium, 43 g carb., 3 g fiber, 27 g pro. **Diabetic Exchanges:** 3 lean meat, 2½ starch, 2 fat.

SOUTHWESTERN CHICKEN & LIMA BEAN STEW

SLOW-COOKED ORANGE CHICKEN

COCONUT CURRY CHICKEN

GARDEN CHICKEN
CACCIATORE

GARDEN CHICKEN CACCIATORE

Treat company to this perfect Italian meal. You'll have time to visit with your guests while it cooks, and it often earns me enthusiastic reviews. I like to present it with couscous, green beans and a dry red wine.

—MARTHA SCHIRMACHER
STERLING HEIGHTS, MI

PREP: 15 MIN. • **COOK:** 8½ HOURS
MAKES: 12 SERVINGS

- 12 **boneless skinless chicken thighs (about 3 pounds)**
- 2 **medium green peppers, chopped**
- 1 **can (14½ ounces) diced tomatoes with basil, oregano and garlic, undrained**
- 1 **can (6 ounces) tomato paste**
- 1 **medium onion, sliced**
- ½ **cup reduced-sodium chicken broth**
- ¼ **cup dry red wine or additional reduced-sodium chicken broth**
- 3 **garlic cloves, minced**
- ¾ **teaspoon salt**
- ⅛ **teaspoon pepper**
- 2 **tablespoons cornstarch**
- 2 **tablespoons cold water**

1. Place the chicken in a 4- or 5-qt. slow cooker. In a small bowl, combine green peppers, tomatoes, tomato paste, onion, broth, wine, garlic, salt and pepper; pour over chicken. Cook, covered, on low 8-10 hours or until the chicken is tender.
2. In a small bowl, mix cornstarch and water until smooth; gradually stir into slow cooker. Cook, covered, on high 30 minutes or until sauce is thickened.
PER SERVING *1 chicken thigh with scant ½ cup sauce equals 207 cal., 9 g fat (2 g sat. fat), 76 mg chol., 410 mg sodium, 8 g carb., 1 g fiber, 23 g pro.* **Diabetic Exchanges:** *3 lean meat, 1 vegetable, ½ fat.*

PULLED CHICKEN SANDWICHES

I was raised as a Southern girl with the love of barbecue built into my DNA. This recipe allows me to enjoy the flavors I grew up eating, while still following a healthy diet.

—HEIDI MULHOLLAND CUMMING, GA

PREP: 20 MIN. • **COOK:** 4 HOURS
MAKES: 6 SERVINGS

- 1 **medium onion, finely chopped**
- 1 **can (6 ounces) tomato paste**
- ¼ **cup reduced-sodium chicken broth**
- 2 **tablespoons brown sugar**
- 1 **tablespoon cider vinegar**
- 1 **tablespoon yellow mustard**
- 1 **tablespoon Worcestershire sauce**
- 2 **garlic cloves, minced**
- 2 **teaspoons chili powder**
- ¾ **teaspoon salt**
- ⅛ **teaspoon cayenne pepper**
- 1½ **pounds boneless skinless chicken breasts**
- 6 **whole wheat hamburger buns, split**

1. In a small bowl, mix the first 11 ingredients. Place chicken in a 3-qt. slow cooker. Pour sauce over the top.
2. Cook, covered, on low 4-5 hours or until chicken is tender. Remove chicken; cool slightly. Shred meat with two forks. Return to slow cooker; heat through. Serve in buns.
FREEZE OPTION *Freeze the cooled chicken mixture in freezer containers. To use, partially thaw in refrigerator overnight. Heat through in a saucepan, stirring occasionally and adding a little broth if necessary.*
PER SERVING *1 sandwich equals 296 cal., 5 g fat (1 g sat. fat), 63 mg chol., 698 mg sodium, 35 g carb., 5 g fiber, 29 g pro.* **Diabetic Exchanges:** *3 lean meat, 2 starch.*

SAUCY RASPBERRY CHICKEN

I first had this dish as a teenage baby sitter—the mom prepared it for us before heading out. The kids loved it, and so did I! Now I make it for my own kids.

—MELISSA WALES
ELEPHANT BUTTE, NM

PREP: 15 MIN. • **COOK:** 5 HOURS
MAKES: 5 SERVINGS

- 5 **chicken leg quarters, skin removed**
- ⅓ **cup seedless raspberry spreadable fruit**
- 3 **tablespoons reduced-sodium soy sauce**
- 1 **teaspoon spicy brown mustard**
- ¼ **teaspoon pepper**
- 2 **tablespoons cornstarch**
- 2 **tablespoons cold water**

1. Place chicken in a 3-qt. slow cooker. In a small bowl, combine the spreadable fruit, soy sauce, mustard and pepper; pour over chicken. Cover and cook on low for 5-6 hours or until meat is tender.
2. Remove chicken to a serving platter; keep warm. Skim fat from cooking juices; transfer juices to a saucepan. Bring to a boil. Combine cornstarch and water until smooth; gradually stir into the pan. Bring to a boil; cook and stir for 2 minutes or until thickened. Serve with chicken.
PER SERVING *1 chicken leg quarter with ⅓ cup sauce equals 337 cal., 16 g fat (4 g sat. fat), 105 mg chol., 468 mg sodium, 14 g carb., trace fiber, 31 g pro.*

ITALIAN CHICKEN
AND PEPPERS

SAVORY LEMONADE CHICKEN

I don't know where this recipe originally came from, but my mother used to prepare it for our family when I was little. Now I love to make it! A sweet and tangy sauce nicely coats chicken that's ready to serve in just a few hours.
—**JENNY COOK** EAU CLAIRE, WI

PREP: 10 MIN. • **COOK:** 3 HOURS
MAKES: 6 SERVINGS

- 6 **boneless skinless chicken breast halves (4 ounces each)**
- ¾ **cup thawed lemonade concentrate**
- 3 **tablespoons ketchup**
- 2 **tablespoons brown sugar**
- 1 **tablespoon cider vinegar**
- 2 **tablespoons cornstarch**
- 2 **tablespoons cold water**

1. Place chicken in a 5-qt. slow cooker. In a small bowl, combine the lemonade concentrate, ketchup, brown sugar and vinegar; pour over chicken. Cover and cook on low for 2½ hours or until chicken is tender.
2. Remove chicken and keep warm. Combine cornstarch and water until smooth; gradually stir into cooking juices. Cover and cook on high for 30 minutes or until thickened. Return chicken to the slow cooker; heat through.
PER SERVING *1 chicken breast half with ¼ cup sauce equals 208 cal., 3 g fat (1 g sat. fat), 63 mg chol., 147 mg sodium, 22 g carb., trace fiber, 23 g pro.* **Diabetic Exchanges:** *3 lean meat, 1½ fruit.*

ITALIAN CHICKEN AND PEPPERS

I put this chicken recipe together one day when I had leftover peppers and wanted something easy. To my delight, the taste reminded me of pizza—something I love but can no longer eat! It pairs nicely with steamed broccoli.
—**BRENDA NOLEN** SIMPSONVILLE, SC

PREP: 20 MIN. • **COOK:** 4 HOURS
MAKES: 6 SERVINGS

- 6 **boneless skinless chicken breast halves (4 ounces each)**
- 1 **jar (24 ounces) garden-style spaghetti sauce**
- 1 **medium onion, sliced**
- ½ **each small green, sweet yellow and red peppers, julienned**
- ¼ **cup grated Parmesan cheese**
- 2 **garlic cloves, minced**
- 1 **teaspoon dried oregano**
- 1 **teaspoon dried basil**
- ½ **teaspoon salt**
- ¼ **teaspoon pepper**
- 4½ **cups uncooked spiral pasta Shaved Parmesan cheese, optional**

1. Place chicken in a 3-qt. slow cooker. In a large bowl, combine the spaghetti sauce, onion, peppers, cheese, garlic, oregano, basil, salt and pepper. Pour over the chicken. Cover and cook on low for 4-5 hours or until a thermometer reads 170°.
2. Cook the pasta according to package directions; drain. Serve with chicken and sauce. Top with shaved Parmesan cheese if desired.
PER SERVING *1 chicken breast half with ¾ cup pasta and ⅔ cup sauce (calculated without the Parmesan topping) equals 396 cal., 7 g fat (2 g sat. fat), 70 mg chol., 770 mg sodium, 50 g carb., 5 g fiber, 32 g pro.*

FREEZE IT
CHIPOTLE-MARMALADE CHICKEN

Big on flavor and simple to throw together, my chicken recipe is so appealing. The sweet-hot sauce gets its heat from chipotle pepper. I like to serve the chicken with a side of rice to use up every delectable drop of sauce.

—**CITTIE** TASTEOFHOME.COM

PREP: 15 MIN. • **COOK:** 4 HOURS
MAKES: 4 SERVINGS

- 4 **boneless skinless chicken breast halves (6 ounces each)**
- ¼ **teaspoon salt**
  Dash pepper
- ½ **cup chicken broth**
- ⅓ **cup orange marmalade**
- 1 **tablespoon canola oil**
- 1 **tablespoon balsamic vinegar**
- 1 **tablespoon minced chipotle pepper in adobo sauce**
- 1 **tablespoon honey**
- 1 **teaspoon chili powder**
- ¼ **teaspoon garlic powder**
- 4 **teaspoons cornstarch**
- 2 **tablespoons cold water**

1. Sprinkle chicken with salt and pepper. Transfer to a 3-qt. slow cooker. In a small bowl, combine the broth, marmalade, oil, vinegar, chipotle pepper, honey, chili powder and garlic powder; pour over the chicken. Cover and cook on low for 4-5 hours or until a thermometer reads 170°.

2. Remove chicken to a serving platter; keep warm. Place cooking juices in a small saucepan; bring to a boil. Combine cornstarch and water until smooth. Gradually stir into the pan. Bring to a boil; cook and stir for 2 minutes or until thickened. Serve with chicken.

FREEZE OPTION *Cool chicken mixture. Freeze in freezer containers. To use, partially thaw in refrigerator overnight. Heat through slowly in a covered skillet until a thermometer inserted in chicken reads 165°, stirring occasionally and adding a little broth or water if necessary.*
PER SERVING *1 chicken breast half with ⅓ cup sauce equals 315 cal., 8 g fat (1 g sat. fat), 95 mg chol., 400 mg sodium, 26 g carb., 1 g fiber, 35 g pro.* **Diabetic Exchanges:** *5 lean meat, 2 starch, ½ fat.*

INDONESIAN PEANUT CHICKEN

For this make-ahead recipe, I cut up fresh chicken, put it in a bag with the remaining slow cooker ingredients and freeze the bag. To cook, remove the bag a day ahead to thaw in the fridge, then pour all the contents into the slow cooker.

—**SARAH NEWMAN** MAHTOMEDI, MN

PREP: 15 MIN. • **COOK:** 4 HOURS
MAKES: 6 SERVINGS

- 1½ **pounds boneless skinless chicken breasts, cut into 1-inch cubes**
- ⅓ **cup chopped onion**
- ⅓ **cup water**
- ¼ **cup reduced-fat creamy peanut butter**
- 3 **tablespoons chili sauce**
- ¼ **teaspoon salt**
- ¼ **teaspoon cayenne pepper**
- ¼ **teaspoon pepper**
- 3 **cups hot cooked brown rice**
- 6 **tablespoons chopped salted peanuts**
- 6 **tablespoons chopped sweet red pepper**

1. Place chicken in a 4-qt. slow cooker. In a small bowl, combine the onion, water, peanut butter, chili sauce, salt, cayenne and pepper; pour over chicken. Cover and cook on low for 4-6 hours or until chicken is no longer pink.

2. Shred meat with two forks and return to slow cooker; heat through. Serve with rice and sprinkle with the peanuts and red pepper.

PER SERVING *½ cup chicken mixture with ½ cup rice equals 353 cal., 12 g fat (2 g sat. fat), 63 mg chol., 370 mg sodium, 31 g carb., 3 g fiber, 31 g pro.* **Diabetic Exchanges:** *3 lean meat, 2 starch, 2 fat.*

CHIPOTLE-MARMALADE CHICKEN

CHICKEN & TURKEY

SOUTHERN BARBECUE SPAGHETTI SAUCE

I revamped our favorite sloppy joe recipe into a thick spaghetti sauce that simmers in the slow cooker. The flavor is bold enough to interest adults, yet mild enough for the kids to enjoy.

—**RHONDA MELANSON** SARNIA, ON

PREP: 20 MIN. • **COOK:** 4 HOURS
MAKES: 12 SERVINGS

- 1 **pound lean ground turkey**
- 2 **medium onions, chopped**
- 1½ **cups sliced fresh mushrooms**
- 1 **medium green pepper, chopped**
- 2 **garlic cloves, minced**
- 1 **can (14½ ounces) diced tomatoes, undrained**
- 1 **can (12 ounces) tomato paste**
- 1 **can (8 ounces) tomato sauce**
- 1 **cup ketchup**
- ½ **cup beef broth**
- 2 **tablespoons Worcestershire sauce**
- 2 **tablespoons brown sugar**
- 1 **tablespoon ground cumin**
- 2 **teaspoons chili powder**
- 12 **cups hot cooked spaghetti**

1. In a large nonstick skillet, cook the turkey, onions, mushrooms and green pepper over medium heat until meat is no longer pink. Add garlic; cook 1 minute longer. Drain.
2. Transfer to a 3-qt. slow cooker. Stir in the tomatoes, tomato paste, tomato sauce, ketchup, beef broth, Worcestershire sauce, brown sugar, cumin and chili powder. Cover and cook on low for 4-5 hours or until vegetables are tender. Serve with spaghetti.

PER SERVING *⅔ cup sauce with 1 cup spaghetti equals 342 cal., 4 g fat (1 g sat. fat), 30 mg chol., 491 mg sodium, 60 g carb., 5 g fiber, 17 g pro.*

SOUTHERN BARBECUE SPAGHETTI SAUCE

SLOW-COOKED ITALIAN CHICKEN

With its seasoned tomato sauce, this enticing chicken entree is particularly good over pasta. My father especially loved this dish.
—**DEANNA D'AURIA** BANNING, CA

PREP: 20 MIN. • **COOK:** 4 HOURS
MAKES: 4 SERVINGS

- 4 boneless skinless chicken breast halves (4 ounces each)
- 1 can (14½ ounces) reduced-sodium chicken broth
- 1 can (14½ ounces) stewed tomatoes, cut up
- 1 can (8 ounces) tomato sauce
- 1 medium green pepper, chopped
- 1 green onion, chopped
- 1 garlic clove, minced
- 3 teaspoons chili powder
- 1 teaspoon ground mustard
- ½ teaspoon pepper
- ¼ teaspoon garlic powder
- ¼ teaspoon onion powder
- ⅓ cup all-purpose flour
- ½ cup cold water
  Hot cooked pasta

1. Place chicken in a 3-qt. slow cooker. In a bowl, combine the broth, tomatoes, tomato sauce, green pepper, onion, garlic and seasonings; pour over chicken. Cover and cook on low for 4-5 hours or until meat is tender. Remove the chicken and keep warm.

2. Pour cooking juices into a large saucepan; skim fat. Combine the flour and cold water until smooth; stir into juices. Bring to a boil; cook and stir for 2 minutes or until thickened. Serve with chicken and pasta.

PER SERVING *1 chicken breast half with ½ cup sauce (calculated without pasta) equals 231 cal., 3 g fat (1 g sat. fat), 63 mg chol., 818 mg sodium, 22 g carb., 3 g fiber, 28 g pro.* **Diabetic Exchanges:** *3 lean meat, 1 starch, 1 vegetable.*

SLOW-COOKED ITALIAN CHICKEN

TENDER TURKEY BREAST WITH WHITE WINE GRAVY

I modified a well-loved dish for the slow cooker. The turkey comes out tender every time and is perfectly complemented by the white wine gravy. It's best to make with drinking wine, not cooking wine.

—TINA MACKISSOCK
MANCHESTER, NH

PREP: 20 MIN. • **COOK:** 6 HOURS
MAKES: 8 SERVINGS

- 1 cup white wine
- 1 medium apple, chopped
- ½ cup sliced fennel bulb
- ⅓ cup chopped celery
- ⅓ cup chopped carrot
- 3 garlic cloves, minced
- 1 teaspoon ground mustard
- 1 bay leaf
- ½ teaspoon dried rosemary, crushed
- ½ teaspoon dried thyme
- ½ teaspoon rubbed sage
- ¼ teaspoon pepper
- 1 package (3 pounds) frozen boneless turkey breast roast, thawed
- 2 tablespoons plus 1½ teaspoons cornstarch
- ½ cup half-and-half cream

1. In a 6-qt. slow cooker, combine wine, apple, fennel, celery, carrot, garlic, mustard and bay leaf. In a small bowl, combine the rosemary, thyme, sage and pepper; rub over turkey. Add turkey to slow cooker. Cover and cook on low for 6-8 hours or until meat is tender.

2. Remove the meat to a serving platter and keep warm. Strain the drippings into a measuring cup to measure 1 cup. Skim fat. In a small saucepan, combine cornstarch and cream; stir until smooth. Gradually add the drippings. Bring to a boil; cook and stir for 2 minutes or until thickened. Serve with turkey.

PER SERVING *5 ounces cooked turkey with 3 tablespoons gravy equals 238 cal., 3 g fat (1 g sat. fat), 113 mg chol., 102 mg sodium, 7 g carb., 1 g fiber, 43 g pro.* **Diabetic Exchanges:** *6 lean meat, ½ starch.*

SAUSAGE PASTA STEW

This delicious dish is packed with turkey sausage, beans and veggies. My family inhales it without even realizing it's healthy.

—SARA BOWEN UPLAND, CA

PREP: 20 MIN. • **COOK:** 7¼ HOURS
MAKES: 8 SERVINGS

- 1 pound turkey Italian sausage links, casings removed
- 4 cups water
- 1 jar (24 ounces) meatless spaghetti sauce
- 1 can (16 ounces) kidney beans, rinsed and drained
- 1 medium yellow summer squash, halved lengthwise and cut into 1-inch pieces
- 2 medium carrots, sliced
- 1 medium sweet red or green pepper, diced
- ⅓ cup chopped onion
- 1½ cups uncooked spiral pasta
- 1 cup frozen peas
- 1 teaspoon sugar
- ½ teaspoon salt
- ¼ teaspoon pepper

1. In a nonstick skillet, cook the sausage over medium heat until no longer pink; drain and place in a 5-qt. slow cooker. Stir in the water, spaghetti sauce, kidney beans, summer squash, carrots, red pepper and onion.

2. Cover; cook on low for 7-9 hours or until vegetables are tender.

3. Stir in the pasta, peas, sugar, salt and pepper. Cover and cook on high for 15-20 minutes or until the pasta is tender.

PER SERVING *1⅓ cups equals 276 cal., 6 g fat (2 g sat. fat), 30 mg chol., 1,111 mg sodium, 38 g carb., 6 g fiber, 18 g pro.*

TENDER TURKEY BREAST WITH WHITE WINE GRAVY

SAUSAGE
PASTA STEW

THAI CHICKEN THIGHS

THAI CHICKEN THIGHS

Thanks to the slow cooker, a traditional Thai dish with peanut butter, jalapeno peppers and chili sauce becomes incredibly easy to make. If you want to crank up the heat, use more jalapeno.
—*TASTE OF HOME* TEST KITCHEN

PREP: 25 MIN. • **COOK:** 5 HOURS
MAKES: 8 SERVINGS

- 8 **bone-in chicken thighs (about 3 pounds), skin removed**
- ½ **cup salsa**
- ¼ **cup creamy peanut butter**
- 2 **tablespoons lemon juice**
- 2 **tablespoons reduced-sodium soy sauce**
- 1 **tablespoon chopped seeded jalapeno pepper**
- 2 **teaspoons Thai chili sauce**
- 1 **garlic clove, minced**
- 1 **teaspoon minced fresh gingerroot**
- 2 **green onions, sliced**
- 2 **tablespoons sesame seeds, toasted**
   Hot cooked basmati rice, optional

1. Place chicken in a 3-qt. slow cooker. In a small bowl, combine salsa, peanut butter, lemon juice, soy sauce, jalapeno, Thai chili sauce, garlic and ginger; pour over chicken.
2. Cover and cook on low 5-6 hours or until the chicken is tender. Sprinkle with green onions and sesame seeds. Serve with rice if desired.
NOTE *Wear disposable gloves when cutting hot peppers; the oils can burn skin. Avoid touching your face.*
PER SERVING *1 chicken thigh with ¼ cup sauce (calculated without rice) equals 261 cal., 15 g fat (4 g sat. fat), 87 mg chol., 350 mg sodium, 5 g carb., 1 g fiber, 27 g pro.* **Diabetic Exchanges:** *4 lean meat, 1 fat, ½ starch.*

⑤ INGREDIENTS

CRANBERRY TURKEY BREAST WITH GRAVY

I'll often serve this for a holiday meal because it's so convenient and satisfying. You can use additional slow cookers to prepare side dishes such as homemade stuffing.

—SHIRLEY WELCH TULSA, OK

PREP: 15 MIN. • **COOK:** 5 HOURS
MAKES: 12 SERVINGS (3 CUPS GRAVY)

- 1 **bone-in turkey breast (5 to 6 pounds)**
- 1 **can (14 ounces) whole-berry cranberry sauce**
- ¼ **cup orange juice**
- 1 **envelope onion soup mix**
- ¼ **teaspoon salt**
- ¼ **teaspoon pepper**
- 3 **to 4 teaspoons cornstarch**
- 1 **tablespoon water**

1. Place turkey in a 5-qt. slow cooker. In a small bowl, combine the cranberry sauce, orange juice, onion soup mix, salt and pepper; pour over turkey. Cover and cook on low for 5-6 hours or until tender.
2. Remove turkey to a serving platter; keep warm. Skim the fat from cooking juices; transfer juices to a small saucepan. Bring to a boil. Combine cornstarch and water until smooth. Gradually stir into the pan. Bring to a boil; cook and stir for 2 minutes or until thickened. Serve with turkey.

PER SERVING *5 ounces cooked turkey with ¼ cup gravy equals 318 cal., 10 g fat (3 g sat. fat), 102 mg chol., 346 mg sodium, 15 g carb., 1 g fiber, 40 g pro.* **Diabetic Exchanges:** *5 lean meat, 1 starch.*

CRANBERRY TURKEY BREAST WITH GRAVY

CHICKEN THIGHS WITH GINGER-PEACH SAUCE

CHICKEN THIGHS WITH GINGER-PEACH SAUCE

We often enjoy this chicken on Sundays. It's a cinch to prepare and requires very little cleanup.
—**LISA RENSHAW** KANSAS CITY, MO

PREP: 15 MIN. • **COOK:** 4 HOURS
MAKES: 10 SERVINGS

- 10 **boneless skinless chicken thighs (about 2½ pounds)**
- 1 **cup sliced peeled fresh or frozen peaches**
- 1 **cup golden raisins**
- 1 **cup peach preserves**
- ⅓ **cup chili sauce**
- 2 **tablespoons minced crystallized ginger**
- 1 **tablespoon reduced-sodium soy sauce**
- 1 **tablespoon minced garlic**
  Hot cooked rice, optional

1. Place chicken in a 4-qt. slow cooker coated with cooking spray. Top with peaches and raisins. In a small bowl, combine the preserves, chili sauce, ginger, soy sauce and garlic. Spoon over top.
2. Cover and cook on low for 4-5 hours or until the chicken is tender. Serve with rice if desired.
PER SERVING *1 serving (calculated without rice) equals 314 cal., 8 g fat (2 g sat. fat), 76 mg chol., 250 mg sodium, 39 g carb., 1 g fiber, 22 g pro.*

TOP TIP

PEACH SEASON

The peak season for fresh peaches is June through September. However, you can always substitute frozen peaches (thawed and drained) or well-drained canned peaches in equal amounts.

TURKEY IN CREAM SAUCE

I've relied on this recipe for tender turkey since I first moved out on my own. I serve it whenever I invite new guests to the house, and I'm always asked to share the recipe.
—**KATHY-JO WINTERBOTTOM** POTTSTOWN, PA

PREP: 20 MIN. • **COOK:** 7 HOURS
MAKES: 8 SERVINGS

- 1¼ **cups white wine or chicken broth**
- 1 **medium onion, chopped**
- 2 **garlic cloves, minced**
- 2 **bay leaves**
- 2 **teaspoons dried rosemary, crushed**
- ½ **teaspoon pepper**
- 3 **turkey breast tenderloins (¾ pound each)**
- 3 **tablespoons cornstarch**
- ½ **cup half-and-half cream or whole milk**
- ½ **teaspoon salt**

1. In a 3-qt. slow cooker, combine wine, onion, garlic and bay leaves. Combine rosemary and pepper; rub over turkey. Place in slow cooker. Cover and cook on low for 7-9 hours or until turkey is tender.
2. Remove the turkey to a serving platter; keep warm. Strain and skim fat from cooking juices; transfer juices to a small saucepan. Bring to a boil. Combine cornstarch, cream and salt until smooth. Gradually stir into the pan. Bring to a boil; cook and stir for 2 minutes or until thickened. Serve with turkey.
PER SERVING *1 serving equals 205 cal., 3 g fat (1 g sat. fat), 58 mg chol., 231 mg sodium, 6 g carb., trace fiber, 32 g pro.* **Diabetic Exchanges:** *4 lean meat, ½ starch, ½ fat.*

SPICY CHICKEN AND RICE

As a working mom with two kids, I have little time to prepare dinner during the week. This recipe is quick to toss together and fabulous to eat later. Both of my picky eaters love it!
—**JESSICA COSTELLO** FITCHBURG, MA

PREP: 20 MIN. • **COOK:** 5½ HOURS
MAKES: 8 SERVINGS

- 1½ **pounds boneless skinless chicken breast halves**
- 2 **cans (14½ ounces each) diced tomatoes with mild green chilies, undrained**
- 2 **medium green peppers, chopped**
- 1 **medium onion, chopped**
- 1 **garlic clove, minced**
- 1 **teaspoon smoked paprika**
- ¾ **teaspoon salt**
- ½ **teaspoon ground cumin**
- ½ **teaspoon ground chipotle pepper**
- 6 **cups cooked brown rice**
- 1 **can (15 ounces) black beans, rinsed and drained**
- ½ **cup shredded cheddar cheese**
- ½ **cup reduced-fat sour cream**

1. Place chicken in a 4- or 5-qt. slow cooker. In a bowl, combine tomatoes, green peppers, onion, garlic, paprika, salt, cumin and chipotle pepper; pour over chicken. Cover and cook on low for 5-6 hours or until chicken is tender.
2. Remove chicken; cool slightly. Shred with two forks and return to the slow cooker. Stir in rice and beans; heat through. Garnish with cheese and sour cream.
PER SERVING *1⅓ cups chicken mixture with 1 tablespoon cheese and 1 tablespoon sour cream equals 389 cal., 7 g fat (3 g sat. fat), 59 mg chol., 817 mg sodium, 53 g carb., 7 g fiber, 27 g pro.*

TURKEY THIGH SUPPER

This family-pleasing meal has it all—tender turkey thighs, tasty vegetables and a scrumptious sauce. You can substitute chicken breasts for the turkey or honey barbecue sauce for the soup mix.
—**BETTY GINGRICH** OXFORD, AR

PREP: 10 MIN. • **COOK:** 6 HOURS
MAKES: 4 SERVINGS

- 3 **medium red potatoes, cut into chunks**
- ½ **pound fresh baby carrots**
- 2 **medium onions, cut into chunks**
- 4 **turkey thighs, skin removed**
- 1 **can (10¾ ounces) condensed tomato soup, undiluted**
- ⅓ **cup water**
- 1 **teaspoon minced garlic**
- 1 **teaspoon Italian seasoning**
- ½ **to 1 teaspoon salt**

In a 5-qt. slow cooker, layer the potatoes, carrots and onions. Top with turkey. Combine the soup, water, garlic, Italian seasoning and salt; pour over turkey. Cover and cook on low for 6-8 hours or until a thermometer reads 170°-175° and vegetables are tender.
PER SERVING *1 serving equals 173 cal., 2 g fat (trace sat. fat), 6 mg chol., 773 mg sodium, 36 g carb., 4 g fiber, 6 g pro.*

TOP TIP

MIX IT UP

If you don't have Italian seasoning, you can mix up your own with equal amounts of basil, thyme, rosemary and oregano. You can also add parsley flakes, marjoram, sage, savory or garlic powder.

FREEZE IT
MUSHROOM MEAT LOAF

I'm a beginner cook, but this recipe is one I'm really proud of. The mushrooms and ground turkey are a nice combination, and it's a cool twist on regular meat loaf.
—**TYLER SHERMAN** WILLIAMSBURG, VA

PREP: 30 MIN. • **COOK:** 3¼ HOURS
MAKES: 6 SERVINGS

- 2 **large eggs, lightly beaten**
- 1⅓ **cups soft bread crumbs**
- ½ **pound large portobello mushrooms, stems removed, finely chopped**
- 1 **small onion, finely chopped**
- 2 **garlic cloves, minced**
- ¾ **teaspoon salt**
- ½ **teaspoon dried thyme**
- ¼ **teaspoon pepper**
- 1 **pound lean ground turkey**
- ¼ **cup chili sauce**
- 2 **teaspoons stone-ground mustard**
- ⅛ **teaspoon cayenne pepper**

1. Cut three 20x3-in. strips of heavy-duty foil; crisscross them so they resemble spokes of a wheel. Place strips on the bottom and up the sides of a 3-qt. slow cooker. Coat strips with cooking spray.
2. In a large bowl, combine eggs, bread crumbs, mushrooms, onion, garlic, salt, thyme and pepper. Crumble the ground turkey over this mixture and mix well. Shape into a 7½x4-in. loaf. Cook loaf immediately or wrap and freeze for up to 3 months.
3. Place meat loaf in the center of the strips. Cover and cook on low for 3-4 hours or until no pink remains and a thermometer reads 160°. Combine the chili sauce, mustard and cayenne; pour over meat. Cover and cook 15 minutes longer or until heated through. Using foil strips as handles, remove the meat loaf to a platter.

TO USE FROZEN MEAT LOAF
Thaw in the refrigerator overnight. Unwrap and cook as directed.
PER SERVING *1 slice equals 194 cal., 8 g fat (2 g sat. fat), 130 mg chol., 648 mg sodium, 12 g carb., 1 g fiber, 17 g pro. Diabetic Exchanges: 2 lean meat, 1 starch, 1 vegetable.*

FREEZE IT **⑤INGREDIENTS**
MAPLE MUSTARD CHICKEN

My husband loves this chicken dish. It calls for only five ingredients, and we try to have them all on hand for a delicious and cozy dinner anytime!
—**JENNIFER SEIDEL** MIDLAND, MI

PREP: 5 MIN. • **COOK:** 3 HOURS
MAKES: 6 SERVINGS

- 6 **boneless skinless chicken breast halves (6 ounces each)**
- ½ **cup maple syrup**
- ⅓ **cup stone-ground mustard**
- 2 **tablespoons quick-cooking tapioca**
   Hot cooked brown rice

Place chicken in a 3-qt. slow cooker. In a small bowl, combine the syrup, mustard and tapioca; pour over chicken. Cover and cook on low for 3-4 hours or until tender. Serve with rice.
FREEZE OPTION *Cool chicken in sauce. Freeze in freezer containers. To use, partially thaw in the refrigerator overnight. Heat through slowly in a covered skillet until a thermometer inserted in chicken reads 165°, stirring occasionally and adding a little broth or water if necessary.*
PER SERVING *1 chicken breast half with 3 tablespoons sauce (calculated without rice) equals 289 cal., 4 g fat (1 g sat. fat), 94 mg chol., 296 mg sodium, 24 g carb., 2 g fiber, 35 g pro. Diabetic Exchanges: 5 lean meat, 1½ starch.*

TURKEY THIGH
SUPPER

MUSHROOM
MEAT LOAF

MAPLE MUSTARD
CHICKEN

SAGE TURKEY
THIGHS

SAGE TURKEY THIGHS

I created this for my boys, who love dark meat. It reminds me of our traditional Thanksgiving turkey, but it's more convenient than cooking a whole bird.

—**NATALIE SWANSON** BALTIMORE, MD

PREP: 15 MIN. • **COOK:** 6 HOURS
MAKES: 4 SERVINGS

- 4 **medium carrots, halved**
- 1 **medium onion, chopped**
- ½ **cup water**
- 2 **garlic cloves, minced**
- 1½ **teaspoons rubbed sage, divided**
- 2 **turkey thighs or turkey drumsticks (2 pounds total), skin removed**
- 1 **tablespoon cornstarch**
- ¼ **cup cold water**
- ¼ **teaspoon salt**
- ⅛ **teaspoon pepper**
- 1 **teaspoon browning sauce, optional**

1. In a 3-qt. slow cooker, combine the carrots, onion, water, garlic and 1 teaspoon sage. Top with turkey. Sprinkle with the remaining sage. Cover and cook on low for 6-8 hours or until a thermometer reads 170°-175°.

2. Remove turkey to a serving platter; keep warm. Strain broth, reserving vegetables. Skim fat from cooking juices; transfer juices to a small saucepan.

3. Place the vegetables in a food processor; cover and process until smooth. Add to the cooking juices. Bring to a boil. Combine cornstarch and water until smooth. Gradually stir into the pan. Add salt, pepper and, if desired, browning sauce. Bring to a boil; cook and stir for 2 minutes or until thickened. Serve with turkey.

PER SERVING *4 ounces cooked turkey with ¼ cup gravy equals 277 cal., 8 g fat (3 g sat. fat), 96 mg chol., 280 mg sodium, 15 g carb., 3 g fiber, 34 g pro.* **Diabetic Exchanges:** *4 lean meat, 3 vegetable.*

TURKEY MEATBALLS AND SAUCE

In an effort to eat healthier, I came up with a lighter take on meatballs. They're easy!

—**JANE WHITTAKER** PENSACOLA, FL

PREP: 40 MIN. • **COOK:** 6 HOURS
MAKES: 8 SERVINGS

- ¼ **cup egg substitute**
- ½ **cup seasoned bread crumbs**
- ⅓ **cup chopped onion**
- ½ **teaspoon pepper**
- ¼ **teaspoon salt-free seasoning blend**
- 1½ **pounds lean ground turkey**

SAUCE

- 1 **can (15 ounces) tomato sauce**
- 1 **can (14½ ounces) diced tomatoes, undrained**
- 1 **small zucchini, chopped**
- 1 **medium green pepper, chopped**
- 1 **medium onion, chopped**
- 1 **can (6 ounces) tomato paste**
- 2 **bay leaves**
- 2 **garlic cloves, minced**
- 1 **teaspoon dried oregano**
- 1 **teaspoon dried basil**
- 1 **teaspoon dried parsley flakes**
- ¼ **teaspoon crushed red pepper flakes**
- ¼ **teaspoon pepper**
- 1 **package (16 ounces) whole wheat spaghetti**

1. In a large bowl, combine the egg substitute, bread crumbs, onion, pepper and seasoning blend. Crumble turkey over mixture and mix well. Shape into 1-in. balls; place on a rack coated with cooking spray in a shallow baking pan. Bake at 400° for 15 minutes or until no longer pink.

2. Meanwhile, in a 4- or 5-qt. slow cooker, combine the tomato sauce, tomatoes, zucchini, green pepper, onion, tomato paste, bay leaves, garlic and seasonings. Stir in the meatballs. Cover and cook on low for 6 hours. Cook the spaghetti according to package directions; serve with meatballs and sauce.

PER SERVING *4 meatballs with ¾ cup sauce and 1 cup spaghetti equals 416 cal., 8 g fat (2 g sat. fat), 67 mg chol., 533 mg sodium, 61 g carb., 10 g fiber, 28 g pro.*

CHICKEN MUSHROOM STEW

The flavors blend beautifully in this pot of chicken, vegetables and herbs. It's perfect for busy days when you still want to enjoy a comforting meal.

—**KIM VAN RHEENEN** MENDOTA, IL

PREP: 20 MIN. • **COOK:** 4 HOURS
MAKES: 6 SERVINGS

- 6 **boneless skinless chicken breast halves (4 ounces each)**
- 2 **tablespoons canola oil, divided**
- 8 **ounces fresh mushrooms, sliced**
- 1 **medium onion, diced**
- 3 **cups diced zucchini**
- 1 **cup chopped green pepper**
- 4 **garlic cloves, minced**
- 3 **medium tomatoes, chopped**
- 1 **can (6 ounces) tomato paste**
- ¾ **cup water**
- 2 **teaspoons each dried thyme, oregano, marjoram, and basil**

1. Cut chicken into 1-in. cubes; brown in 1 tablespoon oil in a large skillet. Transfer to a 3-qt. slow cooker. In the same skillet, saute the mushrooms, onion, zucchini and green pepper in the remaining oil until crisp-tender; add garlic; cook 1 minute longer.

2. Place in slow cooker. Add the tomatoes, tomato paste, water and seasonings. Cover and cook on low for 4-5 hours or until the meat is no longer pink and the vegetables are tender.

PER SERVING *1⅓ cups equals 237 cal., 8 g fat (1 g sat. fat), 63 mg chol., 82 mg sodium, 15 g carb., 3 g fiber, 27 g pro.* **Diabetic Exchanges:** *3 lean meat, 1 starch, 1 fat.*

SESAME PULLED PORK
SANDWICHES, PAGE 145

PORK

147

168

154

CRANBERRY PORK TENDERLOIN

Canned cranberry sauce creates a sweet accompaniment for tender pork. I dress up the cranberries with orange juice, mustard, brown sugar and cloves.

—**BETTY HELTON** MELBOURNE, FL

PREP: 10 MIN. • **COOK:** 5¼ HOURS
MAKES: 4 SERVINGS

- 1 **pork tenderloin (1 pound)**
- 1 **can (14 ounces) whole-berry cranberry sauce**
- ½ **cup orange juice**
- ¼ **cup sugar**
- 1 **tablespoon brown sugar**
- 1 **teaspoon ground mustard**
- ¼ **to ½ teaspoon ground cloves**
- 2 **tablespoons cornstarch**
- 3 **tablespoons cold water**

1. Place pork in a 3-qt. slow cooker. In a small bowl, combine cranberry sauce, orange juice, sugars, mustard and cloves; pour over pork. Cover and cook on low for 5-6 hours or until meat is tender.
2. Remove pork and keep warm. Combine cornstarch and cold water until smooth; gradually stir into the cranberry mixture. Cover and cook on high for 15 minutes or until thickened. Serve with pork.
PER SERVING *3 ounces cooked pork equals 388 cal., 4 g fat (1 g sat. fat), 63 mg chol., 71 mg sodium, 65 g carb., 2 g fiber, 23 g pro.*

TOP TIP

MAKE IT SAUCY

Cornstarch needs just a few minutes of boiling or stirring to thicken a sauce or gravy. If it cooks too long, the cornstarch begins to lose its thickening power. Carefully follow the recipe for the best results.

---

⑤INGREDIENTS
CIDER PORK ROAST

Apple cider, dried cherries and fresh rosemary put the pizzazz in this pleasing pork roast. It's even more flavorful when drizzled with the sweet pan juices.

—**TERRY DANNER** ROCHELLE, IL

PREP: 20 MIN. • **COOK:** 5 HOURS 10 MIN.
MAKES: 6 SERVINGS

- 1 **boneless pork loin roast (2 pounds)**
- ¾ **teaspoon salt**
- ¼ **teaspoon pepper**
- 2 **cups apple cider or unsweetened apple juice, divided**
- 3 **sprigs fresh rosemary**
- ½ **cup dried cherries**
- 5 **teaspoons cornstarch**

1. Sprinkle the pork with salt and pepper. In a nonstick skillet coated with cooking spray, brown pork for about 4 minutes on each side. Pour 1 cup apple cider in a 3-qt. slow cooker. Place two sprigs rosemary in slow cooker; top with meat and remaining rosemary. Place cherries around roast. Cover and cook on low for 5-6 hours or until meat is tender. Remove meat; keep warm.
2. Strain cooking liquid; reserve the liquid and transfer to a small saucepan. Stir in ¾ cup cider; bring to a boil. Combine the cornstarch and remaining cider until smooth. Gradually whisk into cider mixture. Bring to a boil; cook and stir for 1-2 minutes or until thickened. Serve with meat.
PER SERVING *1 serving (4 ounces cooked pork with ¼ cup gravy) equals 298 cal., 9 g fat (3 g sat. fat), 89 mg chol., 368 mg sodium, 20 g carb., 1 g fiber, 32 g pro.* **Diabetic Exchanges:** *4 lean meat, 1½ fruit.*

GRANDMA EDNA'S CAJUN PORK

My grandma used to make this every year as part of our Christmas dinner. These days I make it for my family at the holidays. We love to carry on the delicious tradition of Grandma's Cajun pork.

—**TONYA CLINE** GREENVILLE, OH

PREP: 35 MIN. • **COOK:** 6 HOURS
MAKES: 12 SERVINGS (2¼ CUPS SAUCE)

- 1 **small onion**
- 1 **celery rib**
- 1 **small green pepper**
- 3 **tablespoons butter**
- 3 **garlic cloves, minced**
- 2 **teaspoons dried thyme**
- 1 **teaspoon paprika**
- ½ **teaspoon each salt, white pepper and pepper**
- ½ **teaspoon ground mustard**
- ½ **teaspoon hot pepper sauce**
- 1 **boneless pork loin roast (4 pounds)**
- 2 **tablespoons cornstarch**
- 2 **tablespoons cold water**

1. Finely chop vegetables. In a large skillet, saute the vegetables in butter until tender. Add garlic; cook 1 minute longer. Stir in seasonings and pepper sauce.
2. Cut several slits in the roast to within ½ in. of bottom. Place in a 5-qt. slow cooker. Spoon the onion mixture between slits and over the top of meat. Cover and cook on low for 6-8 hours or until pork is tender.
3. Transfer the roast to a serving platter; keep warm. Pour cooking juices into a saucepan. Combine cornstarch and water until smooth; stir into the pan. Bring to a boil; cook and stir for 2 minutes or until thickened. Serve with roast.
PER SERVING *4 ounces cooked pork with 3 tablespoons gravy equals 225 cal., 10 g fat (4 g sat. fat), 83 mg chol., 167 mg sodium, 3 g carb., 1 g fiber, 29 g pro.* **Diabetic Exchanges:** *4 lean meat, ½ fat.*

GRANDMA EDNA'S
CAJUN PORK

**SESAME PULLED
PORK SANDWICHES**

SESAME PULLED PORK SANDWICHES

I wanted to build a better pork sandwich, and this Asian-style filling was a huge hit with my husband and co-workers. Top with wasabi mayo if you'd like an extra kick.

—**JENNIFER BERRY** LEXINGTON, OH

PREP: 15 MIN. • **COOK:** 4½ HOURS
MAKES: 12 SERVINGS

- 3 pork tenderloins (1 pound each)
- 1¾ cups reduced-fat sesame ginger salad dressing, divided
- ¼ cup packed brown sugar

SLAW

- 1 package (14 ounces) coleslaw mix
- 4 green onions, chopped
- ¼ cup minced fresh cilantro
- 2 tablespoons reduced-fat sesame ginger salad dressing
- 2 teaspoons sesame oil
- 1 teaspoon sugar
- 1 teaspoon reduced-sodium soy sauce

TO SERVE

- 12 multigrain hamburger buns, split
  Wasabi mayonnaise, optional

1. Place the tenderloins in a 5-qt. slow cooker coated with cooking spray; pour ¾ cup salad dressing over pork, turning to coat. Cook, covered, on low 4-5 hours or until meat is tender.
2. Remove pork; cool slightly. Shred meat into bite-size pieces; return to slow cooker. Stir in brown sugar and remaining salad dressing. Cook, covered, for 30-45 minutes longer or until heated through.
3. Combine slaw ingredients. Serve pork on buns with slaw and, if desired, mayonnaise.
NOTE *This recipe was tested with Newman's Own Sesame Ginger Dressing.*

PER SERVING *1 sandwich (calculated without mayonnaise) equals 324 cal., 9 g fat (2 g sat. fat), 64 mg chol., 756 mg sodium, 33 g carb., 3 g fiber, 27 g pro.* **Diabetic Exchanges:** *3 lean meat, 2 starch.*

⑤ INGREDIENTS

BBQ PORK & PEPPERS

My husband taught me how to make this dish. It was the first time I ever prepared something in a slow cooker, but now I turn to it often. I'll usually pair this entree with white rice or a salad.

—**RACHAEL HUGHES**
SOUTHAMPTON, PA

PREP: 10 MIN. • **COOK:** 8 HOURS
MAKES: 4 SERVINGS

- 4 bone-in pork loin chops (7 ounces each)
- 1 large onion, chopped
- 1 large sweet red pepper, chopped
- 1 large green pepper, chopped
- 1 cup barbecue sauce

Place chops in a 4-qt. slow cooker coated with cooking spray. Top with onion, peppers and barbecue sauce. Cover and cook on low 8-10 hours or until pork is tender.

PER SERVING *1 chop with ¾ cup sauce equals 291 cal., 10 g fat (3 g sat. fat), 86 mg chol., 638 mg sodium, 17 g carb., 3 g fiber, 33 g pro.* **Diabetic Exchanges:** *4 lean meat, 1 vegetable, ½ starch.*

SLOW-COOKED
PORK BURRITOS

FREEZE IT
SLOW-COOKED PORK BURRITOS

I've been making this recipe for 20 years, changing it here and there until this delectable version came together one day.

—SHARON BELMONT LINCOLN, NE

PREP: 20 MIN. • **COOK:** 8 HOURS
MAKES: 14 SERVINGS

- 1 **boneless pork sirloin roast (3 pounds)**
- ¼ **cup reduced-sodium chicken broth**
- 1 **envelope reduced-sodium taco seasoning**
- 1 **tablespoon dried parsley flakes**
- 2 **garlic cloves, minced**
- ½ **teaspoon pepper**
- ¼ **teaspoon salt**
- 1 **can (16 ounces) refried beans**
- 1 **can (4 ounces) chopped green chilies**
- 14 **flour tortillas (8 inches), warmed**
  Optional toppings: shredded lettuce, chopped tomatoes, chopped green pepper, guacamole, reduced-fat sour cream and shredded reduced-fat cheddar cheese

1. Cut roast in half; place in a 4- or 5-qt. slow cooker. In a small bowl, mix broth, taco seasoning, parsley, garlic, pepper and salt; pour over roast. Cover and cook on low 8-10 hours or until meat is very tender.
2. Remove pork from slow cooker; cool slightly. Shred meat with two forks. Skim fat from cooking juices. Return cooking juices and pork to slow cooker. Stir in the beans and chilies; heat through.
3. Spoon ½ cup pork mixture across center of each tortilla; add toppings as desired. Fold bottom and sides of tortilla over filling and roll up.
TO FREEZE BURRITOS *Roll up burritos without toppings. Wrap individually in paper towels, and then foil. Transfer to a resealable plastic bag. May be frozen for up to 2 months. To use frozen burritos, remove foil. Place paper towel-wrapped burritos on a microwave-safe plate. Microwave on high for 3-4 minutes or until heated through. Serve with toppings as desired.*

PER SERVING *1 burrito (calculated without optional toppings) equals 320 cal., 9 g fat (3 g sat. fat), 61 mg chol., 606 mg sodium, 33 g carb., 2 g fiber, 26 g pro.* **Diabetic Exchanges:** *2 starch, 2 lean meat, 1 fat.*

FRUITY PORK ROAST

I like using the slow cooker because it frees up the oven for other dishes. This pork roast, which I created by adapting other recipes, shines with the fruit.

—MARY JEPPESEN-DAVIS ST. CLOUD, MN

PREP: 25 MIN.
COOK: 8 HOURS + STANDING
MAKES: 8 SERVINGS

- ½ **medium lemon, sliced**
- ½ **cup dried cranberries**
- ⅓ **cup golden raisins**
- ⅓ **cup unsweetened apple juice**
- 3 **tablespoons sherry or additional unsweetened apple juice**
- 1 **teaspoon minced garlic**
- ½ **teaspoon ground mustard**
- 1 **boneless pork loin roast (3 pounds)**
- ½ **teaspoon salt**
- ¼ **teaspoon pepper**
- ⅛ **to ¼ teaspoon ground ginger**
- 1 **medium apple, peeled and sliced**
- ½ **cup packed fresh parsley sprigs**

1. In a small bowl, combine the first seven ingredients; set aside. Cut roast in half; sprinkle with salt, pepper and ginger.
2. Transfer to a 3-qt. slow cooker. Pour the fruit mixture over roast. Place apple and parsley around roast. Cover and cook on low for 8-10 hours or until meat is tender.
3. Transfer meat to a serving platter. Let stand for 10-15 minutes before slicing.

PER SERVING *5 ounces cooked pork with ¼ cup fruit mixture equals 272 cal., 8 g fat (3 g sat. fat), 85 mg chol., 200 mg sodium, 15 g carb., 1 g fiber, 33 g pro.* **Diabetic Exchanges:** *5 lean meat, 1 fruit.*

HAM TETRAZZINI

I modified a recipe that came with my slow cooker to reduce the fat without sacrificing the familiar taste. Family and friends are pleasantly surprised when they find out they're eating healthy.

—SUSAN BLAIR STERLING, MI

PREP: 15 MIN. • **COOK:** 4 HOURS
MAKES: 5 SERVINGS

- 1 **can (10¾ ounces) reduced-fat reduced-sodium condensed cream of mushroom soup, undiluted**
- 1 **cup sliced fresh mushrooms**
- 1 **cup cubed fully cooked ham**
- ½ **cup fat-free evaporated milk**
- 2 **tablespoons white wine or water**
- 1 **teaspoon prepared horseradish**
- 1 **package (7 ounces) spaghetti**
- ½ **cup shredded Parmesan cheese**

1. In a 3-qt. slow cooker, combine the soup, mushrooms, ham, milk, wine and horseradish. Cover and cook on low for 4 hours.
2. Cook spaghetti according to package directions; drain. Add the spaghetti and cheese to slow cooker; toss to coat.

PER SERVING *1 cup equals 290 cal., 6 g fat (3 g sat. fat), 24 mg chol., 759 mg sodium, 39 g carb., 2 g fiber, 16 g pro.* **Diabetic Exchanges:** *2½ starch, 1 lean meat, ½ fat.*

HONEY-GLAZED HAM

The simple ham is perfect for family dinners where time in the kitchen is as valuable as space in the oven.

—JACQUIE STOLZ LITTLE SIOUX, IA

PREP: 10 MIN. • **COOK:** 4½ HOURS
MAKES: 14 SERVINGS

- 1 boneless fully cooked ham (4 pounds)
- 1½ cups ginger ale
- ¼ cup honey
- ½ teaspoon ground mustard
- ½ teaspoon ground cloves
- ¼ teaspoon ground cinnamon

1. Cut ham in half; place in a 5-qt. slow cooker. Pour ginger ale over ham. Cover and cook on low for 4-5 hours or until heated through.
2. Combine the honey, mustard, cloves and cinnamon; stir until smooth. Spread over ham; cook 30 minutes longer.

PER SERVING *4 ounces cooked ham equals 166 cal., 5 g fat (2 g sat. fat), 66 mg chol., 1,347 mg sodium, 8 g carb., trace fiber, 24 g pro.*

CITRUS-HERB PORK ROAST

The genius combo of seasonings and citrus in this tender roast is exactly what you're looking for.

—LAURA BRODINE
COLORADO SPRINGS, CO

PREP: 25 MIN. • **COOK:** 8 HOURS
MAKES: 8 SERVINGS

- 1 boneless pork sirloin roast (3 to 4 pounds)
- 1 teaspoon dried oregano
- ½ teaspoon ground ginger
- ½ teaspoon pepper
- 2 medium onions, cut into thin wedges
- 1 cup plus 3 tablespoons orange juice, divided
- 1 tablespoon sugar
- 1 tablespoon white grapefruit juice
- 1 tablespoon steak sauce
- 1 tablespoon reduced-sodium soy sauce
- 1 teaspoon grated orange peel
- ½ teaspoon salt
- 3 tablespoons cornstarch
  Hot cooked egg noodles

1. Cut the roast in half. In a small bowl, combine the oregano, ginger and pepper; rub over pork. In a large nonstick skillet coated with cooking spray, brown the roast on all sides. Transfer to a 4-qt. slow cooker and add the onions.
2. In a small bowl, combine 1 cup orange juice, sugar, grapefruit juice, steak sauce and soy sauce; pour over roast. Cover and cook on low for 8-10 hours or until meat is tender. Remove the meat and onions to a serving platter; keep warm.
3. Skim fat from cooking juices; transfer to a small saucepan. Add the orange peel and salt. Bring to a boil. Combine the cornstarch and remaining orange juice until smooth. Gradually stir into the pan. Bring to a boil; cook and stir for 2 minutes or until thickened. Serve with pork and noodles.

PER SERVING *5 ounces cooked pork with 2 tablespoons gravy (calculated without egg noodles) equals 289 cal., 10 g fat (4 g sat. fat), 102 mg chol., 326 mg sodium, 13 g carb., 1 g fiber, 35 g pro.* **Diabetic Exchanges:** *5 lean meat, 1 starch.*

HONEY-GLAZED HAM

CITRUS-HERB
PORK ROAST

GLAZED ROSEMARY PORK ROAST

For a change of pace, I'll serve this pork roast at holiday gatherings. It's a welcome break from traditional turkey or ham, and when dressed with an herb-infused glaze featuring rosemary, thyme and sage, the flavor is unbeatable.

—JOYCE MANIER BEECH GROVE, IN

PREP: 20 MIN. • **COOK:** 4 HOURS
MAKES: 8 SERVINGS

- 1 **boneless pork loin roast (3 pounds)**
- 1 **tablespoon butter**
- 1 **teaspoon olive oil**
- 1 **large onion, sliced**
- 1 **tablespoon brown sugar**
- 1 **tablespoon minced fresh rosemary**
- 1 **teaspoon dried thyme**
- 1 **teaspoon rubbed sage**
- 1 **teaspoon grated orange peel**
- ½ **teaspoon pepper**
- ¼ **teaspoon salt**
- ⅔ **cup apricot jam**
- ½ **cup orange juice**
- 1 **bay leaf**

1. Cut the roast in half. In a large skillet, brown the roast in butter and oil on all sides. Transfer to a 4- or 5-qt. slow cooker.
2. Add onion to the same skillet; cook and stir until tender. Stir in the brown sugar, herbs, orange peel, pepper and salt. Spread over pork. Combine the jam and orange juice; pour over top. Add bay leaf.
3. Cover and cook on low for 4 hours or until a thermometer reads 160°. Discard bay leaf.
PER SERVING *5 ounces cooked pork equals 314 cal., 10 g fat (4 g sat. fat), 88 mg chol., 145 mg sodium, 22 g carb., 1 g fiber, 33 g pro.*

GLAZED ROSEMARY PORK ROAST

SLOW-COOKED SWEET 'N' SOUR PORK

A co-worker gave me this recipe more than 20 years ago, and my family still enjoys it today. No need to order takeout tonight when you can come home to this meal.

—MARTHA NICKERSON
HANCOCK, ME

PREP: 20 MIN. • **COOK:** 6½ HOURS
MAKES: 6 SERVINGS

- 2 tablespoons plus 1½ teaspoons paprika
- 1½ pounds boneless pork loin roast, cut into 1-inch strips
- 1 tablespoon canola oil
- 1 can (20 ounces) unsweetened pineapple chunks
- 1 medium onion, chopped
- 1 medium green pepper, chopped
- ¼ cup cider vinegar
- 3 tablespoons brown sugar
- 3 tablespoons reduced-sodium soy sauce
- 1 tablespoon Worcestershire sauce
- ½ teaspoon salt
- 2 tablespoons cornstarch
- ¼ cup cold water
  Hot cooked rice, optional

1. Place paprika in a large resealable plastic bag. Add pork, a few pieces at a time, and shake to coat. In a nonstick skillet, brown pork in oil in batches over medium-high heat. Transfer to a 3-qt. slow cooker.
2. Drain pineapple, reserving juice; refrigerate the pineapple. Add the pineapple juice, onion, green pepper, vinegar, brown sugar, soy sauce, Worcestershire sauce and salt to slow cooker. Cover and cook on low for 6-8 hours or until meat is tender.
3. Combine cornstarch and water until smooth; stir into pork mixture. Add pineapple. Cover and cook 30 minutes longer or until sauce is thickened. Serve over rice if desired.
PER SERVING *1 cup pork mixture (calculated without rice) equals 312 cal., 10 g fat (3 g sat. fat), 73 mg chol., 592 mg sodium, 28 g carb., 2 g fiber, 27 g pro.* **Diabetic Exchanges:** *3 lean meat, 1 fruit, ½ starch, ½ fat.*

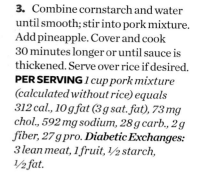

(5)INGREDIENTS
LEMON PORK CHOPS

These pork chops can simmer all day on low and be ready to serve by dinnertime. I serve them with a crisp salad or mac and cheese on the side.

—BARBARA DE FRANG HAZEN, ND

PREP: 5 MIN. • **COOK:** 6 HOURS
MAKES: 4 SERVINGS

- 4 bone-in pork chops (7 ounces each)
- ½ teaspoon salt
- ¼ teaspoon pepper
- 1 medium onion, thinly sliced
- 1 medium lemon, thinly sliced
- ¼ cup packed brown sugar
- ¼ cup ketchup

1. Place the pork chops in a 3-qt. slow cooker. Sprinkle with salt and pepper. Top with onion and lemon. Sprinkle with brown sugar; drizzle with ketchup.
2. Cover and cook on low for 6-8 hours or until meat is tender.
PER SERVING *1 serving equals 290 cal., 8 g fat (3 g sat. fat), 86 mg chol., 543 mg sodium, 22 g carb., 1 g fiber, 31 g pro.*

SLOW-COOKED SWEET 'N' POUR PORK

CANADIAN PORK
ROAST WITH GRAVY

ASIAN PORK
ROAST

SLOW-COOKED
PORK AND BEANS

CANADIAN PORK ROAST WITH GRAVY

My son asked if I had a slow cooker meal he could make to impress his girlfriend. They loved this!

—**MARILYN McCRORY** CRESTON, BC

PREP: 20 MIN. • **COOK:** 5 HOURS
MAKES: 10 SERVINGS

- 1 boneless pork loin roast (3 pounds)
- ⅓ cup maple syrup
- 1 tablespoon lemon juice
- 1 tablespoon Dijon mustard
- 1 garlic clove, minced
- 2 tablespoons cornstarch
- ¼ cup cold water

1. Cut roast in half. Transfer to a 5-qt. slow cooker. Combine the maple syrup, lemon juice, mustard and garlic; pour over pork. Cover and cook on low for 5-6 hours or until meat is tender.

2. Remove the meat to a serving platter; keep warm. Strain cooking juices; transfer 1 cup to a saucepan. Combine the cornstarch and water until smooth; stir into the cooking juices. Bring to a boil; cook and stir for 2 minutes or until thickened. Slice roast; serve with gravy.

PER SERVING *1 serving equals 205 cal., 6 g fat (2 g sat. fat), 68 mg chol., 76 mg sodium, 9 g carb., trace fiber, 26 g pro.* **Diabetic Exchanges:** *4 lean meat, ½ starch.*

HOW-TO

SAVE LEMON JUICE

When a recipe calls for lemon juice, you can either use fresh, frozen or bottled lemon juice in equal amounts. You can also freeze fresh lemon juice in ice cube trays for later.

ASIAN PORK ROAST

We can't get enough of this pork roast with honey, soy and spices. It's particularly perfect on chilly nights. The aroma will draw everyone to the kitchen.

—**SHEREE SHOWN** JUNCTION CITY, OR

PREP: 25 MIN. • **COOK:** 4 HOURS
MAKES: 12 SERVINGS

- 2 large onions, thinly sliced
- 3 garlic cloves, minced
- ½ teaspoon salt
- ½ teaspoon pepper
- 1 boneless pork loin roast (3 pounds)
- 1 tablespoon canola oil
- 3 bay leaves
- ¼ cup hot water
- ¼ cup honey
- ¼ cup reduced-sodium soy sauce
- 2 tablespoons rice vinegar
- 1 teaspoon ground ginger
- ½ teaspoon ground cloves
- 3 tablespoons cornstarch
- ¼ cup cold water
- 2 tablespoons sesame seeds, toasted
  Hot cooked rice and sliced green onion tops, optional

1. Place onions in a 5-qt. slow cooker. In a small bowl, combine the garlic, salt and pepper. Cut roast in half; rub with garlic mixture. In a large nonstick skillet coated with cooking spray, brown pork in oil on all sides. Transfer to slow cooker; add bay leaves.

2. In a small bowl, combine hot water and honey; stir in soy sauce, vinegar, ginger and cloves. Pour over pork. Cover and cook on low for 4-5 hours or until meat is tender.

3. Remove meat and onions from slow cooker; keep warm. Discard bay leaves. Combine cornstarch and cold water until smooth; gradually stir into slow cooker.

4. Cover and cook on high for 30 minutes or until thickened, stirring twice. Slice the pork; top with sauce and sprinkle with

sesame seeds. Serve with rice and garnish with green onion tops if desired.

PER SERVING *3 ounces cooked pork with 3 tablespoons onions and 3 tablespoons sauce (calculated without optional ingredients) equals 203 cal., 7 g fat (2 g sat. fat), 56 mg chol., 342 mg sodium, 11 g carb., 1 g fiber, 23 g pro.* **Diabetic Exchanges:** *3 lean meat, 1 starch.*

SLOW-COOKED PORK AND BEANS

I like to get this dish started before leaving for work in the morning. Then when I get home, my supper is ready. It's a hearty meal that's also good for a potluck. Place a generous helping of the pork and beans next to a slice of warm corn bread.

—**PATRICIA HAGER**
NICHOLASVILLE, KY

PREP: 15 MIN. • **COOK:** 6 HOURS
MAKES: 12 SERVINGS

- 1 boneless pork loin roast (3 pounds)
- 1 medium onion, sliced
- 3 cans (15 ounces each) pork and beans
- 1½ cups barbecue sauce
- ¼ cup packed brown sugar
- 1 teaspoon garlic powder

1. Cut the roast in half; place in a 5-qt. slow cooker. Top with onion. In a large bowl, combine the beans, barbecue sauce, brown sugar and garlic powder; pour over the meat. Cover and cook on low for 6-8 hours or until meat is tender.

2. Remove roast; shred with two forks. Return meat to slow cooker; heat through.

PER SERVING *1 serving (1 cup) equals 217 cal., 6 g fat (2 g sat. fat), 56 mg chol., 404 mg sodium, 16 g carb., 2 g fiber, 24 g pro.*

THAI-STYLE PORK

A creamy Thai peanut sauce coats tender pork in this delectable dish. The recipe comes from a friend in my cooking club and it's always a crowd favorite.

—AMY VAN ORMAN ROCKFORD, MI

PREP: 15 MIN. • **COOK:** 6¼ HOURS
MAKES: 6 SERVINGS

- **2 pounds boneless pork loin chops**
- **¼ cup teriyaki sauce**
- **2 tablespoons rice vinegar**
- **1 teaspoon crushed red pepper flakes**
- **1 teaspoon minced garlic**
- **1 tablespoon cornstarch**
- **¼ cup cold water**
- **¼ cup creamy peanut butter**
  Hot cooked rice
- **½ cup chopped green onions**
- **½ cup dry roasted peanuts**
  Lime juice, optional

1. Place pork chops in a 3-qt. slow cooker. In a small bowl, combine the teriyaki sauce, vinegar, pepper flakes and garlic; pour over meat. Cover and cook on low for 6-8 hours or until meat is tender.

2. Remove the pork and cut into bite-size pieces; keep warm. Place cooking juices in a small saucepan; bring to a boil. Combine cornstarch and water until smooth. Gradually stir into the pan. Bring to a boil; cook and stir for 2 minutes or until thickened. Stir in peanut butter; add meat.

3. Serve with rice and sprinkle with onions and peanuts. Drizzle with lime juice if desired.

PER SERVING *⅔ cup (calculated without rice) equals 357 cal., 20 g fat (5 g sat. fat), 73 mg chol., 598 mg sodium, 9 g carb., 2 g fiber, 35 g pro.* **Diabetic Exchanges:** *5 lean meat, 2 fat, ½ starch.*

SLOW-COOKED PORK ROAST DINNER

You can cut this roast with a fork, and it's just as moist and tender later—if there are any leftovers.

—JANE MONTGOMERY PIQUA, OH

PREP: 25 MIN. • **COOK:** 6 HOURS
MAKES: 8 SERVINGS

- **1 cup hot water**
- **¼ cup sugar**
- **3 tablespoons cider vinegar**
- **2 tablespoons reduced-sodium soy sauce**
- **1 tablespoon ketchup**
- **½ teaspoon salt**
- **½ teaspoon pepper**
- **¼ teaspoon garlic powder**
- **¼ teaspoon chili powder**
- **1 large onion, halved and sliced**
- **1 boneless pork loin roast (2½ pounds), halved**
- **4 medium potatoes (about 1¾ pounds), peeled and cut into 1-inch pieces**
- **1 package (16 ounces) frozen sliced carrots, thawed**
- **2 tablespoons cornstarch**
- **2 tablespoons cold water**

1. In a small bowl, whisk first nine ingredients until blended. Place onion in a 5-qt. slow cooker. Place roast, potatoes and carrots over the onion. Pour sauce mixture over top. Cook, covered, on low 6-8 hours or until pork and potatoes are tender.

2. Remove roast and vegetables from the slow cooker; keep warm. Transfer cooking juices to a small saucepan; skim fat. Bring juices to a boil. In a bowl, mix the cornstarch and water until smooth; stir into juices. Bring to a boil; cook and stir 1-2 minutes or until thickened. Serve with roast and vegetables.

PER SERVING *4 ounces cooked pork with ⅔ cup vegetables and ⅓ cup sauce equals 304 cal., 7 g fat (2 g sat. fat), 70 mg chol., 401 mg sodium, 30 g carb., 3 g fiber, 29 g pro.* **Diabetic Exchanges:** *4 lean meat, 1½ starch, 1 vegetable.*

THAI-STYLE PORK

SLOW-COOKED
PORK ROAST DINNER

LIGHT GLAZED
PORK ROAST

LIGHT GLAZED PORK ROAST

My roast with a hint of orange is popular with adults and children alike. It's an excellent take-along meal for potlucks.

—RADELLE KNAPPENBERGER
OVIEDO, FL

PREP: 30 MIN. • **COOK:** 4 HOURS
MAKES: 16 SERVINGS

- 1 boneless pork loin roast (4 pounds), trimmed
- 1 tablespoon olive oil
- 1 tablespoon butter, melted
- ⅔ cup thawed orange juice concentrate
- ⅓ cup water
- 3 garlic cloves, minced
- 1½ teaspoons salt
- ½ teaspoon pepper

GLAZE

- ¼ cup packed brown sugar
- 2 tablespoons balsamic vinegar
- 1 tablespoon thawed orange juice concentrate
- 1 garlic clove, minced
- 1 can (11 ounces) mandarin oranges, drained, optional

1. Cut the roast in half. In a large skillet, brown roast in oil and butter on all sides.

2. Transfer to a 5-qt. slow cooker. Add the orange juice concentrate, water, garlic, salt and pepper. Cover and cook on low for 4-6 hours or until meat is tender.

3. For glaze, in a small saucepan, combine the brown sugar, vinegar, orange juice concentrate and garlic. Bring to a boil. Reduce the heat and simmer, uncovered, for 3-5 minutes or until reduced to about ¼ cup. Brush over roast. Garnish with oranges if desired.

PER SERVING *3 ounces cooked pork (calculated without oranges) equals 190 cal., 7 g fat (2 g sat. fat), 58 mg chol., 263 mg sodium, 9 g carb., trace fiber, 22 g pro.* **Diabetic Exchanges:** *3 lean meat, ½ starch.*

PORK CHOP CACCIATORE

It's hard to believe that so much flavor can come from such an easy recipe. Serve it with noodles and a simple green salad.

—**TRACY HIATT GRICE** SOMERSET, WI

PREP: 30 MIN. • **COOK:** 8 HOURS
MAKES: 6 SERVINGS

- 6 bone-in pork loin chops (7 ounces each)
- ¾ teaspoon salt, divided
- ¼ teaspoon pepper
- 1 tablespoon olive oil
- 1 cup sliced fresh mushrooms
- 1 small onion, chopped
- 1 celery rib, chopped
- 1 small green pepper, chopped
- 2 garlic cloves, minced
- 1 can (14½ ounces) diced tomatoes
- ½ cup water, divided
- ½ teaspoon dried basil
- 2 tablespoons cornstarch
- 4½ cups cooked egg noodles

1. Sprinkle chops with ½ teaspoon salt and pepper. In a large skillet, brown the chops in oil in batches. Transfer to a 4-or 5-qt. slow cooker coated with cooking spray. Saute the mushrooms, onion, celery and green pepper in drippings until tender. Add garlic; cook 1 minute longer. Stir in the tomatoes, ¼ cup water, basil and remaining salt; pour over chops.

2. Cover and cook on low for 8-10 hours or until pork is tender. Remove meat to a serving platter; keep warm. Skim fat from cooking juices if necessary; transfer juices to a small saucepan. Bring liquid to a boil. Combine the cornstarch and remaining water until smooth. Gradually stir into the pan. Bring to a boil; cook and stir for 2 minutes or until thickened. Serve with meat and noodles.

PER SERVING *1 pork chop with ¾ cup noodles and ½ cup sauce equals 371 cal., 12 g fat (4 g sat. fat), 110 mg chol., 458 mg sodium, 29 g carb., 3 g fiber, 35 g pro.* **Diabetic Exchanges:** *4 lean meat, 1½ starch, 1 vegetable, ½ fat.*

SOUTHERN PULLED PORK

Here's my New England take on a Southern favorite. The sweet and tangy pork takes just a few minutes to get going in the slow cooker. It's irresistible piled high on cooked sweet potatoes.

—**KATIE GRADY** WEST BOYLSTON, MA

PREP: 20 MIN. • **COOK:** 6½ HOURS
MAKES: 10 SERVINGS

- 1 boneless pork shoulder butt roast (3 pounds)
- ⅓ cup spicy brown mustard
- ⅓ cup molasses
- ¼ cup packed brown sugar
- 1½ teaspoons soy sauce
- 1 tablespoon cornstarch
- ¼ cup cold water
    Baked sweet potatoes, optional

1. Place pork in a 3- or 4-qt. slow cooker. Combine the mustard, molasses, brown sugar and soy sauce; pour over roast. Cover and cook on low for 6-8 hours or until meat is tender.

2. Remove meat; cool slightly. Skim the fat from cooking juices; transfer juices to a large saucepan. Bring to a boil. Combine cornstarch and water until smooth; gradually stir into the juices. Return to a boil; cook and stir for 2 minutes or until the sauce has thickened.

3. Shred the meat with two forks; return to slow cooker. Stir in sauce. Cover and cook 15 minutes longer or until heated through. Serve with sweet potatoes if desired.

PER SERVING *½ cup (calculated without potatoes) equals 282 cal., 14 g fat (5 g sat. fat), 81 mg chol., 240 mg sodium, 14 g carb., trace fiber, 23 g pro.* **Diabetic Exchanges:** *3 medium-fat meat, 1 starch.*

PORK CHOP CACCIATORE

SWEETENED
PORK ROAST

SWEETENED PORK ROAST

Need to keep cool during the summer? Try this entree that doesn't need the oven to cook. It's sure to become a favorite.

—MARION LOWERY MEDFORD, OR

PREP: 20 MIN.
COOK: 6 HOURS + STANDING
MAKES: 12 SERVINGS

- 2 cans (8 ounces each) unsweetened crushed pineapple, undrained
- 1 cup barbecue sauce
- 2 tablespoons unsweetened apple juice
- 1 tablespoon minced fresh rosemary or 1 teaspoon dried rosemary, crushed
- 1 teaspoon minced garlic
- 2 teaspoons grated lemon peel
- 1 teaspoon liquid smoke, optional
- ½ teaspoon salt
- ¼ teaspoon pepper
- 1 boneless pork loin roast (3 to 4 pounds)

1. In a large saucepan, combine the first nine ingredients. Bring to a boil. Reduce the heat and simmer, uncovered, for 3 minutes.
2. Meanwhile, cut roast in half. In a nonstick skillet coated with cooking spray, brown pork roast on all sides.
3. Place the roast in a 5-qt. slow cooker. Pour sauce over the roast and turn to coat. Cover and cook on low for 6-7 hours or until meat is tender. Let stand for 10 minutes before slicing.
PER SERVING *3 ounces cooked pork with ¼ cup sauce equals 202 cal., 7 g fat (2 g sat. fat), 66 mg chol., 306 mg sodium, 8 g carb., 1 g fiber, 26 g pro.* **Diabetic Exchanges:** *3 lean meat, ½ starch.*

PORK CHOPS WITH SCALLOPED POTATOES

My sister gave me this recipe to make as a casserole baked in the oven, but I've also fixed it on the stovetop and in the slow cooker. Everyone who has tasted it loves it.

—ELIZABETH JOHNSTON GLENDALE, AZ

PREP: 30 MIN. • **COOK:** 8 HOURS
MAKES: 6 SERVINGS

- 4 medium potatoes, peeled and thinly sliced
- 6 bone-in pork loin chops (7 ounces each)
- 1 tablespoon canola oil
- 2 large onions, sliced and separated into rings
- 2 teaspoons butter
- 3 tablespoons all-purpose flour
- ¼ teaspoon salt
- ¼ teaspoon pepper
- 1 can (14½ ounces) reduced-sodium chicken broth
- 1 cup fat-free milk

1. Place potatoes in a 5- or 6-qt. slow cooker coated with cooking spray. In a large nonstick skillet, brown pork chops in oil in batches.
2. Place chops over potatoes. Saute onions in drippings until tender; place over chops. Melt the butter in a skillet. Combine the flour, salt, pepper and broth until smooth; stir into pan. Add the milk. Bring to a boil; cook and stir for 2 minutes or until thickened.
3. Pour sauce over onions. Cover and cook on low for 8-10 hours or until pork is tender. Skim fat and thicken cooking juices if desired.
PER SERVING *1 pork chop with ¾ cup potatoes equals 372 cal., 12 g fat (4 g sat. fat), 90 mg chol., 389 mg sodium, 29 g carb., 2 g fiber, 35 g pro.* **Diabetic Exchanges:** *4 lean meat, 2 starch, 1 fat.*

FRUITED PORK CHOPS

Here's one of my best dishes. I often prepare these juicy pineapple pork chops with brown rice.

—CINDY RAGAN
NORTH HUNTINGDON, PA

PREP: 10 MIN. • **COOK:** 6¼ HOURS
MAKES: 6 SERVINGS

- 3 tablespoons all-purpose flour
- 1½ teaspoons dried oregano
- ¾ teaspoon salt
- ¼ teaspoon garlic powder
- ¼ teaspoon pepper
- 6 boneless pork loin chops (5 ounces each)
- 1 tablespoon olive oil
- 1 can (20 ounces) unsweetened pineapple chunks
- ¾ cup unsweetened pineapple juice
- ¼ cup water
- 2 tablespoons brown sugar
- 2 tablespoons dried minced onion
- 2 tablespoons tomato paste
- ¼ cup raisins

1. In a large resealable plastic bag, combine the flour, oregano, salt, garlic powder and pepper; add the pork chops, one at a time, and shake to coat. In a nonstick skillet, brown chops in oil on both sides. Transfer to a 5-qt. slow cooker.
2. Drain pineapple, reserving juice; set the pineapple aside. In a bowl, combine the ¾ cup pineapple juice with reserved pineapple juice. Stir in water, brown sugar, onion and tomato paste; pour over the chops. Sprinkle with raisins.
3. Cover and cook on low for 6-8 hours or until meat is tender. Stir in reserved pineapple. Cover and cook 15 minutes longer or until heated through.
PER SERVING 1 serving equals 366 cal., 12 g fat (4 g sat. fat), 79 mg chol., 353 mg sodium, 31 g carb., 2 g fiber, 32 g pro. **Diabetic Exchanges:** 4 lean meat, 2 fruit.

CRANBERRY-APRICOT PORK ROAST WITH POTATOES

I got this recipe from one of my dearest friends. Perfect for the chilly fall and winter months, the comfy entree features apricots, whole-berry cranberry sauce and a hint of cayenne to accent the pork.

—PAT BARNES PANAMA CITY, FL

PREP: 15 MIN. • **COOK:** 5 HOURS
MAKES: 8 SERVINGS

- 4 medium potatoes, peeled and quartered
- 1 boneless pork loin roast (3 pounds)
- 1 can (14 ounces) whole-berry cranberry sauce
- 1 can (15 ounces) apricot halves, drained
- 1 medium onion, quartered
- ½ cup chopped dried apricots
- 1 tablespoon sugar
- ½ teaspoon ground mustard
- ¼ teaspoon cayenne pepper

1. Place potatoes in a 5-qt. slow cooker. Add pork.
2. In a blender, combine the cranberry sauce, apricots, onion, dried apricots, sugar, mustard and cayenne. Cover and process for 30 seconds or until almost smooth. Pour over pork.
3. Cover and cook on low for 5-6 hours or until meat is tender. Serve meat and potatoes with cooking juices.
PER SERVING 1 serving equals 433 cal., 8 g fat (3 g sat. fat), 85 mg chol., 71 mg sodium, 56 g carb., 4 g fiber, 35 g pro.

LIME-CHIPOTLE CARNITAS TOSTADAS

At your next party, set out various toppings and garnishes so guests can customize their own tostadas.

—JAN VALDEZ CHICAGO, IL

PREP: 20 MIN. • **COOK:** 8 HOURS
MAKES: 16 SERVINGS

- ½ cup chicken broth
- 4 teaspoons ground chipotle pepper
- 4 teaspoons ground cumin
- 1 teaspoon salt
- 1 boneless pork shoulder roast (4 to 5 pounds), halved
- 1 large onion, peeled and halved
- 8 garlic cloves, peeled
- 1 to 2 limes, halved
- 16 tostada shells
  Optional toppings: warmed refried beans, salsa, sour cream, shredded lettuce, chopped avocado, crumbled queso fresco and minced fresh cilantro
  Lime wedges

1. Add broth to a 5-qt. slow cooker. Mix the seasonings; rub over all sides of pork. Place in slow cooker. Add onion and garlic cloves. Cook, covered, on low 8-10 hours or until meat is tender.
2. Remove the pork; cool slightly. Strain cooking juices, reserving garlic cloves; discard onion. Skim fat from cooking juices. Mash the garlic with a fork. Shred the pork with two forks.
3. Return cooking juices, garlic and pork to slow cooker. Squeeze the lime juice over pork; heat through, stirring to combine. Layer tostada shells with the pork mixture and toppings as desired. Serve with the lime wedges.
PER SERVING 1 tostada (calculated without optional toppings) equals 269 cal., 15 g fat (5 g sat. fat), 76 mg chol., 279 mg sodium, 9 g carb., 1 g fiber, 23 g pro. **Diabetic Exchanges:** 3 medium-fat meat, ½ starch.

LIME-CHIPOTLE
CARNITAS TOSTADAS

PORK ROAST
DINNER

TUSCAN
PORK STEW

TANGY
PORK CHOPS

PORK ROAST DINNER

I love to cook, so I often make meals for friends. They love trying my new recipes, and this was one of their favorites. Use any leftover meat to create barbecue pork sandwiches the next day.

—LISA CHAMBERLAIN ST. CHARLES, IL

PREP: 30 MIN. + MARINATING
COOK: 8 HOURS • **MAKES:** 8 SERVINGS

- 2 teaspoons minced garlic
- 2 teaspoons fennel seed, crushed
- 1½ teaspoons dried rosemary, crushed
- 1 teaspoon dried oregano
- 1 teaspoon paprika
- ¾ teaspoon salt
- ¼ teaspoon pepper
- 1 boneless whole pork loin roast (3 to 4 pounds)
- 1½ pounds medium potatoes, peeled and cut into chunks
- 1½ pounds large sweet potatoes, peeled and cut into chunks
- 2 large sweet onions, cut into eighths
- ½ cup chicken broth

1. Combine the garlic, fennel, rosemary, oregano, paprika, salt and pepper; rub over pork. Cover and refrigerate for 8 hours.
2. Place potatoes and onions in a 5-qt. slow cooker. Top with pork. Pour broth over meat. Cover and cook on low for 8-10 hours or until meat and vegetables are tender.
3. Let meat stand 10-15 minutes before slicing.
PER SERVING *5 ounces cooked pork with 1 cup vegetables equals 369 cal., 9 g fat (3 g sat. fat), 99 mg chol., 349 mg sodium, 29 g carb., 3 g fiber, 41 g pro.* **Diabetic Exchanges:** *5 lean meat, 2 starch.*

TANGY PORK CHOPS

My husband and I discovered this convenient recipe after the birth of our first child. I could start it during nap time and we'd enjoy an easy, satisfying dinner that night.

—KAROL HINES KITTY HAWK, NC

PREP: 15 MIN. • **COOK:** 5½ HOURS
MAKES: 4 SERVINGS

- 4 bone-in pork loin chops
- ⅛ teaspoon pepper
- 2 medium onions, chopped
- 2 celery ribs, chopped
- 1 large green pepper, sliced
- 1 can (14½ ounces) no-salt-added stewed tomatoes
- ½ cup ketchup
- 2 tablespoons cider vinegar
- 2 tablespoons Worcestershire sauce
- 2 tablespoons brown sugar
- 1 tablespoon lemon juice
- 1 teaspoon beef bouillon granules
- 2 tablespoons cornstarch
- 2 tablespoons cold water
  Hot cooked rice, optional

1. Place the chops in a 3-qt. slow cooker; sprinkle with pepper. Add onions, celery, green pepper and tomatoes. Combine the ketchup, vinegar, Worcestershire sauce, brown sugar, lemon juice and bouillon; pour over the vegetables. Cover and cook on low for 5-6 hours or until meat is tender.
2. Mix cornstarch and water until smooth; stir into liquid in the slow cooker. Cover and cook on high for 30 minutes or until thickened. Serve with rice if desired.
PER SERVING *1 serving equals 349 cal., 9 g fat (3 g sat. fat), 86 mg chol., 757 mg sodium, 34 g carb., 4 g fiber, 32 g pro.*

TUSCAN PORK STEW

Tender chunks of pork cook slowly in a seasoned, wine-infused sauce. Add some crushed red pepper flakes for a little extra kick.

—PENNY HAWKINS MEBANE, NC

PREP: 15 MIN. • **COOK:** 8½ HOURS
MAKES: 8 SERVINGS

- 1½ pounds boneless pork loin roast, cut into 1-inch cubes
- 2 tablespoons olive oil
- 2 cans (14½ ounces each) Italian diced tomatoes, undrained
- 2 cups reduced-sodium chicken broth
- 2 cups frozen pepper stir-fry vegetable blend, thawed
- ½ cup dry red wine or additional reduced-sodium chicken broth
- ¼ cup orange marmalade
- 2 garlic cloves, minced
- 1 teaspoon dried oregano
- ½ teaspoon fennel seed
- ½ teaspoon pepper
- ⅛ teaspoon crushed red pepper flakes, optional
- 2 tablespoons cornstarch
- 2 tablespoons cold water
  Hot cooked fettuccine, optional

1. In a large skillet, brown the pork in oil; drain. Transfer to a 5-qt. slow cooker.
2. Stir in the tomatoes, broth, vegetable blend, wine, marmalade, garlic, oregano, fennel seed, pepper and, if desired, red pepper flakes. Cover and cook on low 8-10 hours or until meat is tender.
3. Combine cornstarch and water until smooth; gradually stir into stew. Cover and cook on high for 30 minutes or until thickened. Serve with fettuccine if desired.
PER SERVING *1 cup (calculated without fettuccine) equals 232 cal., 7 g fat (2 g sat. fat), 42 mg chol., 614 mg sodium, 19 g carb., 1 g fiber, 19 g pro.* **Diabetic Exchanges:** *2 lean meat, 1 starch, 1 vegetable, ½ fat.*

ALL-DAY RED BEANS & RICE

My family loves New Orleans-style cooking, so I make this authentic dish often. I appreciate how simple it is to throw together.
—CELINDA DAHLGREN NAPA, CA

PREP: 20 MIN. + SOAKING
COOK: 8½ HOURS • **MAKES:** 6 SERVINGS

- 1 cup dried red beans
- 7 cups water, divided
- 2 smoked ham hocks
- 1 medium onion, chopped
- 1½ teaspoons minced garlic
- 1 teaspoon ground cumin
- 1 medium tomato, chopped
- 1 medium green pepper, chopped
- 1 teaspoon salt
- 4 cups hot cooked rice

1. Sort beans and rinse in cold water. Place beans in a 3-qt. slow cooker. Add 4 cups water; cover and let stand overnight.

2. Drain and rinse the beans, discarding liquid. Return beans to slow cooker; add the ham hocks, onion, garlic, cumin and remaining water. Cover and cook on low for 8-10 hours or until beans are tender.

3. Remove the ham hocks; cool slightly. Remove meat from bones. Finely chop meat and return to slow cooker; discard bones. Stir in tomato, pepper and salt; cover and cook on high for 30 minutes or until pepper is tender. Serve with rice.

FREEZE OPTION *Freeze the cooled bean mixture in freezer containers. To use, partially thaw in the refrigerator overnight. Microwave, covered, on high in a microwave-safe dish until heated through, stirring and adding a little water if necessary.*

PER SERVING *⅔ cup beans with ⅔ cup rice equals 297 cal., 7 g fat (3 g sat. fat), 33 mg chol., 441 mg sodium, 50 g carb., 12 g fiber, 17 g pro.*

ALL-DAY RED
BEANS & RICE

SHREDDED PORK WITH BEANS

A friend gave me this recipe, which my sons all say is a keeper. For a change of pace, spoon the pork into corn or whole wheat tortillas.
—SARAH JOHNSTON LINCOLN, NE

PREP: 20 MIN. • **COOK:** 8 HOURS
MAKES: 12 SERVINGS

- 3 pounds pork tenderloin, cut into 3-inch lengths
- 2 cans (15 ounces each) black beans, rinsed and drained
- 1 jar (24 ounces) picante sauce
  Hot cooked rice, optional

Place the pork, beans and picante sauce in a 5-qt. slow cooker. Cover and cook on low for 8 hours or until pork is tender. Shred the pork; return to slow cooker. Serve with rice if desired.

PER SERVING *1 cup (calculated without rice) equals 207 cal., 4 g fat (1 g sat. fat), 64 mg chol., 595 mg sodium, 14 g carb., 3 g fiber, 26 g pro.* **Diabetic Exchanges:** *3 lean meat, 1 starch.*

TOP TIP

WHICH RICE?

When picking the most nutritious rice option, many point to brown rice. Brown rice has the husk removed but not the bran layer—the bran layer retains more vitamin, mineral and fiber content than white rice.

SHREDDED PORK
WITH BEANS

CRANBERRY PORK ROAST

PORK CHOP DINNER

Family and friends call me the Crock-Pot Queen. Of my many slow-cooked specialties, this fabulous dish gets a thumbs-up from my husband every time.
—**JANET PHILLIPS** MEADVILLE, PA

PREP: 10 MIN. • **COOK:** 4 HOURS
MAKES: 6 SERVINGS

- 6 **pork loin chops (¾ inch thick)**
- 1 **tablespoon canola oil**
- 1 **large onion, sliced**
- 1 **medium green pepper, chopped**
- 1 **can (4 ounces) mushroom stems and pieces, drained**
- 1 **can (8 ounces) tomato sauce**
- 1 **tablespoon brown sugar**
- 2 **teaspoons Worcestershire sauce**
- 1½ **teaspoons cider vinegar**
- ½ **teaspoon salt**
  Hot cooked rice, optional

In a skillet, brown pork chops on both sides in oil; drain. Place chops in a 3-qt. slow cooker. Add onion, green pepper and mushrooms. In a bowl, combine the tomato sauce, brown sugar, Worcestershire sauce, vinegar and salt. Pour over meat and vegetables. Cover and cook on low for 4-5 hours or until meat is tender. Serve with rice if desired.
PER SERVING *1 serving equals 199 cal., 8 g fat (2 g sat. fat), 59 mg chol., 507 mg sodium, 10 g carb., 1 g fiber, 22 g pro.* **Diabetic Exchange:** *3 lean meat.*

CRANBERRY PORK ROAST

The colorful cranberry sauce in this recipe accompanies the juicy pork wonderfully. There's plenty of sauce for each serving.
—**JESSICA PHILLEO** CARMEL, IN

PREP: 25 MIN. • **COOK:** 8 HOURS
MAKES: 10 SERVINGS (5 CUPS SAUCE)

- 1 **package (12 ounces) fresh or frozen cranberries, thawed**
- 1 **package (12 ounces) frozen pitted dark sweet cherries, thawed**
- ¼ **cup packed brown sugar**
- ¼ **cup Marsala wine or unsweetened apple juice**
- ⅓ **cup raspberry vinaigrette**
- 1 **large red onion, sliced**
- 1 **large apple, peeled and sliced**
- 1 **boneless whole pork loin roast (4 pounds)**
- 1 **teaspoon minced fresh rosemary or ¼ teaspoon dried rosemary, crushed**
- 1 **teaspoon coarsely ground pepper**
- 2 **teaspoons cornstarch**
- 2 **teaspoons water**

1. In a large saucepan, combine the cranberries, cherries, brown sugar and wine. Cook over medium heat until berries pop, about 15 minutes. Stir in vinaigrette.

2. Place half of the onion and apple in a 4- or 5-qt. slow cooker. Cut the roast in half; add to slow cooker. Top with remaining onion and apple. Pour cranberry mixture over top. Sprinkle with the rosemary and pepper. Cover and cook on low for 8-10 hours or until meat is tender.

3. Remove meat to a serving platter; keep warm. Skim fat from cooking juices; transfer juices to a small saucepan. Bring liquid to a boil. Combine cornstarch and water until smooth. Gradually stir into the pan. Bring to a boil; cook and stir for 2 minutes or until thickened. Serve with meat.
PER SERVING *5 ounces cooked pork with ½ cup sauce equals 294 cal., 11 g fat (3 g sat. fat), 68 mg chol., 110 mg sodium, 21 g carb., 3 g fiber, 27 g pro.* **Diabetic Exchanges:** *4 lean meat, 1 fruit, 1 fat, ½ starch.*

THE SKINNY

CHOOSE LEAN

If you want to eat lean protein, try pork (round, loin or tenderloin), or skinless chicken or turkey. All of these options will fill you up in a healthy way.

COUNTRY-STYLE PORK LOIN

This pork roast tops my son's list of favorite foods. The meat practically melts in your mouth. Good with a variety of sides, we enjoy it with mashed potatoes.

—CORINA FLANSBERG
CARSON CITY, NV

PREP: 20 MIN.
COOK: 5 HOURS + STANDING
MAKES: 8 SERVINGS

- 1 boneless pork loin roast (3 pounds)
- ½ cup all-purpose flour
- 1 teaspoon onion powder
- 1 teaspoon ground mustard
- 2 tablespoons canola oil
- 2 cups reduced-sodium chicken broth
- ¼ cup cornstarch
- ¼ cup cold water
  Hot mashed potatoes, optional

1. Cut the roast in half. In a large resealable plastic bag, combine the flour, onion powder and mustard. Add pork, one portion at a time, and shake to coat. In a large skillet, brown pork in oil on all sides.

2. Transfer to a 5-qt. slow cooker. Pour broth over pork. Cover and cook on low for 5-6 hours or until tender. Remove the pork and keep warm; let stand for 10-15 minutes before slicing.

3. Strain cooking juices, reserving 2½ cups; skim the fat from the reserved juices. Transfer to a small saucepan. Bring the liquid to a boil. Combine the cornstarch and water until smooth; gradually stir into the pan. Bring to a boil; cook and stir for 2 minutes or until thickened. Serve the pork and gravy with mashed potatoes if desired.

FREEZE OPTION *Cool pork and gravy. Freeze sliced pork and gravy in freezer containers. To use, partially thaw in the refrigerator overnight. Heat through slowly in a covered skillet, stirring occasionally and adding a little broth or water if necessary. Serve as directed.*

PER SERVING *5 ounces cooked pork with ¼ cup gravy (calculated without potatoes) equals 291 cal., 11 g fat (3 g sat. fat), 85 mg chol., 204 mg sodium, 10 g carb., trace fiber, 34 g pro.* ***Diabetic Exchanges:*** *5 lean meat, ½ starch, ½ fat.*

COUNTRY-STYLE
PORK LOIN

CARNE GUISADA

After temporarily moving out of state, my boyfriend and I really started to miss the spicy flavors of Texas, so we made this recipe often. We serve it with homemade flour tortillas or brown rice.
—**KELLY EVANS** DENTON, TX

PREP: 25 MIN. • **COOK:** 7 HOURS
MAKES: 12 SERVINGS
(ABOUT 2 QUARTS)

- 1 **bottle (12 ounces) beer**
- ¼ **cup all-purpose flour**
- 2 **tablespoons tomato paste**
- 1 **jalapeno pepper, seeded and chopped**
- 4 **teaspoons Worcestershire sauce**
- 1 **bay leaf**
- 2 **to 3 teaspoons crushed red pepper flakes**
- 2 **teaspoons chili powder**
- 1½ **teaspoons ground cumin**
- ½ **teaspoon salt**
- ½ **teaspoon paprika**
- 2 **garlic cloves, minced**
- ½ **teaspoon red wine vinegar**
     Dash liquid smoke, optional
- 1 **boneless pork shoulder butt roast (3 pounds), cut into 2-inch pieces**
- 2 **large unpeeled red potatoes, chopped**
- 1 **medium onion, chopped**
     Whole wheat tortillas or hot cooked brown rice, lime wedges and chopped fresh cilantro, optional

1. In a 4- or 5-qt. slow cooker, combine the first 13 ingredients. If desired, stir in liquid smoke. Add pork, potatoes and onion; toss to combine. Cook, covered, 7-9 hours or until pork is tender.
2. Discard bay leaf; skim fat from cooking juices. Shred pork slightly with two forks. If desired, serve with tortillas, lime and cilantro.
NOTE *Wear disposable gloves when cutting hot peppers; the oils can burn skin. Avoid touching your face.*

PER SERVING *⅔ cup (calculated without tortillas) equals 261 cal., 12 g fat (4 g sat. fat), 67 mg chol., 200 mg sodium, 16 g carb., 2 g fiber, 21 g pro.* **Diabetic Exchanges:** *3 medium-fat meat, 1 starch.*

PORK ROAST WITH PEACH SAUCE

My husband loves this roast with spiced peaches. Easy to make, it's ideal for special occasions or weeknight meals when it's chilly.
—**JANICE CHRISTOFFERSON** EAGLE RIVER, WI

PREP: 20 MIN. • **COOK:** 6 HOURS
MAKES: 8 SERVINGS (2½ CUPS SAUCE)

- 1 **boneless pork loin roast (3 to 4 pounds)**
- 2 **teaspoons canola oil**
- ¼ **teaspoon onion salt**
- ¼ **teaspoon pepper**
- 1 **can (15¼ ounces) sliced peaches**
- ½ **cup chili sauce**
- ⅓ **cup packed brown sugar**
- 3 **tablespoons cider vinegar**
- 1 **teaspoon pumpkin pie spice**
- 2 **tablespoons cornstarch**
- 2 **tablespoons cold water**

1. Cut the roast in half. In a large skillet, brown the pork in oil on all sides. Transfer to a 4- or 5-qt. slow cooker. Sprinkle with the onion salt and pepper.
2. Drain peaches, reserving juice in a small bowl; stir chili sauce, brown sugar, vinegar and pie spice into the juice. Spoon peaches over the roast; top with juice mixture. Cover and cook on low for 6-8 hours or until meat is tender.
3. Remove meat and peaches to a serving platter; keep warm. Skim fat from cooking juices; transfer juices to a saucepan. Bring liquid to a boil. Combine the cornstarch and water until smooth; gradually stir into the pan. Bring to a boil; cook and stir for 2 minutes or until thickened. Serve with pork and peaches.
PER SERVING *5 ounces cooked pork with about ⅓ cup sauce equals 318 cal., 8 g fat (3 g sat. fat), 85 mg chol., 344 mg sodium, 25 g carb., trace fiber, 33 g pro.* **Diabetic Exchanges:** *4 lean meat, 1 starch, ½ fruit.*

PORK ROAST WITH PEACH SAUCE

CARNE
GUISADA

TOMATO-TOPPED
ITALIAN PORK CHOPS

TOMATO-TOPPED ITALIAN PORK CHOPS

When you're only seven ingredients away from a delicious meal, what's not to love?

—KRYSTLE CHASSE
RADIUM HOT SPRINGS, BC

PREP: 25 MIN. • **COOK:** 8 HOURS
MAKES: 6 SERVINGS

- 6 bone-in pork loin chops (7 ounces each)
- 1 tablespoon canola oil
- 1 small onion, chopped
- ½ cup chopped carrot
- 1 can (14½ ounces) diced tomatoes, drained
- ¼ cup reduced-fat balsamic vinaigrette
- 2 teaspoons dried oregano

1. In a large skillet, brown the chops in oil in batches. Transfer to a 4- or 5-qt. slow cooker coated with cooking spray. Saute the onion and carrot in drippings until tender. Stir in the tomatoes, vinaigrette and oregano; pour over chops.
2. Cover and cook on low for 8-10 hours or until meat is tender.
PER SERVING *1 pork chop equals 267 cal., 12 g fat (3 g sat. fat), 86 mg chol., 234 mg sodium, 7 g carb., 2 g fiber, 31 g pro.* **Diabetic Exchanges:** *4 lean meat, 1 vegetable, 1 fat.*

TOP TIP

GETTING VITAMIN A

You probably heard that you should eat carrots because they're good for your eyes, right? Turns out it might be true! Carrots are an excellent source of vitamin A, which can promote good eyesight. In addition, carrots contain vitamin K, which helps blood clot properly.

CHOPS 'N' BEANS

Combine tender pork chops and two kinds of beans for a satisfying supper right from your slow cooker.

—DOROTHY PRITCHETT
WILLS POINT, TX

PREP: 15 MIN. • **COOK:** 5 HOURS
MAKES: 4 SERVINGS

- 4 pork loin chops (½ inch thick)
- ¼ teaspoon salt
- ¼ teaspoon pepper
- 1 tablespoon canola oil
- 2 medium onions, chopped
- 2 garlic cloves, minced
- ¼ cup chili sauce
- 1½ teaspoons brown sugar
- 1 teaspoon prepared mustard
- 1 can (16 ounces) kidney beans, rinsed and drained
- 1¾ cups frozen lima beans, thawed

1. Sprinkle pork chops with salt and pepper. In a large skillet, heat oil over medium-high heat. Brown chops on both sides. Transfer to a 3-qt. slow cooker. Discard the drippings, reserving 1 tablespoon drippings in skillet. Add onions; cook and stir until tender. Add garlic; cook and stir 1 minute. Stir in the chili sauce, brown sugar and mustard. Pour over chops.
2. Cook, covered, on low 4 hours or until meat is almost tender. Stir in beans. Cook, covered, 1 to 2 hours longer or until heated through.
PER SERVING *1 serving equals 297 cal., 5 g fat (1 g sat. fat), 14 mg chol., 607 mg sodium, 45 g carb., 11 g fiber, 19 g pro.* **Diabetic Exchanges:** *3 starch, 3 lean meat.*

SLOW-COOKED PORK TACOS

Sometimes I'll substitute Bibb lettuce leaves for the tortillas to make crunchy lettuce wraps instead of tacos. It's good either way.

—**KATHLEEN WOLF** NAPERVILLE, IL

PREP: 20 MIN. • **COOK:** 4 HOURS
MAKES: 10 SERVINGS

- 2 pounds boneless pork sirloin, cut into 1-inch pieces
- 1½ cups salsa verde
- 1 medium sweet red pepper, chopped
- 1 medium onion, chopped
- ¼ cup chopped dried apricots
- 2 tablespoons lime juice
- 2 garlic cloves, minced
- 1 teaspoon ground cumin
- ½ teaspoon salt
- ¼ teaspoon white pepper
  Dash hot pepper sauce
- 10 flour tortillas (8 inches), warmed
  Reduced-fat sour cream, thinly sliced green onions, cubed avocado, shredded reduced-fat cheddar cheese and chopped tomato, optional

1. In a 3-qt. slow cooker, combine the first 11 ingredients. Cover and cook on high for 4-5 hours or until meat is tender.

2. Shred pork with two forks. Place about ½ cup pork mixture in the center of each tortilla. Serve with toppings if desired.

PER SERVING *1 taco (calculated without optional toppings) equals 301 cal., 8 g fat (2 g sat. fat), 54 mg chol., 616 mg sodium, 32 g carb., 1 g fiber, 24 g pro.* **Diabetic Exchanges:** *3 lean meat, 2 starch.*

SLOW-COOKED PORK TACOS

HERBED PORK ROAST

A quick rub of butter and herbs adds awesome flavor to this roast. I like to serve the roast with parsley-tossed potatoes and a green salad.

—SHELIA LETCHWORTH
VERSAILLES, MO

PREP: 25 MIN.
COOK: 8 HOURS + STANDING
MAKES: 12 SERVINGS

- 1 **boneless pork loin roast (4 pounds)**
- 1 **cup water**
- ¼ **cup butter, softened**
- 2 **tablespoons rubbed sage**
- 2 **tablespoons dried parsley flakes**
- 2 **teaspoons pepper**
- 1 **teaspoon minced garlic**
- 1 **teaspoon dried oregano**
- ½ **teaspoon salt**
- 1 **small onion, thinly sliced**
- 1 **teaspoon browning sauce, optional**

Cut roast in half. Place pork and water in a 4-qt. slow cooker. Spread butter over meat. Combine the sage, parsley, pepper, garlic, oregano and salt; sprinkle over meat. Top with onion. Cover and cook on low for 8-10 hours or until meat is tender. If desired, thicken cooking juices. Stir in browning sauce if desired. Let the meat stand 10 minutes before slicing.

PER SERVING *4 ounces cooked meat with about 2 tablespoons gravy (calculated without browning sauce) equals 227 cal., 11 g fat (5 g sat. fat), 85 mg chol., 171 mg sodium, 1 g carb., trace fiber, 29 g pro.* **Diabetic Exchanges:** *4 lean meat, 1 fat.*

HERBED PORK ROAST

VEGETARIAN STUFFED
PEPPERS, PAGE 181

OTHER ENTREES

180

179

176

LAMB WITH ORZO

Looking to switch up your slow-cooked staples? Consider this lamb entree with some traditional Greek flavors. A splash of lemon juice and zesty lemon peel complement the spinach and feta cheese.

—DAN KELMENSON
WEST BLOOMFIELD, MI

PREP: 30 MIN. • **COOK:** 8 HOURS
MAKES: 9 SERVINGS

- 1 boneless lamb shoulder roast (3 pounds)
- 3 tablespoons lemon juice
- 3 garlic cloves, minced
- 2 teaspoons dried oregano
- 2 teaspoons grated lemon peel
- ¼ teaspoon salt
- 1 package (16 ounces) orzo pasta
- 2 packages (9 ounces each) fresh spinach, torn divided
- 1 cup (4 ounces) crumbled feta cheese, divided

1. Cut the roast in half. Place in a 5-qt. slow cooker. Drizzle with lemon juice. Sprinkle with garlic, oregano, lemon peel and salt. Cover and cook on low for 8-10 hours or until meat is tender.

2. Cook orzo according to package directions. Remove lamb from slow cooker. Shred meat with two forks; set aside and keep warm.

3. Skim the fat from cooking juices if necessary; return 1 cup cooking juices to the slow cooker. Add a package of spinach. Cook on high for 5-10 minutes or until spinach is wilted. Drain orzo; add to spinach mixture. Stir in reserved meat and ½ cup feta cheese.

4. To serve, arrange remaining fresh spinach on nine individual plates. Top with lamb mixture. Sprinkle each with the remaining feta cheese.

PER SERVING *1 cup lamb mixture with ½ cup spinach equals 438 cal., 11 g fat (4 g sat. fat), 105 mg chol., 333 mg sodium, 41 g carb., 3 g fiber, 41 g pro.*

LAMB WITH ORZO

TANGY LAMB TAGINE

I love lamb stew but wanted to try something different, so I created this recipe that uses Moroccan spices. The stew tastes even better served a day or two later, when the flavors have had a chance to meld.

—BRIDGET KLUSMAN OTSEGO, MI

PREP: 40 MIN. • **COOK:** 8 HOURS
MAKES: 8 SERVINGS

- 3 pounds lamb stew meat, cut into 1½-inch cubes
- 1 teaspoon salt
- 1 teaspoon pepper
- 4 tablespoons olive oil, divided
- 6 medium carrots, sliced
- 2 medium onions, chopped
- 6 garlic cloves, minced
- 2 teaspoons grated lemon peel
- ¼ cup lemon juice
- 1 tablespoon minced fresh gingerroot
- 1½ teaspoons ground cinnamon
- 1½ teaspoons ground cumin
- 1½ teaspoons paprika
- 2½ cups reduced-sodium chicken broth
- ¼ cup sweet vermouth
- ¼ cup honey
- ½ cup pitted dates, chopped
- ½ cup sliced almonds, toasted

1. Sprinkle lamb with salt and pepper. In a Dutch oven, brown meat in 2 tablespoons oil in batches. Using a slotted spoon, transfer to a 4- or 5-qt. slow cooker.

2. In the Dutch oven, saute the carrots, onions, garlic and lemon peel in remaining oil until crisp-tender. Add the lemon juice, ginger, cinnamon, cumin and paprika; cook and stir 2 minutes longer. Add to slow cooker.

3. Stir in the broth, vermouth, honey and dates. Cover and cook on low for 8-10 hours or until lamb is tender. Sprinkle with almonds.

PER SERVING *1¼ cups equals 440 cal., 19 g fat (4 g sat. fat), 111 mg chol., 620 mg sodium, 28 g carb., 4 g fiber, 38 g pro.*

TANGY LAMB TAGINE

**SWEET POTATO
LENTIL STEW**

SWEET POTATO LENTIL STEW

Years ago, I first experienced the spiciness and wonderful aroma of this hearty dish. You can serve the stew alone or as a topper for meat or poultry. It's great either way!

—HEATHER GRAY LITTLE ROCK, AR

PREP: 15 MIN. • **COOK:** 5 HOURS
MAKES: 6 SERVINGS

- 1¼ **pounds sweet potatoes (about 2 medium), peeled and cut into 1-inch pieces**
- 1½ **cups dried lentils, rinsed**
- 3 **medium carrots, cut into 1-inch pieces**
- 1 **medium onion, chopped**
- 4 **garlic cloves, minced**
- ½ **teaspoon ground cumin**
- ¼ **teaspoon ground ginger**
- ¼ **teaspoon cayenne pepper**
- 1 **carton (32 ounces) vegetable broth**
- ¼ **cup minced fresh cilantro**

In a 3-qt. slow cooker, combine first nine ingredients. Cook, covered, on low 5-6 hours or until vegetables and lentils are tender. Stir in the cilantro.

PER SERVING *1⅓ cups equals 290 cal., 1 g fat (trace sat. fat), 0 chol., 662 mg sodium, 58 g carb., 15 g fiber, 15 g pro.*

SIMPLE POACHED SALMON

My kind of recipe is healthy and almost effortless. The salmon here always cooks to perfection!
—**ERIN CHILCOAT** CENTRAL ISLIP, NY

PREP: 10 MIN. • **COOK:** 1½ HOURS
MAKES: 4 SERVINGS

- 2 **cups water**
- 1 **cup white wine**
- 1 **medium onion, sliced**
- 1 **celery rib, sliced**
- 1 **medium carrot, sliced**
- 2 **tablespoons lemon juice**
- 3 **fresh thyme sprigs**
- 1 **fresh rosemary sprig**
- 1 **bay leaf**
- ½ **teaspoon salt**
- ¼ **teaspoon pepper**
- 4 **salmon fillets (1¼ inches thick and 6 ounces each)**
  Lemon wedges

1. In a 3-qt. slow cooker, combine first 11 ingredients. Cook, covered, on low 45 minutes.
2. Carefully place fillets in liquid; add additional warm water (120° to 130°) to cover if needed. Cook, covered, 45-55 minutes or just until fish flakes easily with a fork (a thermometer inserted in fish should read at least 145°). Remove the fish from cooking liquid. Serve warm or cold with lemon wedges.
PER SERVING *1 salmon fillet equals 272 cal., 16 g fat (3 g sat. fat), 85 mg chol., 115 mg sodium, 1 g carb., trace fiber, 29 g pro.* **Diabetic Exchange:** *4 lean meat.*

FREEZE IT
RED CLAM SAUCE

While this luscious sauce may taste like you've worked on it all day, it actually cooks hands-free! What a great way to jazz up pasta.
—**JOANN BROWN** LATROBE, PA

PREP: 25 MIN. • **COOK:** 3 HOURS
MAKES: 4 SERVINGS

- 1 **medium onion, chopped**
- 1 **tablespoon canola oil**
- 2 **garlic cloves, minced**
- 2 **cans (6½ ounces each) chopped clams, undrained**
- 1 **can (14½ ounces) diced tomatoes, undrained**
- 1 **can (6 ounces) tomato paste**
- ¼ **cup minced fresh parsley**
- 1 **bay leaf**
- 1 **teaspoon sugar**
- 1 **teaspoon dried basil**
- ½ **teaspoon dried thyme**
- 6 **ounces linguine, cooked and drained**

1. In a small skillet, saute the onion in oil until tender. Add garlic; cook 1 minute longer.
2. Transfer to a 1½- or 2-qt. slow cooker. Stir in the clams, tomatoes, tomato paste, parsley, bay leaf, sugar, basil and thyme.
3. Cover and cook on low for 3-4 hours or until heated through. Discard bay leaf. Serve with linguine.
FREEZE OPTION *Cool sauce before placing in a freezer container. Cover and freeze for up to 3 months. To use, thaw in refrigerator overnight. Place in a large saucepan; heat through, stirring occasionally. Serve with linguine.*
PER SERVING *1 cup sauce with ¾ cup cooked linguine equals 305 cal., 5 g fat (trace sat. fat), 15 mg chol., 553 mg sodium, 53 g carb., 7 g fiber, 15 g pro.*

RED CLAM SAUCE

ENCHILADA PIE

Stacked high with layers of beans, veggies and cheese, this mile-high pie makes for a fun fiesta night with the family. Who would have guessed it all comes together so easily in the slow cooker?

—JACQUELINE CORREA LANDING, NJ

PREP: 40 MIN. • **COOK:** 4 HOURS
MAKES: 8 SERVINGS

- 1 package (12 ounces) frozen vegetarian meat crumbles
- 1 cup chopped onion
- ½ cup chopped green pepper
- 2 teaspoons canola oil
- 1 can (16 ounces) kidney beans, rinsed and drained
- 1 can (15 ounces) black beans, rinsed and drained
- 1 can (10 ounces) diced tomatoes and green chilies, undrained
- ½ cup water
- 1½ teaspoons chili powder
- ½ teaspoon ground cumin
- ¼ teaspoon pepper
- 6 whole wheat tortillas (8 inches)
- 2 cups (8 ounces) shredded reduced-fat cheddar cheese

1. Cut three 25x3-in. strips of heavy-duty foil; crisscross so they resemble spokes of a wheel. Place strips on the bottom and up the sides of a 5-qt. slow cooker. Coat strips with cooking spray.

2. In a large saucepan, cook the meat crumbles, onion and green pepper in oil until vegetables are tender. Stir in both cans of beans, tomatoes, water, chili powder, cumin and pepper. Bring to a boil. Reduce heat; simmer, uncovered, for 10 minutes.

3. In prepared slow cooker, layer about a cup of bean mixture, one tortilla and ⅓ cup cheese. Repeat layers five times. Cover and cook on low for 4-5 hours or until heated through and cheese is melted.

4. Using foil strips as handles, remove the pie to a platter.

NOTE *Vegetarian meat crumbles are a nutritious protein source made from soy. Look for them in the natural foods freezer section.*
PER SERVING *1 piece equals 367 cal., 11 g fat (4 g sat. fat), 20 mg chol., 818 mg sodium, 41 g carb., 9 g fiber, 25 g pro.* **Diabetic Exchanges:** *3 starch, 2 lean meat, 1 fat.*

CORN BREAD-TOPPED FRIJOLES

My family often requests this savory entree. It's loaded with fresh Southwestern flavors.

—SUZANNE CALDWELL ARTESIA, NM

PREP: 20 MIN. • **COOK:** 3 HOURS
MAKES: 8 SERVINGS

- 1 medium onion, chopped
- 1 medium green pepper, chopped
- 1 tablespoon canola oil
- 2 garlic cloves, minced
- 1 can (16 ounces) kidney beans, rinsed and drained
- 1 can (15 ounces) pinto beans, rinsed and drained
- 1 can (14½ ounces) diced tomatoes, undrained
- 1 can (8 ounces) tomato sauce
- 1 teaspoon chili powder
- ½ teaspoon pepper
- ⅛ teaspoon hot pepper sauce

CORN BREAD TOPPING

- 1 cup all-purpose flour
- 1 cup yellow cornmeal
- 1 tablespoon sugar
- 1½ teaspoons baking powder
- ½ teaspoon salt
- 2 large eggs, lightly beaten
- 1¼ cups fat-free milk
- 1 can (8¾ ounces) cream-style corn
- 3 tablespoons canola oil

1. In a large skillet, saute onion and green pepper in oil until tender. Add garlic; cook 1 minute longer. Transfer to a greased 5-qt. slow cooker.

2. Stir in beans, tomatoes, tomato sauce, chili powder, pepper and pepper sauce. Cover and cook on high for 1 hour.

3. In a large bowl, combine flour, cornmeal, sugar, baking powder and salt. Combine the eggs, milk, corn and oil; add to the dry ingredients and mix well. Spoon evenly over bean mixture.

4. Cover and cook on high for 2 hours or until a toothpick inserted near the center of corn bread comes out clean.

PER SERVING *1 serving equals 367 cal., 9 g fat (1 g sat. fat), 54 mg chol., 708 mg sodium, 59 g carb., 9 g fiber, 14 g pro.*

CORN BREAD-TOPPED
FRIJOLES

VEGETARIAN STUFFED PEPPERS

I slightly updated my mom's stuffed peppers, which were a favorite when I was growing up. Whenever I make them, I'm reminded of home.
—**MELISSA MCCABE** VICTOR, NY

PREP: 30 MIN. • **COOK:** 3½ HOURS
MAKES: 6 SERVINGS

- 2 cups cooked brown rice
- 3 small tomatoes, chopped
- 1 cup frozen corn, thawed
- 1 small sweet onion, chopped
- ¾ cup cubed Monterey Jack cheese
- ⅓ cup chopped ripe olives
- ⅓ cup canned black beans, rinsed and drained
- ⅓ cup canned red beans, rinsed and drained
- 4 fresh basil leaves, thinly sliced
- 3 garlic cloves, minced
- 1 teaspoon salt
- ½ teaspoon pepper
- 6 large sweet peppers
- ¾ cup meatless spaghetti sauce
- ½ cup water
- 4 tablespoons grated Parmesan cheese, divided

1. Place the first 12 ingredients in a large bowl; mix lightly to combine. Cut and discard tops from sweet peppers; remove seeds. Fill the peppers with rice mixture.

2. In a small bowl, mix spaghetti sauce and water; pour half of the mixture into an oval 5-qt. slow cooker. Add filled peppers. Top with remaining sauce. Sprinkle with 2 tablespoons cheese.

3. Cook, covered, on low for 3½-4 hours or until peppers are tender. Sprinkle with remaining Parmesan cheese.

PER SERVING *1 stuffed pepper equals 261 cal., 8 g fat (4 g sat. fat), 18 mg chol., 815 mg sodium, 39 g carb., 7 g fiber, 11 g pro.* **Diabetic Exchanges:** *2 starch, 1 lean meat, 1 vegetable, 1 fat.*

VEGETARIAN STUFFED PEPPERS

STRAWBERRY RHUBARB SAUCE,
PAGE 189

SNACKS & SWEETS

184

186

189

SWEET & SPICY PEANUTS

These crunchy peanuts have a caramel-like coating, and hot sauce gives them a touch of heat. They make a tasty snack any time of day.

—TASTE OF HOME TEST KITCHEN

PREP: 10 MIN.
COOK: 1½ HOURS + COOLING
MAKES: 4 CUPS

- 3 cups salted peanuts
- ½ cup sugar
- ⅓ cup packed brown sugar
- 2 tablespoons hot water
- 2 tablespoons butter, melted
- 1 tablespoon Sriracha Asian hot chili sauce or hot pepper sauce
- 1 teaspoon chili powder

1. Place the peanuts in a greased 1½-qt. slow cooker. In a small bowl, combine the sugars, water, butter, hot sauce and chili powder. Pour over peanuts. Cover and cook on high for 1½ hours, stirring once.
2. Spread on waxed paper to cool. Store in an airtight container.
PER SERVING *⅓ cup equals 284 cal., 20 g fat (4 g sat. fat), 5 mg chol., 214 mg sodium, 22 g carb., 3 g fiber, 10 g pro.*

SWEET & SPICY PEANUTS

SLOW-COOKED PEACH SALSA

Fresh peaches and tomatoes make my salsa a hands-down winner over store versions. As a treat, I give my co-workers several jars throughout the year.

—PEGGI STAHNKE CLEVELAND, OH

PREP: 20 MIN. • **COOK:** 3 HOURS
MAKES: 11 CUPS

- 4 pounds tomatoes (about 12 medium), chopped
- 1 medium onion, chopped
- 4 jalapeno peppers, seeded and finely chopped
- ½ to ⅔ cup packed brown sugar
- ¼ cup minced fresh cilantro
- 4 garlic cloves, minced
- 1 teaspoon salt
- 4 cups chopped peeled fresh peaches (about 4 medium), divided
- 1 can (6 ounces) tomato paste

1. In a 5-qt. slow cooker, combine the first seven ingredients; stir in 2 cups peaches. Cook, covered, on low 3-4 hours or until the onion is tender.
2. Stir tomato paste and remaining peaches into slow cooker. Transfer to covered containers. (If freezing, use freezer-safe containers and fill to within ½ in. of tops.) Refrigerate salsa up to 1 week or freeze up to 12 months. Thaw frozen salsa in refrigerator before serving.
NOTE *Wear disposable gloves when cutting hot peppers; the oils can burn skin. Avoid touching your face.*
PER SERVING *¼ cup equals 28 cal., trace fat (trace sat. fat), 0 chol., 59 mg sodium, 7 g carb., 1 g fiber, 1 g pro.* **Diabetic Exchange:** *½ starch.*

SLOW-COOKED
PEACH SALSA

WARM SPICED
CIDER PUNCH

sticks on a double thickness of cheesecloth; bring up corners of cloth and tie with string to form a bag. Place bag in slow cooker.

2. Cover and cook on low for 4-5 hours or until heated through. Remove and discard spice bag. Garnish with orange slices and additional cinnamon sticks if desired.

PER SERVING *¾ cup equals 108 cal., trace fat (trace sat. fat), 0 chol., 13 mg sodium, 26 g carb., trace fiber, 1 g pro.*

⑤INGREDIENTS

SLOW-COOKED APPLESAUCE

My chunky applesauce works as either a light snack or alongside main dishes. Because it's prepared in the slow cooker, you can fix it and forget it so you and the family can head out for some fun.

—SUSANNE WASSON
MONTGOMERY, NY

PREP: 20 MIN. • **COOK:** 6 HOURS
MAKES: 12 CUPS

6	pounds apples (about 18 medium), peeled and sliced
1	cup sugar
1	cup water
1	teaspoon salt
1	teaspoon ground cinnamon
¼	cup butter, cubed
2	teaspoons vanilla extract

1. In a 5-qt. slow cooker, combine the apples, sugar, water, salt and cinnamon. Cover and cook on low for 6-8 hours or until tender.
2. Turn off heat; stir in butter and vanilla. Mash if desired. Serve warm or cold.

PER SERVING *½ cup equals 105 cal., 2 g fat (1 g sat. fat), 5 mg chol., 112 mg sodium, 23 g carb., 2 g fiber, trace pro.* **Diabetic Exchanges:** *1 fruit, ½ starch, ½ fat.*

WARM SPICED CIDER PUNCH

Nothing warms you up on a chilly night the way hot apple cider does, so ladle up some love!

—SUSAN SMITH FOREST, VA

PREP: 5 MIN. • **COOK:** 4 HOURS
MAKES: 8 SERVINGS

4	cups apple cider or unsweetened apple juice
2¾	cups water
¾	cup orange juice concentrate
¾	teaspoon ground nutmeg
¾	teaspoon ground ginger
3	whole cloves
2	cinnamon sticks
	Orange slices and additional cinnamon sticks, optional

1. In a 3-qt. slow cooker, combine the apple cider, water, orange juice concentrate, nutmeg and ginger. Place the cloves and cinnamon

CHERRY & SPICE RICE PUDDING

Cinnamon and cherries sweeten the deal in this dessert. If you've never tried rice pudding, here's an excellent place to start.

—**DEB PERRY** TRAVERSE CITY, MI

PREP: 10 MIN. • **COOK:** 2 HOURS
MAKES: 12 SERVINGS

- 4 **cups cooked long grain rice**
- 1 **can (12 ounces) evaporated milk**
- 1 **cup 2% milk**
- ⅓ **cup sugar**
- ¼ **cup water**
- ¾ **cup dried cherries**
- 3 **tablespoons butter, softened**
- 2 **teaspoons vanilla extract**
- ½ **teaspoon ground cinnamon**
- ¼ **teaspoon ground nutmeg**

1. In a large bowl, combine the rice, evaporated milk, milk, sugar and water. Stir in the remaining ingredients. Transfer to a 3-qt. slow cooker coated with cooking spray.

2. Cover and cook on low for 2-3 hours or until the mixture is thickened. Stir pudding lightly before serving. Serve warm or cold. Refrigerate leftovers.

PER SERVING *1/2 cup equals 193 cal., 5 g fat (4 g sat. fat), 19 mg chol., 61 mg sodium, 31 g carb., trace fiber, 4 g pro.* **Diabetic Exchanges: 2 starch, 1 fat.**

TOP TIP

MILK SAVINGS

Using 2% milk instead of whole milk in the Cherry & Spice Rice Pudding recipe cuts back on calories, fat and saturated fat. That means you can feel great about enjoying it.

CHERRY & SPICE
RICE PUDDING

APPLE PIE OATMEAL DESSERT

APPLE PIE OATMEAL DESSERT

This warm and comforting dessert brings back memories of time spent with my family around the kitchen table. I usually serve the dish with sweetened whipped cream or vanilla ice cream as a topper.

—**CAROL GREER** EARLVILLE, IL

PREP: 15 MIN. • **COOK:** 4 HOURS
MAKES: 6 SERVINGS

- 1 cup quick-cooking oats
- ½ cup all-purpose flour
- ⅓ cup packed brown sugar
- 2 teaspoons baking powder
- 1½ teaspoons apple pie spice
- ¼ teaspoon salt
- 3 large eggs
- 1⅔ cups 2% milk, divided
- 1½ teaspoons vanilla extract
- 3 medium apples, peeled and finely chopped
  Vanilla ice cream, optional

1. In a large bowl, whisk the oats, flour, brown sugar, baking powder, pie spice and salt. In a small bowl, whisk eggs, 1 cup milk and vanilla until blended. Add to oat mixture, stirring just until moistened. Fold in apples.
2. Transfer to a greased 3-qt. slow cooker. Cook, covered, on low 4-5 hours or until apples are tender and top is set.
3. Stir in remaining milk. Serve warm or cold, with ice cream if desired.
PER SERVING ¾ cup (calculated without ice cream) equals 238 cal., 5 g fat (2 g sat. fat), 111 mg chol., 306 mg sodium, 41 g carb., 3 g fiber, 8 g pro.

STRAWBERRY RHUBARB SAUCE

A neighbor shared with me the recipe for this wonderful fruit sauce. It's a great way to use up a bumper crop of rhubarb. We like it over ice cream, pancakes and even fresh, hot biscuits.

—**NANCY COWLISHAW** BOISE, ID

PREP: 15 MIN. • **COOK:** 4¼ HOURS
MAKES: 4½ CUPS

- 6 cups sliced fresh or frozen rhubarb, thawed
- 1 cup sugar
- ½ cup unsweetened apple juice
- 3 cinnamon sticks (3 inches)
- ½ teaspoon grated orange peel
- ¼ teaspoon ground ginger
- 1 pint fresh strawberries, halved
  Vanilla ice cream

1. Place the rhubarb, sugar, juice, cinnamon sticks, orange peel and ginger in a 3-qt. slow cooker. Cover and cook on low for 4-5 hours or until rhubarb is tender.
2. Stir in strawberries; cover and cook 15 minutes longer or until heated through. Discard cinnamon sticks. Serve with ice cream.
PER SERVING ¼ cup (calculated without ice cream) equals 60 cal., trace fat (trace sat. fat), 0 chol., 2 mg sodium, 15 g carb., 1 g fiber, trace pro. **Diabetic Exchange:** 1 fruit.

CHOCOLATE COVERED CHERRY PUDDING CAKE

Remembering how much my grandfather loved the chocolate-covered cherries we brought him for Christmas, I came up with this rich recipe in his honor. It's delicious, especially when served with whipped topping.

—MEREDITH COE CHARLOTTESVILLE, VA

PREP: 20 MIN.
COOK: 2 HOURS + STANDING
MAKES: 8 SERVINGS

- ½ cup reduced-fat sour cream
- 2 tablespoons canola oil
- 1 tablespoon butter, melted
- 2 teaspoons vanilla extract
- 1 cup all-purpose flour
- ¼ cup sugar
- ¼ cup packed brown sugar
- 3 tablespoons baking cocoa
- 2 teaspoons baking powder
- ½ teaspoon ground cinnamon
- ⅛ teaspoon salt
- 1 cup fresh or frozen pitted dark sweet cherries, thawed
- 1 cup fresh or frozen pitted tart cherries, thawed
- ⅓ cup 60% cacao bittersweet chocolate baking chips

PUDDING

- ½ cup packed brown sugar
- 2 tablespoons baking cocoa
- 1¼ cups hot water

1. In a large bowl, beat the sour cream, oil, butter and vanilla until blended. Combine the flour, sugars, cocoa, baking powder, cinnamon and salt. Add to sour cream mixture just until combined. Stir in cherries and chips. Pour into a 3-qt. slow cooker coated with cooking spray.
2. In a small bowl, combine the brown sugar and cocoa. Stir in the hot water until blended. Pour over the batter (do not stir). Cover and cook on high for 2 to 2½ hours or until set. Let stand for 15 minutes. Serve warm.

PER SERVING *1 serving equals 291 cal., 9 g fat (3 g sat. fat), 9 mg chol., 167 mg sodium, 51 g carb., 2 g fiber, 4 g pro.*

SPICED POMEGRANATE SIPPER

Your entire house will fill with the wonderful aroma of spices and simmering fruit juices when you make this.

—LISA RENSHAW KANSAS CITY, MO

PREP: 10 MIN. • **COOK:** 1 HOUR
MAKES: 16 SERVINGS (¾ CUP EACH)

- 1 bottle (64 ounces) cranberry-apple juice
- 2 cups unsweetened apple juice
- 1 cup pomegranate juice
- ⅔ cup honey
- ½ cup orange juice
- 10 whole cloves
- 3 cinnamon sticks (3 inches)
- 2 tablespoons grated orange peel

In a 5-qt. slow cooker, combine the first five ingredients. Place cloves, cinnamon sticks and orange peel on a double thickness of cheesecloth. Gather up corners of cloth to wrap seasonings; tie securely with string. Add to slow cooker. Cook, covered, on low 1-2 hours or until heated through. Discard spice bag.
PER SERVING *¾ cup equals 131 cal., trace fat (trace sat. fat), 0 chol., 21 mg sodium, 33 g carb., trace fiber, trace pro.*

CREAMY ARTICHOKE DIP

Enjoy a lighter take on a treasured family favorite. It's just as ooey-gooey good as before!

—MARY SPENCER GREENDALE, WI

PREP: 20 MIN. • **COOK:** 1 HOUR
MAKES: 5 CUPS

- 2 cans (14 ounces each) water-packed artichoke hearts, rinsed, drained and coarsely chopped
- 1 package (8 ounces) reduced-fat cream cheese, cubed
- ¾ cup (6 ounces) plain yogurt
- 1 cup (4 ounces) shredded part-skim mozzarella cheese
- 1 cup reduced-fat ricotta cheese
- ¾ cup shredded Parmesan cheese, divided
- ½ cup shredded reduced-fat Swiss cheese
- ¼ cup reduced-fat mayonnaise
- 2 tablespoons lemon juice
- 1 tablespoon chopped seeded jalapeno pepper
- 1 teaspoon garlic powder
- 1 teaspoon seasoned salt
  Tortilla chips

1. In a 3-qt. slow cooker, combine artichokes, cream cheese, yogurt, mozzarella cheese, ricotta cheese, ½ cup Parmesan cheese, Swiss cheese, mayonnaise, lemon juice, jalapeno, garlic powder and seasoned salt. Cover and cook on low for 1 hour or until heated through.
2. Sprinkle with remaining cheese. Serve with tortilla chips.
NOTE *Wear disposable gloves when cutting hot peppers; the oils can burn skin. Avoid touching your face.*
PER SERVING *¼ cup (calculated without tortilla chips) equals 104 cal., 6 g fat (3 g sat. fat), 20 mg chol., 348 mg sodium, 5 g carb., trace fiber, 7 g pro.*

THE SKINNY

GIVE A MAKEOVER

This makeover Creamy Artichoke Dip recipe has about ⅓ the calories and ½ of the fat per serving compared to the original. The secret? We scaled back some ingredients, such as mayonnaise, and either added or increased a low-fat counterpart, such as plain yogurt.

CREAMY ARTICHOKE DIP

CHOCOLATE COVERED CHERRY PUDDING CAKE

SPICED POMEGRANATE SIPPER

HEIRLOOM TOMATO
& ZUCCHINI SALAD, PAGE 197

BONUS:
QUICK SIDES, SALADS & BREADS

198

209

209

BRUSSELS SPROUTS
WITH GARLIC

1. In a large skillet, saute onion and carrot in butter until crisp-tender. Stir in the barley; cook and stir for 1 minute. Stir in 1 cup broth. Bring to a boil. Reduce heat; cook and stir until most of the liquid is absorbed.
2. Add the asparagus. Cook for 15-20 minutes or until the barley is tender and liquid is absorbed, stirring occasionally and adding more broth as needed. Stir in the marjoram and pepper; sprinkle with cheese.
PER SERVING *¾ cup equals 226 cal., 5 g fat (2 g sat. fat), 9 mg chol., 396 mg sodium, 39 g carb., 9 g fiber, 9 g pro.* **Diabetic Exchanges:** *2 starch, 1 vegetable, ½ fat.*

⑤INGREDIENTS

MINTY WATERMELON-CUCUMBER SALAD

Capturing many of the fantastic flavors of summer, this refreshing, beautiful salad will be the talk of any picnic or potluck.
—**ROBLYNN HUNNISETT** GUELPH, ON

START TO FINISH: 20 MIN.
MAKES: 16 SERVINGS (¾ CUP EACH)

- 8 **cups cubed seedless watermelon**
- 2 **English cucumbers, halved lengthwise and sliced**
- 6 **green onions, chopped**
- ¼ **cup minced fresh mint**
- ¼ **cup balsamic vinegar**
- ¼ **cup olive oil**
- ½ **teaspoon salt**
- ½ **teaspoon pepper**

In a large bowl, combine the watermelon, cucumbers, green onions and mint. In a small bowl, whisk the remaining ingredients. Pour over salad and toss to coat. Serve immediately or refrigerate, covered, for up to 2 hours before serving the salad.
PER SERVING *¾ cup equals 60 cal., 3 g fat (trace sat. fat), 0 chol., 78 mg sodium, 9 g carb., 1 g fiber, 1 g pro.* **Diabetic Exchanges:** *½ fruit, ½ fat.*

⑤INGREDIENTS

BRUSSELS SPROUTS WITH GARLIC

These Brussels sprouts are special enough for company, and so I like to serve them for Thanksgiving dinner. If you can't find fresh sprouts, try using frozen ones.
—**MYRA INNES** AUBURN, KS

START TO FINISH: 30 MIN.
MAKES: 6 SERVINGS

- 1½ **pounds fresh Brussels sprouts**
- 2 **teaspoons olive oil**
- 3 **teaspoons butter, divided**
- 4 **garlic cloves, chopped**
- ½ **cup reduced-sodium chicken broth**
- ¼ **teaspoon salt**
- ⅛ **teaspoon pepper**

1. Trim Brussels sprout stems. Using a paring knife, cut an "X" in the bottom of each.
2. In a large saucepan, heat oil and 1 teaspoon butter over medium heat. Add the garlic; cook and stir 1-2 minutes or until garlic begins to color. Immediately add Brussels sprouts, stirring to coat.
3. Stir in broth, salt and pepper; bring to a boil. Reduce the heat;

simmer, covered, 8-10 minutes or until Brussels sprouts are tender. Drain. Add the remaining butter; toss to coat.
PER SERVING *⅔ cup equals 83 cal., 3 g fat (1 g sat. fat), 5 mg chol., 198 mg sodium, 11 g carb., 4 g fiber, 4 g pro.* **Diabetic Exchanges:** *2 vegetable, ½ fat.*

SPRINGTIME BARLEY

While working as a sorority house mother, I would occasionally cook for the girls. They loved this medley.
—**SHARON HELMICK** COLFAX, WA

START TO FINISH: 30 MIN.
MAKES: 4 SERVINGS

- 1 **small onion, chopped**
- 1 **medium carrot, chopped**
- 1 **tablespoon butter**
- 1 **cup quick-cooking barley**
- 2 **cups reduced-sodium chicken broth, divided**
- ½ **pound fresh asparagus, trimmed and cut into 1-inch pieces**
- ¼ **teaspoon dried marjoram**
- ⅛ **teaspoon pepper**
- 2 **tablespoons shredded Parmesan cheese**

MINTY WATERMELON-
CUCUMBER SALAD

LEMON HERB
QUINOA

(5) INGREDIENTS

LEMON HERB QUINOA

My family is turning to quinoa more and more these days. It's a super grain that's packed with nutrients. Plus, it can be paired with any kind of main course.

—JENN TIDWELL FAIR OAKS, CA

START TO FINISH: 25 MIN.
MAKES: 4 SERVINGS

- 2 cups water
- 1 cup quinoa, rinsed
- ½ teaspoon salt, divided
- 1 tablespoon minced fresh basil
- 1 tablespoon minced fresh cilantro
- 1½ teaspoons minced fresh mint
- 1 teaspoon grated lemon peel

1. In a small saucepan, bring the water to a boil. Add the quinoa and ¼ teaspoon salt. Reduce heat; cover and simmer for 12-15 minutes or until liquid is absorbed.

2. Remove from the heat. Add the basil, cilantro, mint, lemon peel and remaining salt; fluff with a fork.

NOTE *Look for quinoa in the cereal, rice or organic food aisle.*

PER SERVING *⅔ cup equals 160 cal., 2 g fat (trace sat. fat), 0 chol., 304 mg sodium, 29 g carb., 3 g fiber, 6 g pro.* **Diabetic Exchange:** *2 starch.*

TOP TIP

WHY QUINOA?

Quinoa (really a seed) is often referred to as the "the perfect grain" because, unlike most grains, it offers complete proteins. So it's an excellent choice for vegetarian and vegan meals, which can be low in protein.

(5)INGREDIENTS

DILLED NEW POTATOES

With six kids at home, I try to grow as much of our food as possible. Our big potato patch means easy and affordable meals for a good part of the year. And this side is a hit!

—**JENNIFER FERRIS** BRONSON, MI

START TO FINISH: 25 MIN.
MAKES: 8 SERVINGS

- 2 **pounds baby red potatoes (about 24)**
- ¼ **cup butter, melted**
- 2 **tablespoons snipped fresh dill**
- 1 **tablespoon lemon juice**
- 1 **teaspoon salt**
- ½ **teaspoon pepper**

1. Place potatoes in a Dutch oven; add water to cover. Bring to a boil. Reduce heat; cook, uncovered, 15-20 minutes or until tender.

2. Drain; return to the pan. Mix remaining ingredients; drizzle over potatoes and toss to coat.

PER SERVING *¾ cup equals 180 cal., 8 g fat (5 g sat. fat), 20 mg chol., 447 mg sodium, 27 g carb., 2 g fiber, 3 g pro.* **Diabetic Exchanges:** *2 starch, 1½ fat.*

HEIRLOOM TOMATO & ZUCCHINI SALAD

Tomato wedges give this salad a juicy bite. It's a smart use of fresh herbs and veggies from your own garden or the farmers market.

—**MATTHEW HASS** FRANKLIN, WI

START TO FINISH: 25 MIN.
MAKES: 12 SERVINGS (¾ CUP EACH)

- 7 **large heirloom tomatoes (about 2½ pounds), cut into wedges**
- 3 **medium zucchini, halved lengthwise and thinly sliced**
- 2 **medium sweet yellow peppers, thinly sliced**
- ⅓ **cup cider vinegar**
- 3 **tablespoons olive oil**
- 1 **tablespoon sugar**
- 1½ **teaspoons salt**
- 1 **tablespoon each minced fresh basil, parsley and tarragon**

1. In a large bowl, combine the tomatoes, zucchini and peppers. In a small bowl, whisk vinegar, oil, sugar and salt until blended. Stir in herbs.

2. Just before serving, drizzle dressing over salad; toss gently to coat.

PER SERVING *1 cup equals 68 cal., 4 g fat (1 g sat. fat), 0 chol., 306 mg sodium, 8 g carb., 2 g fiber, 2 g pro.* **Diabetic Exchanges:** *1 vegetable, ½ fat.*

MUSHROOM & PEA RICE PILAF

Almost anything can be in a rice pilaf, so add peas and portobello mushrooms for a burst of color and a variety of textures.
—**STACY MULLENS** GRESHAM, OR

START TO FINISH: 25 MIN.
MAKES: 6 SERVINGS

- 1 **package (6.6 ounces) rice pilaf mix with toasted almonds**
- 1 **tablespoon butter**
- 1½ **cups fresh or frozen peas**
- 1 **cup sliced baby portobello mushrooms**

1. Prepare pilaf according to the package directions.
2. In a large skillet, heat butter over medium heat. Add the peas and mushrooms; cook and stir 6-8 minutes or until tender. Stir in the rice.
PER SERVING *⅔ cup equals 177 cal., 6 g fat (2 g sat. fat), 10 mg chol., 352 mg sodium, 28 g carb., 3 g fiber, 5 g pro. **Diabetic Exchanges:** 2 starch, ½ fat.*

HONEY-THYME BUTTERNUT SQUASH

Instead of potatoes, try whipping up mashed butternut squash with honey, butter and thyme. More than a delightful Thanksgiving side, this 30-minute dish is a new fall favorite for weeknight meals, too.
—**BIANCA NOISEUX** BRISTOL, CT

START TO FINISH: 30 MIN.
MAKES: 10 SERVINGS

- 1 **large butternut squash (about 5 pounds), peeled and cubed**
- ¼ **cup butter, cubed**
- 3 **tablespoons half-and-half cream**
- 2 **tablespoons honey**
- 2 **teaspoons dried parsley flakes**
- ½ **teaspoon salt**

- ⅛ **teaspoon dried thyme**
- ⅛ **teaspoon coarsely ground pepper**

1. In a large saucepan, bring 1 in. of water to a boil. Add squash; cover and cook for 10-15 minutes or until tender.
2. Drain. Mash squash with the remaining ingredients.
PER SERVING *¾ cup equals 145 cal., 5 g fat (3 g sat. fat), 14 mg chol., 161 mg sodium, 26 g carb., 7 g fiber, 2 g pro. **Diabetic Exchanges:** 1½ starch, 1 fat.*

EASY GARDEN TOMATOES

Simple as it is, this is one of my go-to dishes. I made three batches the first time, and a few stray olive slices were the only things left on the platter by the end of the meal.
—**HEATHER AHRENS** COLUMBUS, OH

START TO FINISH: 15 MIN.
MAKES: 6 SERVINGS

- 3 **large tomatoes, thinly sliced**
- 1 **large red onion, thinly sliced**
- ⅓ **cup olive oil**
- ¼ **cup red wine vinegar**
- 2 **garlic cloves, minced**
- 1 **tablespoon minced fresh basil or 1 teaspoon dried basil**
- 1½ **teaspoons minced fresh oregano or ½ teaspoon dried oregano**
- ¾ **cup crumbled feta cheese**
- 1 **can (2¼ ounces) sliced ripe olives, drained**

Arrange the tomatoes and onion on a serving platter. In a small bowl, whisk the oil, vinegar, garlic, basil and oregano; drizzle over the salad. Top salad with cheese and olives. Chill until serving.
PER SERVING *1 serving equals 184 cal., 16 g fat (3 g sat. fat), 8 mg chol., 234 mg sodium, 8 g carb., 2 g fiber, 4 g pro.*

FAVORITE MASHED SWEET POTATOES

My family begs me to make this recipe during the holidays. They like it because pumpkin pie spice really brings out the best in the sweet potatoes. And I love that I can make it the day before!
—**SENJA MERRILL** SANDY, UT

START TO FINISH: 25 MIN.
MAKES: 8 SERVINGS

- 3 **pounds sweet potatoes (about 6 medium), peeled and cubed**
- 3 **tablespoons orange juice**
- 2 **tablespoons brown sugar**
- 2 **tablespoons maple syrup**
- ¼ **teaspoon pumpkin pie spice**

Place the sweet potatoes in a 6-qt. stockpot; add water to cover. Bring to a boil. Reduce heat; cook, uncovered, 10-15 minutes or until tender. Drain; return to pan. Mash potatoes, gradually adding orange juice, brown sugar, syrup and pie spice to reach desired consistency.
PER SERVING *⅔ cup equals 117 cal., trace fat (trace sat. fat), 0 chol., 10 mg sodium, 28 g carb., 3 g fiber, 1 g pro. **Diabetic Exchange:** 2 starch.*

TOP TIP

SWEET PERKS

In addition to tasting delicious, sweet potatoes contain a lot of good-for-you nutrients! They're an excellent source of vitamin A and a good source of vitamins C and B6, fiber and potassium. All the more reason to enjoy these taters!

MUSHROOM & PEA RICE PILAF

FAVORITE MASHED SWEET POTATOES

EASY GARDEN TOMATOES

LEMON
PARMESAN ORZO

⑤INGREDIENTS
LEMON PARMESAN ORZO

Fresh lemon peel and minced parsley make this springtime orzo side. My family asks for it all the time. It's fantastic with chicken, pork and fish.

—**LESLIE PALMER** SWAMPSCOTT, MA

START TO FINISH: 20 MIN.
MAKES: 4 SERVINGS

- 1 **cup uncooked whole wheat orzo pasta**
- 1 **tablespoon olive oil**
- ¼ **cup grated Parmesan cheese**
- 2 **tablespoons minced fresh parsley**
- ½ **teaspoon grated lemon peel**
- ¼ **teaspoon salt**
- ¼ **teaspoon pepper**

Cook orzo according to package directions; drain. Transfer to a small bowl; drizzle with oil. Stir in the remaining ingredients.
PER SERVING ½ cup equals 191 cal., 6 g fat (1 g sat. fat), 4 mg chol., 225 mg sodium, 28 g carb., 7 g fiber, 7 g pro. **Diabetic Exchanges:** 2 starch, ½ fat.

⑤INGREDIENTS
ROASTED CARROT FRIES

Turn carrot sticks into crispy baked fries with a healthy twist. They are simply delicious with sweet and spicy ketchup.

—**TASTE OF HOME** TEST KITCHEN

START TO FINISH: 20 MIN.
MAKES: 5 SERVINGS

- 1 **pound fresh carrots, cut into ½-inch sticks**
- 2 **teaspoons olive oil**
- ½ **teaspoon salt**

Place the carrots in a greased 15x10x1-in. baking pan. Drizzle with oil and sprinkle with salt; toss to coat. Bake, uncovered, at 450° for 10-12 minutes or until crisp-tender.

HOLIDAY BRUSSELS SPROUTS

PER SERVING ½ cup equals 53 cal., 2 g fat (trace sat. fat), 0 chol., 299 mg sodium, 9 g carb., 3 g fiber, 1 g pro. **Diabetic Exchange:** 2 vegetable.

HOLIDAY BRUSSELS SPROUTS

Make Brussels sprouts extra special for the holidays with peas, celery and, of course, bacon. It's easy to double the recipe if needed.

—**JODIE BECKMAN** COUNCIL BLUFFS, IA

START TO FINISH: 25 MIN.
MAKES: 6 SERVINGS

- 1 **package (16 ounces) frozen Brussels sprouts**
- 1 **package (10 ounces) frozen peas**
- 2 **tablespoons butter**
- 2 **celery ribs, chopped**
- 2 **bacon strips, cooked and crumbled**
- 2 **tablespoons minced fresh chives**

1. Cook Brussels sprouts and peas according to the package directions; drain.
2. In a large skillet, heat the butter over medium-high heat. Add celery; cook and stir until crisp-tender. Add Brussels sprouts, peas, bacon and chives; toss to combine.
PER SERVING ⅔ cup equals 115 cal., 5 g fat (3 g sat. fat), 12 mg chol., 147 mg sodium, 13 g carb., 5 g fiber, 6 g pro. **Diabetic Exchanges:** 2 vegetable, 1 fat.

⑤INGREDIENTS

ROASTED ASPARAGUS WITH FETA

Pretty and easy to assemble, this simple side dish is delicious. With its festive appearance, it fits right in during the holidays.
—**PHYLLIS SCHMALZ** KANSAS CITY, KS

START TO FINISH: 25 MIN.
MAKES: 6 SERVINGS

- 2 **pounds fresh asparagus, trimmed**
- 1 **tablespoon olive oil**
  Kosher salt to taste
- 2 **medium tomatoes, seeded and chopped**
- ½ **cup crumbled feta cheese**

1. Arrange the asparagus in an ungreased 13x9-in. baking dish. Drizzle with the oil and sprinkle with salt.
2. Bake, uncovered, at 400° for 15-20 minutes or until tender. Transfer to a serving dish; sprinkle with tomatoes and feta cheese. Serve immediately.
PER SERVING *1 serving (calculated without salt) equals 72 cal., 4 g fat (1 g sat. fat), 5 mg chol., 103 mg sodium, 6 g carb., 2 g fiber, 4 g pro.* **Diabetic Exchanges:** *1 vegetable, 1 fat.*

⑤INGREDIENTS

SAUTEED SQUASH WITH TOMATOES & ONIONS

I love cooking food for family. My zucchini dish with tomatoes is like ratatouille without the eggplant.
—**ADAN FRANCO** MILWAUKEE, WI

START TO FINISH: 20 MIN.
MAKES: 8 SERVINGS

- 2 **tablespoons olive oil**
- 1 **medium onion, finely chopped**
- 4 **medium zucchini, chopped**
- 2 **large tomatoes, finely chopped**
- 1 **teaspoon salt**
- ¼ **teaspoon pepper**

1. In a large skillet, heat oil over medium-high heat. Add the onion; cook and stir 2-4 minutes or until tender. Add zucchini; cook and stir for 3 minutes.
2. Stir in tomatoes, salt and pepper; cook and stir 4-6 minutes longer or until squash is tender. Serve with a slotted spoon.
PER SERVING *¾ cup equals 60 cal., 4 g fat (1 g sat. fat), 0 chol., 306 mg sodium, 6 g carb., 2 g fiber, 2 g pro.* **Diabetic Exchanges:** *1 vegetable, ½ fat.*

TOP TIP

WHEN SHOULD YOU BUY ORGANIC?

Most of us have a budget to watch. So when should you buy organic fruit and veggies to avoid high levels of pesticide residue (ick!), and when can you buy conventional ones that don't have so much (yay!)?

- **Splurge on organic:** peppers, zucchini, celery, tomatoes, cucumbers, grapes, leafy greens, apples, nectarines, peaches, potatoes, snap peas and strawberries.
- **Save with conventional:** pineapple, avocados, cabbage, cantaloupe, eggplant, asparagus, cauliflower, kiwifruit, onions, sweet corn and mangoes.

SAUTEED SQUASH WITH TOMATOES & ONIONS

PESTO PASTA
& POTATOES

PESTO PASTA & POTATOES

Although this healthy pasta dish is pretty easy to begin with, the cooking method makes it even easier. You can throw the green beans and pasta into one big pot.

—LAURA FLOWERS MOSCOW, ID

START TO FINISH: 30 MIN.
MAKES: 12 SERVINGS

- 1½ pounds small red potatoes, halved
- 12 ounces uncooked whole grain spiral pasta
- 3 cups cut fresh or frozen green beans
- 1 jar (6½ ounces) prepared pesto
- 1 cup grated Parmigiano-Reggiano cheese

1. Place the potatoes in a large saucepan; add water to cover. Bring to a boil. Reduce heat; cook, uncovered, 9-11 minutes or until tender. Drain water; transfer to a large bowl.

2. Meanwhile, cook the pasta according to package directions, adding green beans during the last 5 minutes of cooking; drain, reserving ¾ cup pasta water.

3. Add the pasta and green beans to potatoes. Stir in the pesto, cheese and enough reserved pasta water to coat.

PER SERVING *¾ cup equals 261 cal., 10 g fat (3 g sat. fat), 11 mg chol., 233 mg sodium, 34 g carb., 5 g fiber, 11 g pro.* **Diabetic Exchanges:** *2 starch, 2 fat.*

PROSCIUTTO
BREADSTICKS

⑤INGREDIENTS

PARTY TORTELLINI SALAD

Introduce this crowd-pleasing salad with a light vinaigrette dressing at your next gathering. It's an appealing addition to cookouts and picnics.
—**MARY WILT** IPSWICH, MA

START TO FINISH: 25 MIN.
MAKES: 10 SERVINGS

- 1 **package (19 ounces) frozen cheese tortellini**
- 2 **cups fresh broccoli florets**
- 1 **medium sweet red pepper, chopped**
- ½ **cup pimiento-stuffed olives, halved**
- ¾ **cup reduced-fat red wine vinaigrette**
- ½ **teaspoon salt**

1. Cook tortellini according to the package directions; drain and rinse in cold water.
2. In a large bowl, combine the tortellini, broccoli, red pepper and olives. Drizzle with dressing and sprinkle with salt; toss to coat. Cover and refrigerate until serving.
PER SERVING *¾ cup equals 156 cal., 7 g fat (2 g sat. fat), 8 mg chol., 596 mg sodium, 19 g carb., 1 g fiber, 6 g pro.* **Diabetic Exchanges:** *1 starch, 1 lean meat, ½ fat.*

THE SKINNY

VEGGIE-FULL SALAD

This pasta salad gets over a third of its volume from healthy veggies. Adding veggies is a great way to stretch fat- and calorie-loaded ingredients (meat, cheese and tortellini for example), so toss in even more if you'd like.

⑤INGREDIENTS

PROSCIUTTO BREADSTICKS

Pair these breadsticks with your favorite pasta or egg dish. They're a tasty substitute for bacon and toast at brunch or any time.
—**MARIA REGAKIS** SAUGUS, MA

START TO FINISH: 30 MIN.
MAKES: 1 DOZEN

- 6 **thin slices prosciutto or deli ham**
- 1 **tube (11 ounces) refrigerated breadsticks**
- 1 **large egg, lightly beaten**
- ¼ **teaspoon fennel seed, crushed**
- ¼ **teaspoon pepper**

1. Preheat oven to 375°. Cut each slice of prosciutto into four thin strips. Unroll dough; separate into breadsticks. Top each with two strips prosciutto, pressing gently to adhere. Twist each breadstick; place on ungreased baking sheet, pressing the ends down firmly. Brush with beaten egg.
2. Combine fennel and pepper; sprinkle over breadsticks. Bake breadsticks for 10-13 minutes or until golden brown.
PER SERVING *1 breadstick equals 86 cal., 2 g fat (1 g sat. fat), 8 mg chol., 323 mg sodium, 13 g carb., trace fiber, 4 g pro.* **Diabetic Exchange:** *1 starch.*

PEAS A LA FRANCAISE

I love peas, especially in this recipe. With tiny pearl onions and accents of thyme and chervil, the dish is lovely to present.
—**CHRISTINE FRAZIER**
AUBURNDALE, FL

START TO FINISH: 30 MIN.
MAKES: 12 SERVINGS (½ CUP EACH)

- 1½ cups pearl onions, trimmed
- ¼ cup butter, cubed
- ¼ cup water
- 1 tablespoon sugar
- 1 teaspoon salt
- ¼ teaspoon dried thyme
- ¼ teaspoon dried chervil
- ¼ teaspoon pepper
- 2 packages (16 ounces each) frozen peas, thawed
- 2 cups shredded lettuce

1. In a Dutch oven, bring 6 cups water to a boil. Add pearl onions; boil for 3 minutes. Drain and rinse in cold water; peel and set aside.
2. In the same saucepan, melt butter over medium heat. Stir in the onions, water, sugar and seasonings. Add peas and lettuce; stir until blended. Cover and cook for 6-8 minutes or until vegetables are tender. Serve vegetables with a slotted spoon.
PER SERVING ½ cup equals 112 cal., 4 g fat (2 g sat. fat), 10 mg chol., 315 mg sodium, 15 g carb., 4 g fiber, 4 g pro. **Diabetic Exchanges:** 1 starch, 1 fat.

FREEZE IT
BLUEBERRY OATMEAL MUFFINS

Grab one of these tender muffins and go. Oats, blueberries and yogurt make them tasty and nutritious.
—**DONNA BROCKETT** KINGFISHER, OK

START TO FINISH: 30 MIN.
MAKES: 1 DOZEN

- 1¼ cups all-purpose flour
- 1 cup quick-cooking oats
- ½ cup packed brown sugar
- 2 teaspoons baking powder
- ½ teaspoon salt
- ½ teaspoon ground cinnamon
- ¼ teaspoon baking soda
- ¼ teaspoon ground nutmeg
- 1 large egg, lightly beaten
- 1 cup (8 ounces) plain yogurt
- ¼ cup butter, melted
- 1 cup fresh blueberries

1. In a large bowl, combine the first eight ingredients. Combine the egg, yogurt and butter; stir into the dry ingredients just until moistened. Fold in blueberries.
2. Coat the muffin cups with cooking spray or use paper liners; fill three-fourths full with batter. Bake at 400° for 18-22 minutes or until a toothpick inserted in the muffin comes out clean. Cool for 5 minutes before removing from pan to a wire rack. Serve warm.
FREEZE OPTION *Wrap muffins in foil; transfer to a resealable plastic freezer bag. May be frozen for up to 3 months. To use frozen muffins: Remove the foil. Thaw at room temperature. Serve warm.*
PER SERVING 1 muffin equals 167 cal., 6 g fat (3 g sat. fat), 31 mg chol., 249 mg sodium, 26 g carb., 1 g fiber, 4 g pro. **Diabetic Exchanges:** 1½ starch, 1 fat.

ARTICHOKE TOMATO SALAD

Dress up this salad by adding shredded rotisserie chicken or crumbling feta cheese on top.
—**DEBORAH WILLIAMS** PEORIA, AZ

START TO FINISH: 20 MIN.
MAKES: 8 SERVINGS

- 5 large tomatoes (about 2 pounds), cut into wedges
- ¼ teaspoon salt
- ¼ teaspoon pepper
- 1 jar (7½ ounces) marinated quartered artichoke hearts, drained
- 1 can (2¼ ounces) sliced ripe olives, drained
- 2 tablespoons minced fresh parsley
- 2 tablespoons white wine vinegar
- 2 garlic cloves, minced

Arrange the tomato wedges on a large platter; sprinkle with salt and pepper. In a small bowl, toss the remaining ingredients; spoon over tomatoes.
PER SERVING ¾ cup equals 74 cal., 5 g fat (1 g sat. fat), 0 chol., 241 mg sodium, 7 g carb., 2 g fiber, 1 g pro. **Diabetic Exchanges:** 1 vegetable, 1 fat.

HOW-TO
MINCE PARSLEY

1. Holding the handle of a chef's knife with one hand, rest fingers of your other hand on the top of the blade near tip.
2. Using the handle to guide and apply pressure, move knife in an arc across the parsley leaves, cutting with a rocking motion until the pieces are no larger than ⅛ in.

ARTICHOKE TOMATO SALAD

THYME-ROASTED CARROTS

THYME-ROASTED CARROTS

Cutting the carrots lengthwise makes this dish look extra pretty. For even more elegance, garnish with sprigs of either fresh thyme or parsley.

—DEIRDRE COX KANSAS CITY, MO

START TO FINISH: 30 MIN.
MAKES: ABOUT 12 SERVINGS
(2 CARROT HALVES EACH)

- 3 **pounds medium carrots, halved lengthwise**
- 2 **tablespoons minced fresh thyme or 2 teaspoons dried thyme**
- 2 **tablespoons canola oil**
- 1 **tablespoon honey**
- 1 **teaspoon salt**

Preheat the oven to 400°. Divide the carrots between two greased 15x10x1-in. baking pans. In a small bowl, mix the thyme, oil, honey and salt; brush over the carrots. Roast 20-25 minutes or until tender.

PER SERVING *2 carrot halves equals 73 cal., 3 g fat (trace sat. fat), 0 chol., 275 mg sodium, 12 g carb., 3 g fiber, 1 g pro.* **Diabetic Exchanges:** *1 vegetable, ½ starch, ½ fat.*

TENDER BISCUITS

These rolls are low in fat but not in flavor. They'll dress up a weeknight meal with ease.

—ANE BURKE BELLA VISTA, AR

START TO FINISH: 30 MIN.
MAKES: 2 BISCUITS

- ⅓ **cup self-rising flour**
- 1 **tablespoon grated Parmesan cheese**
- ⅛ **teaspoon garlic salt**
- 3 **tablespoons reduced-fat cream cheese**
- 3 **tablespoons fat-free milk**
- 1 **tablespoon fat-free plain yogurt**

1. In a small bowl, combine the flour, Parmesan cheese and garlic salt. Cut in cream cheese until mixture resembles coarse crumbs. Stir in milk and yogurt just until mixture is moistened.

2. Drop by scant ⅓ cupfuls 2 in. apart onto a baking sheet coated with cooking spray. Bake biscuits at 400° for 12-15 minutes or until golden brown. Serve warm.

PER SERVING *1 biscuit equals 142 cal., 5 g fat (4 g sat. fat), 18 mg chol., 497 mg sodium, 17 g carb., trace fiber, 6 g pro.* **Diabetic Exchanges:** *1 starch, 1 fat.*

TENDER BISCUITS

ORANGE POMEGRANATE SALAD WITH HONEY

ORANGE POMEGRANATE SALAD WITH HONEY

I discovered this special fruit salad in a cooking class. If you can, try to find orange flower water (also called orange blossom water)—it perks up the orange segments. But orange juice works well, too!

—CAROL RICHARDSON MARTY
LYNWOOD, WA

START TO FINISH: 15 MIN.
MAKES: 6 SERVINGS

> 5 **medium oranges or**
>   **10 clementines**
> ½ **cup pomegranate seeds**
> 2 **tablespoons honey**
> 1 **to 2 teaspoons orange flower**
>   **water or orange juice**

1. Cut a thin slice from top and bottom of each orange; stand orange upright on a cutting board. With a knife, cut off peel and outer membrane from oranges. Cut crosswise into ½-in. slices.
2. Arrange the orange slices on a serving platter; sprinkle with pomegranate seeds. In a small bowl, mix the honey and orange flower water; drizzle over fruit.
PER SERVING *⅔ cup equals 62 cal., trace fat (trace sat. fat), 0 chol., 2 mg sodium, 15 g carb., trace fiber, 1 g pro.* **Diabetic Exchange:** *1 fruit.*

TOP TIP

EDIBLE SEEDS
Yes, pomegranate seeds are edible! The seeds and surrounding juice sacs (arils) are the only parts of the pomegranate you can eat. One medium pomegranate (weighing about 8 ounces) yields roughly ¾ cup arils.

GRILLED SWEET POTATO WEDGES

I love it when an entire meal can be cooked outside on the grill and I don't have to fuss around in the kitchen. This recipe is easy and healthy at the same time. It's fun dipping the wedges in spicy sauce.
—**NATALIE KNOWLTON** KAMAS, UT

START TO FINISH: 30 MIN.
MAKES: 8 SERVINGS

- 4 **large sweet potatoes, cut into ½-inch wedges**
- ½ **teaspoon garlic salt**
- ¼ **teaspoon pepper**

DIPPING SAUCE
- ½ **cup reduced-fat mayonnaise**
- ½ **cup fat-free plain yogurt**
- 1 **teaspoon ground cumin**
- ½ **teaspoon seasoned salt**
- ½ **teaspoon paprika**
- ½ **teaspoon chili powder**

1. Place the potatoes in a large saucepan and cover with water. Bring to a boil. Reduce heat; cover and simmer 4-5 minutes or until crisp-tender. Drain; pat dry with paper towels. Sprinkle potatoes with garlic salt and pepper.

2. Grill, covered, over medium heat for 10-12 minutes or until tender, turning once. In a small bowl, combine the mayonnaise, yogurt and seasonings. Serve with sweet potato wedges.

PER SERVING *¾ cup with 2 tablespoons sauce equals 166 cal., 5 g fat (1 g sat. fat), 6 mg chol., 349 mg sodium, 28 g carb., 3 g fiber, 3 g pro.* **Diabetic Exchanges:** *1½ starch, 1 fat.*

GRILLED SWEET POTATO WEDGES

CRUNCHY
BROCCOLI SALAD

CRUNCHY BROCCOLI SALAD

I never liked broccoli when I was younger, but now I'm hooked on this salad's light, sweet taste. It gives broccoli a whole new look and taste, in my opinion.

—**JESSICA CONREY** CEDAR RAPIDS, IA

START TO FINISH: 25 MIN.
MAKES: 10 SERVINGS

- 8 **cups fresh broccoli florets (about 1 pound)**
- 1 **bunch green onions, thinly sliced**
- ½ **cup dried cranberries**
- 3 **tablespoons canola oil**
- 3 **tablespoons seasoned rice vinegar**
- 2 **tablespoons sugar**
- ¼ **cup sunflower kernels**
- 3 **bacon strips, cooked and crumbled**

In a large bowl, combine broccoli, green onions and cranberries. In a small bowl, whisk oil, vinegar and sugar until blended; drizzle over broccoli mixture and toss to coat. Refrigerate until serving. Sprinkle with sunflower kernels and bacon before serving.

PER SERVING *¾ cup equals 121 cal., 7 g fat (1 g sat. fat), 2 mg chol., 233 mg sodium, 14 g carb., 3 g fiber, 3 g pro. **Diabetic Exchanges:** 1 vegetable, 1 fat, ½ starch.*

---

(5)INGREDIENTS

SWISS CHARD WITH ONIONS & GARLIC

I like to serve Swiss chard prepared this way with pasta, but it's also a tasty side dish on its own. My boys love it and ask for it often.

—**REBEKAH CHAPPEL** PORTALES, NM

START TO FINISH: 25 MIN.
MAKES: 6 SERVINGS

- 2 **tablespoons olive oil**
- 2 **medium onions, chopped**
- 6 **garlic cloves, sliced**
- ½ **cup white balsamic vinegar**
- 2 **bunches Swiss chard, coarsely chopped (about 16 cups)**
- ½ **cup walnut halves, toasted**
- ¼ **teaspoon salt**
- ¼ **teaspoon pepper**

1. In a 6-qt. stockpot, heat oil over medium-high heat. Add onions; cook and stir until tender. Add garlic; cook 1 minute longer.
2. Add vinegar, stirring to loosen any browned bits from pot. Add the remaining ingredients; cook for 4-6 minutes or until chard is tender, stirring occasionally.
NOTE *To toast the nuts, bake in a shallow pan in a 350° oven for 5-10 minutes or cook in a skillet over low heat until they are lightly browned, stirring occasionally.*
PER SERVING *⅔ cup equals 159 cal., 10 g fat (1 g sat. fat), 0 chol., 381 mg sodium, 16 g carb., 3 g fiber, 4 g pro. **Diabetic Exchanges:** 2 fat, 1 starch.*

HOW-TO

TOAST NUTS IN MICROWAVE

Really in a pinch and need toasted nuts for a recipe? Place nuts in a microwave-safe dish. Microwave, uncovered, on high for 2-3 minutes or until lightly toasted, stirring twice. Watch carefully to avoid burning the nuts. You may need to adjust the time, depending on your microwave's power and the amount of nuts you are toasting.

EASY BAKED MUSHROOMS

Bet you've never had mushrooms quite like these! Skipping the deep fryer keeps them low in fat.
—**DENISE DIPACE** MEDFORD, NJ

START TO FINISH: 30 MIN.
MAKES: 4 SERVINGS

- 1 **pound medium fresh mushrooms, halved**
- 2 **tablespoons olive oil**
- ¼ **cup seasoned bread crumbs**
- ¼ **teaspoon garlic powder**
- ¼ **teaspoon pepper**
  Fresh parsley, optional

1. Place mushrooms on a baking sheet. Drizzle with oil; toss to coat. In a small bowl, combine the bread crumbs, garlic powder and pepper; sprinkle over mushrooms.
2. Bake, uncovered, at 425° for 18-20 minutes or until lightly browned. Garnish with parsley if desired.
PER SERVING *¾ cup equals 116 cal., 8 g fat (1 g sat. fat), 0 chol., 112 mg sodium, 10 g carb., 2 g fiber, 4 g pro.* **Diabetic Exchanges:** *1½ fat, ½ starch.*

LEMON-THYME ASPARAGUS

Out of thyme? No worries, the beauty of this dish is its versatility. Use another herb instead.
—**SARAH REID** OSHAWA, ON

START TO FINISH: 20 MIN.
MAKES: 4 SERVINGS

- 1 **pound fresh asparagus, trimmed and cut into 1-inch pieces**
- ½ **pound sliced fresh mushrooms**
- 1 **tablespoon butter**
- 1 **teaspoon olive oil**
- 1½ **teaspoons minced fresh thyme or ½ teaspoon dried thyme**
- 1 **teaspoon grated lemon peel**
- ½ **teaspoon salt**
- ½ **teaspoon lemon juice**
- ¼ **teaspoon pepper**

In a large skillet, saute asparagus and mushrooms in butter and oil until tender. Stir in the remaining ingredients.
PER SERVING *1 cup equals 64 cal., 4 g fat (2 g sat. fat), 8 mg chol., 324 mg sodium, 5 g carb., 2 g fiber, 3 g pro.* **Diabetic Exchanges:** *1 vegetable, 1 fat.*

CRUNCHY APPLE SALAD

A salad with fiber-rich fruit, creamy dressing and crunchy walnuts wins lots of fans. Add some low-fat granola for even more crunch.
—**KATHY ARMSTRONG** POST FALLS, ID

START TO FINISH: 15 MIN.
MAKES: 5 SERVINGS

- ⅓ **cup fat-free sugar-free vanilla yogurt**
- ⅓ **cup reduced-fat whipped topping**
- ¼ **teaspoon plus ⅛ teaspoon ground cinnamon, divided**
- ¼ **cup dried cranberries**
- 2 **medium red apples, chopped**
- 1 **large Granny Smith apple, chopped**
- 2 **tablespoons chopped walnuts**

In a large bowl, combine yogurt, whipped topping and ¼ teaspoon cinnamon. Add cranberries and apples; toss to coat. Refrigerate until serving. Sprinkle with the walnuts and remaining cinnamon before serving.
PER SERVING *¾ cup equals 109 cal., 3 g fat (1 g sat. fat), trace chol., 12 mg sodium, 22 g carb., 3 g fiber, 2 g pro.* **Diabetic Exchanges:** *1 fruit, ½ starch, ½ fat.*

HOW-TO

MAKE YOUR OWN SEASONED BREAD CRUMBS

Break slices of dried bread into pieces and process in a blender or food processor until you have fine crumbs, then season the crumbs as you like. A basic recipe might include dried basil and oregano, garlic and onion powder, grated Parmesan cheese, salt and paprika. Start with small amounts of the seasonings and add more as needed. One slice of dried bread will yield about ¼ cup of fine, dry bread crumbs.

EASY BAKED MUSHROOMS

LEMON-THYME ASPARAGUS

CRUNCHY APPLE SALAD

SHREDDED GINGERED
BRUSSELS SPROUTS

SHREDDED GINGERED BRUSSELS SPROUTS

If you know folks who usually turn away from Brussels sprouts, have them try these. One bite just might make them converts.

—JAMES SCHEND
PLEASANT PRAIRIE, WI

START TO FINISH: 25 MIN.
MAKES: 6 SERVINGS

- 1 **pound fresh Brussels sprouts (about 5½ cups)**
- 1 **tablespoon olive oil**
- 1 **small onion, finely chopped**
- 1 **tablespoon minced fresh gingerroot**
- 1 **garlic clove, minced**
- ½ **teaspoon salt**
- 2 **tablespoons water**
- ¼ **teaspoon pepper**

1. Trim Brussels sprouts. Cut sprouts lengthwise in half; cut crosswise into thin slices.

2. Place a large skillet over medium-high heat. Add Brussels sprouts; cook and stir 2-3 minutes or until sprouts begin to brown lightly. Add oil and toss to coat. Stir in the onion, ginger, garlic and salt. Add water; reduce heat to medium and cook, covered, for 1-2 minutes or until vegetables are tender. Stir in the pepper.

PER SERVING *¾ cup equals 56 cal., 2 g fat (trace sat. fat), 0 chol., 214 mg sodium, 8 g carb., 3 g fiber, 2 g pro.* ***Diabetic Exchanges:*** *1 vegetable, ½ fat.*

TENDER WHOLE WHEAT MUFFINS

Want oven-baked treats but need something to fit your diet? Simple whole wheat muffins are wonderful paired with soup or spread with a little jam for breakfast.

—KRISTINE CHAYES SMITHTOWN, NY

START TO FINISH: 30 MIN.
MAKES: 10 MUFFINS

- 1 **cup all-purpose flour**
- 1 **cup whole wheat flour**
- 2 **tablespoons sugar**
- 2½ **teaspoons baking powder**
- 1 **teaspoon salt**
- 1 **large egg**
- 1¼ **cups milk**
- 3 **tablespoons butter, melted**

1. Preheat oven to 400°. In a large bowl, whisk flours, sugar, baking powder and salt. In another bowl, whisk egg, milk and melted butter until blended. Add to flour mixture; stir just until moistened.

2. Fill greased muffin cups three-fourths full. Bake muffins 15-17 minutes or until a toothpick inserted in the center comes out clean. Cool for 5 minutes before removing from pan to a wire rack. Serve warm.

PER SERVING *1 muffin equals 152 cal., 5 g fat (3 g sat. fat), 35 mg chol., 393 mg sodium, 22 g carb., 2 g fiber, 5 g pro.* ***Diabetic Exchanges:*** *1½ starch, 1 fat.*

TENDER WHOLE WHEAT MUFFINS

BONUS: LIGHT DESSERTS

BONUS:
LIGHT DESSERTS

243

229

220

CHOCOLATE ANGEL CUPCAKES WITH COCONUT CREAM FROSTING

Sweeten any meal with these fun, creamy frosted chocolate cupcakes that take just minutes to make. Their finger-licking flavor packs far fewer calories and less fat than you'll find in most traditional desserts!

—**MANDY RIVERS** LEXINGTON, SC

PREP: 15 MIN.
BAKE: 15 MIN. + COOLING
MAKES: 2 DOZEN

- 1 **package (16 ounces) angel food cake mix**
- ¾ **cup baking cocoa**
- 1 **cup (8 ounces) reduced-fat sour cream**
- 1 **cup confectioners' sugar**
- ⅛ **teaspoon coconut extract**
- 2½ **cups reduced-fat whipped topping**
- ¾ **cup flaked coconut, toasted**

1. Prepare cake mix according to package directions for cupcakes, adding cocoa when mixing.
2. Fill foil- or paper-lined muffin cups two-thirds full. Bake at 375° for 11-15 minutes or until the cake springs back when lightly touched and the cracks feel dry. Cool for 10 minutes before removing the cupcakes from pans to wire racks to cool completely.
3. For frosting, in a large bowl, combine sour cream, confectioners' sugar and extract until smooth. Fold in whipped topping. Frost cupcakes. Sprinkle with coconut. Refrigerate leftovers.
PER SERVING *1 cupcake equals 142 cal., 3 g fat (2 g sat. fat), 3 mg chol., 154 mg sodium, 27 g carb., 1 g fiber, 3 g pro.* **Diabetic Exchanges:** *1½ starch, ½ fat.*

⑤INGREDIENTS
LEMON-APRICOT FRUIT POPS

With just 31 calories, a kiss of sugar and lots of vitamin C, this is one lightly refreshing summer dessert everyone can find room for.

—**AYSHA SCHURMAN** AMMON, ID

PREP: 15 MIN. + FREEZING
MAKES: 6 SERVINGS

- ¼ **cup orange juice**
- 1 **teaspoon grated lemon peel**
- ¼ **cup lemon juice**
- 4 **teaspoons sugar**
- 1 **cup sliced fresh apricots (4-5 medium)**
- ½ **cup ice cubes**
- 1 **teaspoon minced fresh mint, optional**
- 6 **freezer pop molds or 6 paper cups (3 ounces each) and wooden pop sticks**

1. Place the first six ingredients in a blender; cover and process until blended. If desired, stir in mint.
2. Pour into molds or paper cups. Top molds with holders. If using cups, top with foil and insert sticks through foil. Freeze until firm.
PER SERVING *1 pop equals 31 cal., trace fat (trace sat. fat), 0 chol., trace sodium, 8 g carb., 1 g fiber, trace pro.* **Diabetic Exchange:** *½ fruit.*

THE SKINNY

NO-GUILT POPS

With only 11 little calories from added sugar in these pops, they're a fresh and tasty, low-cal way to beat the heat.

CHOCOLATE ANGEL CUPCAKES WITH COCONUT CREAM FROSTING

LEMON-APRICOT
FRUIT POPS

HOT FUDGE
CAKE

HOT FUDGE CAKE

What better way to top off a great meal than with a rich, chocolaty cake that makes its own sauce? Mom served it with a scoop of ice cream or a drizzle of cream, but why not try the lower fat versions?

—**VERA REID** LARAMIE, WY

PREP: 20 MIN. • **BAKE:** 35 MIN.
MAKES: 9 SERVINGS

- 1 **cup all-purpose flour**
- ¾ **cup sugar**
- 6 **tablespoons baking cocoa, divided**
- 2 **teaspoons baking powder**
- ¼ **teaspoon salt**
- ½ **cup 2% milk**
- 2 **tablespoons canola oil**
- 1 **teaspoon vanilla extract**
- 1 **cup packed brown sugar**
- 1¾ **cups hot water**
  Ice cream or whipped cream, optional

1. Preheat oven to 350°. In a bowl, whisk flour, sugar, 2 tablespoons cocoa, baking powder and salt. In another bowl, whisk milk, oil and vanilla until blended. Add to flour mixture; stir just until moistened.
2. Transfer to an ungreased 9-in. square baking pan. In a small bowl, mix brown sugar and remaining cocoa; sprinkle over batter. Pour hot water over all; do not stir.
3. Bake 35-40 minutes. Serve cake warm. If desired, top with ice cream or whipped cream.
PER SERVING *1 serving (calculated without whipped cream or ice cream) equals 253 cal., 4 g fat (1 g sat. fat), 2 mg chol., 171 mg sodium, 54 g carb., 1 g fiber, 3 g pro.*

BANANA PUDDING

My son enlisted in the Marines after high school and I didn't see him for more than two years. When he finally arrived back home, I grabbed hold of him at the airport and burst out crying. And when we got to our house, the first thing he ate was two bowls of my banana pudding.

—STEPHANIE HARRIS
MONTPELIER, VA

PREP: 35 MIN. + CHILLING
MAKES: 9 SERVINGS

¾ **cup sugar**
¼ **cup all-purpose flour**
¼ **teaspoon salt**
3 **cups 2% milk**

3 **large eggs**
1½ **teaspoons vanilla extract**
8 **ounces vanilla wafers (about 60 cookies), divided**
4 **large ripe bananas, cut into ¼-inch slices**

1. In a large saucepan, mix sugar, flour and salt. Whisk in milk. Cook and stir over medium heat until thickened and bubbly. Reduce heat to low; cook and stir for 2 minutes longer. Remove from heat.

2. In a small bowl, whisk the eggs. Whisk a small amount of the hot mixture into eggs; return all to pan, whisking constantly. Bring to a gentle boil; cook and stir 2 minutes. Remove from the heat. Stir in vanilla. Cool 15 minutes, stirring occasionally.

3. In an ungreased 8-in. square baking dish, layer 25 vanilla wafers, half of the banana slices and half of the pudding. Repeat layers.

4. Press plastic wrap onto surface of pudding. Refrigerate 4 hours or overnight. Just before serving the pudding, crush remaining wafers and sprinkle over top.

PER SERVING *1 serving equals 302 cal., 7 g fat (2 g sat. fat), 80 mg chol., 206 mg sodium, 55 g carb., 2 g fiber, 7 g pro.*

BANANA
PUDDING

ZUCCHINI CHOCOLATE
CAKE WITH ORANGE GLAZE

ZUCCHINI CHOCOLATE CAKE WITH ORANGE GLAZE

This lightened-up version of a family favorite has a lovely chocolate flavor with a hint of orange—and crunch from walnuts. Applesauce takes the place of some fat, cutting calories.

—BARBARA WORREL GRANBURY, TX

PREP: 20 MIN.
BAKE: 50 MIN. + COOLING
MAKES: 16 SERVINGS

- ½ cup butter, softened
- 1½ cups sugar
- 2 large eggs
- ¼ cup unsweetened applesauce
- 1 teaspoon vanilla extract
- 2½ cups all-purpose flour
- ½ cup baking cocoa
- 1¼ teaspoons baking powder
- 1 teaspoon salt
- 1 teaspoon ground cinnamon
- ½ teaspoon baking soda
- ½ cup fat-free milk
- 3 cups shredded zucchini
- ½ cup chopped walnuts
- 1 tablespoon grated orange peel

GLAZE
- 1¼ cups confectioners' sugar
- 2 tablespoons orange juice
- 1 teaspoon vanilla extract

1. Coat a 10-in. fluted tube pan with cooking spray and sprinkle with flour.
2. In a large bowl, cream the butter and sugar until light and fluffy. Add the eggs, one at a time, beating well after each addition. Beat in the applesauce and vanilla.
3. Combine flour, cocoa, baking powder, salt, cinnamon and baking soda; add to the creamed mixture alternately with milk, beating well after each addition. Fold in the zucchini, walnuts and orange peel.
4. Transfer to prepared pan. Bake at 350° for 50-60 minutes or until a toothpick inserted near the center comes out clean.
5. Cool for 10 minutes before removing from pan to a wire rack to cool completely. Combine glaze ingredients; drizzle over cake.
PER SERVING *1 slice equals 282 cal., 9 g fat (4 g sat. fat), 42 mg chol., 273 mg sodium, 47 g carb., 2 g fiber, 4 g pro.*

APPLE OATMEAL COOKIES

When I took these yummy cookies to work, they were gone in seconds. They're a wonderfully welcome snack that's low in calories!

—NICKI WOODS SPRINGFIELD, MO

PREP: 10 MIN. • **BAKE:** 15 MIN./BATCH
MAKES: ABOUT 5 DOZEN

- 1 package yellow cake mix (regular size)
- 1½ cups quick-cooking oats
- ½ cup packed brown sugar
- 2 teaspoons ground cinnamon
- 1 large egg
- ¾ cup unsweetened applesauce
- 1 cup finely chopped peeled apple
- ½ cup raisins

1. In a large bowl, combine the cake mix, oats, brown sugar and cinnamon. In a small bowl, combine the egg, applesauce, apple and raisins. Stir into oat mixture and mix well.
2. Drop by heaping teaspoonfuls 2 in. apart onto baking sheets coated with cooking spray. Bake at 350° for 12-14 minutes or until cookies are golden brown. Let stand 2 minutes before removing to wire racks to cool.
PER SERVING *1 cookie equals 57 cal., 1 g fat (trace sat. fat), 0 chol., 55 mg sodium, 12 g carb., 1 g fiber, 1 g pro.* **Diabetic Exchange:** *1 starch.*

LEMON MERINGUE CUPCAKES

Classic lemon meringue pie was the inspiration for these gorgeous little cupcakes. The tangy treats hide an indulging lemon pie filling beneath the fluffy toasted meringue. Make them for your next gathering—they'll be a big hit.

—ANDREA QUIROZ CHICAGO, IL

PREP: 30 MIN.
BAKE: 25 MIN. + COOLING
MAKES: 2 DOZEN

1 package lemon cake mix (regular size)
1⅓ cups water
⅓ cup canola oil
3 large eggs
1 tablespoon grated lemon peel
1 cup lemon creme pie filling
MERINGUE
3 large egg whites
½ teaspoon cream of tartar
½ cup sugar

1. In a large bowl, combine cake mix, water, oil, eggs and lemon peel; beat on low speed for 30 seconds. Beat on medium for 2 minutes.
2. Fill paper-lined muffin cups two-thirds full. Bake at 350° for 18-22 minutes or until a toothpick inserted near the center comes out clean.
3. Cut a small hole in corner of a pastry or plastic bag; insert a very small tip. Fill with pie filling. Push tip into top of each cupcake to fill.
4. In a large bowl, beat the egg whites and cream of tartar on medium speed until soft peaks form. Gradually beat in the sugar, 1 tablespoon at a time, on high until stiff glossy peaks form and the sugar is dissolved. Pipe meringue over tops of cupcakes.
5. Bake at 400° for 5-8 minutes or until the meringue is golden brown. Cool the cupcakes for 10 minutes before removing from pans to wire racks to cool completely. Store in an airtight container in refrigerator.

PER SERVING *1 cupcake equals 153 cal., 5 g fat (1 g sat. fat), 28 mg chol., 176 mg sodium, 25 g carb., trace fiber, 2 g pro.* **Diabetic Exchanges:** *1½ starch, 1½ fat.*

UPSIDE-DOWN BERRY CAKE

Here's a summery cake that's delicious warm or cold. It soaks up loads of flavor from the berries.

—CANDICE SCHOLL
WEST SUNBURY, PA

PREP: 20 MIN.
BAKE: 30 MIN. + COOLING
MAKES: 15 SERVINGS

½ cup chopped walnuts
1 cup fresh or frozen blueberries
1 cup fresh or frozen raspberries, halved
1 cup sliced fresh strawberries
¼ cup sugar
1 package (3 ounces) raspberry gelatin
1 package yellow cake mix (regular size)
2 large eggs
1¼ cups water
2 tablespoons canola oil
1½ cups miniature marshmallows

1. In a well-greased 13x9-in. baking pan, layer the walnuts and berries; sprinkle with sugar and gelatin. In a large bowl, combine the cake mix, eggs, water and oil; beat on low speed for 30 seconds. Beat on medium 2 minutes. Fold in marshmallows. Pour over top.
2. Bake at 350° for 35-40 minutes or until a toothpick inserted near the center comes out clean. Cool for 5 minutes before inverting onto a serving platter. Refrigerate any leftovers.

PER SERVING *1 piece equals 276 cal., 7 g fat (2 g sat. fat), 28 mg chol., 249 mg sodium, 51 g carb., 1 g fiber, 3 g pro.*

WARM CHOCOLATE MELTING CUPS

These creamy, chocolaty desserts are surprisingly decadent and oh so smooth. Even more surprising, each one has fewer than 200 calories and only 6 grams of fat.

—KISSA VAUGHN TROY, TX

PREP: 20 MIN. • **BAKE:** 20 MIN.
MAKES: 10 SERVINGS

1¼ cups sugar, divided
½ cup baking cocoa
2 tablespoons all-purpose flour
⅛ teaspoon salt
¾ cup water
¾ cup plus 1 tablespoon semisweet chocolate chips
1 tablespoon brewed coffee
1 teaspoon vanilla extract
2 large eggs
1 large egg white
10 fresh strawberry halves, optional

1. In a small saucepan, combine ¾ cup sugar, cocoa, flour and salt. Gradually stir in water. Bring to a boil; cook and stir for 2 minutes or until thickened. Remove from the heat; stir in the chocolate chips, coffee and vanilla until smooth. Transfer to a large bowl.
2. In another bowl, beat eggs and egg white until slightly thickened. Gradually add the remaining sugar, beating until thick and lemon-colored. Fold the egg mixture into the chocolate mixture.
3. Transfer to ten 4-oz. ramekins coated with cooking spray. Place the ramekins in a baking pan; add 1 in. of boiling water to pan. Bake, uncovered, at 350° for 20-25 minutes or just until centers are set. Garnish with strawberry halves if desired. Serve immediately.

PER SERVING *1 dessert equals 197 cal., 6 g fat (3 g sat. fat), 42 mg chol., 51 mg sodium, 37 g carb., 2 g fiber, 3 g pro.*

LEMON MERINGUE
CUPCAKES

WARM CHOCOLATE
MELTING CUPS

UPSIDE-DOWN
BERRY CAKE

CHOCOLATY
S'MORES BARS

(5) INGREDIENTS
CHOCOLATY S'MORES BARS

One night, my husband had some friends over to play poker, and he asked for these bars. When they polished off the pan, I shared the recipe so his friends could make them at home, too.
—**REBECCA SHIPP** BEEBE, AR

PREP: 15 MIN. + COOLING
MAKES: 1½ DOZEN

- ¼ **cup butter, cubed**
- 1 **package (10 ounces) large marshmallows**
- 1 **package (12 ounces) Golden Grahams**
- ⅓ **cup milk chocolate chips, melted**

1. In a large saucepan, melt the butter over low heat. Add the marshmallows; cook and stir until blended. Remove from heat. Stir in cereal until coated.
2. Using a buttered spatula, press evenly into a greased 13x9-in. pan. Drizzle with the melted chocolate chips. Cool completely. Cut into bars. Store in an airtight container.
PER SERVING *1 bar equals 159 cal., 4 g fat (2 g sat. fat), 7 mg chol., 197 mg sodium, 30 g carb., 1 g fiber, 1 g pro.*

HOW-TO

MELT CHOCOLATE
Place chocolate in a microwave-safe bowl. Microwave for 1 minute; stir. Then microwave for additional 10- to 20-second intervals; stir until smooth. Do not overheat.

ROOT BEER FLOAT PIE

(5) INGREDIENTS
ROOT BEER FLOAT PIE

Your kids will always remember this pie. And you can stay cool in the kitchen making it—no need to turn on the oven or stand over a stove!
—**CINDY REAMS** PHILIPSBURG, PA

PREP: 15 MIN. + CHILLING
MAKES: 8 SERVINGS

- 1 **carton (8 ounces) frozen reduced-fat whipped topping, thawed, divided**
- ¾ **cup cold diet root beer**
- ½ **cup fat-free milk**
- 1 **package (1 ounce) sugar-free instant vanilla pudding mix**
- 1 **graham cracker crust (9 inches)**
  Maraschino cherries, optional

1. Set aside and refrigerate ½ cup whipped topping for garnish. In a large bowl, whisk the root beer, milk and pudding mix for 2 minutes. Fold in half of remaining whipped topping. Spread into the graham cracker crust.
2. Spread the remaining whipped topping over pie. Refrigerate for at least 8 hours or overnight.
3. Dollop the reserved whipped topping over each serving; top with a maraschino cherry if desired.
PER SERVING *1 piece equals 185 cal., 8 g fat (4 g sat. fat), trace chol., 275 mg sodium, 27 g carb., trace fiber, 1 g pro.* **Diabetic Exchanges:** *2 starch, 1 fat.*

RHUBARB-PINEAPPLE CRISP

We grow our own rhubarb, so I enjoy finding new ways to use it. I first tried this combination with tropical fruit years ago, becoming an instant fan.

—JUDY SCHUT GRAND RAPIDS, MI

PREP: 15 MIN. • **BAKE:** 30 MIN.
MAKES: 6 SERVINGS

- **2 cups sliced fresh or frozen rhubarb, thawed and drained**
- **1 can (20 ounces) unsweetened pineapple tidbits, drained**
- **½ cup sugar, divided**
- **2 tablespoons plus ⅓ cup all-purpose flour, divided**
- **⅓ cup quick-cooking oats**
- **¾ teaspoon ground cinnamon**
- **⅛ teaspoon salt**
- **¼ cup cold butter**
  Whipped cream, optional

1. In a large bowl, combine the rhubarb, pineapple, ¼ cup sugar and 2 tablespoons flour. Transfer to a 9-in. deep-dish pie plate coated with cooking spray.

2. In a small bowl, combine the oats, cinnamon, salt and remaining sugar and flour. Cut in the butter until crumbly. Sprinkle over the fruit. Bake, uncovered, at 350° for 30-35 minutes or until the filling is bubbly and the topping is golden brown. Cool for 5 minutes; serve with whipped cream if desired.

NOTE *If using frozen rhubarb, measure rhubarb while still frozen, then thaw completely. Drain in a colander, but do not press liquid out.*
PER SERVING *1 serving (calculated without whipped cream) equals 232 cal., 8 g fat (5 g sat. fat), 20 mg chol., 106 mg sodium, 39 g carb., 2 g fiber, 2 g pro.*

RHUBARB-PINEAPPLE CRISP

---

(5) INGREDIENTS

OLD-FASHIONED RICE PUDDING

As a child, I always waited eagerly for the first heavenly bite of this rice pudding. Talk about a dish with the taste of homemade love!

—SANDRA MELNYCHENKO GRANDVIEW, MB

PREP: 10 MIN. • **BAKE:** 1 HOUR
MAKES: 6 SERVINGS

- **3½ cups 2% milk**
- **½ cup uncooked long-grain rice**
- **⅓ cup sugar**
- **½ teaspoon salt**
- **½ cup raisins**
- **1 teaspoon vanilla extract**
  Ground cinnamon, optional

1. In a large saucepan, combine milk, rice, sugar and salt. Bring to a boil over medium heat, stirring constantly. Pour into a greased 1½-qt. baking dish.

2. Cover and bake at 325° for 45 minutes, stirring the pudding every 15 minutes. Add the raisins and vanilla; cover and bake for 15 minutes longer or until rice is tender. Sprinkle with cinnamon if desired. Serve warm or chilled. Store in the refrigerator.

PER SERVING *¾ cup equals 208 cal., 3 g fat (2 g sat. fat), 11 mg chol., 270 mg sodium, 40 g carb., 1 g fiber, 6 g pro.*

OLD-FASHIONED
RICE PUDDING

**VANILLA
MERINGUE COOKIES**

⑤ INGREDIENTS

VANILLA MERINGUE COOKIES

These sweet little swirls are light as can be. They're all you need after a big, special dinner.

—**JENNI SHARP** MILWAUKEE, WI

PREP: 20 MIN.
BAKE: 40 MIN. + STANDING
MAKES: ABOUT 5 DOZEN

   3 **large egg whites**
1½ **teaspoons clear or regular vanilla extract**
   ¼ **teaspoon cream of tartar**
      Dash salt
   ⅔ **cup sugar**

1. Place the egg whites in a small bowl; let stand at room temperature 30 minutes.

2. Preheat the oven to 250°. Add vanilla, cream of tartar and salt to egg whites; beat on medium speed until foamy. Gradually add sugar, 1 tablespoon at a time, beating on high after each addition until sugar is dissolved. Continue beating until stiff glossy peaks form, about 7 minutes.

3. Cut a small hole in the tip of a pastry bag or in a corner of a food-safe plastic bag; insert a #32 star tip. Transfer meringue to bag. Pipe 1¼-in.-diameter cookies 2 in. apart onto parchment paper-lined baking sheets.

4. Bake 40-45 minutes or until firm to the touch. Turn off oven (do not open oven door); leave meringues in oven 1 hour. Remove from oven; cool completely on baking sheets. Remove meringues from paper; store in an airtight container at room temperature.

PER SERVING *1 cookie equals 10 cal., trace fat (0 sat. fat), 0 chol., 5 mg sodium, 2 g carb., 0 fiber, trace pro.* **Diabetic Exchange:** *Free food.*

LEMON-BERRY SHORTCAKE

Bake a simple cake using fresh strawberries, and enjoy this summertime classic with whipped topping and more berries.

—**MERYL HERR** GRAND RAPIDS, MI

PREP: 30 MIN.
BAKE: 20 MIN. + COOLING
MAKES: 8 SERVINGS

- 1⅓ cups all-purpose flour
- ½ cup sugar
- 2 teaspoons baking powder
- ¼ teaspoon salt
- 1 large egg
- ⅔ cup buttermilk
- ¼ cup butter, melted
- 1 teaspoon grated lemon peel
- 1 tablespoon lemon juice
- 1 teaspoon vanilla extract
- 1 cup sliced fresh strawberries

TOPPING
- 1 cup fresh blackberries
- 1 cup sliced fresh strawberries
- 1 tablespoon lemon juice
- 1 teaspoon sugar
- 2 cups reduced-fat whipped topping

1. Preheat oven to 350°. Grease and flour a 9-in. round baking pan.
2. In a large bowl, whisk the flour, sugar, baking powder and salt. In another bowl, whisk the egg, buttermilk, melted butter, lemon peel, lemon juice and vanilla. Add to the dry ingredients; stir just until moistened. Fold in 1 cup of strawberries. Transfer to the prepared pan.
3. Bake 20-25 minutes or until a toothpick inserted in center comes out clean. Cool 10 minutes before removing from pan to a wire rack to cool completely.
4. For topping, toss berries with lemon juice and sugar. To serve, spread whipped topping over cake. Top with berries.

PER SERVING *1 slice equals 252 cal., 9 g fat (6 g sat. fat), 42 mg chol., 245 mg sodium, 40 g carb., 2 g fiber, 4 g pro.*

LEMON-BERRY SHORTCAKE

**STRAWBERRY
SORBET SENSATION**

5 INGREDIENTS
STRAWBERRY SORBET SENSATION

On hot days in Colorado, we chill out with slices of this berries-and-cream dessert. The layered effect is so much fun. Use any flavor of sorbet you like.

—KENDRA DOSS COLORADO SPRINGS, CO

PREP: 20 MIN. + FREEZING
MAKES: 8 SERVINGS

- 2 cups strawberry sorbet, softened if necessary
- 1 cup cold fat-free milk
- 1 package (1 ounce) sugar-free instant vanilla pudding mix
- 1 carton (8 ounces) frozen reduced-fat whipped topping, thawed
  Sliced fresh strawberries

1. Line an 8x4-in. loaf pan with foil. Spread sorbet onto bottom of pan; place in freezer 15 minutes.
2. In a small bowl, whisk milk and pudding mix 2 minutes. Let stand 2 minutes or until soft-set. Fold the whipped topping into the pudding; spread over sorbet. Freeze, covered, 4 hours or overnight.
3. Remove dessert from freezer 10-15 minutes before serving. Unmold dessert onto a serving plate; remove foil. Cut into slices. Serve with strawberries.
PER SERVING *1 slice equals 153 cal., 3 g fat (3 g sat. fat), 1 mg chol., 163 mg sodium, 27 g carb., 2 g fiber, 1 g pro.* **Diabetic Exchanges:** *2 starch, ½ fat.*

RHUBARB OAT BARS

These soft rhubarb bars provide just the right balance of tartness and sweetness. They're hard to beat when you're craving a sweet treat.
—RENETTE CRESSEY FORT MILL, SC

PREP: 20 MIN.
BAKE: 25 MIN. + COOLING
MAKES: 16 BARS

- 1½ cups chopped fresh or frozen rhubarb
- 1 cup packed brown sugar, divided
- 4 tablespoons water, divided
- 1 teaspoon lemon juice
- 4 teaspoons cornstarch
- 1 cup old-fashioned oats
- ¾ cup all-purpose flour
- ½ cup flaked coconut
- ½ teaspoon salt
- ⅓ cup butter, melted

1. In a large saucepan, combine rhubarb, ½ cup brown sugar, 3 tablespoons water and lemon juice. Bring to a boil. Reduce the heat to medium; cook and stir for 4-5 minutes or until the rhubarb is tender.
2. Combine the cornstarch and remaining water until smooth; gradually stir into rhubarb mixture. Bring to a boil; cook and stir for 2 minutes or until thickened. Remove from the heat; set aside.
3. In a large bowl, combine oats, flour, coconut, salt and remaining brown sugar. Stir in butter until mixture is crumbly.
4. Press half of the oats mixture into a greased 8-in. square baking dish. Spread with rhubarb mixture. Sprinkle with the remaining oat mixture and press down lightly.
5. Bake at 350° for 25-30 minutes or until golden brown. Cool on a wire rack. Cut into squares.
NOTE *If using frozen rhubarb, measure rhubarb while still frozen, then thaw completely. Drain in a colander, but do not press liquid out.*

PER SERVING *1 bar equals 145 cal., 5 g fat (3 g sat. fat), 10 mg chol., 126 mg sodium, 24 g carb., 1 g fiber, 2 g pro.* **Diabetic Exchanges:** *1½ starch, 1 fat.*

TROPICAL CRISP

One bite of this juicy, crunchy fruit crisp and you just might hear the crash of ocean waves!
—TASTE OF HOME TEST KITCHEN

PREP: 20 MIN. • **BAKE:** 30 MIN.
MAKES: 9 SERVINGS

- 1 fresh pineapple, peeled and cubed
- 4 medium bananas, sliced
- ¼ cup packed brown sugar
- 2 tablespoons all-purpose flour

TOPPING
- ⅓ cup old-fashioned oats
- ¼ cup all-purpose flour
- 2 tablespoons flaked coconut, toasted
- 2 tablespoons brown sugar
- ¼ teaspoon ground nutmeg
- ¼ cup cold butter, cubed

1. Preheat oven to 350°. In a large bowl, combine the pineapple and bananas. Sprinkle with brown sugar and flour; toss to coat. Transfer to an 11x7-in. baking dish coated with cooking spray.
2. In a small bowl, mix the first five topping ingredients; cut in the butter until crumbly. Sprinkle over the pineapple mixture.
3. Bake 30-35 minutes or until filling is bubbly and topping is golden brown. Serve warm or at room temperature.
NOTE *To toast coconut, bake in a shallow pan in a 350° oven for 5-10 minutes or cook in a skillet over low heat until golden brown, stirring occasionally.*
PER SERVING *1 serving equals 188 cal., 6 g fat (4 g sat. fat), 13 mg chol., 44 mg sodium, 34 g carb., 3 g fiber, 2 g pro.* **Diabetic Exchanges:** *1 starch, 1 fruit, 1 fat.*

GRAN'S APPLE CAKE

My grandmother would occasionally bring over this wonderful cake while it was still warm from the oven. The spicy apple flavor, plus the sweet cream cheese frosting, made the dessert a standout. I've lightened up the recipe, but we love this family favorite just as much as ever.

—LAURIS CONRAD TURLOCK, CA

PREP: 20 MIN.
BAKE: 35 MIN. + COOLING
MAKES: 18 SERVINGS

- 1⅔ cups sugar
- 2 large eggs
- ½ cup unsweetened applesauce
- 2 tablespoons canola oil
- 2 teaspoons vanilla extract
- 2 cups all-purpose flour
- 2 teaspoons baking soda
- 2 teaspoons ground cinnamon
- ¾ teaspoon salt
- 6 cups chopped peeled tart apples
- ½ cup chopped pecans

FROSTING

- 4 ounces reduced-fat cream cheese
- 2 tablespoons butter, softened
- 1 teaspoon vanilla extract
- 1 cup confectioners' sugar

1. Preheat the oven to 350°. Coat a 13x9-in. baking pan well with cooking spray.

2. In a large bowl, beat sugar, eggs, applesauce, oil and vanilla until well blended. In another bowl, whisk flour, baking soda, cinnamon and salt; gradually beat into the sugar mixture. Fold in apples and pecans.

3. Transfer to prepared pan. Bake 35-40 minutes or until top is golden brown and a toothpick inserted in the center comes out clean. Cool completely in pan on a wire rack.

4. In a small bowl, beat cream cheese, butter and vanilla until smooth. Gradually beat in the confectioners' sugar (the mixture will be soft). Spread over the cake. Refrigerate leftovers.

PER SERVING 1 piece equals 241 cal., 7g fat (2g sat. fat), 29mg chol., 284mg sodium, 42g carb., 1g fiber, 3g pro.

⑤ INGREDIENTS

BANANA BOATS

This recipe, a long-ago gift from a good friend, is quick, fun to make and scrumptious. My family always requests it when we go camping.

—BRENDA LOVELESS GARLAND, TX

START TO FINISH: 20 MIN.
MAKES: 4 SERVINGS

- 4 medium unpeeled ripe bananas
- 4 teaspoons miniature chocolate chips
- 4 tablespoons miniature marshmallows

1. Cut the banana peel lengthwise about ½ in. deep, leaving ½ in. at both ends. Open peel wider to form a pocket. Fill each with 1 teaspoon chocolate chips and 1 tablespoon marshmallows. Crimp and shape four pieces of heavy-duty foil (about 12 in. square) around the bananas, forming boats.

2. Grill bananas, covered, over medium heat for 5-10 minutes or until the marshmallows melt and are golden brown.

PER SERVING 1 banana boat equals 136 cal., 2 g fat (1 g sat. fat), 0 chol., 3 mg sodium, 32 g carb., 3 g fiber, 1 g pro.

MAKEOVER DIRT DESSERT

Break out the spoons and make sure you get a bite before everyone else when you take this lightened-up treat to your next potluck, because it won't be around very long.

—KRISTI LINTON BAY CITY, MI

PREP: 30 MIN. + CHILLING
MAKES: 20 SERVINGS

- 1 package (8 ounces) fat-free cream cheese
- 3 ounces cream cheese, softened
- ¾ cup confectioners' sugar
- 3½ cups cold fat-free milk
- 2 packages (1 ounce each) sugar-free instant vanilla pudding mix
- 1 carton (12 ounces) frozen reduced-fat whipped topping, thawed
- 1 package (15½ ounces) reduced-fat Oreo cookies, crushed

1. In a large bowl, beat cream cheeses and confectioners' sugar until smooth. In a large bowl, whisk the milk and pudding mixes for 2 minutes; let stand for 2 minutes or until soft-set. Gradually stir into cream cheese mixture. Fold in the whipped topping.

2. Spread 1⅓ cups of the crushed Oreo cookies into an ungreased 13x9-in. dish. Layer with half the pudding mixture and half of the remaining cookies. Repeat layers. Refrigerate the dessert for at least 1 hour before serving.

PER SERVING ½ cup equals 208 cal., 6 g fat (4 g sat. fat), 6 mg chol., 364 mg sodium, 33 g carb., 1 g fiber, 5 g pro. **Diabetic Exchanges:** 2 starch, 1 fat.

THE SKINNY

LIGHTER DESSERT

By finding a low-fat or no-fat equivalent for almost every ingredient in the original Dirt Dessert, we trimmed more than 100 calories and 10g of fat from every serving!

GRAN'S APPLE
CAKE

BANANA
BOATS

MAKEOVER DIRT
DESSERT

ARCTIC
ORANGE PIE

⑤ INGREDIENTS
ARCTIC ORANGE PIE

This frosty pie is so easy to make—and versatile. Instead of orange, I have tried lemonade, mango and pineapple juice concentrates, and my family loves each version.
—MARIE PRZEPIERSKI ERIE, PA

PREP: 20 MIN. + FREEZING
MAKES: 8 SERVINGS

- 1 package (8 ounces) fat-free cream cheese
- 1 can (6 ounces) frozen orange juice concentrate, thawed
- 1 carton (8 ounces) frozen reduced-fat whipped topping, thawed
- 1 reduced-fat graham cracker crust (8 inches)
- 1 can (11 ounces) mandarin oranges, drained

In a large bowl, beat cream cheese and orange juice concentrate until smooth. Fold in whipped topping; pour into crust. Cover and freeze for 4 hours or until firm. Remove from the freezer about 10 minutes before cutting. Garnish with oranges.
PER SERVING *1 piece equals 241 cal., 7 g fat (4 g sat. fat), 2 mg chol., 251 mg sodium, 36 g carb., 1 g fiber, 6 g pro.* **Diabetic Exchanges:** *1½ fat, 1 starch, 1 fruit.*

DATE OAT BARS

My mother found this recipe many years ago. I love the surprise citrus zip just as much now as I did then.
—JOYCE EASTMAN
GARDEN GROVE, CA

PREP: 30 MIN.
BAKE: 30 MIN. + COOLING
MAKES: 3 DOZEN

- 1¾ cups chopped dates
- ½ cup water
- 2 tablespoons brown sugar
- 1 teaspoon grated orange peel
- 2 tablespoons orange juice
- 1 teaspoon lemon juice

CRUST
- 1½ cups all-purpose flour
- 1 teaspoon baking powder
- ½ teaspoon baking soda
- ¼ teaspoon salt
- 1 cup cold butter
- 1½ cups old-fashioned oats
- 1 cup packed brown sugar

1. In a small saucepan, combine the dates, water, brown sugar and orange peel. Cook and stir over medium heat until mixture comes to a boil, about 4 minutes. Cook and stir 3 minutes longer or until liquid is absorbed. Remove from the heat. Stir in the orange and lemon juices. Cool to room temperature.
2. In a large bowl, combine flour, baking powder, baking soda and salt. Cut in butter until crumbly. Add oats and brown sugar; mix well. Set aside half for the topping. Press remaining crumb mixture into a greased 13x9-in. baking pan.
3. Drop the date mixture by small spoonfuls onto crust. Sprinkle with the reserved crumb mixture; press down gently. Bake at 325° for 30-35 minutes or until golden brown. Cool on a wire rack. Cut into bars.
PER SERVING *1 bar equals 126 cal., 5 g fat (3 g sat. fat), 14 mg chol., 100 mg sodium, 19 g carb., 1 g fiber, 1 g pro.* **Diabetic Exchanges:** *1 starch, 1 fat.*

STRAWBERRY CREAM CHEESE PIE

Cheesecake lovers will savor every bite of this creamy strawberry pie. Everyone in my family is a fan.
—KIM VAN RHEENEN MENDOTA, IL

PREP: 20 MIN. + CHILLING
BAKE: 30 MIN. + COOLING
MAKES: 8 SERVINGS

- Pastry for a single-crust pie (9 inches)
- 1 package (8 ounces) reduced-fat cream cheese

- ½ cup egg substitute
- 3 tablespoons honey
- 1 teaspoon vanilla extract
- 3½ cups sliced fresh strawberries
- 1 tablespoon cornstarch
- ½ cup cold water
- ½ cup reduced-sugar strawberry preserves
- Fat-free whipped topping, optional

1. Roll out pastry to fit a 9-in. pie plate; transfer pastry to plate. Trim pastry to ½ in. beyond edge of plate; flute edges. Bake at 350° for 13-15 minutes or until the crust is lightly browned.
2. Meanwhile, in a large bowl, beat the cream cheese, egg substitute, honey and vanilla until smooth. Pour into crust. Bake 15-18 minutes longer or until center is almost set. Cool completely on a wire rack.
3. Arrange strawberries over the filling. In a saucepan, combine cornstarch and water until smooth. Stir in preserves. Bring to a boil; cook and stir for 2 minutes or until thickened. Spoon or brush over the strawberries. Refrigerate pie for 2 hours before cutting. Garnish with whipped topping if desired.
PER SERVING *1 piece (calculated without whipped topping) equals 268 cal., 12 g fat (6 g sat. fat), 21 mg chol., 119 mg sodium, 34 g carb., 2 g fiber, 5 g pro.*

THE SKINNY

EGG SUB
By using egg substitute instead of whole eggs in this pie, you save about 10 calories per slice. In addition, egg substitute cuts back on cholesterol while keeping the protein.

PUMPKIN
OATMEAL BARS

APPLE-SPICE ANGEL FOOD CAKE

Angel food cake mix is lower in fat and calories than regular cake mix. Apple pie spice and toasted nuts add a festive fall flavor, but you'll want to make this year-round!

—JOAN BUEHNERKEMPER
TEUTOPOLIS, IL

PREP: 10 MIN.
BAKE: 35 MIN. + COOLING
MAKES: 16 SERVINGS

- 1 package (16 ounces) angel food cake mix
- 1 cup water
- ⅔ cup unsweetened applesauce
- ½ cup finely chopped pecans, toasted
- 1 teaspoon apple pie spice
  Reduced-fat whipped topping and/or apple slices, optional

1. In a large bowl, combine cake mix and water. Beat on low speed for 30 seconds. Beat on medium speed for 1 minute. Fold in the applesauce, pecans and pie spice.
2. Gently spoon into an ungreased 10-in. tube pan. Cut through batter with a knife to remove air pockets. Bake on the lowest oven rack at 350° for 35-45 minutes or until lightly browned and entire top appears dry. Immediately invert pan; cool completely, about 1 hour.
3. Run a knife around side and center tube of pan. Remove cake to a serving plate. Garnish with whipped topping and/or apple slices if desired.
PER SERVING *1 slice (calculated without optional ingredients) equals 136 cal., 3 g fat (trace sat. fat), 0 chol., 209 mg sodium, 26 g carb., 1 g fiber, 3 g pro.* ***Diabetic Exchanges:*** *1½ starch, ½ fat.*

PUMPKIN OATMEAL BARS

It took me a long time to perfect these bars, but I'm so happy with how they turned out in the end. They have it all: sugar and spice and a light, creamy pumpkin layer that's especially nice!

—ERIN ANDREWS EDGEWATER, FL

PREP: 30 MIN.
BAKE: 30 MIN. + COOLING
MAKES: 2 DOZEN

- 1 package yellow cake mix (regular size)
- 2½ cups quick-cooking oats
- 5 tablespoons butter, melted
- 3 tablespoons honey
- 1 tablespoon water

FILLING

- 1 can (15 ounces) solid-pack pumpkin
- ¼ cup reduced-fat cream cheese
- ¼ cup fat-free milk
- 3 tablespoons brown sugar
- 2 tablespoons maple syrup
- 1 teaspoon ground cinnamon
- 1 teaspoon vanilla extract
- ¼ teaspoon ground allspice
- ¼ teaspoon ground cloves
- 1 large egg

- 1 large egg white
- ¼ cup chopped walnuts
- 1 tablespoon butter, melted

1. In a large bowl, combine the cake mix and oats; set aside ½ cup for topping. Add the butter, honey and water to the remaining cake mixture. Press onto the bottom of a 13x9-in. baking pan coated with cooking spray.
2. For the filling, in a large bowl, beat the pumpkin, cream cheese, milk, brown sugar, maple syrup, cinnamon, vanilla, allspice and cloves until blended. Add egg and egg white; beat on low speed just until combined. Pour over crust. In a small bowl, combine the walnuts, butter and reserved cake mixture; sprinkle over filling.
3. Bake at 350° for 30-35 minutes or until set and edges are lightly browned. Cool on a wire rack. Cut into bars.
PER SERVING *1 bar equals 186 cal., 7 g fat (3 g sat. fat), 18 mg chol., 180 mg sodium, 30 g carb., 2 g fiber, 3 g pro.* ***Diabetic Exchanges:*** *2 starch, 1 fat.*

APPLE-SPICE
ANGEL FOOD CAKE

RASPBERRY SORBET

RASPBERRY SORBET

With an abundant crop of fresh raspberries from the backyard, I rely on this recipe for a tasty frozen dessert that's pure simplicity.

—**KAREN BAILEY** GOLDEN, CO

PREP: 5 MIN. + FREEZING
MAKES: 6 SERVINGS

- ¼ cup plus 1½ teaspoons fresh lemon juice
- 3¾ cups fresh or frozen unsweetened raspberries
- 2¼ cups confectioners' sugar

Place all ingredients in a blender or food processor; cover and process until smooth. Transfer to a freezer container; freeze until firm.
PER SERVING *1 serving equals 216 cal., trace fat (trace sat. fat), 0 chol., 1 mg sodium, 55 g carb., 5 g fiber, 1 g pro.*

TOP TIP

KEEP THE SUGAR

When making sorbet, don't skimp on the amount of sugar in the recipe. The high sugar content keeps it from freezing into a block of ice. Sugar also helps give sorbet its smooth texture, so keep things sweet.

LOW-FAT PEANUT BUTTER COOKIES

When you bite into one of these yummy cookies, you'll never guess it's low in fat. It's our little secret.

—MARIA REGAKIS SAUGUS, MA

PREP: 15 MIN. + FREEZING
BAKE: 10 MIN. + COOLING
MAKES: ABOUT 2 DOZEN

- 3 **tablespoons butter**
- 2 **tablespoons reduced-fat peanut butter**
- ½ **cup packed brown sugar**
- ¼ **cup sugar**
- 1 **large egg white**
- 1 **teaspoon vanilla extract**
- 1 **cup all-purpose flour**
- ¼ **teaspoon baking soda**
- ⅛ **teaspoon salt**

1. In a large bowl, cream butter, peanut butter and sugars until light and fluffy. Add egg white; beat until blended. Beat in vanilla. Combine the flour, baking soda and salt; gradually add to the creamed mixture and mix well. Shape into an 8-in. roll; wrap in plastic wrap. Freeze for 2 hours or until firm.

2. Unwrap and cut into slices, just over ¼-in. thick. Place 2 in. apart on baking sheets coated with cooking spray. Press with a fork to make crisscross pattern. Bake at 350° for 6-8 minutes for chewy cookies or 8-10 minutes for crisp cookies. Cool for 1-2 minutes before removing cookies to wire racks; cool completely.

PER SERVING *1 cookie equals 62 cal., 2 g fat (1 g sat. fat), 4 mg chol., 64 mg sodium, 11 g carb., trace fiber, 1 g pro.* **Diabetic Exchanges:** *½ starch, ½ fat.*

LOW-FAT PEANUT
BUTTER COOKIES

PICNIC BERRY
SHORTCAKES

PICNIC BERRY SHORTCAKES

You can make the berry sauce ahead of time and chill. Then assemble the entire dessert a couple of hours before serving.
—TASTE OF HOME TEST KITCHEN

PREP: 20 MIN. + CHILLING
MAKES: 4 SERVINGS

- 2 **tablespoons sugar**
- ½ **teaspoon cornstarch**
- 2 **tablespoons water**
- 2 **cups sliced fresh strawberries, divided**
- ½ **teaspoon grated lime peel**
- 2 **individual round sponge cakes**
- 2 **cups fresh blueberries**
  Whipped topping, optional

1. In a small saucepan, mix sugar and cornstarch. Stir in water. Add 1 cup strawberries; mash mixture. Bring to a boil; cook and stir for 1-2 minutes or until thickened. Remove from heat; stir in the lime peel. Transfer to a small bowl; refrigerate, covered, until chilled.
2. Cut sponge cakes crosswise in half; trim each to fit in the bottoms of four wide-mouth half-pint canning jars. In a small bowl, mix the blueberries and remaining strawberries; spoon over cakes. Top with sauce. If desired, serve with whipped topping.

PER SERVING *1 dessert (calculated without whipped topping) equals 124 cal., 1 g fat (trace sat. fat), 10 mg chol., 67 mg sodium, 29 g carb., 3 g fiber, 2 g pro.* **Diabetic Exchanges:** *1 starch, 1 fruit.*

IRISH CREAM CUPCAKES

IRISH CREAM CUPCAKES

If you're looking for big, grown-up taste in a lightened-up little package, give these cute cupcake treats a try. No need to wait for St. Patrick's Day.
—JENNY LEIGHTY WEST SALEM, OH

PREP: 25 MIN.
BAKE: 20 MIN. + COOLING
MAKES: 2 DOZEN

- ½ **cup butter, softened**
- 1½ **cups sugar**
- 2 **large eggs**
- ¾ **cup unsweetened applesauce**
- 2 **teaspoons vanilla extract**
- 2½ **cups all-purpose flour**
- 3 **teaspoons baking powder**
- ½ **teaspoon salt**
- ½ **cup Irish cream liqueur**

FROSTING
- ⅓ **cup butter, softened**
- 4 **ounces reduced-fat cream cheese**
- 6 **tablespoons Irish cream liqueur**
- 4 **cups confectioners' sugar**

1. In a large bowl, beat the butter and sugar until crumbly, about 2 minutes. Add eggs, one at a time, beating well after each addition. Beat in the applesauce and vanilla (the mixture may appear curdled). Combine flour, baking powder and salt; add to the creamed mixture alternately with liqueur, beating well after each addition.
2. Fill paper-lined muffin cups two-thirds full. Bake at 350° for 18-22 minutes or until a toothpick inserted near the center comes out clean. Cool for 10 minutes before removing from pans to wire racks to cool completely.
3. For frosting, in a large bowl, beat butter and cream cheese until fluffy. Beat in liqueur. Add confectioners' sugar; beat until smooth. Pipe over tops of the cupcakes. Refrigerate the leftovers.

PER SERVING *1 cupcake equals 273 cal., 9 g fat (5 g sat. fat), 38 mg chol., 170 mg sodium, 45 g carb., trace fiber, 2 g pro.*

GENERAL RECIPE INDEX

Find every recipe by food category and major ingredient.

GENERAL INDEX

ALPHABETICAL RECIPE INDEX
Find every recipe by title.